THE HISTORY
OF
THE SOMERSET LIGHT INFANTRY
(PRINCE ALBERT'S)
1919–1945

HIS MAJESTY KING GEORGE VI
COLONEL-IN-CHIEF

THE HISTORY OF THE SOMERSET LIGHT INFANTRY
(PRINCE ALBERT'S)
1919–1945

COMPILED BY
GEORGE MOLESWORTH

WITH FIVE PORTRAITS AND THIRTY SKETCH MAPS

REGIMENTAL COMMITTEE
SOMERSET LIGHT INFANTRY

First published 1951

LIEUTENANT-GENERAL SIR JOHN G. DES R. SWAYNE, K.C.B., C.B.E.
COLONEL OF THE REGIMENT FROM OCTOBER 1947

FOREWORD

THIS third volume of the History of The Somerset Light Infantry (Prince Albert's) deals with the period from 1919 to 1945. It covers the years between the two wars when the Regiment played an important part in the mechanisation, re-equipment and reorganisation of the Army for the tasks which lay ahead. It also covers the years of the Second World War in which the Regiment, like so many others, had to throw off new units and spend a long period carrying out essential garrison duties while training itself for the decisive fighting which was to come.

Years of waiting and training in time of war are apt to disappoint and discourage men who are anxious to fight for their country, but *esprit de corps* was proof against this danger. Battalions of the Regiment, both old and new, steadily increased in efficiency, inspired by the spirit of service and comradeship which has ever been a characteristic of the Somerset Light Infantry and, when the chance came, were ready to acquit themselves with honour in bitter fighting in many lands.

Regimental *esprit de corps* has always been the main strength of the British Army and this volume shows that in the late war it again brought us through the dark days to victory. If we continue to cherish that spirit, so that it remains an inspiration in whatever circumstances modern conditions of war may require the Regiment to serve, we need have no fear for the future.

We owe a deep debt of gratitude to George Molesworth, whose devotion to his old Regiment has led him voluntarily to devote so much time and skill to the writing of this volume.

J. G. DES R. SWAYNE
Colonel, The Somerset Light Infantry
(Prince Albert's)

COMPILER'S PREFACE

THIS narrative has been compiled in haste, for two reasons. Firstly, it was desirable to produce some record of the achievements of the Regiment in the 1939–45 War while the events were still fresh in the memory of those who took part in them. Secondly, it was necessary to prepare and produce this volume before the ever-rising costs of printing and binding rendered any publication at a reasonable price, accessible to the many, prohibitive. Thus the blemishes of haste will be very apparent.

Too little time has passed, since fighting ceased, to produce an authentic "history" of the various campaigns, between 1939 and 1945, in which battalions of the Regiment took part. The various components of the world-wide struggle have not yet been brought into focus and, while parts of the vast picture are still out of the true proportion, others are hazy and ill-defined. No authoritative accounts of the various campaigns, nor of the war as a whole, have yet appeared and it is unlikely that they will be ready for some years. Thus, though all reasonable care has been taken to ensure accuracy of detail, this volume must not be regarded as "history", but merely as a narrative giving some record of particular campaigns and the parts played in them by various battalions.

For the record of the period "between the two wars", the main sources of information have been Digests of Services, correspondence in possession of Colonels of the Regiment, some data available at the Depot and the volumes of the *Light Bob Gazette*. The information available is scanty, for in times of peace there is, generally, little of major interest to record.

In the absence of any official accounts of the 1939–45 War, reliance has been placed, in the main, on War Diaries. Battalion War Diaries have been made available by Record Offices. Some of them are full and clear. Others are not so clear. In others there are unfortunate gaps. In many cases references to individuals—particularly Other Ranks—omit any initials or regimental numbers. Thus, in certain instances, it has not been possible to identify an individual and include mention of him in the narrative.

In addition to the battalion diaries, the relevant Corps, Division and Brigade Diaries have been consulted. These are extremely voluminous and examination of them in meticulous detail has been impossible in the time available. In the diaries of the higher formations, the "narrative" is in skeleton form only, the details being hidden in numerous and extensive appendices, containing orders, situation reports, intelligence summaries and a great mass of administrative matter. It is clear, however, that many plans for operations were discussed in conference and that many of the orders were issued verbally, being only briefly reflected in subsequent orders, or messages, on paper. This has made it difficult, on many occasions, to ascertain the actual rôle assigned to a brigade, or battalion.

In order to supplement information obtained from War Diaries, a number of "personal" accounts from eye-witnesses of events has been consulted. These descriptions have been valuable in providing local colour and details not included in the brief narratives of the Diaries. In many cases, the recollections of the eye-witnesses contain discrepancies in dates, times, places and the names of persons mentioned. Thus they have had to be accepted with caution. Among such information, much assistance has been obtained from *The History of the 4th Battalion, The Somerset Light Infantry, June 1944–May 1945* and *Incidents with the Seventh Battalion, The Somerset Light Infantry in France and Germany from June 1944 to June 1945*. These two books were published privately.

Considerable difficulty has arisen owing to the absence of adequate maps. Many of the War Diaries refer to places by means of four- or six-figure co-ordinates. Some of these references seem to refer to Field Surveys and others to maps which are not at present available to the public. There are also discrepancies in the spelling of place names, due to typing and manuscript errors and some confusion owing to similarity in place names and the fact that, in some areas, more than one village is called by the same name. So far as has been possible these discrepancies have been resolved. But some differences in spelling may remain, possibly due to variations in language; e.g. "Molbergen", for "Morbergen".

The maps referred to in the War Diaries range from 1/500,000 to 1/25,000 in scale. In the main the 1/100,000 series has been consulted, since these have been more readily available at the Historical Section of the Cabinet Offices. From tracings of these sheets the majority of the towns and villages mentioned in the text has been reflected in the sketch maps to this volume. It has not been possible to identify a certain number of hamlets, chateaux, suburbs, copses, etc. The sketch maps do not lay claim to any high degree of accuracy They are, however, sufficiently accurate to enable the reader to follow the movements of formations and battalions as described in the text and to give some idea of the distances involved. Owing to the present high cost of draughtsman's work, a great deal of topographical detail has had to be omitted.

No attempt has been made to provide an index to this volume. To prepare this would have entailed great delay in publication if the index was to be of any real value. As an alternative, a detailed synopsis of contents, is given at the head of each chapter, to facilitate easy reference.

ACKNOWLEDGMENTS

The thanks of the Regiment are due to many who have contributed information, or given most valuable assistance in the compilation of this volume. In particular, acknowledgments are made to:

Lieut.-General Sir John Swayne, K.C.B., C.B.E.

Major-General V. H. B. Majendie, C.B., D.S.O.

Colonel V. W. Roche.

Major G. H. Wood, M.C.

Major F. M. Turner.

Lieut.-Colonel A. Hunt.

Brigadier E. H. C. Frith, C.B.E.

Lieut.-Colonel P. Lewis.

Lieut.-Colonel G. H. Cole.

Lieut.-Colonel W. H. F. Routh.

Lieut.-Colonel J. R. I. Platt, D.S.O.

Lieut.-Colonel J. D. Gage-Brown.

Major K. J. Whitehead.

Major R. F. Stileman.

Major T. L. Ingram.

Captain C. W. Smart, M.B.E.

General Sir Bernard Paget, G.C.B., D.S.O., M.C.

Lieut.-Colonel H. F. Lazier, The Royal Hamilton Light Infantry.

Major J. McGrath, Australian Army Staff.

Lieut.-Colonel R. B. Rowett (R.A.), Somerset T. and A.F. Association.

C. V. Owen, Esq., Archivist, Cabinet Offices.

The Staff of the Officer i/c Infantry and A.A.C. Records, Exeter.

CONTENTS

CHAP.		PAGE
I.	THE BRAVE DAYS OF OLD	1

A retrospect of the origins of the Regiment and the major episodes in its record of service between 1685 and 1918.

| II. | BETWEEN TWO WARS—THE FIRST DECADE 1919–28 | 10 |

The aftermath of the war 1914–18 in the international field—Demobilisation—Peace service of regular and territorial army battalions—The Colonel in Chief—The Royal Hamilton Regiment of Canada.

| III. | BETWEEN TWO WARS—THE SECOND DECADE 1928–39 | 21 |

The evolution of Mechanised Forces—Trends in the evolution of infantry—Changes in badges and dress—The Territorial Army—The Royal Hamilton Light Infantry—alliance with the 13th Australian Infantry—Various regimental institutions—Developments in defence—Events in the international field leading to the War 1939–45.

| IV. | THE PATTERN OF THE CONFLICT | 40 |

The beginning of the war and the expansion of the Regiment—A chronological account of the main developments of the conflict and the part played, in each year by the various battalions of the Regiment.

| V. | THE "PHONEY WAR"—AUGUST 1939 TO MAY 1940. | 58 |

Operations of the 1st Battalion in India and the Ahmadzai Salient—Embodiment and raising of the 4th, 5th, 6th, 7th, 8th (Home Defence) and 11th (Holding) Battalions—Formation of the Somerset L.I. Brigade.

| VI. | THE BATTLE OF BRITAIN—JUNE TO OCTOBER 1940 | 67 |

The German invasions of the Low Countries—Dunkirk—the Battle of France—Italy enters the war—Collapse of France—The Battle of Britain—raising of 9th Battalion and formation of 50th (Holding) Battalion.

| VII. | THE BATTLE FOR EXISTENCE—NOVEMBER 1940 TO DECEMBER 1941 | 74 |

Situation in Russia and France—Dominions war effort—Events in Britain 1940—Air attacks—50th Battalion redesignated 10th Battalion—8th Battalion redesignated 30th Battalion—Moves of battalions in Britain—2nd Battalion in Gibraltar—1st Battalion in India—The international field—The United States enters the war.

| VIII. | FIGHTING BACK—1942 | 83 |

Japan enters the war—Reversal of military policy in India—1st Battalion operations in Waziristan—Greenwood's Corner—Datta Khel—Situation in Burma and Assam—Insurrection in India—2nd Battalion at Gibraltar—The battalions in Britain—10th Battalion converted to 7th Battalion (L.I.) The Parachute Regiment, Army Air Corps.

| IX. | OPERATIONS IN THE ARAKAN—1943 TO APRIL 1944 | 94 |

A record of the operations of the 1st Battalion in this campaign.

| X. | TEMPERING THE BLADE—JANUARY 1943 TO MAY 1944 | 120 |

Training problems—Objects and methods of training—The status of infantry—The results of infantry training—Preparations for D-day—30th Battalion to Algiers and Sicily—2nd Battalion to Egypt and Italy.

CHAP.		PAGE
XI.	THE CAMPAIGN IN ITALY: I—OPENING GAMBITS, MAY 1943 TO APRIL 1944	133

Opening of the Italian campaign—Invasion of Sicily—Invasion of Italy—Salerno—30th Battalion in Sicily—General situation—2nd Battalion moves to Italy—Operations on R. Garigliano—30th Battalion in Italy.

XII. THE BATTLES OF NORMANDY—JUNE TO AUGUST 1944 139

Operation "Overlord"—Plans and factors affecting the invasion of Normandy—7th Battalion (L.I.) Para Regt. in airborne landings—Operations in Bois de Bavent area—Landings of 4th and 7th Battalions—Operations on R. Odon—Attacks on point 112—Offensive east of R. Orne—Operations at Briquessard and St. Pierre du Fresne—Mont Pincon—Battle of the Falaise Pocket—Advance to R. Seine—Operations of 7th Battalion (L.I.) Para Regt. near Bois de Bavent—The advance eastwards.

XIII. THE CAMPAIGN IN ITALY: II—THE CROSSING OF THE R. LIRI AND THE FALL OF ROME 163

The situation in March 1944—Operations in Valvori and Belvedere sectors—The spring offensive—The Battle of the R. Garigliano—The advance to Rome.

XIV. NORTHERN EUROPE—SEPTEMBER TO DECEMBER 1944 171

Regrouping of forces for the pursuit—The advance into Belgium—The Battle for Arnhem—Operations on the R. Waal and R. Maas—General situation at the end of September 1944—Operations near Geilenkirchen—The Battle of the Ardennes.

XV. THE CAMPAIGN IN ITALY: III—ROME TO FLORENCE 1944 186

Situation in June 1944—The Battle for Vaiano—Operations near Lake Trasemene—The advance to Arezzo—The action at Ricasoli—The advance to and capture of Florence.

XVI. THE BATTLES OF THE ROER AND THE RHINELAND 195

Situation in January 1945—Clearing of the Ardennes Pocket—7th Battalion (L.I.) Para Regt. near Grimbiermont—Advance to R. Ourthe—The clearance of the Roermond triangle—The Battle of the Rhineland, Phase I—Actions at Cleve and Bedburg—The Battle of the Rhineland, Phase II—Operations near Goch and Xanten—7th Battalion (L.I.) Para Regt. in Holland—The Royal Hamilton Light Infantry.

XVII. 8TH ARMY OPERATIONS IN THE ADRIATIC SECTOR: ITALY—AUTUMN 1944 . . 214

The general situation in August 1944—2nd Battalion moves to Adriatic Sector—Crossing of R. Marano—Advance to R. Ausa and R. Marecchia—Operations near San Giustina—Crossing of R. Savio and R. Ronco—Crossing of R. Montone and R. Cosina—2nd Battalion preparations for move to Greece—30th Battalion in Italy—Surrender of German Armies in Italy.

XVIII. THE RHINE TO THE ELBE 225

General situation in March 1945—Plans for crossing the R. Rhine—7th Battalion (L.I.) Para Regt. near Wesel—The crossing of the R. Rhine—Expansion of the bridge-heads—7th Battalion (L.I.) Para Regt. advance to Erle—The Break Out—Capture of Varsseveld and Lochem—7th Battalion (L.I.) Para Regt. advance to Osnabruch—The advance on Bremen—7th Battalion (L.I.) Para Regt. advance to R. Leine—Advance to Cloppenburg—The attack on and capture of Bremen—7th Battalion (L.I.) Para Regt. advance to R. Elbe and the Baltic—Advance east of Bremen on Hamburg—The closing scene—The Surrender.

XIX. THE WAR IN GREECE 245

An account of developments in Greece and the part played by the 2nd Battalion in the reoccupation of Greece in December 1944.

XX. THE CURTAIN FALLS 253

An account of immediate post war events, with the demobilisation and disbandment of various battalions and the move of others to peace stations.

EPILOGUE 259

APPENDICES

		PAGE
A.	Succession of Colonels of the Regiment	261
B.	Succession of Lieut.-Colonels	263
C.	Succession of Adjutants and Quarter-Masters	264
D.	List of Regimental Sergeant-Majors	265
E.	Obituaries of some Old Comrades	266
F.	Records of service of General Officers 1939–45	270
G.	Records of service of Brigadiers and Colonels who served away from the Regiment 1939–45	272
H.	Note on No. 7 (Somerset L.I.) Troop of No. 8 (London District) Commando	274
I.	Note on services of 13th and 2/13th Australian Infantry Battalions 1939–45	275
J.	The Roll of Honour	278
K.	Honours and Awards	279
L.	The History of the Regimental Dinner Club	285

LIST OF ILLUSTRATIONS

His Majesty King George VI . . . . *Frontispiece*
   Colonel-in-Chief.

Lieut.-General Sir John Swayne, K.C.B., C.B.E. . . . . *Facing Foreword*
   Colonel of the Regiment from October 1947.

                                                                                                   FACING PAGE

General Sir Walter Braithwaite, G.C.B. 261
   Colonel of the Regiment, August 1929–October 1938.

Major-General V. H. B. Majendie, C.B., D.S.O. 262
   Colonel of the Regiment, October 1938–October 1947.

Lieut.-General Sir John Harding, K.C.B., C.B.E., D.S.O., M.C. 270

Lieut. George Albert Cairns, V.C. 278

SKETCH MAPS

(NOTE: *Insufficient data has been available to allow of the preparation of tactical maps of actions*)

GENERAL MAPS

NO.		FACING PAGE
1.	THE ARAKAN	98
2.	NORMANDY	162
3.	THE PURSUIT FROM THE R. SEINE (FRANCE AND BELGIUM)	184
4.	SOUTHERN ITALY	224
5.	NORTHERN GERMANY (Routes of 43rd Div. and 6th Airborne Div.)	244
6.	GREECE	248
7.	GERMANY	258

SPECIAL MAPS OF LOCALITIES

8.	THE AHMADZAI SALIENT, N.W.F., INDIA	60
9.	OPERATIONS IN WAZIRISTAN, 1941	88
10.	THE PYINSHE RIDGES, ARAKAN	112
11.	THE KALAPANZIN VALLEY, ARAKAN	118
12.	THE INVASION OF SICILY	134
13.	NORMANDY: SEA LANDINGS AND ADVANCE TO R. ODON	146
14.	NORMANDY: CROSSING OF R. ODON	152
15.	NORMANDY: THE APPROACH TO MONT PINCON	154
16.	NORMANDY: OPERATIONS NEAR MONT PINCON	158
17.	NORMANDY: LANDING OF 6TH AIRBORNE DIVISION	162
18.	ITALY: OPERATIONS NEAR NAPLES	170
19.	THE BATTLE FOR ARNHEM	180
20.	ITALY: THE ADVANCE TO FLORENCE	194
21.	OPERATIONS IN THE ROER POCKET	202
22.	BATTLES OF THE RHINELAND	212
23.	ITALY: THE ADRIATIC SECTOR	222
24.	THE CROSSING OF THE R. RHINE	232
25.	GERMANY: SINDEREN TO OLDENZAAL	236
26.	GERMANY: OLDENZAAL TO HEERSUM	238
27.	GERMANY: HASELUNNE TO WILDESHAUSEN	240
28.	GERMANY: WILDESHAUSEN TO BREMEN	242
29.	GREECE: ATHENS	252
30.	MACEDONIA AND NORTHERN GREECE	258

CHAPTER I

THE BRAVE DAYS OF OLD

Early changes in title—Connection with the County of Somerset—Constituted a Corps of Light Infantry—Formation of 2nd Battalion and Depot—Title of Prince Albert's—Militia, Volunteers and Territorial Force—Wars of William III—War of the Spanish Succession—War of the Austrian Succession—The rebellion of 1745—Napoleonic Wars—Campaigns in Burma and Afghanistan—The Defence of Jellalabad—The Crimean War—The Indian Mutiny—Campaigns in South Africa—The Second Burmese War—The South African War—The War of 1914–18—Battle Honours for 1914–18—Record of service at home and abroad—Shorter title

THE history of a regiment of the British Army is closely related to the history of the nation. It follows closely the pattern of national growth and expansion; of economic and scientific developments; of foreign policy and colonial extensions.

As, with the passing of the years, national administration became more complex and centralised, so the nature of the army—its command and organisation—passed, from the hands of noblemen and adventurers and the special prerogative of the Crown, to the State. This process has continued until the British Army has ceased to be a strictly professional force and has become merged in the National Forces.

Although the history of a regiment is, largely, the history of the nation and—in later years—the history of the British Commonwealth of Nations, it looms more strongly in the mind of the soldier than does the broader, impersonal record of the nation as a whole. The latter he may learn, in a rudimentary fashion, at school. Regimental history becomes part of his life.

In most regiments the history of past years is carefully taught and the lessons to be learned from it inculcated. The tradition of the past is fostered, whether it be of victory or glorious disaster. It tells a story of loyalty to Crown and State and devotion to duty; of great achievements; of honours and coveted distinctions won on the battlefield; of the deeds of heroic men; of hardships and dangers resolutely faced; of fortitude on the stricken field; of the capacity of men to suffer misfortune and rise again to conquer.

Regimental history is the story of fighting-men. Thus, it is the most human of all histories. It lays the foundation of morale by pointing to the traditions of the past. It has been proved, time and again, that the knowledge of past glories, the will to emulate them and the desire to maintain a great reputation untarnished, are factors which, in desperate circumstances, will give to a soldier, or a unit, the extra determination which makes the difference between success or failure.

The first volume of this history gives the record of the Somerset Light

Infantry from the time when it was raised up to the period before the 1914–18 War. The second volume contains the story of the First World War. This volume carries the narrative forward to the close of the 1939–45 World War.

During the period covered by this volume, the Regiment, in 1935, celebrated the 250th year of life. It is therefore fitting to look back, briefly, at some of the outstanding features in its history and the background to the movements of the Regiment at home and abroad. It is well, also, to trace the growth of the various units who played their part in the Second World War. History is said to repeat itself. That may, or may not, be so. But, as the years go by, there is seen to be a continuity in the life of the various battalions. They fight again and again over the same battlefields of the world, with the same place names recurring. The pattern of war shows little change, though the form of the Regiment, its organisation, armament and equipment is ever changing.

EARLY CHANGES IN TITLE

In 1685 Charles II died and was succeeded by James II. In that year Theophilus, 7th Earl of Huntingdon, was authorised to raise the Regiment as "Huntingdon's Foot".

Between 1685 and 1767, the Regiment was known by the name of the Colonel at the time, though in 1700, when the army was engaged in the War of the Spanish Succession, the number 13, in the Order of Battle, was allotted to it. It has retained this number ever since.

During this period it was successively "Hasting's", "Jacob's", "Barrymore's", "Pearce's Dragoons", "Cotton's 13th", "Lord Mark Kerr's 13th", "Pulteney's 13th", until, in 1767, when commanded by Major-General Murray, it was designated "The 13th Regiment of Foot".

CONNECTION WITH THE COUNTY OF SOMERSET

On 11th October 1782, during the reign of George III, it was ordered that "our 13th Regiment of Foot . . . shall take the County name of the 1st Somersetshire Regiment and be attached to that County." This order authorised the raising of men from the County for the regiment and the connection has remained ever since.

CONSTITUTED A CORPS OF LIGHT INFANTRY

On 25th December 1822, during the reign of George IV, the Regiment was constituted a Corps of Light Infantry. The initiative for this may have come from the Commanding Officer, Lieutenant-Colonel Lewis Butler, who was transferred to the command from the 60th Rifles. Or it may have been the result of tactics adopted by the Regiment during forest warfare against the Americans during the campaign on the Canadian Border in 1813–15. The Regiment was then styled "The 1st Somersetshire Light Infantry."

FORMATION OF 2ND BATTALION AND DEPOT

In 1858, during the reign of Queen Victoria, the 2nd Battalion was raised at Winchester. In 1873 the Depot was formed at Taunton and the 1st and 2nd Battalions affiliated to it.

TITLE OF "PRINCE ALBERT'S"

On the 26th August 1842, in consideration of the part played by the Regiment in the campaigns in Burma and Afghanistan, Queen Victoria approved of the Regiment assuming the title of 'The 13th or Prince Albert's Regiment of Light Infantry". The facings of the Regiment were then changed from yellow to blue. Since that time the Regiment has worn Royal facings without being a Royal Regiment.

MILITIA, VOLUNTEERS AND TERRITORIAL FORCE

Up to 1601, local forces for home defence were known as the Fyrd, which was established by Alfred the Great. In 1604, James I abolished the Fyrd and replaced it by the "Trained (or Train) Bands". These were, at first, under local control. But, during the reign of Charles II, they were taken under control of the Crown. They were then known as Militia and were much neglected until 1757. In that year, while the bulk of the regular forces was absent for the Seven Years War, the Militia was carefully organised for the defence of the country. Later, distinctions arose between Militiamen, who were conscripted by ballot, and Volunteers who served voluntarily. The Volunteer organisations received much increased support during the Napoleonic Wars.

The County of Somerset has a long tradition of Volunteer and Militia service. Among the units raised, from time to time, were:

The Bath Volunteers;
The West Somerset Yeomanry;
The North Somerset Yeomanry;
The Somerset Provisional Cavalry;
The Somerset Volunteers; and
The 1st, 2nd and 3rd Volunteer Battalions, Somerset Light Infantry.

In 1907, Lord Haldane's "Territorial and Reserve Forces Act" came into force, by which the Militia ceased to exist. The 3rd (Militia) Battalion became the 3rd (Reserve) Battalion, while the 4th (Militia) Battalion was disbanded. The 1st, 2nd and 3rd Volunteer Battalions were reorganised into the 4th (T.F.) and 5th (T.F.) Battalions, with headquarters at Bath and Taunton, respectively. When first constituted these battalions formed part of the Regiment, but were not permitted to wear the badges, nor place on their colours the Battle Honours, of the Regiment.

WARS OF WILLIAM III

William of Orange landed at Torbay in 1688. James II was deposed and the army swore allegiance to William. James's supporters started troubles in Scotland and Ireland. In 1689 the Regiment was sent to Scotland and fought its first battle at Killiecrankie. Here, when William's forces met with disaster, almost alone it stood firm and left the field with ranks unbroken. Thus were laid the foundations of later tradition and reputation which have grown steadily ever since.

When this campaign was over the Regiment went, under the command of King William, to Ireland, where it fought at the Battle of the Boyne. Later, under Marlborough, it took part in the capture of Cork and Kinsale.

William now embroiled England in the long struggle he had waged against Louis XIV of France. In 1701, the Regiment joined Marlborough's forces in Flanders and fought at Nimeguen, Venloo and Liege. In 1703 it was engaged in the siege and capture of Huy.

WAR OF THE SPANISH SUCCESSION

In 1703, during the reign of Queen Anne, a treaty of alliance was signed with Portugal, proclaiming Charles of Austria as King of Spain. During 1704–5 the Regiment was engaged in the siege and capture of Gibraltar. This became the first Battle Honour on the colours. From there it took part in the siege and capture of Barcelona.

In 1706, as a reward for its services it was mounted as a Regiment of Dragoons. As such it took part in the conquest of Valencia and displayed great gallantry at the disastrous battle of Almanza. The cavalry pattern mess-jacket and waistcoat, worn by officers up to 1909, was a memento of this period of mounted service.

In 1708 the Regiment was re-converted to infantry and, in 1709, was involved in the disaster on the River Caya, in Portugal. Here it was taken prisoner, but, later, exchanged as the result of Marlborough's victories. In 1710 hostilities in Spain ended and the Regiment went to Gibraltar, where it remained for 16 years.

In 1726 the Spaniards resumed hostilities and attacked Gibraltar. The Regiment took part in the successful defence, which ended in 1729.

WAR OF THE AUSTRIAN SUCCESSION

This began in 1740. In 1742, the Regiment was sent to Flanders and that year fought at Dettingen. This became the second Battle Honour. In 1745 it was present at Fontenoy. Shortly afterwards it was sent home to meet the threat from Prince Charles Edward.

THE REBELLION OF 1745

On arriving in Scotland it joined the force under the Duke of Cumberland. It was engaged first at Falkirk Muir and then at Culloden. Here it greatly distinguished itself. As a reward the Sergeants were permitted to knot the sash on the same side as the officers—a unique distinction which has been preserved ever since.

THE BRAVE DAYS OF OLD

After the defeat of the Pretender, the Regiment returned to Flanders and fought in the battles of Roncoux and Val. In 1760 George III became King and the War of the Austrian Succession terminated in 1767 with the Peace of Aix-la-Chapelle.

NAPOLEONIC WARS

The French Revolution took place in 1789 and the British Government was much concerned at the spread of ideas of liberty and equality which threatened Europe with anarchy. These doctrines began to spread to the negro populations of the West Indies. Accordingly, in 1790, the Regiment was sent to Barbados and Jamaica. In 1793 it took part in the expedition to San Domingo and remained in the West Indies till 1795.

In 1798 Napoleon, with the French "Army of the East", conquered Egypt with a view to establishing a base for further operations against India. The French fleet was destroyed by Nelson in Aboukir Bay (the Battle of the Nile) after which Napoleon unsuccessfully attacked Acre and then returned to France.

In 1800 Spain allied herself with France. The Regiment joined a force under General Pulteney which landed at Corunna. Later an attack on Ferrol failed. The force joined a detachment under General Abercromby, but failed to take Cadiz. It was then moved to Gibraltar.

In 1801, under Abercromby's command, the regiment landed at Aboukir Bay and engaged in the operations near Alexandria, which led to the surrender of the French Army under General Menou. As a reward for these services "The Sphinx", with the word Egypt, was placed in the centre of the Regimental Colour, replacing the numeral 13.

In 1807 the Regiment was ordered to take part in an expedition against the Spanish possessions in South America. In 1808 it arrived in Bermuda, and from there, in 1809–10, it took part in the capture of Guadaloupe and Martinique from the French. "Martinique, 1809" is the third Battle Honour.

In 1812, measures by Napoleon to destroy British commerce involved us in war with the United States. The scene of the conflict was the Frontier of Canada. In 1813 the Regiment was sent to Halifax and, later, to Quebec and Montreal. During 1814 it fought minor actions near Lake Champlain and held posts on the Richelieu River. In that year Napoleon was defeated and sent to Elba. War with the United States was concluded in 1815, in which year Napoleon escaped. The Regiment was hastily sent to England, but arrived too late for the Waterloo campaign.

CAMPAIGNS IN BURMA AND AFGHANISTAN

In 1823 the 13th Somersetshire Light Infantry arrived at Calcutta, on their first tour of duty in India. Relations with the Burmese King of Ava had become strained, owing to outrages and acts of aggression against the possessions of the East India Company. The first Burmese War of 1824–6 followed, in which the Regiment distinguished itself. The fourth Battle Honour, "Ava", was added to the colours as a reward. In 1826 the Regiment returned to India and served in various stations until 1838.

Queen Victoria ascended the throne in 1837. During this year and the next, the Persians, instigated by the Russians, besieged Herat and appeared to be contemplating an advance through Afghanistan to invade India. Amir Dost Mahomed of Afghanistan attacked Ranjit Singh, ruler of the Punjab and ally of Britain. In 1838 the Regiment joined the force under Sir Willoughby Cotton to invade Afghanistan.

In 1839, moving through the Bolan Pass, Kandahar was occupied and Ghazni taken by storm. In August the force entered Kabul. With the Regiment were Robert Sale, known as "Fighting Bob", and Henry Havelock. The former gained undying fame at Jellalabad and, later, died of wounds received at the battle of Mudki, in 1845. The latter, also, became famous during the Indian Mutiny.

During 1840 there were numerous engagements near Kabul. In 1841 conditions had improved and the Regiment was ordered to return to India via the Kabul and Khyber Passes. In October 1841 traditional Afghan treachery was encountered and the situation deteriorated. After severe fighting round Gandamak and in the Kabul Passes, the Regiment, with Sale's Brigade, reached Jellalabad.

THE DEFENCE OF JELLALABAD

The town was at once besieged by an Afghan Army and the defenders were much harassed by earthquakes, which repeatedly destroyed the fortifications. In January 1842 the main British forces, evacuating Kabul, were destroyed by the Afghans in the Passes. Dr. Brydon alone escaped to reach Jellalabad. Here first mention is made of the Bugles which play such a part in the life of the Regiment. Every half-hour, from the ramparts of the town, the Bugles sounded the advance, to direct stragglers from the defeated army to a place of safety.

Two sorties from the town failed. But, on the 7th April, 1842, the garrison sallied out and utterly defeated the Afghans under Mohamed Akbar. The siege was raised. In his despatch to Her Majesty, Lord Ellenborough, Governor General of India, referred to Sale's Brigade as "The Illustrious Garrison". In addition to the change of title and facings, already mentioned, the Regiment was authorised to bear on its colours and appointments a Mural Crown, superscribed Jellalabad. A special medal was struck and awarded to the garrison.

Each year all units of the Regiment celebrate the 7th April as Jellalabad Day. Throughout the 1939–45 War all units celebrated this day, unless in actual contact with the enemy.

Later in 1842 the Regiment re-entered Kabul in the campaign of retribution. In 1844 it returned to England. As a result of this campaign, the fifth, sixth and seventh Battle Honours were added to the Colours—"Ghuznee, 1839", "Affghanistan, 1839", and "Cabool, 1842".

THE CRIMEAN WAR

In 1854, while the Regiment was at Gibraltar, Russia attempted to dismember Turkey. Britain and France allied with Turkey to resist her. In 1855 the Regiment went to the Crimea, taking part in the final stages of the siege of Sevastopol. The eighth Battle Honour, "Sevastopol", was added to the Colours.

THE INDIAN MUTINY

This broke out in 1857 and the Regiment arrived in Calcutta in October of that year. Under Sir Colin Campbell it was employed in Oudh. On the 6th April 1858 it fought a very gallant convoy action at Azimghur. Here Sergeant William Napier and Private Patrick Carlin won the first two Victoria Crosses for the Regiment.

CAMPAIGNS IN SOUTH AFRICA

As already mentioned the 2nd Battalion was raised in 1858. In 1860 it was sent to Cape Colony, moving to Mauritius in 1862.

In 1875 the 1st Battalion moved to Cape Colony and thence to Natal. In 1877 it was at Pretoria and in 1878 took part in the campaign against Sekukini, distinguishing itself in the action of Tolyana Spruit. The First Zulu War followed, with the actions of Kambula (29th March 1879) and Ulundi (5th July 1879). The ninth Battle Honour, "South Africa, 1878-9" commemorates these campaigns.

THE SECOND BURMESE WAR

In 1878 the 2nd Battalion went to India and to Burma in 1883. The Second Burmese War followed in 1885. The battalion was employed in detachments and took part in many minor engagements. This gained the tenth Battle Honour of "Burma, 1885-7". The battalion returned to Madras in 1893, where it was relieved by the 1st Battalion.

In 1897 the 1st Battalion, stationed at Peshawar, took part in the Mohmand Campaign, being engaged at the relief of Shabkadr and the assault on the Bedmanai Pass.

THE SOUTH AFRICAN WAR

This began in 1899. The 2nd Battalion was sent to Natal and took part in the "Relief of Ladysmith". This became the eleventh Battle Honour. In 1900 it fought at Spion Kop, Valkrantz and in the relief of Wepener. Later it was divided into two wings and engaged in the various sweeps for De Wet.

The wings rejoined in 1901 when a successful action was fought at Mooifontein. When peace was declared the twelfth Battle Honour, "South Africa, 1889–1902" was added to the colours.

THE WAR OF 1914-18

When, in 1914, war was declared with Germany, the 1st Battalion was in England and the 2nd Battalion in India. The Regiment was expanded greatly, the battalions and their record of service being as follows:

1st	(Regular)	France and Flanders.
2nd	(Regular)	India and 3rd Afghan War 1919.
3rd	(Reserve)	Draft finding.
4th	(Reserve)	Draft finding.
1/4th	(T.F.)	India and Mesopotamia.
2/4th	(T.F.)	India and Palestine.
3/4th	(T.F.)	Draft finding.
1/5th	(T.F.)	India and Palestine.
2/5th	(T.F.)	Burma.
3/5th	(T.F.)	Draft finding.
6th	(Service)	France.
7th	(Service)	France.
8th	(Service)	France.
9th	(Service)	Home service. Later became 45th Territorial Reserve Battalion and left the Regiment.
11th	(T.F.)	France as Garrison Battalion.
12th	(T.F.)	Palestine. Formed in Egypt from West Somerset Yeomanry.
13th	(T.F.)	Home service.
1st	(Garrison)	Home service.
30th		Home service.

BATTLE HONOURS FOR WAR 1914-18

Battalions which helped to gain these 10 Honours were as follows:

"Marne, 1914", "Aisne, 1914", "Ypres, 1915"—1st Battalion.
"Somme, 1916"—1st, 6th, 7th and 8th Battalions.
"Ypres, 1917", "Arras, 1917", "Albert, 1916", "Cambrai, 1917"—1st, 6th, 7th and 8th Battalions.
"Tigris, 1916"—1/4th Battalion.
"Palestine, 1917-18"—2/4th, 1/5th and 12th Battalions.
"Hindenburg Line"—1st, 7th, 8th and 12th Battalions.
"Ypres, 1918", "Marne, 1918", "Somme, 1918", "Albert, 1918", "Cambrai, 1918"—1st, 2/4th, 6th, 7th, 8th and 12th Battalions.
An additional Battle Honour was:
"Afghanistan, 1919", gained by the 2nd Battalion.

THE BRAVE DAYS OF OLD

RECORD OF SERVICE AT HOME AND ABROAD

This survey of the history of the Regiment may well conclude with details of its services during its 250 years of existence, up to 1935. The 1st Battalion has been in being for 250 years; the 2nd Battalion for 77 years—a total of 327 years. The stations served in by the regular battalions, with the periods in years, are as follows:

	Years		Years
England	78	Scotland	15
Ireland	36	Channel Islands	6
Total Home service			135 years
India	63	Spain	$2\frac{1}{2}$
West Indies	15	Burma	7
Minorca	7	Mauritius	4
Flanders	6	Canada	2
South Africa	13	China	4
France and Belgium	5	Crimea	1
Portugal	$4\frac{1}{2}$	Palestine	1
Afghanistan	4	Soudan	1
Malta	7	Germany	1
Egypt	3	Gibraltar	38
Total service abroad			192 years

PRESENT TITLE

In 1912 the title of the Regiment was changed in two minor respects to make it shorter, namely, the omission of "The" before "Prince Albert's" and the omission of the suffix "shire" in "Somersetshire". The new title then read "Prince Albert's (Somerset Light Infantry.") The present title, however, is "The Somerset Light Infantry (Prince Albert's)."

CHAPTER II

BETWEEN TWO WARS—THE FIRST DECADE, 1919–1928

The aftermath of war—The rise of the U.S.S.R.—Readjustment of European frontiers—The League of Nations—The nature of British Defence Forces—The period of demobilisation—1st and 2nd Battalions—Change of Colonelcy—Battle Honours, 1914–18—H.R.H. the Duke of York becomes Colonel-in-Chief—War Memorials (Wells and Sandhurst)—Colours of 4th Battalion—Cadet Training Units—Marriage of H.R.H. the Colonel-in-Chief—2nd Battalion in India, Soudan and Home—1st Battalion (Home, Egypt and China)—4th and 5th Battalions—Royal Hamilton Regt.—The International field

THE AFTERMATH OF WAR

YEARS of peace, in the history of a regiment, seldom chronicle any spectacular events. They are, however, of much importance, for they are periods of reorganisation, re-equipment and training for whatever fresh struggle may come. They are the years in which morale, skill at arms and physical fitness are built up. During such periods, however, the march of events requires study, for from them, in many fields, may be seen the pattern of things to come.

The War of 1914–18 began and ended on high notes of enthusiasm and hope. In 1914 the country was anxious to come to grips with arrogant German Imperialism and was tired of the sword-rattling antics of Kaiser Wilhelm. There had been no British Army on the continent since the Crimean War in 1855–7. The army of 1914 was trained and equipped on the lessons learned in the South African War. The infantry was, probably, more highly trained and efficient than at any previous period in history. There was, however, little artillery and fewer automatic weapons. The infantry relied mainly on skill with the rifle and bayonet to get to grips with the enemy. Opinion generally seemed to imagine that the armament and tactics which had, ultimately, been successful against an enemy few in numbers and inadequately equipped, fighting in open country, were sufficient for action in enclosed country, against continental masses, well provided with all forms of artillery and machine-guns.

Unorthodox military thinkers, who pressed for more guns and more automatics, were regarded with some disapproval. When war broke out and the Expeditionary Force—pitifully weak—was sent to France, few of those in authority expected the conflict to last longer than six months. The French Army was expected to settle the matter in a short space of time. Fewer still foresaw the enormous expansion of our forces which would be required; the outpouring of men, materials and money; the terrible casualties arising from siege warfare conditions on the Western Front; the coming of the Armoured

Fighting Vehicle and the disappearance of horsed cavalry; the rapid development of the aeroplane; nor the world-wide nature of the struggle and the part which the Dominions would play in it.

In 1918 there was also enthusiasm. The widespread and complex nature of the conflict had fostered the growth of democratic ideas. No longer was war a matter for the professional sailor and soldier. It had become a national commitment. The whole nation was thankful that the "blood bath" was at an end. Men believed that they had been victorious in a war which "would end war." They also believed that a new Britain would emerge, "fit for heroes to live in". It was not long before these illusions were shattered.

After the rush for demobilisation and the profligate spending of war gratuities, the stark facts began to appear. The inevitable reaction set in. Men from the services found it difficult to obtain either work or homes. In many great cities the lamentable spectacle of parties of begging ex-servicemen appeared. The brief post-war boom was followed, later, by a depression, with unemployment, hardship and growing discontent.

The situation became difficult in the national field, but internationally it worsened even more rapidly. The peacemakers at Versailles had before them a task which was, perhaps, beyond human capacity to accomplish to the satisfaction of all. The quarrels which began and the errors which were made sowed the seeds of bitterness and disunity which, later, were to produce a fearful harvest of bloodshed and destruction. Among the most grievous errors of the Allies, was the failure to occupy Germany and dictate terms of Peace at Berlin. The German people never suffered the full humiliation of defeat. They saw neither the armies of their conquerors, nor the devastation they had wrought on the lands of their enemies.

THE RISE OF THE U.S.S.R.

Three major factors emerged from the aftermath of war which had their repercussions on Europe. Tsarist Russia had crumbled before the German impact and was replaced by a Communist State, headed by Lenin and Trotsky, pledged to further the cause of international communism. In 1919, Lenin founded the Third International in Moscow. At first the U.S.S.R. was fully occupied with internal reconstruction and a series of Five Year Plans to reorganise its internal industrial and transportation systems. Behind these plans was a desire to ensure security in the event of any further European conflict. Later, however, the New Russia was to enter the international field as an ominous portent, following a policy of "peaceful penetration" and the encouragement of underground subversive activities.

READJUSTMENT OF EUROPEAN FRONTIERS

The second factor arose from the terms of the Treaty of Versailles. These were dictated at Versailles in April 1919 and were known by the Germans as the "Diktat". The German people were left, somewhat bewildered, to argue with the Navy and Army as to who was responsible for their defeat. Russia was not represented at Versailles and had no say in the peace terms.

Among the territorial dispensations were:

(a) The addition of Eupen and Malmedy to Belgium.

(b) The creation of plebiscite areas in Schleswig, East Prussia and Upper Silesia.

(c) The placing of the Saar for 15 years under the League of Nations.

(d) The cessation of part of the German-speaking Tyrol to Italy.

(e) The addition of 3 million Germans in the Sudeten-land to Czecho-slovakia.

(f) The reduction of Austria to a small and impotent state.

(g) The removal from Hungary of 61 per cent. of population and 71 per cent. of territory.

(h) The formation, from Russian territory, of the Baltic States of Finland, Lithuania, Latvia and Estonia.

(i) The creation of the Free State of Danzig.

(j) The cession of Posen and West Prussia to Poland, who, also, received a "corridor" to the sea at Gydnia, which isolated East Prussia from the rest of Germany.

All this rearrangement of frontiers and populations was calculated to cause confusion, discontent, bitterness and wranglings. Later, it was the arguments which arose about the readjustment of Poland which provided the spark to fire the magazine in 1939.

THE LEAGUE OF NATIONS

A third factor was the launching of the League of Nations as a body capable of settling European and World disputes by discussion without recourse to war. It originated in the mind of President Wilson, the author of the famous "14 points". When it took shape there were high hopes that it would, effectively, discharge its responsibilities. Unfortunately, the refusal of the United States to join it, in practice, sounded its death knell from its inception. The U.S.S.R. did not join it. Later, Germany, under a Nazi régime, joined it for a short time. It did good work in many fields. But, as the years went by, it became increasingly apparent that, on major conflicts of policy, it was impotent and it fell into disrepute. The hopes which attended its birth were not fulfilled.

THE NATURE OF BRITISH DEFENCE FORCES

The War of 1914–18 brought many changes in the texture of our main lines of defence. The Royal Navy, as of old, remained the first line. The army, having passed through the stages of "Private" and "Professional", had become a national force, closely linked with and dependent on, the man-power, productive potential and economic development of the nation. National

Service had been accepted as inescapable. Democratic ideas were in the ascendant. They found expression in the disappearance of much of the old "officer class", who served without much regard for rates of pay. Improvements were necessary in pay for all ranks and in conditions affecting accommodation and amenities.

Mechanisation had come to stay. Even more important were the developments in the Air Arm, superimposed on, but essential to, both the Navy and Army. Amid much heated argument the Independent Air Force emerged.

All these factors were of paramount importance in determining the organisation, equipment and training of the army in the period between the two wars. The British Army had always been designed to fight outside the confines of Great Britain, whether in Europe or in areas where there were colonial and commercial interests. This had necessitated transportation by sea, and frequently landings on foreign coasts, either unopposed or in the face of the enemy. Prior to 1914 there had been close co-operation with the Royal Navy in such operations. But, with the coming of the Air arm it became increasingly apparent that each arm of the services was complementary to the others. Thus the need for training in Combined Operations—sea, land and air—became more important as the years went by.

THE PERIOD OF DEMOBILISATION

After all great wars, the outpouring of money, materials and men, necessary to achieve victory is followed by drastic reductions in expenditure and the strength of forces, often regardless of actual immediate, or future, requirements. Sometimes the pendulum, pushed by economic and political necessity, swings from lavish spending to dangerous cheese-paring. With the coming of peace in 1918, the economy axe was wielded with gusto. Committees of all kinds delved into details of strengths and expenditure, both at home and abroad. Establishments were cut to the bone. During the years 1919–22 there were gradual, but sweeping, reductions in the strength of the armed forces.

Within the Regiment the 6th, 7th, 8th and 9th (Service) battalions were the first to go. The King's Colour of the 7th Battalion was deposited in Bath Abbey on 17th April 1920. The identity of the 7th and 8th (Service) battalions was preserved in Clubs, for annual re-unions and other social functions.

Many of the Territorial battalions, raised during the war, suffered the same fate. On 27th September 1919, the remaining personnel of the 3rd (Reserve) Battalion were absorbed into the 1st Battalion. The 3rd Battalion was disembodied and reduced to cadre form.

By 1923 only the 1st (Regular), 2nd (Regular), 3rd (Reserve), 4th (T.F.) and 5th (T.F.) Battalions remained.

1st AND 2nd BATTALIONS

During the latter part of 1918 and the major part of 1919, the 1st Battalion remained in France. In September 1919 it was reduced to cadre in Belgium, under command of Lieut.-Colonel V. H. B. Majendie, D.S.O. The cadre returned to England under Captain E. H. C. Frith and the Battalion was reformed in Belfast under Lieut.-Colonel P. M. Wardlaw, D.S.O. The 2nd Battalion, in 1918, was at Peshawar. During 1919 it was engaged in the 3rd Afghan War, gaining the Battle Honour "Afghanistan 1919."

In February 1920, reduced to cadre form by demobilisation, it moved to Palestine under Major C. A. Williams. There it was joined by the Foreign Service Details under Lieut.-Colonel W. J. Bowker, C.M.G., D.S.O.; 16 officers and 876 other ranks which had left Devonport on 17th September 1919 for Palestine via France and Egypt.

The Battalion moved to Helmieh, near Cairo, in September. On 20th December 1920, it sailed, in H.T. "Maine," for India and was stationed at Lucknow, where it remained for two years. In 1921, while at Lucknow, it proceeded to Calcutta, for the visit of H.R.H. the Prince of Wales.

CHANGE OF COLONELCY

Early in 1920, Major-General R. Lloyd Payne, C.B., D.S.O., who had been Colonel since 1914, resigned on grounds of ill-health. He was succeeded by Lieut-General Sir T. D'O. Snow, K.C.B., K.C.M.G.

BATTLE HONOURS, 1914–18

For some time the Colonel was in correspondence with battalions regarding the selection of Battle Honours to be placed on the regimental colours. With so many theatres of war and major battles to consider, the choice was a difficult one, if the final selection was to do justice to the claims of all. Early in 1923 the War Office called for these lists. The following were finally submitted and approved:

Marne, 1914, 1918.	Aisne, 1914.
Ypres, 1915, 1917, 1918.	Somme, 1916, 1918.
Albert, 1916, 1918.	Tigris, 1916.
Arras, 1917, 1918.	Hindenburg Line.
Cambrai, 1917, 1918.	Palestine, 1917, 1918.

"Ypres, 1914" was, also, submitted, but was not approved. Details of the battalions who gained these honours are given in Chapter I.

H.R.H. THE DUKE OF YORK BECOMES COLONEL-IN-CHIEF

In May 1921, H.M. The King honoured the Regiment by appointing H.R.H. The Duke of York, K.G., K.T., G.C.V.O., to be Colonel-in-Chief. Thus the association of the Regiment with the Royal Family, which had begun with his great-grandfather the Prince Consort in 1842, was resumed. On 31st May 1921, representatives of the Regiment, headed by the Colonel (Lieut.-General Sir T. D'O. Snow), Major-General H. J. Everett, Lieut.-Colonel A. H.

1919–1928

Yatman and Major L. A. Jones-Mortimer were received by the Colonel-in-Chief at Buckingham Palace. On 20th June 1922, H.R.H. the Colonel-in-Chief paid his first visit to the Depot (Major L. A. Jones-Mortimer) at Taunton. He was received by the Colonel and the Lord Lieutenant of Somerset (the Marquis of Bath). The first act of H.R.H. was to present the Distinguished Conduct Medal to R.S.M. Gange.

WAR MEMORIALS (WELLS AND SANDHURST)

In October 1922 H.R.H. the Colonel-in-Chief attended the dedication of the Memorial to the men of Somerset who fell in the War, 1914–18, in the Cathedral Church at Wells. The Memorial included the restoration of the Chapels of St. Martin and St. Calixtus, the placing of a Golden Book of Remembrance in the Cathedral and the endowment of an educational fund for the benefit of children of Somerset Soldiers and Sailors who were killed, or disabled, during the conflict. The Golden Book contains 11,278 names, of which 8,000 were natives of Somerset.

The Golden Book contains the names of many in addition to those who served in and lost their lives with the Somerset Light Infantry. The regimental statistics for the years 1914–18 show that over 700 officers and 13,000 other ranks were trained and sent overseas. The regimental casualty lists for the war period show the numbers of those killed, died of wounds, or died on service as:

Officers	269
Other ranks	4487
Total	4756

In October 1923 the Regimental Memorial Panel, in the Chapel of the Royal Military College, Sandhurst, was completed. Much care had been bestowed on the design of the regimental badge which surmounts the Panel. 30 officers of the Regiment, formerly Cadets of the College, who lost their lives during 1914–18, are commemorated. The dedication ceremony, in the presence of T.M. the King and Queen, took place on 2nd May 1936.

COLOURS OF 4TH BATTALION

In April 1923 the 4th Battalion (Lieut.-Colonel C. H. Little) received back their Colours from the hands of the Mayor of Bath (Alderman Cedric Chivers). They had been in the keeping of the city since August 1914. After handing over the Colours the Mayor, accompanied by the Lord Lieutenant of Somerset (the Marquis of Bath), took the salute as the battalion marched off with bugles playing and colours flying.

CADET TRAINING UNITS

In addition to the Militia, Volunteer and Territorial units mentioned in Chapter I, the County of Somerset had, prior to 1914, a strong Cadet organisation. It had its origin in the desire for military training which spread to many schools when the Volunteer Force was raised in 1859, cadets being affiliated to Volunteer units. For some years the training of cadets was in the hands of the 1st, 2nd and 3rd Volunteer Battalions of the Somerset Light Infantry.

During the latter part of the nineteenth century the movement in Somerset was confined mainly to the Public Schools, except for two units of the Church Lads' Brigade. The Public School units were part of the Officers Training Corps and existed at Taunton, Wellington and Bath. During 1914–18, many new open and school units were formed. In 1918 these units were under the general designation of the 1st, 2nd and 3rd Volunteer Battalions of the Somerset Light Infantry. In 1923 the units of the Cadet force, in Somerset, were:

1st (Ilminster), 2nd (Bridgwater) and 3rd (Minehead) Cadet Corps, 5th Somerset L.I.
2nd Cadet Corps, 4th Somerset L.I.
4th Bath and Wells Cadet Battalion.
Queen's College (Taunton) Cadet Battalion.
Crewkerne, Yeovil and Sexey's School (Blackford) Cadet Corps.
1st Wessex Battalion, The Boys' Brigade.
Chard School and Wells Boys' Blue School Cadet Coys.

MARRIAGE OF H.R.H. THE COLONEL-IN-CHIEF

On 26th April 1923 an event of great interest to all ranks of the Regiment took place. H.R.H. the Colonel-in-Chief was married to the Lady Elizabeth Bowes-Lyon at Westminster Abbey. The Regiment was represented by the Colonel (Lieut.-General Sir T. D'O. Snow), Lieut.-Colonel A. H. Yatman, D.S.O. (Commanding 1st Battalion), Major R. H. E. Bennett, M.C. (Depot and 3rd Battalion), Captain G. W. R. Bishop (4th Battalion), Captain H. F. Calway (5th Battalion), one Warrant Officer and nine Other Ranks. The detachment lined the pavement at the West Door of the Abbey.

All ranks of the Regiment combined to present to T.R.H. a silver statuette of an officer of the Regiment in the uniform of 1843.

1st BATTALION

On 8th July 1920 Lieut.-Colonel A. H. Yatman, D.S.O., succeeded Lieut.-Colonel P. M. Wardlaw in command of the 1st Battalion, which sustained a number of "battle casualties" during the Belfast Riots. The Battalion moved from Ireland to England in 1921 for Strike Duty and on 15th November was transferred to Devonport. There, in July 1921, Lieut.-Colonel J. S. N. Harrison, D.S.O., succeeded Lieut.-Colonel Yatman in command.

A Trooping of the Colour Parade was held at Raglan Barracks in June 1925 and in the following year the Battalion was moved by sea in connection with the General Strike of 1926. At the end of the year it proceeded overseas to Ismailia on the Suez Canal.

1919–1928

2ND BATTALION: INDIA, SOUDAN AND HOME

In February 1922 the 2nd Battalion moved from Lucknow to Agra and in April Lieut.-Colonel W. J. Bowker, C.M.G., D.S.O., vacated command, being succeeded by Lieut.-Colonel A. W. S. Paterson, D.S.O.

At an inspection by Lord Rawlinson, Commander-in-Chief in India, he recorded:

"A fine body of men and a particularly nice lot of keen, sporting young officers. They are lucky to have such good senior men at the head of affairs; and I was specially pleased to see a good, old-fashioned type of N.C.O. The men looked fit and healthy."

In September 1923 the battalion was engaged in dealing with communal riots in Agra—an unpleasant and difficult task. When tranquillity had been restored a number of leading Indian gentlemen of the city subscribed a substantial sum for the entertainment of the men as a tribute to their exemplary tact and forbearance in maintaining order in every part of the city. The *Pioneer* of Allahabad, dated 17th September 1923, stated:

"The frank recognition by prominent Indians of the services rendered by British soldiers at a time when feeling between Hindus and Mohammedans was running so high that neither would trust the other, does honour to both the givers and the recipients. Incidentally it serves as a significant reminder of the utility of British Troops in holding the scales even between the two factions, without the slightest possibility of any suspicion of their impartiality arising."

In June 1925 Lieut.-Colonel Paterson, D.S.O., vacated command and was succeeded by Lieut.-Colonel H. I. R. Allfrey, D.S.O., M.C. In that year a memorial tablet was erected in the Garrison Church at Lucknow, dedicated to Lieut. L. J. Hansford White and Privates J. W. Jeffrey, H. E. Francis and H. J. Peppiatt, who lost their lives while stationed there.

On 12th December 1925 the battalion sailed from Bombay in H.T. "Derbyshire", landing at Port Soudan and moving to Khartoum. It sailed for England on 4th January 1927, in H.T. "Assaye", leaving 300 ranks to join the 1st Battalion at Ismailia.

On arrival in England the battalion was stationed at Tidworth.

On this tour of duty the 2nd Battalion spent just over 18 years abroad, during which period it made seven sea voyages to Malta, North China, India, Palestine, India (again), the Soudan and England. After serving in Malta and North China (where it saw active service during the disturbances arising from the Revolution of 1911–13) it was unlucky to be retained, as one of six regular battalions, to hold the North-West Frontier during the 1914–18 War. Had it proceeded to Lebong—to which station it was originally ordered—instead of going to Quetta in 1913, it might have left India for a theatre of war with one of the Divisions which were despatched at an early date after the outbreak of hostilities.

It took an active part, however, on the Khyber Front, during the 3rd Afghan War in 1919, particularly in the actions of Bagh and Dakar, in both of which engagements the Afghan Army was routed. At one time it was under short notice to proceed to Jellalabad, where it might have revisited the site of the glorious episode of 1842. This advance was, however, cancelled owing to lack of transport to maintain the force. At the final assault on "Somerset Hill" during the action at Dakar, on the 16th/17th May 1919, the bugles of the battalion sounded the charge—perhaps for the last time in war.

1st BATTALION: EGYPT, CHINA

On the 12th June 1927, H.R.H. the Colonel-in-Chief passed through the Suez Canal in H.M.S. "Renown", on return from his Empire tour. He landed at Moascar, specially to inspect the 1st Battalion and, later, sent the following signal:

"Please inform all ranks how delighted I was to see them this morning and I was much impressed with their smart appearance. I wish I could have stayed longer. Albert."

In October 1927, the battalion moved to Cairo, sending a detachment to Cyprus. In July 1928 Lieut.-Colonel C. H. Little, D.S.O., took over command from Lieut.-Colonel J. S. N. Harrison. On 17th December the Battalion sailed from Suez in H.T. "City of Marseilles" and arrived at Hong-Kong on 11th January 1929, being stationed on the mainland at Kowloon.

4TH AND 5TH BATTALIONS

On 6th August 1924 the 4th (Lieut.-Colonel G. Flemming, O.B.E., M.C.) and 5th (Lieut.-Colonel R. A. Giffard, T.D.) Battalions went into camp together at Weston-super-Mare. While there they were inspected by the Colonel of the Regiment. H.R.H. the Colonel-in-Chief sent messages to both battalions congratulating all ranks on the high standard of training attained and the general efficiency of the units.

On 25th September 1925 a War Memorial to the 4th Battalion was unveiled at Bridgwater by the Earl of Cavan, Chief of the Imperial General Staff, in the presence of Lieut.-Colonel R. A. Giffard, T.D., the Band, Bugles and No. 3 Company 4th Battalion.

13TH ROYAL HAMILTON REGIMENT OF CANADA

In the early years of the twentieth century the Regiment formed an alliance with the 13th Royal Hamilton Regiment of the Canadian Forces. This regiment was raised in 1862. The association had been fostered by the interchange of visits between officers of the two regiments.

In 1924 Major-General Sir John Gibson, K.C.M.G., was Honorary Colonel and Major-General S. C. Newburn, C.M.G., M.P., Honorary Lieut.-Colonel. Lieut.-Colonel G. W. Black was in command and was succeeded in 1926 by Lieut.-Colonel Thomas Morrison.

In 1927, the Royal Hamilton Regiment, with the full concurrence of the Colonel of the Somerset Light Infantry, applied to be formed into a regiment of Light Infantry. It also asked that H.R.H. the Duke of York should become Colonel-in-Chief and that the words "Prince Albert's" should be added to the title.

On 1st April 1927, H.R.H. was gazetted Colonel-in-Chief. In July 1927 the title of the Regiment was changed to "The Royal Hamilton Light Infantry". It was pointed out by National Defence Headquarters, Canada, that the title of "Prince Albert's" referred to the late Prince Consort and was conferred on the Somerset Light Infantry, by Queen Victoria, as a unique honour and distinction for the illustrious services rendered by the Regiment at Jellalabad in 1841–42. Thus its application to any other regiment was inappropriate. The request to be allowed to assume this title was, therefore, withdrawn.

The regimental badge adopted by the Royal Hamilton Light Infantry displays the Light Infantry Bugle, on which is imposed the roman numeral XIII. The whole is surmounted by the Maple Leaf badge.

In 1929 the 1st Battalion Somerset Light Infantry presented a silver bugle to the Royal Hamilton Light Infantry. Following this the whole Bugle Band of the Regiment was equipped with silver bugles of the same pattern.

During 1929 Lieut-Colonel T. Morrison was succeeded in command by Lieut.-Colonel D. K. Baldwin. On his retirement Lieut.-Colonel C. W. G. Gibson, M.C., V.D., A.D.C., assumed command.

THE INTERNATIONAL FIELD

In addition to the complications arising from the Treaty of Versailles, referred to at the start of this Chapter, certain other major events began to cast their dark shadows over Europe.

With the coming of peace the German Imperial Family went into exile. A revolution took place in Berlin, from which the Social-Democratic Party emerged victorious and, probably, saved Germany from Bolshevism, as represented by the K.P.D., or German Communist Party. The Social-Democrats were bourgeois and relied greatly on the favour of disgruntled army officers.

In October 1923 Adolf Hitler made his first appearance when, with the National Socialist Party, he made his first attempt, at Munich, to seize power. Although he then failed, his adherents grew rapidly in numbers, consisting mainly of members of the younger generation who had experienced the misery of the period of German economic inflation.

The economic situation in Germany caused much anxiety and great hardship. In May 1921 an Allied Reparations Commission fixed the indemnity to be paid by Germany at 132 billions of gold marks. This was followed by the vast printing of German paper money, the complete devaluation of the mark, the ruin of the German middle-classes and the request for a Moratorium in January 1923.

France replied by occupying the Ruhr, to collect what was due to her. By the summer of 1923 business in Germany was at a standstill and the country on the verge of starvation. The Dawes Plan was evolved, with a loan to Germany which served to improve conditions. But divergencies of opinion arose between Britain, the United States and France which led, later, to attempts by France to "encircle" Germany and to her support of the "Little Entente", comprising Yugo-Slavia, Czecho-Slovakia and Roumania. In October 1922 Italian Black Shirts entered Rome and a Fascist Cabinet was set up under the control of Benito Mussolini.

Thus the rise of Communism, the first signs of Nazism and Fascism, disputes between the Allies, the isolationist policy of the United States, discontent of European populations arising from territorial readjustments, inflationary tendencies, economic difficulties, starvation and poverty, all began to play their part in setting the stage for a further European conflict.

In the East, Japan was discontented with her rewards for her share in the 1914–18 War. She was also gravely perturbed at the rise of Communism and feared that it might spread, from Siberia and Mongolia, to the teeming population of the Japanese Islands. She began to further her designs on Manchuria and China itself.

CHAPTER III

BETWEEN TWO WARS—THE SECOND DECADE, 1928-1939

1st Battalion Abroad—New Colours for 2nd Battalion—The evolution of Mechanised forces—The Armoured Force—The 7th (Experimental) Infantry Brigade—Trends of the evolution of infantry—Changes in dress—Green whistle lanyards—Full dress sash—Badges, buttons and titles—Badge for Regimental Colour—Territorial Army—Old Comrades' Association—Families of Lamb and Chambers—Changes in Colonelcy—Alliance with 13th Australian Infantry—The Royal Hamilton Light Infantry—Memorial at Ypres—King's Guard in London—The Colonel-in-Chief—4th and 5th Battalions (T.A.)—2nd Battalion to Gibraltar—Soldiers' Home, Taunton—Regimental Museum—Light Bob Gazette—Regimental Dinner Club—Developments of defence—Events in international field—The events leading to War, 1939

THERE must, of necessity, be an overlap between two arbitrarily fixed periods of time. In the case of this history, the overlap occurs in the story of the 2nd Battalion. As this battalion was to play a pioneer part in the reorganisation of infantry, it will be convenient to deal with its progress as a whole.

1st BATTALION ABROAD

During the years 1928-39 the 1st Battalion served overseas, engaged on normal peacetime duties. It was, however, called upon to take part in various interesting events.

During 1929-30, whilst in Hong-Kong, it provided guards on small coasting vessels, plying between Hong-Kong and Singapore as protection against piracy, which was rife. In 1930 it moved to Wellington, in the Nilgiris of South India, where it remained until 1934. Here it provided large detachments in the Moplah country, at Malapuram, and on the east coast at Calicut in Malabar, where unrest continued since the Moplah Rebellion of 1921. In July 1932 Lieut.-Colonel G. E. M. Whittuck, M.C., succeeded Lieut.-Colonel C. H. Little in command.

In 1934 the Battalion moved to Poona, where it remained until 1939. Between 1935-8 communal rioting was rife in India and on several occasions the Battalion was called on to "show the flag" in Poona and on the borders of Hyderabad State at Sholapur, when disorders had occurred, or threatened. In July 1936 Lieut.-Colonel V. W. Roche succeeded Lieut.-Colonel Whittuck in command.

PRESENTATION OF NEW COLOURS TO THE 2ND BATTALION

Although the question of Colours may seem remote from such material matters as the evolution of infantry, it has a direct bearing on morale, without which weapons and equipment are of little use. The traditions and spirit of a Regiment are enshrined in the visible symbol of the Colours.

In January 1927, on its return from foreign service, the 2nd Battalion was stationed at Tidworth. On the 20th July, while under the command of Lieut.-Colonel H. I. R. Allfrey, D.S.O., M.C., H.R.H. the Colonel-in-Chief presented the new Colours. Among those present were the Colonel of the Regiment, Lieut.-General Sir T. D'O. Snow, K.C.B., K.C.M.G., and the Adjutant-General to the Forces, General Sir W. P. Braithwaite, K.C.B., A.D.C.

The Old Colours were carried by Lieut. E. H. C. Evered and 2/Lieut. H. N. Barlow. The New Colours were received by Lieuts. A. Hunt and R. E. D. Vining. The consecration was carried out by the Chaplain General to the Forces.

H.R.H. the Colonel-in-Chief, addressing the battalion said:

"I am very glad to be here today and to present these New Colours to the Battalion of a Regiment whose record has ever been a splendid one. I myself never fail to be deeply moved by the stirring history of Jellalabad, one of the most glorious episodes in the history of the British Army. You all know the story of that battle and how Queen Victoria gave the Somerset Light Infantry, as a reward, the title of 'Prince Albert's', which in her eyes was the highest honour she could confer on them. I am proud to be your Colonel-in-Chief and to continue in this way the personal association between the Regiment and my family. I know that Jellalabad has come to be regarded by the Regiment as symbolic of the soul and spirit which animates it and that the memory of that day will never die . . . I know, too, that in entrusting these Colours to the direct successors of the Illustrious Garrison, I am handing them to those who will ever maintain the high traditions of the Regiment and prove themselves worthy of the gallant officers and men who served so loyally in the past."

136 Old Comrades, including two Chelsea Pensioners, gathered for the ceremony. They were inspected by H.R.H., who shook hands with them and spoke to each man.

In November 1927 the Old Colours were laid up in St. Mary's Church, Taunton, being placed on the South wall of the Chancel of the Church.

THE EVOLUTION OF MECHANISED FORCES

When the War of 1914–18 was over, certain problems faced the army leaders in preparing and training forces for a future struggle. These problems may be categorised briefly as:

(*a*) the means of moving unarmoured men on the battlefield in the face of fire from automatic weapons;

(*b*) the employment of, and protection from, aircraft, whose development had introduced a new dimension into warfare;

(*c*) protection from, and use of, poison gas;

(*d*) the harnessing of national resources for National War.

As regards movement on the battlefield, two methods, neither very successful, had been evolved during the latter years of the war in France. The French resorted to the massing of artillery and the drenching thereby, of centres of resistance with high explosive. The British combined fire and movement in the armoured fighting vehicle.

Over all, it was abundantly clear that the old theory of "big battalions" and masses of men on the battlefield had failed. It was also clear that warfare of the future necessitated intensive economic preparation in time of peace, with the organised defence of centres of industry. From the lessons learned during four stern years of war, it was generally agreed that forces engaged on land should be small, should contain a considerable armoured element, should be highly mobile and should be supported by aircraft. These conclusions were of importance, for to each one practical effect was given, in the composition, strategy and tactics of the armies which fought between 1939 and 1945.

There were three stages in the preparation and training of the forces which emerged:

First, the administrative change over from the horse drawn vehicle and the man on the horse, to machines for the transport of men, weapons, munitions and supplies.

Second, the strategic mechanisation required to move the forces to the front, to protect them on the move and to maintain them in a theatre of war.

Third, the tactical developments necessary to enable a mechanical and armoured force to fight on the battlefield.

These three stages were not accomplished without many difficulties and a long period of experiment, trial and error. The main difficulties were:

(i) technical limitations in the conflict between weapons and armour. Here it became apparent that speed of movement provided better protection than weight of armour;

(ii) the training of specialists to handle complicated machines and equipment. The types of the latter were constantly changing as experience was gained. A great deal of electrical equipment, including wireless sets, was brought into use, requiring specialist knowledge for its employment and maintenance;

(iii) space was required in which to train forces which were capable of rapid movement over long distances. The movement of forces was no longer governed by the endurance of men and horses.

As the experiments with the new forces progressed, it was found necessary, after transportation to the battlefield, to provide lightly armed men to fight on foot in conjunction with the armoured vehicles. Thus, while cavalry abandoned the horse for the tank, or armoured car, capable of reconnaissance and shock action, the rôle of infantry—particularly Light Infantry—remained just as important and very much the same as it had always been. The new developments gave to infantry increased mobility, activity and more suitable weapons for both offence and defence.

In the air considerable strides were made in co-operation with, and close support of, land forces. The main lines of development were in respect of reconnaissance, artillery co-operation, attack, transportation and supply.

The main lessons of the 1914–18 War, which were studied in great detail during the period between the two wars, were: the necessity for adequate organisation of national resources in time of peace, so as to ensure rapid mobilisation when war came; the development of civil aviation to provide a second-line air force and a reserve of pilots; first line land forces, to take the first shock of war, had to be highly mechanised and armoured.

THE ARMOURED FORCE

In January 1927 the 2nd Battalion joined the 7th Infantry Brigade at Tidworth. It formed part of the Experimental Armoured Force located in the neighbourhood of Salisbury Plain. This included Tanks, Armoured Cars and mechanised artillery, engineer, infantry, medical and supply units.

The 2nd Battalion was converted into a mechanised machine gun battalion, and was first known as the 1st Mechanised M.G. Battalion. It was carried in cross-country vehicles and was the first infantry unit of the British Army to be so organised and equipped. The organisation comprised: Battalion H.Q.; H.Q. Wing; three mechanised machine gun companies, and one rifle company.

The latter was, mainly, employed in training and providing the drafts for the 1st Battalion overseas. The signal section was equipped with wireless sets and motor-cycle despatch riders.

The first transport issued consisted, mainly, of Crossley-Kegresse half-track lorries and a number of motor-cycles. Armament and equipment included:

- 36 Vickers machine guns.
- 10 Lewis guns.
- 14 Light cars, half-track.
- 4 Light, six-wheeled, lorries.
- 32 30-cwt., half-track, lorries.
- 4 Water carts, with kitchen trailers.

The total strength of the four companies was 546 and of the battalion, 728.

As was natural, the Armoured Force experienced many "teething troubles" during the early part of its existence. Much time had to be devoted to individual training of N.C.O.s, specialists and men. Even at an early stage it was found that Salisbury Plain was all too small for the tactical exercises which the force required.

On 20th March 1928, the Experimental Armoured Force paraded at Bulford for the benefit of Amir Amanullah of Afghanistan. This episode was merely interesting as affording an Order of Battle of the Force:

- 2nd Battalion Royal Tank Corps.
- 5th Battalion Royal Tank Corps.
- Light Tank Company of 3rd Battalion Royal Tank Corps.
- 12th Armoured Car Company.
- 17th Mechanised Field Company Royal Engineers.

9th Mechanised Brigade Royal Field Artillery.
9th Mechanised Light Brigade Royal Artillery.
1st Mechanised Medium Brigade Royal Artillery.
1st Mechanised Machine Gun Battalion (Somerset Light Infantry).
Mechanised Medical and Supply Units.
3rd S.S. (Fighter) Squadron Royal Air Force.

THE 7th (EXPERIMENTAL) INFANTRY BRIGADE

By the end of 1928 much preliminary work had been completed and a change of policy came. Early in 1929, the Experimental Armoured Force was dispersed. The 2nd Battalion ceased to be the 1st Mechanised Machine Gun Battalion and became part of the 7th (Experimental) Brigade at Tidworth. It was reorganised as follows: Battalion H.Q. and H.Q. Wing; three rifle companies, and one machine gun company. The machine gun company had one platoon in Carden-Lloyds with trailers and two platoons carried in half-track lorries. Headquarter Wing contained an Anti-tank platoon with four ·8in. Oerlikon guns, each gun with a trailer for the gun team, towed by a Carden-Lloyd. This organisation represented the development of the theory that infantry should be able to defend itself against Tanks and could not rely, solely, on the artillery for protection.

First Line transport remained mechanised, except for the issue of eight chargers and one G.S. Limber, with two light-draught horses. This seems a retrograde step, but arose from the fact that, at that time, no suitable mechanical vehicle had been evolved to enable the battalion commander and company commanders to carry out reconnaissances and perform other duties. The Scout-car and Jeep were still developments of the future. Wireless sets were withdrawn from the Signal Section and visual and line signalling reverted to.

These developments foreshadowed the coming of the Support Company and the provision of armoured carriers within the battalion.

During May 1929 Lieut.-Colonel H. I. R. Allfrey vacated command and was succeeded by Lieut.-Colonel V. H. B. Majendie, D.S.O.

During 1930 two further changes in organisation took place. Rifle platoons were organised on a basis of three rifle sections and one Lewis gun section. Headquarter Wing received a platoon of Vickers machine guns, carried in Carden-Lloyds, without trailers. This marked the first development of "in-fighting weapons" within the battalion. In December 1930 the Battalion moved to Blackdown and became part of the 6th Infantry Brigade, which continued experimental training.

1931 saw the "in-fighting platoon" removed from Headquarter Wing and merged into the Machine Gun Company. The latter then consisted of two platoons of Armoured machine-gun carriers, one with, the other without, trailers, and one horse-drawn platoon. An experimental 3-in. Mortar Platoon was added to Headquarter Wing, carried in Carden-Lloyds with trailers. Rifle platoons were reorganised with one rifle section and two Lewis gun sections.

These developments foreshadowed the increase of fire-power in the infantry battalion and the more even distribution of weapons throughout the unit.

1932 saw the Machine Gun Company become the "Support" Company, organised as three machine-gun platoons and one mortar platoon, all carried in Carden-Lloyds with trailers. This company was inspected by H.M. the King at Aldershot on 22nd April, 1932.

On 7th April 1932 (Jellalabad Day) H.R.H. the Colonel-in-Chief attended the Trooping of the Colour by the 2nd Battalion at Blackdown. In May 1932 Lieut.-Colonel V. H. B. Majendie vacated command and was succeeded by Lieut.-Colonel R. H. Waddy, D.S.O. In 1933 the 6th Infantry Brigade was "de-mechanised" and the 2nd Battalion gave up all its mechanical vehicles, motor-cycles and anti-tank guns. In November 1934 it moved to Colchester. So ended an episode in the history of the Regiment and the British Army. But the work done, in a fresh field, by the 2nd Battalion, was to bear fruit in the years which lay ahead.

TRENDS OF THE EVOLUTION OF INFANTRY

It is fitting to conclude this record of the experimental mechanisation of the 2nd Battalion with a reference to a tentative proposal made by the War Office in 1935. Certain units of the British Army were asked if they would be prepared to accept conversion into "Machine Gun" or "Support" regiments. These proposals appear to have been confined to Infantry of the Line. The alternative to this proposal was to remain as "Rifle Regiments". The following organisations for battalions were envisaged:

"Rifle Battalion";
    Battalion H.Q. Headquarter Company (to include Signal Section, Mortar Section, Light M.G. Section).
    Four Companies; each of four platoons armed with rifles and light machine guns.
    The whole with mechanised transport.

"Machine Gun Battalion";
    Battalion H.Q. Headquarter Company (to include Signal Section and Anti-aircraft M.G. Section).
    Three Companies each of three platoons of machine guns.
    One Anti-tank Company of four platoons, each of four Anti-tank guns.
    The whole with mechanised transport.

These proposals are of interest in showing the ideas on the subject of the organisation of infantry which had emerged from the experience of the Experimental Force.

The views of battalions of the Regiment on these proposals were obtained, having regard to the fact that the 2nd Battalion had already had experience as a Machine Gun battalion. In brief, it was held that the opportunities offered by the Machine Gun battalion organisation for attracting recruits of the best type and for the possible ultimate emergence of a Corps d'Élite, were outweighed by the danger that the Regiment might, if so converted, lose its Light Infantry identity, its County connection and its regimental spirit. These were cherished possessions which could not lightly be cast aside.

It was also felt that, on a long term view, Machine Gun Regiments might, in the face of unforeseen future developments, become redundant and their existence threatened. It was, therefore, decided to remain a "Rifle Regiment".

CHANGES IN DRESS

Although the evolution of infantry was, perhaps, the most important feature during the period between the two wars, from the point of view of the student of military administration, strategy and tactics, there were other aspects of these years of comparative peace which were of interest and importance in the life of a regiment.

Not least among these was the question of dress, which, although not perhaps generally realised, has a marked bearing on morale. Woman is not the only member of the human race engaged in "The Eternal Masquerade". Man, also, likes to dress up and display his finery. Indeed, it is a healthy sign for the young soldier to take a pride in his clothes and his turn out. It is a definite fact that, on active service, those regiments which continue to insist on the cleanliness and smart appearance of their men are usually those which give the best account of themselves in battle. Slovenliness and military efficiency seldom go hand-in-hand.

Among the adjuncts to a high standard of morale are the much prized peculiarities of dress, or ornament, which are the unique possession of certain regiments. These are a source of pride. If a man will go into battle with more confidence in himself and fight better because, say, he wears a peacock's feather in his hat, which no one outside his unit is allowed to wear, this peculiarity should outweigh any considerations of making him conspicuous, or easily identifiable. The criterion, however, is that within a regiment such peculiarities of dress should be uniform.

Thus certain changes in the dress of the Regiment are worthy of record.

GREEN WHISTLE LANYARDS

In August 1928 the wearing of green whistle lanyards and black sword knots by English Regiments of Light Infantry, which had been a prized, but unauthorised, practice for many years, was regularised (W. O. letter 54 (Officers) 2587 (M.G.O. 7. b), dated 2nd August 1928).

THE FULL DRESS SASH

In 1931 H.M. the King was graciously pleased to approve that the long established custom in the Regiment of the officers wearing the Sash, in full dress, knotted on the right side, should be officially recognised (W.O. letter

54/Misc/2846 (M.G.O.7.b), dated 26th February 1931). This custom has a long history and is discussed at some length in Volume I of this history.

In 1764, after the battle of Culloden, the Duke of Cumberland gave orders that the Sergeants of the Regiment should knot the sash on the same side as the Officers. This was a unique distinction and, in the various arguments which arose regarding the custom from time to time, three legends concerning its origin emerged.

Reynolds, in his exhaustive work on Military Uniforms of the British Army (Victoria and Albert Museum, 84 vols.) takes the view that it may have something to do with the period, in 1706, when the Regiment was employed as Dragoons. At that time cavalry sashes were tied on the right and infantry sashes on the left side. There is, however, no record that, at that time, sergeants wore sashes at all.

The second legend ascribes it to a reward for the pulling down of an old wall at Culloden, to allow the cavalry to pass through. The third legend says that the reward was for the determined courage of the regiment at Culloden, which prevented the clansmen from closing in. The latter fled before they could be engaged with the bayonet.

Whatever may have been the real reason for the reward, the custom was regularised for sergeants in 1865. No mention was then made of officers, since, at that time, officers knotted the sash on the right side. In 1898 dress regulations were altered and it was then laid down that all officers in Regiments of the Line should knot the sash on the left side. At that time no application seems to have been made for the officers of the Regiment to knot the sash on the same side as authorised for the sergeants. The practice was, however, continued without sanction until regularised in 1931.

BADGES, BUTTONS AND TITLES

In June 1929 the War Office approved "sealed patterns" of officers cap and Service Dress collar badges for the Regiment, as well as patterns of badges for wear by Other Ranks. This order authorised certain articles of dress which, for many years, had been worn without official sanction. In 1933 sanction was accorded to the Forage Cap button being changed to a pattern similar in design to that worn on Service Dress Caps, but in silver (W.O. letter 54/Infantry/6908 (M.G.O.7.b), dated 20th July 1933).

In 1938 approval was accorded to the issue of shoulder titles of one piece for the Regiment, when stocks of the two-piece design were exhausted (W.O. letter 54/Infantry/7776 (M.G.O.7.b), dated 26th January 1938).

BADGE FOR THE REGIMENTAL COLOUR

In October 1933 the heraldic description of the Centre Badge for the Regimental Colour was approved and defined as: "Within a bugle horn stringed ensigned, with a Mural Crown superscribed 'Jellalabad,' the Roman Numeral XIII" (W.O. letter 20/Gen/5314 (A.G.4.d), dated 31st October 1933).

1928–1939

THE TERRITORIAL ARMY

In April 1929 the Territorial Army "came of age", after 21 years of existence. Some details of its origin are given in Chapter I. The designation had been changed from "Territorial Force" to "Territorial Army" in 1921. In 1917 H.M. the King had approved of Territorial battalions wearing the same badges and placing the same honours on their Colours as the regular battalions.

The 4th and 5th Battalions already had Colours which had been subscribed for by Ladies of the County. They had been presented by H.M. King Edward VII, at Windsor Castle, on 22nd June 1909. They were first carried in the presence of Royalty, when T.R.H. the Prince and Princess of Wales visited Wells and Glastonbury. On that occasion the North Somerset Yeomanry provided the Royal Escort with Standard, and the 4th and 5th Battalions, the Somerset Light Infantry, the Guards of Honour with Colours.

Among county Territorial units which have disappeared, mostly about the year 1918, were:

The West Somerset Yeomanry (perpetuated in the 373rd and 374th (West Somerset Yeomanry) Field Batteries, Royal Artillery).
The Somerset Battery, Royal Horse Artillery.
The 2nd South Western Mounted Brigade Transport and Supply Column, R.A.S.C.
The South Western Infantry Brigade Company, R.A.S.C.
The 2nd South Western Mounted Brigade Field Ambulance, R.A.M.C.

In August 1929 H.R.H. the Colonel-in-Chief inspected the 2nd, 4th and 5th Battalions on Salisbury Plain. He was accompanied by the Marquis of Bath, Lord Lieutenant of Somerset.

OLD COMRADES' ASSOCIATION

The Old Comrades' Association was strengthened and flourished in the period between the two wars. The main headquarters of the Association was at Taunton, but sub-branches were opened in London and cities in Somerset. The connection of the Old Comrades with the Regiment had always been very close.

On the 12th August 1929 the 50th Anniversary of the Battle of Kambula was celebrated at Taunton, many veterans of the Zulu (1879) and Burma (1885) wars being present. Among these were ten out of the twelve Zulu War veterans still living. The Colonel of the Regiment (Lieut.-General Sir T. D'O. Snow) presided and recalled that, at the close of the Zulu War, he shook hands with Cetewayo and gave him a bottle of gin. In return Cetewayo introduced him to his four wives who, at the time, were enjoying a hot bath. Corporal P. Tacchi, aged 85 years, spoke on behalf of the veterans.

On 12th May 1932, H.R.H. the Colonel-in-Chief inspected members of the Association at Taunton. 398 members were on parade under Major-General Sir H. J. Everett, K.C.M.G., C.B., and were drawn up in the order of the campaigns in which they served between 1878 and 1919. All twelve surviving Zulu War veterans were present, the oldest being Mr. A. Ashford (83), Mr. W. Pring (77) and Mr. T. Parkhurst (75). The oldest soldier on parade was Mr. T. Collinson, of Taunton, who joined the Regiment in 1872.

As an example of the close connection of the Regiment with particular families in Somerset, over many years, the history of the Lamb family is deserving of record:

Father:

R. LAMB. Enlisted in 1855 in the Land Transport Corps. Discharged by purchase, with the rank of Sergeant in 1856. Joined the regiment in 1858 and transferred to the Hospital Corps in 1876. Discharged as a Sergeant-Major in 1878, being unfit for further service. Joined up as a Sergeant-Major R.A.M.C., for Home Service in 1899. Died at Golden Hill, Isle of Wight, in 1901. He had 24 years service and the Crimean, Turkish and Long Service and Good Conduct Medals.

Sons:

J. LAMB. Joined the Regiment as a boy in 1873. Colour Sergeant, 1890. Discharged in 1908. Re-enlisted in the Regiment in 1914 and served in Ireland. Posted to 9th Battalion and discharged as unfit in 1916. He had $36\frac{3}{4}$ years' service, the Meritorious Service and Long Service and Good Conduct Medals. He died in December 1935.

R. J. LAMB. Joined the 4th Battalion as a boy in 1900. Sergeant, 1902. Joined the 2nd Battalion in 1903 and became a C.S.M. Promoted Captain in 1918 and served in India as R.T.O. Promoted Major in 1920 and served as D.A.D.R.T. with the Waziristan Field Force and at Lahore. Retired 1922, 22 years' service. G.S., Indian G.S., with clasp, "Waziristan 1919–21," Medals.

Stepson:

R. GOULD. Joined Regiment in 1866. Sergeant, 1878. Bugle Major, 1880. Colour Sergeant, 1882. Q.M. Sergeant, 1887. Discharged, 1890. 24 years' service. Indian G.S. with clasp "Burma 1885–7", and Long Service and Good Conduct Medals.

The aggregate of service for this family was $106\frac{3}{4}$ years.
The record of the Chambers Family is equally remarkable.

Father:

J. D. CHAMBERS. Sergeant Master Tailor. Served with the Regiment for 36 years between 1870 and 1915. Long Service and Good Conduct Medal.

Sons:

J. H. CHAMBERS. Quartermaster Sergeant in the Regiment and on Garrison Staff. 23 years' service between 1891 and 1914. King's, and Queen's South Africa, Long Service and Good Conduct Medals.

G. D. CHAMBERS. Lieutenant and Quartermaster in the Regiment. 24 years' service between 1895 and 1919. British War, Victory, Long Service and Good Conduct Medals.

C. S. CHAMBERS. Captain in the Regiment and the Loyal Regiment. 24 years' service between 1898 and 1922. Queen's South Africa, 1914–15 Star, British War and Victory Medals. Croix de Guerre.

T. S. CHAMBERS. Sergeant in the Regiment. Transferred to Royal Engineers.

P. A. CHAMBERS. Captain R.A.O.C. 33 years' service between 1902 and 1935. 1914 Star, British War, Victory, Long Service and Good Conduct Medals.

I. F. CHAMBERS. Warrant Officer, Class I, Royal Air Force. 23 years' service between 1912 and 1935. 1914 Star, British War, Victory and Long Service and Good Conduct Medals.

The aggregate of service of this family, up to 1935, was 176 years.

During the period between the two wars many links with the past were severed by the death of Old Comrades. Notes regarding the services of some of those who "Passed over" are given in an appendix to this volume.

CHANGES IN COLONELCY

During August 1929 Lieut.-General Sir T. D'O. Snow, K.C.B., K.C.M.G., resigned the colonelcy and was succeeded by General Sir Walter P. Braithwaite, G.C.B., A.D.C., Adjutant-General to the Forces. General Snow resigned "to enable a younger and more able-bodied man to represent the Regiment and because a regiment does not often get the chance of having the Adjutant-General for its Colonel".

On 20th October 1938 General Braithwaite vacated the appointment, and was followed by Major-General V. H. B. Majendie, C.B., D.S.O., who was destined to watch over the interests of the Regiment during the war years, 1939–45. General Braithwaite, announcing his resignation, wrote:

" ... It is over 52 years since I was gazetted to the Regiment and for the past 9 years I have had the honour to be its Colonel. . . . I hand over to a very distinguished officer and a devoted servant of the Regiment who will sound the same clear Bugle Call of service as has been my aim and that of my predecessors."

ALLIANCE WITH 13TH AUSTRALIAN INFANTRY

In September 1928, Major E. W. Sproule, Commanding the 13th Battalion Australian Infantry, wrote to the Colonel of the Regiment suggesting an alliance. He based his proposal on the number 13 borne by both regiments and the fact that many battle honours gained by the Somerset Light Infantry were also borne by the 13th Australian Infantry.

This proposal was welcomed by the Regiment and approved by H.R.H. the Colonel-in-Chief. H.M. the King, also, was graciously pleased to approve (W.O. letter 092/1941 (A.G.4.b), dated 2nd July 1929). Army Orders of July 1929 announced that:

"The 13th Battalion Australian Infantry, Australian Military Forces, is allied to the Somerset Light Infantry (Prince Albert's)."

A similar authorisation is contained in Australian Army Order No. 443, dated 29th September 1929.

The 13th Australian Infantry had its headquarters at West Maitland, New South Wales, and was known as "The Maitland Regiment", with the motto, "Vigor in Arduis". Its area of recruitment included the towns of West Maitland, Kurri Kurri and Singleton. Major Sproule vacated command in October 1930 and was succeeded by Major McPherson.

THE ROYAL HAMILTON LIGHT INFANTRY

In August 1929, Major-General Sir John Gibson, K.C.M.G., died. He had been Honorary Colonel of the Regiment for many years and closely connected with it. In November 1934, Lieut.-Colonel C. W. G. Gibson, M.C., V.D., A.D.C., vacated command and was succeeded by Lieut.-Colonel G. L. Wright, V.D. The latter was followed by Lieut.-Colonel F. C. Thompson, until 1938, when Lieut.-Colonel H. Gordon-Wright assumed command.

MEMORIAL AT YPRES

During November 1935 a Memorial Banner, representing the Regiment, was placed in the Church at Ypres. It had been worked by a committee of the Ladies of Somerset and was first used, after the 1914–18 War, at the Memorial Service to the First Seven Divisions, held at the Albert Hall, London. Since July 1920 it had been kept in St. Mary Magdalene's Church at Taunton.

KING'S GUARD IN LONDON

In August 1936 the 2nd Battalion was selected to replace, temporarily, the Brigade of Guards, engaged in field training. 5 Officers and some 100 Other Ranks furnished the King's Guard at Buckingham Palace and St. James's Palace. A detachment also took over duties at the Tower of London.

As a souvenir of this occasion a silver Reading Lamp, in the shape of three silver bugles, supporting a Mural Crown, was presented by the Officers of the 2nd Battalion to the Officers of the Brigade of Guards, to be used in the King's Guard Mess at St. James's Palace.

THE COLONEL-IN-CHIEF

During January 1936, H.R.H. the Colonel-in-Chief was promoted first to Lieut.-General and then to General. On 20th January King George V died and was succeeded by H.R.H. the Prince of Wales, as King Edward VIII. In December 1936, King Edward abdicated and H.R.H. the Duke of York ascended the throne as King George VI. On the 12th December 1936, the Colonel of the Regiment sent the following telegram to the Private Secretary to H.M.:

"The Somerset Light Infantry (Prince Albert's) tender their humble duty and loyal allegiance to their Colonel-in-Chief on His Majesty's accession."

The Private Secretary replied:

"The King sincerely thanks all ranks for their message of loyal assurances which His Majesty has received with much pleasure."

In April 1937 H.M. the King graciously indicated his intention to continue his association with the Regiment. The following are extracts from the correspondence between the Colonel of the Regiment and the Private Secretary to H.M.:

From the Colonel:

"I received only on Friday a copy of the March Monthly Army List in which the King is shown as Colonel-in-Chief of the Somerset Light Infantry (Prince Albert's). May I, on behalf of the Regiment, ask you with our humble duty to assure His Majesty what an honour is felt by all ranks to have the King for their Colonel-in-Chief. It is now sixteen years since His Majesty, as Duke of York, was appointed Colonel-in-Chief of the Regiment, and it is a source of great pride to all connected with the Regiment that the King has graciously continued his association with it."

From the Private Secretary to H.M., dated 14th April 1937:

"The King was much gratified to receive the kind message which you were good enough to send. . . . His Majesty is very glad to continue his association with the Regiment of which he has been Colonel-in-Chief for so many years. The King would like to hear from time to time how the Regiment is getting on and I shall be much obliged if you will send particulars to me."

On 2nd December 1937 H.M. the Colonel-in-Chief passed through Taunton on a tour to the Duchy of Cornwall. He was received by the Lord Lieutenant of Somerset, the Marquis of Bath, who presented to him the Officers of the Depot. He inspected representatives of the Old Comrades' Association, under Brigadier General H. C. Frith, C.B. Lieut.-Colonel R. H. Waddy, D.S.O., and Mr. T. Collinson (who joined the Regiment in 1872), were also presented to him.

4TH AND 5TH BATTALIONS (T.A.)

In March 1933 Lieut.-Colonel W. O. Gibbs assumed command of the 4th Battalion and was succeeded by Lieut.-Colonel G. W. R. Bishop, T.D., in March 1934. On 27th May 1933 this battalion furnished a Guard of Honour, at Bath, for T.R.H. the Duke and Duchess of York. During the autumn of 1937 the Marquis of Bath, K.G., P.C., C.B., T.D., Lord Lieutenant of Somerset, resigned the Honorary Colonelcy of the 4th Battalion which he had held for sixteen years. He was succeeded by Colonel G. Flemming, O.B.E., M.C.

In March 1933 Lieut.-Colonel G. P. Clarke, M.C., T.D., assumed command of the 5th Battalion, which he held until March 1938, when he was succeeded by Lieut.-Colonel J. R. Ware, T.D.

2ND BATTALION: MOVE TO GIBRALTAR

In April 1937 Lieut.-Colonel R. H. Waddy, D.S.O., vacated command of the 2nd Battalion and was succeeded by Lieut.-Colonel O. G. B. Philby. On 12th January 1939 the battalion left Colchester and sailed in H.T. "Somersetshire" for Gibraltar. H.M. the Colonel-in-Chief sent the following telegram to the battalion:

"I sincerely thank you and all ranks for your loyal message on the departure of the battalion for Gibraltar. In sending my best wishes I am confident that in your new station you will all maintain the high standard for which the Regiment has ever been famous. George R.I., Colonel-in-Chief."

Both regular battalions of the Regiment were now overseas.

OTHER MATTERS

The life of a regiment is not entirely taken up with training and preparation for war, nor with war itself. Thus no history is complete without some mention of those minor social, cultural and recreational activities which go to make up the daily round.

The Old Comrades' Association has been already mentioned. Connected with it was the Soldiers' Home, Taunton, the rebuilding of which was completed in 1923. The new accommodation provided bedrooms, additional bath rooms, a billiards room, coffee bar and improvements to the kitchen.

A Regimental Museum had been in existence at the Depot for some years. After 1919 this was greatly improved and many trophies of war, medals and documents of historical interest added to it.

The Regimental Journal, the *Light Bob Gazette*, took on a new and improved lease of life. It had been started at the Depot in 1893, the Editor being Lieut. H. J. Everett, but in its present form was by no means the first periodical published to carry regimental news. There is mention of the *Camp Followers* (P.A.L.I.), published at Raneeunge, India, in 1857. Such issues of this journal as have survived contain references to an earlier predecessor which seems to have failed. A publication called *The Griff* purported to be the successor of the *Camp Follower* and was published in Allahabad in 1857. This was probably a Station newspaper, though members of the Regiment may have had a hand in it.

The name of *Light Bob*, by which the Regimental Gazette is known, seems originally to have been applied to the Somersetshire and Oxford and Buckinghamshire Regiments of Light Infantry. This title is alleged to have been gained owing to their "light-heartedness and jolly doggishness" when on active service. It seems also to have been applied to all Light Companies of Regiments of the Line, prior to the formation of Light Infantry Regiments. It must be admitted, however, that the origin of the term is obscure.

In 1935 the *Light Bob Gazette* issued a special Souvenir number to commemorate the 250th anniversary of the raising of the Regiment. A similar Souvenir Number was issued in connection with the furnishing of the King's Guard in 1936. During the 1939–45 War some battalions issued their own news sheets. Mention will be made of these journalistic enterprises at the appropriate time.

Since 1870 a Regimental Dinner Club had been in existence. The history of this Club is given in an appendix to this Volume. In 1933 the Somerset Light Infantry Regimental Club was formed.

The Regiment has always been famous in the world of sport, both in the United Kingdom and Overseas. An account of some of its successes are given in an appendix.

DEVELOPMENTS IN DEFENCE

As a generalisation, it may be said that during the decade 1928–39 progress in the evolution of forces was slow. The world economic depression during the early years of the period led to restrictions of expenditure on defence and, prior to 1939, there was little recovery from this stringency. A great deal of planning was done on paper, there was "much argument about it and about", but little concrete action was taken leading to production.

On the higher level of Preparation for War the Committee of Imperial Defence was strengthened, a Minister for Defence Co-ordination was appointed and the Imperial Defence College developed. All these measures were good for planning.

In the army the main activities were, perhaps, on the development of Armoured Fighting Vehicles, self-propelled artillery, anti-tank and anti-aircraft weapons, mechanical vehicles of all kinds, light automatics, mortars and devices for the offensive use of poison gas and protection of men and materials against it. There was, however, the inevitable time lag between the selection of the prototype and the mass production of the equipment.

Much work was carried out to evolve Strategical and Tactical principles for the handling of mechanised forces, during the approach to the battle-field and in battle itself, under the new conditions of warfare. This, naturally, entailed the study of Combined Operations and the complicated problems of supply, maintenance and repair.

The British Army has always fought its campaigns outside the United Kingdom. Thus, in conjunction with the Royal Navy, it has gained much experience in sea voyages and the landing of forces, on foreign coasts, either unopposed, or in the face of an enemy. These operations were now complicated by the developments of the air arm. The new Royal Air Force was very young and had few leaders of experience. The Royal Navy had retained control of the Royal Naval Air Service, but the army had to rely on an independent Air Force, whose main aim was to build up a strong Fighter Force for defence and a Strategic Bomber Force for attack. The task of convincing the new service of the requirements of co-operation with land forces was an uphill one. Thus Army Co-operation, and the provision of the aircraft required for it, proceeded slowly and somewhat acrimoniously.

It was a sign of the times that attempts made, in Middle Eastern areas, to institute spheres of "Air Control", proved abortive. These experiments clearly demonstrated that men in the air cannot take the place of men on the ground; air and land forces are complementary, one to the other, each in its own dimension.

But progress along certain lines was made. A plan for the Defence of Great Britain against air attack was evolved. This entailed the use of Fighter Aircraft, anti-aircraft artillery and an Observer Corps. There was much experiment in types of Fighter, Bomber and Transport aircraft, though the actual strength of available squadrons remained low. It was discovered that the development and maintenance of an Air Force was extremely expensive. From another angle, civilian flying clubs were developed and Auxiliary Air Squadrons proved popular. These provided a potential reserve of pilots and trained personnel.

In the preparations for the defence of the civil population against air attack and the use of poison gas, Great Britain lagged far behind other nations of Europe. Plans for the rapid mobilisation of national man-power and industry were woefully backward. There was much planning of dispersion of industries and the provision of "Shadow Factories". But, from the practical point of view, these plans were even more shadowy than the factories they projected. Stocks of reserve equipment, weapons and ammunition were allowed to fall to dangerously low levels.

Within the Empire, concerted plans for the co-ordination of Commonwealth Forces in the event of War progressed slowly. Even more dilatory were the preparations of the strategic Fortress of Singapore, which was to form a vital link with the Dominions in the South Pacific and a bulwark against any aggression by Japan. Construction of defences and the provision of heavy armaments proceeded by "fits and starts" and much public money was wasted by fluctuations in policy. When the time came the fortress was unprepared.

In Europe, warlike preparations were advancing steadily. Germany, under Adolf Hitler, was rapidly rebuilding her armed forces. Japan was gaining much experience of warfare in her aggressive policy in Manchuria and her war against China. Italy, with increased forces, embarked on schemes of territorial aggrandisement in North Africa, Ethiopia and Albania. Soviet Russia, in spite of the commitments of her Five Year Plans was rearming rapidly. Germany, Italy and Russia, took advantage of Civil War in Spain to try out new weapons and new tactics.

In France, millions of public money were put into the defensive works of the Maginot Line, behind which the French Field Army could manœuvre. The Line, however, left a serious gap on the North Eastern frontier, which, later, the Germans were not slow to take advantage of. Always strong in artillery, France developed her Armoured Fighting Vehicles. But her heavy tanks, much publicised in peace, failed to materialise when war came.

In the face of these alarming portents, the United States remained firmly isolationist. In Great Britain, with returning prosperity after the depression, the public took little heed of warnings, were content to go about their occupations and amusements and preferred "butter" to "guns". Thus, when the final crisis came, in the autumn of 1939, Britain was ill-prepared for the struggle.

EVENTS IN THE INTERNATIONAL FIELD

Some mention of the general situation in post-war Europe has already been made in Chapter II. The main events of the second decade were the revitalisation of Germany under Nazism, the rise of a military dictatorship in Spain under Primo de Rivera, the aggressive policy of Fascist Italy and the expansionist and "Co-prosperity" policy of Japan in China and the Far East, directed against European exploitation of oriental populations. These trends led, in the end, to the formation of the alliance known as the Berlin-Rome-Tokio Axis.

Throughout this series of conflicts the League of Nations steadily lost ground. Not only did the League fail to settle international disputes by conferences between the parties concerned, but the sole weapon of imposing "sanctions" on states who resorted to war in defiance of the League, was found, in practice, to be ineffectual. The war clouds rose steadily on the European horizon and monthly grew blacker. As the effectiveness of the League declined, so did the aggressive tendencies of the totalitarian states increase.

THE EVENTS LEADING TO WAR

In 1929 Germany was still the Pariah of Europe and threatened by the dangers of inflation and starvation. In 1931 the Young Plan for Reparations was suspended and was followed by the one-year Hoover Moratorium. Dr. Brunning was then Chancellor. During 1932 he reorganised the Banks and issued decrees designed to protect the German agricultural market. On 25th May he was dismissed by President Hindenburg, who appointed Von Papen as Chancellor. Von Papen resigned in November 1932, being unable to reconcile the conservative views of the Prussian Landowners, with the rising demands of the Nazi Party.

On 30th January 1933 President Hindenburg could no longer resist Hitler. The latter became Chancellor and at once began the rejuvenation of Germany. After a period during which he firmly established the Nazi Party in the Reich and gained undivided control of all departments of State, in 1936 he re-introduced conscription. His first aim was an army of 500,000 men, organised in 36 Divisions.

Hitler then, with force at his back, began to break what he termed "the encirclement of Germany". His policy was to regain, in the first instance, the territories and populations which Germany had lost by the Treaty of Versailles. The Western Powers were too divided among themselves to resist him. In July 1934 he had already carried out the first Nazi "putsch" in Austria, when Premier Dollfuss was murdered and much of Austria came under Nazi control.

In the meantime Fascist Italy, under Mussolini, had developed military bases in Libya and Tripolitania. In 1931 Italy withdrew from the League of Nations. In October 1935 she declared war on Abyssinia. The campaigns in that country followed which the League failed to prevent. Italy was firmly established on the Red Sea, which, up till then, had been practically a British lake.

Hitler continued his preparations and aggressive tactics, resulting in periodical crises and "wars of nerves" in Europe. By September 1938 his plans to over-run Czecho-Slovakia and reclaim the Sudetenland were well advanced. In an endeavour to counter these, the Munich agreement was signed by Germany, France, Italy and Britain in September. In October President Benes resigned and was replaced by the weakling Hacha. During March 1939 German troops crossed the Czech frontier and Hitler declared the "Protectorate of Bohemia and Moravia". During the same month, after a German ultimatum, Lithuania ceded the Memelland to Germany. Britain and France, thoroughly alarmed, announced guarantees to Poland. In the meantime Mussolini invaded Albania.

In April 1939 Hitler, spurred on by success, denounced the Naval Agreement, regarding construction, with Britain and the 1934 Non-aggression Pact with Poland. He demanded Danzig and a road through the Polish Corridor. The British reply to this was, on 26th April, to announce the introduction of compulsory military training. A Bill to this effect was introduced on 1st May. Registration was ordered on 3rd June and the call-up was for 1st July. This legislation caused some difficulties later, for the Bill dealt, mainly, with "Militia Training". Thus, when it became necessary to embody and expand the Territorial Force, at a later date, some unnecessary duplication occurred. During the next few months the situation deteriorated rapidly. In August an Anglo-French Military Mission to the U.S.S.R. started talks in Moscow. Fortunately they had not proceeded very far when, on 21st August, a Soviet-German Non-aggression Pact was published. Mr. Neville Chamberlain, the Prime Minister, then informed Hitler that the British guarantees to Poland would be fulfilled by force if necessary.   To this Hitler replied that Germany was unable to renounce interests in Danzig and the Corridor.   On 25 August an Anglo-Polish Alliance was signed.   In the meantime appeals from President Roosevelt, M. Daladier, Holland and Belgium to Hitler to keep the peace had been rejected.

At 5.30 a.m. on 1st September 1939, Germany invaded Poland.   The evacuation of children from London and other vulnerable cities in Britain began.   Britain and France issued ultimatums to Germany to withdraw her troops from Poland.   On 3rd September, at 11 a.m., the British ultimatum expired.   The French ultimatum expired at 5 p.m.   Both countries were then at war with Germany.

CHAPTER IV

THE PATTERN OF THE CONFLICT

Beginning of War—Expansion to nine battalions.

1939. Defeat of Poland—Russian invasion of Finland.

1940. April: German invasion of Denmark and Norway—May: German invasion of Holland, Belgium and Luxemburg—Dunkirk—June: Battle of France—Italy enters War—July–October: Battle of Britain—August: Italy invades Somaliland—September: Italian attack on Egypt—December: First Western Desert Offensive.

1941. February: Counter offensives in Somaliland and Abyssinia—April: First German-Italian Counter-offensive in Libya—German-Italian invasion of Greece—Revolt in Iraq and Syria—June: German invasion of Russia—Aggression by Japan in Indo-China—August: Operations in Iran—October: Germans reach Crimea—November: Second Western Desert Offensive—Pearl Harbour—Japan and United States enter War—December: Fall of Hongkong.

1942. January: Second German Counter-Offensive in Libya—Fall of Singapore—Japanese invasion of Burma—Fall of Bataan in Philippines—May: Third German Counter-Offensive in Libya—Battle of the Coral Sea—June: Battle for Egypt—Germans invade Caucasus—August: investment of Stalingrad—October: Battle of El Alamain—November: Allied landings in Algeria—Russian Counter-Offensive at Stalingrad.

1943. Relief of Leningrad—8th Army enters Tripoli—March: Mareth Line broken—Battle of Bismarck Sea—April: Enfidaville Line broken—May: German Surrender in Tunisia—End of North Africa Campaigns—July: Allied invasion of Sicily—South East Asia Command established—September: Allied invasion of Italy—Mussolini Resigns—Landing at Salerno—Surrender of Italy—November: Russian Offensive in Ukraine—Capture of Kiev.

1944. January: British Offensive in Arakan—Anzio landing—February: German Offensives at Anzio—March: Japanese Offensive in Assam—May: Russians take Sevastopol—June: Allies enter Rome—Invasion of Normandy—July: Battle of Caen—August: Battle of Falaise Pocket—Pursuit of Germans in France—British Offensive in Assam—September: Brussels entered—Battle of Arnhem—Gothic Line (Italy) broken—October: Rumania, Bulgaria and Finland eliminated—Naval Battle of Philippines—British invade Burma—British land in Greece—December: German Offensive in Ardennes.

1945. U.S. Counter-attacks in Ardennes—February: move up to Rhine—Breslau taken—March: Crossing of Rhine at Remagen and near Rees—April: British take Bremen—Russians take Stettin—U.S. and Russians meet at Torgau on R. Elbe—Capture of Genoa and Venice—Mussolini shot by partisans—Hitler commits suicide—May: Surrender of German forces in Germany and Italy—VE-Day—Rangoon taken—July: Atom Bombs on Japan—Japan surrenders—VJ-Day.

IN order fully to comprehend the detailed history of the various battalions of the Regiment engaged in the 1939–45 War, it is as well, at the beginning, to have a clear conspectus of the moves which took place on the chess-board of War Strategy. It is only thus that the timing of developments in various theatres of war can be appreciated and the effect of these campaigns, their disasters and successes, on the outcome of the struggle as a whole made clear. Units of the British Army were only pawns in the

THE PATTERN OF THE CONFLICT

Great Game and their tiny moves—widely separated in time and space—must be seen against the background of the Master Plan which finally resulted in the checkmate of the enemy.

As has been seen from Chapter I, the Regiment was expanded to some nineteen battalions during the 1914–18 War, though only sixteen battalions played any serious part in the fighting. In Chapter III it was seen that developments in warfare led to the conclusion that, in future wars, masses of men on the battlefield would no longer be required. Their place would be taken by machines and improved weapons. Among these weapons was gas, for the use of which—and for protection against it—provision was made in time of peace. Between 1939–45, however, Chemical Warfare was not employed by either side, mainly because it is a two-edged weapon. 1945 saw the new and revolutionary development of atomic warfare, which appears likely to change the whole scheme of warfare of the future.

The views on the subject of fewer men and more machines and weapons, formulated in time of peace, were borne out during 1939–45. Although the number of men and women employed in the fighting services was very large, there were actually fewer men on the battlefield. There was, also, practically no siege warfare on an extended scale. These two factors reduced the number of casualties, compared with 1914–18. The new conditions were reflected in the expansion of the Regiment, which was only called upon to provide nine battalions, as follows:

1st (Regular)	served in India and the Arakan.
2nd (Regular)	served in Italy and Greece.
The Depot	expanded into the Infantry Training Centre at Taunton.
4th (T.A.)	served in France and Germany.
5th (T.A.)	served in Great Britain.
6th (T.A.)	served in Great Britain.
7th (T.A.)	served in France and Germany.
8th (Home Defence)	served in Algiers, Sicily, and on Railway Protection in Italy, as 30th Battalion.
9th	served in Great Britain.
10th	served in France and Germany as the 7th Battalion (L.I.) Para Regt.

Ten battalions are listed, but the 3rd (Reserve) Battalion never served as a battalion proper and was only an Infantry Training Centre. The 8th Battalion (Home Defence) became the 30th Battalion in December 1941, and later went to Italy as so designated. The 10th Battalion was raised as the 11th (Holding) Battalion in January 1940. In June 1940 it became the 50th (Holding) Battalion Somerset Light Infantry. In October 1940 it became the 10th Battalion Somerset Light Infantry. In November 1942 it was converted into the 7th Battalion (Light Infantry), The Parachute Regt., Army Air Corps.

In the general review of the War, which follows, with the outline of the parts played by battalions of the Regiment, only the relevant portions of the major strategic events are touched on, which affect the detailed account in the subsequent chapters. Thus little reference will be found to events in the war on sea and in the air, nor to the various international conferences, the economic aspects of the war, nor events in theatres of war in which battalions of the Regiment were not engaged. An attempt has been made, however, without embarking on a history of the War, to correlate the major factors leading to final victory.

1939

After the declaration of war on 3rd September 1939, there was a considerable period of operational passivity on land which was popularly known as "the Phoney War". Affairs did not develop according to preconceived ideas, thus illustrating the dictum that, in war, it is the unexpected which happens.

At first the main scene of operations was in Poland. The Western Allies had guaranteed her safety, but were unable to help her. No attempt was made to invade Germany from the West. On the other hand full-scale preparations for defence and for the organisation of forces and resources were undertaken. The Dominions also made their preparations, but the United States held aloof.

On 10th September the British Expeditionary Force began to move over to France and was employed on the North-East Frontier defences. No battalion of the Regiment accompanied this force. On 17th September Russian troops entered eastern Poland and, on 27th September, Warsaw surrendered.

On 30th November Russian troops, presumably acting in concert with Germany, invaded Finland, and two days later the U.S.S.R. was expelled from the League of Nations. During December the first contingent of Canadian troops reached Britain and an Indian Contingent landed in France.

In Britain Territorial Army battalions of the Regiment were embodied and expanded, vulnerable points were placed under guard, re-equipping and intensive training began.

THE REGIMENT IN 1939

During this period:

1st Battalion was at Poona, moving to Multan as part of the Kohat Brigade in October;
2nd Battalion was at Gibraltar;
4th Battalion was embodied at Bath and moved to Havant in September;
5th Battalion was embodied at Taunton and concentrated at Tiverton;
6th Battalion was formed from the 4th Battalion at Wells and employed in Somerset;
7th Battalion was formed from the 5th Battalion at Bridgewater and employed in Somerset;

8th Battalion was raised as a Home Defence Battalion at Taunton and employed in Somerset.

This was the full extent of the expansion of the Regiment in 1939. The 5th, 6th and 7th Battalions formed the 135th Infantry Brigade of the 45th Division, the first appearance of a Somerset Light Infantry Brigade in the history of the Regiment.

1940

Early in 1940 the first Anzac detachments reached Egypt. On 12th March a Russo-Finnish peace treaty was signed at Moscow and hostilities in Finland ceased. In the same month Hitler and Mussolini had their first meeting on the Brenner Pass, though Italy had not yet entered the war. On land, there was a period of stagnation and of waiting on events.

On 9th April Germany invaded Denmark and Norway and the area of operations began to widen. During April British troops were landed in Norway for operations around Narvick, Namsos and Andalsnes. These were abortive and the bulk of the force was withdrawn during May. Hostilities ceased in Norway on 9th June.

On 10th May the threatened German invasion of Holland, Belgium and Luxemburg began. British and French troops entered Belgium from the West. It became early apparent that affairs were going badly for the French. The Germans broke through across the R. Meuse between Mezieres and Namur, using bridges which were not destroyed. On 15th May the Dutch Army capitulated and the British were forced to withdraw, East of Brussels, to the Escaut Line. By the 21st May the Germans had reached Arras and claimed the total defeat of the 9th French Army. During the last week in May the Germans began to encircle the Belgian, French and British forces in Belgium. On 28th May the Belgian Army capitulated and the evacuation of the British from Dunkirk began.

In the Dunkirk Evacuation some four-fifths of the personnel of the British Force escaped, but it was an unparalleled disaster. Practically all the equipment, weapons, stores and munitions of the force were lost, in addition to six destroyers and twenty-four smaller naval vessels. Britain was, for the time, almost defenceless. The men who returned had to be re-equipped, reorganised and rehabilitated.

In June the Battle for France was fought. The result was a foregone conclusion. On 15th June, Italy seized her opportunity and declared war on Britain and France, invading Southern France. The French Army disintegrated rapidly. On 14th June the Germans entered Paris and began to penetrate the Maginot Line. Metz, Orleans, Verdun and Besançon fell swiftly. On 17th June a Cabinet under Marshal Petain asked for armistice terms, making the same request to Italy two days later. By 25th June all was over in France and the Germans had reached the Channel and Atlantic Ports. The Vichy collaborationist government came into being.

In Britain the period was a critical one. Invasion was expected and preparations to meet it were pressed on. Britain had become a Fortress. Organisations for coastal defence, for defence in depth and against parachute landings were rapidly devised. The Germans began to concentrate troops and shipping preparatory to a cross-channel expedition. Their first requirement was to obtain air superiority to cover the invasion fleet. Thus, on 10th July, the Battle of Britain began.

This was fought in the air and lasted until 31st October. The first large-scale air raid was in the South Wales Dock Area. Between 21st July and 25th August the main targets were the Channel Ports and shipping. From then, until 10th September, airfields were attacked. Throughout September daylight air attacks were made on London. On 8th September all troops in Britain received the code word "Cromwell", indicating "Invasion imminent". In October German fighter-bomber attacks were designed to reduce our fighter strength. Our own fighters were heavily outnumbered. By the end of October the German effort had clearly failed for the time being. From then onward throughout the winter night attacks on London continued with varying severity. But German failure in the air had, for the time, scotched the invasion plans.

During August operations spread to North Africa. The Italians invaded Somaliland, taking Zeila, Hargeisa and Oodwina. In September Italian forces from Libya attacked Egypt. They occupied Sollum and, later, Sidi Barrani.

Italy also picked a quarrel with Greece. On 28th October an Italian ultimatum was rejected and Italian forces invaded Greece and bombed Patras. Help was sent to Greece from Egypt. On 11th/12th November the Fleet Air Arm successfully attacked the Italian Fleet at Taranto.

On 9th December the First Desert Offensive from Egypt began. By the 17th December Sidi Barrani, Sollum and Fort Capuzzo had been taken, together with 35,949 Italian prisoners of war.

In December Spain refused to enter the war. Thus German plans for an attack on Gibraltar, early in January 1941, were frustrated. The United States still remained neutral.

This year saw the close of the "Phoney War", followed by a series of major disasters. The situation at the end of the year was very grave.

THE REGIMENT IN 1940

During this period:

1st Battalion was engaged during March, April and May in operations in the Ahmedzai Salient on the North-West Frontier of India; in May it returned to Multan.

2nd Battalion remained at Gibraltar.

4th Battalion moved to Aylesbury in January and to Coastal Defence near Folkestone in September.

5th, 6th and 7th Battalions moved with 45th Division to Kent and Sussex, being engaged on anti-invasion duties. In November they moved to Yorkshire.

8th Battalion was employed on detachment at vulnerable points in many areas in England.

11th (Holding) Battalion was raised at Ludlow in January and became the 50th (Holding) Battalion Somerset Light Infantry in June. In October it was re-designated the 10th Battalion Somerset Light Infantry with Headquarters at Bridgwater.

9th Battalion was raised at Taunton in July and employed on Coast Defences in Somerset.

1941

January and February saw further British successes in the Western Desert. Bardia and Tobruk were taken with heavy Italian casualties. On 6th February Benghazi was occupied and El Agheila, frontier post of Cyrenaica, two days later. Air attacks were launched on Tripoli where German reinforcements were arriving.

During February South African troops from Kenya began to advance into Somaliland from the South and took Mogadishiu. During March Berbera was retaken. Following the successes in Libya, troops were switched to Abyssinia from the Soudan. After severe fighting near Keren, our forces took Asmara on 1st April and Addis Ababa on 5th April.

German re-inforcements now made an enemy offensive possible in Libya and this started on 30th March. Benghazi was lost on 3rd April and by 13th April Bardia had fallen and Tobruk was encircled. By the 28th April the enemy had reached Sollum.

In Albania an Italian offensive opened on 9th March. On 28th March our Fleet severely handled the Italians at the battle of Cape Matapan. On 6th April the Germans invaded Yugo-Slavia and Greece. Bulgaria also attacked the Yugo-slavs, who withdrew, exposing the Greek flank. The Germans then took Salonica and advanced rapidly into Greece. On 20th April Greek forces in Epirus and Macedonia capitulated and British troops, sent to assist them, withdrew to Thermopylæ. Two days later their evacuation began. On 27th April German forces entered Athens. Our troops withdrew to Crete, while the Germans over-ran Islands in the Ægean Sea. On 20th May the invasion of Crete began. By 1st June our forces, having suffered heavy losses on sea, land and in the air, withdrew to Egypt.

At the end of April a German inspired revolt of Iraqi troops under Rashid Ali began. The R.A.F. Cantonment at Habbaniya was attacked. A force from India was sent to Basra and thence to Baghdad. By 30th May the revolt had collapsed, but the situation in Syria, complicated by Vichy French Forces, deteriorated. Indian troops entered Syria from Iraq and Imperial and Free French forces from Palestine. Palmyra was taken during June and armistice terms were settled at Acre on 12th July.

On 22nd June Germany suddenly declared war on Russia and invaded the Ukraine. By 5th July German troops had reached the River Dneiper. In August Leningrad was attacked. By the end of the month the Russians had been forced to destroy the Dneiper Dam in their retreat from the Ukraine.

For some time there had been much anxiety over the policy of Japan in the Pacific. Encouraged by the disasters to the Western Allies, Japan had been strengthening her hold on the occupied areas of China and, following the collapse of France, began to extend her influence south-westwards towards Indo-China and Siam. She had already declared her policy of a "New Order" in Asia, which was anti-European in aims.

In September 1940 Japanese troops entered Indo-China and in January 1941 she reaffirmed her claims to control in the Pacific. An Australian Division was then sent to Singapore. In March, the question of an attack on Singapore was discussed by the Japanese Foreign Minister in Berlin. Later he visited Rome and from then onwards the Berlin–Rome–Tokyo Axis was firmly established. In July a pact signed at Vichy admitted the Japanese demands for bases in Indo-China. This was followed by the landing of troops at Saigon and the taking over of eight airfields. These moves were, clearly, directed against Singapore.

During the summer, air raids, from bases in Sicily, on Malta increased in intensity and the movement of our convoys in the Mediterranean became extremely hazardous. In Iran German infiltration increased and replies by the Iranian Government to British-Soviet notes were unsatisfactory. On 25th August British and Russian troops entered Iran, occupying Abadan and Tabriz. Hostilities ceased on the 29th August, after which British and Russian zones were occupied and a land route organised for the supply of war material to Russia.

In Russia, during the autumn, the German advance continued steadily. On 19th October a state of siege was proclaimed in Moscow, while further south German forces invaded the Crimea.

In North Africa there was a period of stagnation while German-Italian forces were being built up. We, also, received some re-inforcements. On 18th November the 8th Army opened the Second Western Desert Offensive, with the object of encircling enemy tank concentrations in the rectangle Tobruk–Sollum–Sidi Omar–El Gobi. Between the 20th and 24th November a tank battle was fought with heavy losses on both sides. A further battle took place, with fluctuating successes, between 28th and 30th November. After a pause it was resumed on 6th December and next day the Germans drew off westwards to reform. On the 17th December the German front broke and by the 24th December the 8th Army had retaken Benghazi.

During the autumn events in the Far East moved rapidly to a climax. In November the United States asked the Japanese to explain the reasons for troop concentrations in Indo-China. On 30th November a Japanese fleet was reported off North Borneo, moving south-east. A state of emergency was declared in Malaya and volunteers called up in Hongkong. On 7th December

THE PATTERN OF THE CONFLICT

Japan launched air attacks on Pearl Harbour in Hawaii, 19 United States warships being sunk or damaged. On the same day Japan declared war on Britain and the United States. The latter country ordered general mobilisation.

On 7th December Japanese forces landed in Siam and at Kota Bahru in North-East Malaya. Hongkong was invested and a landing took place in the Philippines. On 10th December H.M.S. "Prince of Wales" and "Repulse" were sunk off the Malayan Coast with the loss of 600 lives. In Malaya our troops withdrew on both sides of the Peninsula, evacuating Penang on 19th December. Hongkong fell on 25th December after a siege of 17 days and by the end of the year Manila was threatened.

The year had seen a rising tide of Axis successes and a vast widening of the area of conflict.

THE REGIMENT IN 1941

During this period:

1st Battalion was engaged on North-West Frontier defence in India;
2nd Battalion remained at Gibraltar;
4th Battalion was employed on coastal defence and training in Kent;
5th, 6th and 7th Battalions were employed in Buckinghamshire and moved to coastal defence in the Colchester area in July;
8th (Home Defence) Battalion was employed in training in Somerset and was re-designated the 30th Battalion, Somerset Light Infantry, in December;
9th Battalion moved to Plymouth in March to join the 48th Division; after a move to Cornwall in August, it went with the 48th Division to the Skegness area;
10th Battalion moved to Portland in April, to the Isle of Wight in July and to Lincolnshire in November.

1942

The year opened well in North Africa, but hopes were short-lived On 6th January the Germans counter-attacked, without success, at Agedabia and were, later, pursued along the coast road. On 12th January Sollum was taken and on the 17th January, Halfya, the last enemy post in Cyrenaica, fell.

The Germans were now reinforced and, on 21st January, opened the Second German Counter-Offensive, advancing east from El Agheila. On 23rd January they reached Agedabia and a tank battle developed to their advantage. Benghazi fell on 29th January and Derna on 4th February. On 14th February the German advance eastwards was resumed.

In the Far East, the Japanese advance on Singapore continued. The Netherlands East Indies were invaded on 10th January. By 9th February Japanese troops had landed on Singapore Island and on 15th February the Fortress surrendered. Between 55,000 and 60,000 British and Imperial troops were captured.

Developments were also taking place in Burma and towards India. During the latter part of December 1941, Japanese troops, after landing at Bangkok, in Siam, advanced overland and entered Lower Burma and Tennaserim. On 31st January 1942 Moulmein was invested and the R. Salween crossed on 9th February. British forces withdrew across the R. Sittang on 24th February and evacuated Rangoon on 7th March.

On 27th February an Allied Naval Squadron engaged the Japanese Fleet and was wiped out with the loss of 5 cruisers and 6 destroyers. Next day Japanese forces landed in Java. On 9th April 35,000 United States troops surrendered on the Bataan Peninsula in the Philippines, a remnant holding out in the Fortress of Corregidor. In Burma, after destroying the oil-fields, the British withdrew and evacuated Mandalay by 1st May. Shortly afterwards the Japanese drove Chinese forces out of Lashio and Bhamo and cut the land route to China. On 8th May Myitkhyna fell and a sea-borne landing took Akyab in the Arakan. By 15th May retreating British forces had reached the Indo-Burma frontier.

In North Africa the Germans opened the 3rd German Offensive on 26th May, in an attempt to outflank the British at Bir Hakeim. By 28th May the battle was raging in the "Cauldron" area, some 25 miles from Tobruk. On 4th June our forces were overrun near "Knightsbridge" and counter-attacks failed to restore the situation. Bir Hakeim fell on 10th June. On 14th June the British withdrawal to the Egyptian Frontier began, a garrison being left at Tobruk. On 21st June Tobruk was taken and the Germans reached Bardia. On 27th June the Battle for Egypt began at Mersa Matruh, which fell on 29th June. By 14th July German and British forces faced each other on the Ruwaisat Ridge, south of El Alamein.

In Russia, the spring and early summer had seen further German successes. Attacks were directed, in the main, against Leningrad, Moscow and the Crimea. A drive was started towards the oil-fields of the Caucasus, penetrating to Maikop. By the end of August the investment of Stalingrad had begun.

In May the United States Fleet in the Pacific successfully engaged the Japanese in the Battle of the Coral Sea, near the Solomon Islands. This checked further Japanese penetration towards Australia. In the Indian Ocean, our Fleet withdrew to the African Coast at Kilindini. British troops landed on Madagascar. In the Arakan, British forces advanced across the Burma Frontier on 21st December, moving on Akyab.

In North Africa the Battle of El Alamein began on 24th October, continuing until 3rd November, when the Germans began to withdraw westwards, with heavy losses of tanks and guns. By 5th November we had advanced 100 miles and, by 12th November, Sollum, Bardia and Tobruk had been retaken. On 8th November Allied forces landed in French North Africa, near Oran and in Algeria. The 8th Army continued to pursue the enemy, and by the end of the year had reached Mejez El Bab.

On 22nd November the Russian Counter-Offensive at Stalingrad opened.

THE PATTERN OF THE CONFLICT

By the end of the year the Germans were in full retreat in the Middle Don area.

1942 was a year of disaster in many theatres. But the close of the year carried with it some gleams of hope.

THE REGIMENT IN 1942

During this period:

- 1st Battalion moved to Waziristan in January and to Delhi in September. In November it was mobilised to train for jungle warfare, as part of 7th Indian Division near Nowshera;
- 2nd Battalion remained at Gibraltar;
- 4th Battalion moved to the Dover Defences in February; 5th and 6th Battalions were on coastal defence in the Colchester area;
- 7th Battalion moved from the Colchester area to the Isle of Wight, in September;
- 30th Battalion was on airfield defence in Somerset; in October it joined 115th Infantry Brigade in Dorset, for coast defence;
- 9th Battalion was on coast defence in Yorkshire, until the autumn when it moved to Northern Ireland;
- 10th Battalion was on coast defence in Yorkshire until September, when it moved to Berkhamstead. In November it was converted to the 7th Battalion (Light Infantry) The Parachute Regt., Army Air Corps. It then moved to Bulford.
- H.Q. First Army Defence Company (Somerset Light Infantry) formed and moved to Algiers, subsequently to Constantine. Platoons went into action temporarily for battle training in Tunisia.

1943

In the early part of the year the Russians continued to drive the Germans back. On 18th January Leningrad was relieved and on 2nd February the remaining German forces near Stalingrad capitulated.

In North Africa our forces began to make ground on both fronts. The 8th Army entered Tripoli on 23rd January and this marked the start of the final phase in this theatre.

On 20th February the 1st Army saw severe fighting near the Kasserine Pass and gave ground near Medjez. On 6th March the Germans counter-attacked the 8th Army, but were held. On 26th March the 8th Army broke through the Mareth Line, later occupying Gabes. On 28th March the 1st Army took the offensive and reached Cap Ferrat on 31st March. During April the offensive continued on both fronts, culminating in the successful assault by the 8th Army on the Enfidaville Line on 20th April.

On 7th May the 1st Army entered Tunis and Bizerta and on 9th May the enemy surrendered unconditionally. 291,000 prisoners were taken. This was followed by the capture of Pantellaria and Lampedusa Islands on 11th and 12th June.

On 9th/10th July the Italian Campaign opened with air and sea landings in Sicily. On 25th July Mussolini was arrested after resignation and King Emmanuel, with Marshal Badoglio, assumed control in Italy. By 16th August Sicily had been cleared and Messina entered.

On 3rd September the 5th Anglo-American Army under General Mark Clarke, U.S.A. landed at Reggio in Italy. On 8th September Italy surrendered unconditionally. The 5th Army was switched to land at Salerno, near Naples, while German forces occupied Rome and began to prepare for the defence of Northern Italy. Counter-attacks developed against the Salerno beach-head on 13th September. On 16th September the 5th Army opened an offensive from the beach-head, while the 8th Army pressed northwards from Southern Italy. By 29th September the 5th Army had reached Pompeii and on 13th October Italy declared war on Germany. By 4th November the 8th Army had begun to link up with the 5th Army near Castel Pietro. On 23rd November the 8th Army crossed the R. Sangro in force and by 2nd December had broken through the German Winter Line on that river.

After the check to the Japanese drive southwards in the Pacific during May 1942, United States and Australian forces began to consolidate their positions, particularly in the Solomons Group, New Guinea and Guadalcanal. In February 1943, the latter Island was cleared. On 2nd March the naval Battle of the Bismarck Sea turned favourably for the Allies. During the summer and autumn operations continued in those areas.

On the Indo-Burma frontier pressure by land and air was maintained against the Japanese; but the period was one of the build-up and training of our forces prior to resuming the offensive. In the Arakan the struggle fluctuated. After reaching Rathedaung in December 1942, we were forced to withdraw from Buthidaung and Maungdaw in May 1943. In August, South East Asia Command was set up, to co-ordinate effort in the Burma-Malaya-Netherlands East Indies area. Small scale operations continued, but were overshadowed, materially and psychologically, by the Allied successes in Italy and Russia. All material resources available were directed to exploiting these victories.

In Russia, from the Baltic to the Black Sea, the Germans gave way after bitter fighting. Kharkov was taken in March; Bielgorod and Orel in August. Further successes were gained in the Crimea. In September Smolensk was retaken and an offensive launched in the R. Dneiper area. In November Kiev was recaptured and the end of the year saw the Russians exerting pressure on all fronts.

In brief, 1943 saw the turn of the tide. The enemy had been driven out of Africa; Italy had been eliminated and Southern Italy over-run by Allied troops. The Germans were on the retreat in Russia and the Japanese forced to give ground in the Pacific.

THE PATTERN OF THE CONFLICT

THE REGIMENT IN 1943

During this period:

1st Battalion moved in January to Chindwara for jungle training. In May it reached Calcutta for coast defence. In June it landed at Chittagong, reaching Bawli Bazar, by march route in September. There it engaged in operations towards Taung Bazar, being the first unit of the Regiment to meet the enemy;

2nd Battalion left Gibraltar in December and moved to Ataqa Camp, near Port Said, Egypt;

4th Battalion remained in the Dover area until May. After a period of training in Kent and Sussex it took over coast defence near Dymchurch;

5th and 6th Battalions moved to Northern Ireland in February; and returned to Sussex in December;

7th Battalion moved to Cornwall in May and was mobilised for Foreign Service in June. After a period near Berwick-on-Tweed it moved to Hythe for coast defence in November;

30th Battalion moved to Portland in May and landed in Algiers in September. In October it landed in Sicily and was employed in the Palermo area;

9th Battalion moved to Cornwall in May and to Berwick-on-Tweed in July. It formed part of the 115th Infantry Brigade of 38th Division;

7th (L.I.) Parachute Battalion formed part of the 5th Para Brigade of 6th Airborne Division and was employed training on Salisbury Plain.

On the disbandment of 1st Army, H.Q. 1st Army Defence Coy. (Somerset Light Infantry) was re-designated as H.Q. 15th Army Group Defence Company and moved to Sicily, thence to Italy.

1944

In Italy the 5th Army operated in the Rapido Valley and launched attacks across the R. Garigliano during January. On 22nd January, a landing was made at Anzio, south of Rome, and a beach-head established and widened. By 30th January the Gustav Line had been broken into, in an area north of Cassino.

On 3rd February the Germans launched the first major offensive against the Anzio beach-head. A second offensive developed on 16th February and there was fierce fighting near Cassino. The third offensive at Anzio began on 29th February. Critical fighting went on in this area until 11th May when, all attacks having been held, the 5th and 8th Armies opened an attack in force on the Gustav Line. By 16th May the whole of the front south of the R. Liri had been cleared. On 18th May Monte Cassino was taken. On 23rd May the 5th Army broke out of the Anzio beach-head and, after breaking the Hitler

Line in the Liri Valley, entered Rome on 5th June. Thereafter the 8th Army switched to the Adriatic Front.

In January British-Indian forces opened an offensive in the Arakan, capturing Maungdaw. This was followed by a Japanese counter-offensive which took Taung Bazar and endeavoured to outflank our forces, on the north, at the Ngakyedyauk Pass. This threat was held after severe fighting. On 8th January the enemy withdrew from Taung Bazar. By the end of January the Ngakyedyauk Pass area and the country east of the Mayu Range had been secured. On 11th March we took Buthidaung. Further north United States and Chinese troops, operating from Assam, penetrated the Hukawng Valley as far as Sumprabum. On 17th March airborne forces were landed in an isolated area in Central Burma, to exert pressure on Japanese communications.

Towards the end of March the Japanese staged a major offensive against Assam and India. By 2nd April they had taken Tiddim and isolated Imphal. Later Kohima was invested. Severe and critical fighting followed until, on 5th May, the British took the offensive. By 14th May the siege of Kohima was raised and the Kohima Ridge cleared of enemy. During April and May severe fighting continued in the Arakan, particularly in the area between Maungdaw and Buthidaung, where the Japanese held on in the "tunnels" area and on "Hill 551".

In the Pacific, United States and Australian forces continued to make slow progress in Island Groups and New Guinea.

In Russia the Germans fell back on the 1st, 2nd and 3rd Ukrainian fronts. On 17th January the blockade of Leningrad was lifted. Krivoi Rog was taken in February. During April there was severe fighting in the Crimea and on 7th May Sevastopol was captured.

June saw the opening of the Invasion of Normandy. On the night of 5th/6th June Allied Airborne troops landed behind the German coastal defences. 6th June was D-Day. Landings were made on the coast between the Cherbourg Peninsula and Le Havre, with United States forces on the West and British and Canadian troops on the East. Bayeux was taken on 7th June. On 10th June British Armour reached Tilly and by 12th June after taking Carentan and clearing the Foret De Cerisy, the beach-heads were linked up on a front of 50 miles. Cherbourg was isolated on 17th June and captured on 26th June.

On 8th July the assault on Caen began and on 18th July the British 2nd Army broke through south east of Caen. Between 25th and 27th July United States forces broke through near St. Lo and Lessay, exploiting towards Rennes and Redon in Brittany. By 6th August the Brest Peninsula had been sealed off.

Fighting continued on the British front near Caen, Villers Bocage and Mortain. By 12th August the German reserves had been committed and resistance broken. The general German Retreat from Normandy began. The allied pursuit pivoted on the British on the coast, with the United States forces sweeping in an arc to the south, through Nantes and across the R. Loire.

THE PATTERN OF THE CONFLICT

On 15th August Allied forces landed in Southern France, between Toulon and Nice on a front of 50 miles. Between 15th and 19th August, in the north, the Battle of the Falaise Pocket went in our favour and was followed by the crossing of the R. Seine on 25th August. Paris was liberated by French Resistance Forces on 23rd August. The pursuit continued, with United States forces on the south, British in the centre and Canadians along the coast. By the end of August United States troops had crossed the R. Meuse and the British 2nd Army was in Amiens.

In Italy, during the summer, the advance of the 5th and 8th Armies was slowed by strong German opposition and difficult terrain. By 11th August Florence was taken and on 31st August the 8th Army began an attack on the Gothic Line in the Adriatic Sector.

In June the United States attack on Leyte in the Philippines began to develop and on 10th August Guam was taken. On the Assam border our advance continued. Tamu fell on 5th August and by 16th August the Japanese had been cleared from India. In the Arakan we took Pinbaw near Mogaung.

In June the first Russian offensive against Finland was launched. On 3rd July Minsk was taken. This was followed by offensives across the R. Bug and in the Ukraine. On 23rd August Rumania accepted armistice terms.

In Britain the first Flying Bomb (V 1) fell on the night of 13th/14th June. Thereafter attacks from this weapon increased in intensity against the London area, until our forces over-ran the launching sites. Special anti-aircraft, fighter and balloon defences were installed to control the menace. The first Rocket Bomb (V 2) fell at Chiswick on 8th September and attacks from this weapon, from sites in Holland, continued until 27th March 1945.

On 3rd September British Forces entered Brussels and Tournai, linking up, on 5th September, with United States forces at Namur and Charleroi. On 7th September the British 2nd Army crossed the Albert Canal. In the meantime Nieuport and Ostend had been occupied and Calais was taken on 30th September. United States troops crossed the German frontier near Trier and Aachen on 11th September, later taking Thionville. The Siegfried Line was breached on 15th September.

On 17th September Allied Airborne troops landed in Holland, near Nijmegen, and Eindhoven; the British 1st Airborne Division dropped at Arnhem, to seize bridges over the rivers Maas, Waal and Lower Rhine. Armour of the British 2nd Army made contact with these forces at Eindhoven on 18th and Nijmegen on 20th September. By 24th September the 2nd Army had reached the Lower Rhine in force and, after severe fighting, the remnants of the 1st Airborne Division were withdrawn on the night 25th/26th September.

During October Allied forces were moving up to the R. Rhine. By the end of the month the Canadians had reached the Walcheren Channel. During November we increased pressure on the R. Maas and R. Seille. By the end of the month United States forces had crossed the R. Saar and Strasbourg had fallen. On 26th November the Port of Antwerp was opened and, in the South, Belfort and Mulhouse were taken.

On 16th December the German counter-offensive in the Ardennes was launched. This fell on the 7th United States Army on a front of 70 miles, between Monchau and Trier. By 20th December the Germans had penetrated to Stavelot, but were held there. On 31st December the U.S. 3rd Army counter-attacked between Bastogne and St. Hubert.

In Italy progress was slow. On 2nd September the 5th Army took Pisa and crossed the R. Arno, while the 8th Army offensive broke through the Gothic Line in the east. On 26th September the 8th Army crossed the R. Rubicon and the R. Savio on 22nd October. This Army continued to advance, taking Forli and crossing the R. Montone in November. By 16th December Ravenna and Faenza had been occupied.

In Burma we captured Tiddim on 19th October. In the Pacific the Second Naval Battle of the Philippines, on 23rd October, caused heavy Japanese losses. U.S. troops, on Leyte, continued to advance.

On 9th September operations in Bulgaria ceased and next day an armistice with Finland was signed. On 23rd October Russian forces entered East Prussia.

During August and September the situation in Greece began to cause anxiety. On 5th October a British Force was landed at Patras, later occupying Corinth. Fighting began between the Greek factions of E.A.M. and E.D.E.S. On 14th October we entered Athens, but fighting between the factions continued in the city to the end of the year.

It will be seen that 1944 saw the tide of Victory flowing strongly.

THE REGIMENT IN 1944

During 1944:

1st Battalion engaged in operations in the Arakan until April, when it returned to India and moved to Peshawar;

2nd Battalion arrived at Naples on 15th March, as part of 28th Infantry Brigade of 4th Division, 10th Corps, 8th Army. On 24th November it left Forli and landed at Piraeus (Greece) on 15th December;

4th Battalion landed at Arromanches (Normandy) on 19th June as part of 129th Infantry Brigade. At the end of the year it had reached Hulsberg (Holland);

5th Battalion moved to Seaford in March and became a draft-finding unit. In August it was reorganised to train Light Anti-Aircraft Artillery (R.A.) to be Infantry.

6th Battalion moved to Harwich in January and was disbanded at Peacehaven on 14th July;

7th Battalion landed at La Riviere (Normandy) on 24th June as part of 214th Infantry Brigade of 43rd Division. By the end of the year it had reached the Moorveld area;

30th Battalion was employed on Railways Protection duties in Southern Italy;

THE PATTERN OF THE CONFLICT

9th Battalion was employed in Hampshire and was disbanded at Bustard Camp, Salisbury Plain, on 16th September;

7th Battalion (L.I.) Parachute Regt., dropped at Ranville on 6th June as part of 5th Para Brigade of 6th Airborne Division. It returned to Bulford on 5th September and landed at Calais on 25th December, moving up to Corenne.

H.Q. 15th Army Group Defence Coy. (Somerset Light Infantry) was disbanded, and personnel posted as reinforcements to 2nd Battalion.

1945

This was the year of Victory.

On 1st January the Germans launched an attack near Saarguemines and, later, re-crossed the R. Rhine north of Strasbourg. Two days later United States forces attacked on the north of the Ardennes Salient, towards Houffalize and on 9th January attacked the Salient from the south. On 16th January the British 2nd Army attacked the Salient east of the R. Maas, the subsequent fighting seeing the virtual end of this German offensive.

On 2nd February the British 2nd Army crossed the R. Maas directed on Breda and positions south-east of Nijmegen. By 9th February the first of the Siegfried Line zones had been penetrated and the R. Rhine reached at Millingen. The advance continued to Cleve and by 13th February the Reichswald had been cleared. Canadian troops reached the R. Rhine north-east of Calcar.

Early in March United States troops retook Trier. On 7th March they crossed the R. Rhine by an undestroyed bridge at Remagen and completed the clearance of Cologne. The next day British troops entered Xanten and by 10th March the German bridge-head across the R. Rhine in the Wesel-Xanten area was abandoned. Further south, United States troops crossed the R. Moselle south-west of Coblenz, taking Bitche, Kaiserslautern and Saarbrucken. On 23rd March they crossed the R. Rhine south of Mainz.

On 24th March 21st Army Group crossed the Rhine at four places between Rees and a point south of Wesel, aided by air-borne landings. The next day United States troops broke out of the Remagen bridgehead. Canadian troops took Emmerich and Netterden and U.S. troops, Frankfurt and Aschaffenburg.

In the meantime Russian forces were pressing into central Prussia and, on 6th February crossed the R. Oder south of Breslau. By 15th February Breslau was surrounded and Danzig threatened. Poznan (Poland) fell on 23rd February and Brandenburg, in East Prussia, on 17th March. On 22nd March Zoppot was taken and Danzig isolated. Further breaks through followed to the west of Budapesth and in the Vertes Mountains.

In Greece, terms of truce were signed by E.L.A.S. in January and hostilities virtually ceased in Athens and the Piraeus.

On 9th January United States forces landed on Luzon in the Philippines and by 17th February the whole of the Bataan Peninsula had been occupied. In Burma we took Yeu on 3rd January and Akyab two days later. Meiktila fell on 28th February and Maymyo on 13th March.

In Italy the 5th Army staged an offensive on the R. Serchio in February, retaking Gallicano. On 18th February a new attack began west of the Bologna-Pistoia Road, capturing heights in the Upper Reno Valley after heavy fighting.

April was an eventful month in Germany on all fronts. On 3rd April Canadian troops crossed the Twenthe Canal and took Rheine. Minden fell on 5th April and the R. Wesser crossed. On 6th April United States troops crossed the R. Wesser at Hameln. By 15th April we had taken Zutphen, Wildenhausen and Hanover and crossed the R. Ijssel.

In the meantime the 2nd British Army crossed the R. Leine on 11th April while United States forces captured Essen and crossed the R. Elbe south of Magdeburg. On 14th April the Ruhr Pocket was split at Hagen and finally eliminated on 18th April. The same day the British 2nd Army reached Luneburg, while United States forces entered Czecho-Slovakia and occupied Magdeburg and Dusseldorf.

Between 19th and 21st April the British 2nd Army reached the R. Elbe at Lauenburg and captured Buxtehude, while United States troops cleared Leipzig, Halle and Nuremberg. On 24th April British and Canadian forces entered Bremen which surrendered on 26th April. On 25th April United States and Russian forces met at Torgau on the R. Elbe and on 30th April Hitler committed suicide at Berlin.

During April the Russians pressed forward rapidly. Konigsberg was taken on 8th April and by 21st April Russian troops were fighting in the suburbs of Berlin. Simultaneously with the fall of Bremen, the Russians took Stettin.

In Italy, by the 11th April, the 5th Army had taken Monte Folgorita, overlooking the Ligurian Plain, Massa and Carrara. By 23rd April both the 5th and 8th Armies were on the line of the R. Po. Next day Ferrara, Spezia and Modena were occupied and the R. Po crossed at several places. On 27th April the 5th Army entered Genoa and the next day Brescia and Bergamo fell, while United States troops reached Como. The 8th Army entered Venice on 29th April.

THE CLOSING SCENE IN EUROPE

At the beginning of May the German forces, compressed between the Allied advances on the West, South and East, began to disintegrate. The two Dictators were dead; Hitler from suicide on 30th April and Mussolini at the hands of partisans, who shot him while he was attempting to escape into Switzerland on 28th April.

On 2nd May Berlin surrendered to the Russians. On the same day the German forces in Italy capitulated. On 7th May Germany surrendered unconditionally. The 8th May was celebrated by the Allies as VE-Day. Hostilities in Europe were at an end.

THE CLOSING SCENE IN THE FAR EAST

So far as the history of the Somerset Light Infantry is concerned, in this Volume, it ends with VE-Day. There was, however, a brief period of occupation of enemy territories before the final disbandment of battalions raised during the war and the disembodiment of Territorial Army units. But the War against Japan went on for a time ; though not for so long as was expected.

On 3rd May the 14th Army took Rangoon and began to force the Japanese out of Lower Burma. On 5th July the whole of the Philippines were liberated. In South East Asia Command preparations began for the liberation of Malaya, Singapore and the Netherlands East Indies. These, if they had been put into execution would, probably, have been lengthy and very costly in lives. But all operations in the Far East were cut short by the introduction of Atomic Warfare.

On 16th July the first Atom Bomb was exploded, as a test, in New Mexico. On 6th August the first Atom Bomb used in warfare was dropped on Hiroshima, Japan. On the 9th August the second Atom Bomb fell on Nagasaki. On 14th August Japan surrendered unconditionally. The 15th August was celebrated by the Allies as VJ-Day.

THE REGIMENT IN 1945

During this period:

1st Battalion was in India;
2nd Battalion was in Greece;
4th Battalion was in Holland and Germany and was finally disbanded at Buxtehude in August 1946;
5th Battalion served in South Wales and Sussex. It joined the 183rd Infantry Brigade of the 61st (Light) Division in June and was disbanded on 1st January 1946;
7th Battalion was in Holland and Germany and was disbanded at Buxtehude in October 1946;
30th Battalion remained on Railway Protection in Southern Italy and was disbanded in Rome in January 1946;
7th Parachute Battalion (L.I.) served in Holland and Germany and returned to Bulford on 21st May. It disembarked at Bombay on 7th August and moved to Kalyan. On 14th December it landed at Batavia (Java) and subsequently went to Singapore on 19th March 1946.

CHAPTER V

THE "PHONEY WAR"—AUGUST 1939–MAY 1940

1st Battalion at Poona—Move to Multan—Operations in Ahmedzai Salient—2nd Battalion at Gibraltar—Embodiment and raising of Second Line battalions—4th Battalion—5th Battalion—6th Battalion—Formation of Somerset Light Infantry Brigade—7th Battalion—8th (Home Defence) Battalion—11th (Holding) Battalion

"BLESSED is he who expecteth nothing; he shall not be disappointed." Those who looked back to the hectic mobile warfare operations of 1914 in France and held preconceived ideas as to the development of the war in the autumn and winter of 1939, were doomed to disappointment.

The wild national enthusiasm of 1914 was lacking when war finally came in September 1939. In its place was a desire to put an end to the intolerable menace of Nazism and a grim determination, since the nettle had to be grasped, to see the matter through to a decisive end. But operations did not develop on the lines of 1914. Following long months of "appeasement" there was, for some time, a period of inactivity on land. Poland fell an easy prey to German and Russian aggression. Britain and France could do little, in spite of guarantees, to help her. For some months there was no call for large numbers of men for the fighting services. People wondered what the British Expeditionary Force was doing on the Belgian frontier. In the Dominions and India there was a great popular urge to raise forces, but offers to this end received only partial acceptance. In Britain, however, intensive preparations were set on foot and a limited expansion began.

It will be convenient, in recounting the events of this period, within the Regiment, to deal with Battalions in their order of seniority.

The two Regular Battalions were overseas, maintaining normal Watch and Ward in India and Gibraltar. But in Britain the Territorial Army was embodied and began to expand according to plan. There was no attempt to go outside this organisation as there had been, in 1915, when the "Kitchener Armies" were raised. But the expansion and training of these Second Line units—now to become First Line—must be seen against the background of events during the first ten months of war.

The existing Territorial units provided a sound nucleus of trained officers and men; many with experience of war from the 1914–18 campaigns. Many of these units were in annual training camps when the call came. This made embodiment and calling up easier. The existing units, however, had had to cast off duplicate units and take in new recruits. This required a good deal of initial reorganisation. All units had to be equipped and provided with stores,

AUGUST 1939–May 1940

arms and transport. As usual these requirements came in slowly and for some time new units were short of arms and other essentials.

It was essential, also, that all units should have a period in which to settle down and carry out the Primary, or Basic, Training of individuals and specialists. But this training was gravely hampered by duties which had, immediately, to be performed. It was not until late in 1940 and early in 1941, that any attempt could be made to embark on the "collective" training of battalions, brigades, divisions and corps. In the meantime men had to learn as best they could—mainly by experience.

At first there was a great fear of landings on the coast from submarines and landings from the air by parachutists. There was also fear of air and gas attack on a large scale. Fifth Columnists and sabotage had to be guarded against; Ports and communications—both rail and road—had to be secured. New arsenals, dumps, airfields and factories sprang up all over the country and had to be protected. Thus, from the outset units were widely dispersed in detachments.

With all this demand for dispersion, training proceeded slowly. It must be remembered that, in addition to the men themselves and the specialists, junior leaders had to be trained as instructors and in the new weapons and tactics of mechanised warfare. Thus the story of the "Phoney War" is, largely, one of training under difficulties and apparently aimless moves at frequent intervals.

It was not until April and May, with the German invasion of Denmark, Norway and the Low Countries, leading to the Dunkirk evacuation and the collapse of France, that affairs began to crystallise. Then came the move of units and formations—indifferently trained and equipped—to the east, south-east and southern coastal areas and the organisation of defence in depth, prior to the Battle of Britain, which began in July 1940.

THE 1st BATTALION

During 1939 the 1st Battalion was at Poona, in India. In August, Lieut.-Colonel V. W. Roche completed command and was succeeded by Lieut.-Colonel A. F. Harding, M.C. Major H. W. Spurrell, M.C., was 2nd-in-Command and Major A. Hunt, Adjutant.

After a farewell inspection by the G.O.C.-in-C., Southern Command (General Sir John Brind, K.C.B., K.B.E.) the Battalion arrived at Edwardes Barracks, Multan, Punjab, on 4th October, relieving the 2nd Duke of Wellington's Regt. At first it came under command of Ferozepore Brigade Area of Lahore District (Major-General M. Saunders, C.B., D.S.O.). Its rôle was Frontier Defence Reserve, under the orders of H.Q. Northern Command, Rawalpindi. On 19th November it moved to Kohat for training with the Kohat Brigade. About the same time the first draft of non-regular personnel was received from the United Kingdom. On 19th December it returned to Multan.

OPERATIONS IN THE AHMEDZAI SALIENT

On 10th February 1940 the Battalion moved to Kohat as reserve to the Ahmedzai Force. This was commanded by Brigadier Barstow, I.A. (killed later while commanding 17th Indian Division in operations in eastern Malaya). The Force comprised:

1 Somerset L.I.	2/5 Gurkha Rifles.
2 Worcestershire Regt.	5/8 Punjab
13 Frontier Force Rifles.	1/16 Punjab.

For some years the centre of unrest among Wazirs and Mahsuds, in Waziristan, had been the notorious Fakir of Ipi, a Muslim fanatic. This man frequented an inaccessible tribal tract at the head of the Tochi Valley, where he lived in caves with a band of irreconcilables. The caves provided good cover from air attack. Their location was close to the Durand Line, so that, on the approach of troops the Fakir could slip over into Afghanistan, where he could not be followed and where the Afghan Government was averse to taking action against him. From these fastnesses he organised attacks on our troops and communications and raids into the settled districts of the Kohat and Bannu areas of the Indus Valley.

The Ahmedzai Salient—a political anachronism—was a triangular wedge of country lying between the Kohat–Thall road, to the Kurram Valley, on the north and the Bannu–Miranshah road, to the Tochi Valley, on the south. The base of the wedge lay along the fair-weather track from Miranshah to Thall and the apex was close to Bannu, flanking the Bannu–Kohat road.

The Salient itself was a trackless, tangled stretch of scrub-covered hills and ravines, with only a few watering places, one of which was at Daryobe, about the centre of the Salient. In this area gangs could collect and lie up unseen, awaiting a favourable opportunity to raid. Later, the area provided a convenient escape route. It was extremely difficult to intercept such gangs on the track which formed the base of the Salient. To do so effectively would have required numbers of men not available. This raiding had become an intolerable nuisance. It was decided, therefore, to penetrate the Salient and construct a road to, and Post at, Daryobe, thus controlling the area in which gangs collected.

On 19th March 1940, the Battalion moved by M.T., via the Bannu road, to a perimeter camp at Gummatti, on the south of the Salient. Here it joined the 3rd Indian Infantry Brigade (Brigadier Quayle). During the latter part of March it was employed on permanent piquets, construction of posts and road protection. In the meantime, work on the road to Daryobe progressed, with little opposition. On 6th April the Battalion moved up to Daryobe. Heavy rains delayed operations and for some time the force was on half-rations. A great deal of heavy manual labour was necessary to construct the new Post and to carry the pipes for the water supply. On 7th May the operations concluded. There were no casualties. Lieut.-Colonel A. F. Harding was mentioned in

AUGUST 1939–MAY 1940

Dispatches. R.Q.M.S. J. Grant and Corporal (Master Cook) Reed received Meritorious Service Cards from the Army Commander. The Battalion returned to Multan, sending three companies to Dalhousie for the hot weather.

THE 2ND BATTALION

The 2nd Battalion arrived at Gibraltar in January 1939 and was there when war broke out in September.

    Commanding: Lieut.-Colonel O. G. B. Philby.
    2nd-in-Command: Major B. J. Corballis, M.C.
    Adjutant: Lieut. P. D. Maud.

For a considerable time conditions remained almost similar to those in peace-time. Units in Gibraltar did not start to keep War Diaries until February 1941. Consequently details are scanty. The Battalion was employed on manning of defences and providing guards for shipping. At an early stage work on new defences began and went on steadily. There was always a danger that Spain might join, or give right of access to, Axis forces. In which case attacks on Gibraltar would have developed.

Lieut.-Colonel Philby vacated command in May 1940 and was posted to command the I.T.C. (3rd Reserve Battalion) at Taunton.

THE 4TH BATTALION (T.A.)

On 25th August 1939 orders were received to embody "key parties" of this battalion at Bath. This was followed, at once, by the embodiment of H.Q., B, C and D Companies at Bath and A Company at Midsomer Norton. The Battalion also cast off a duplicate unit which became the 6th Battalion (T.A.).

    Commanding Officer: Colonel G. W. R. Bishop, T.D.
    Adjutant: Captain C. L. Firbank.
    R.S.M.:   W. Holley.
    R.Q.M.S.:   W. Wynne.

On 2nd September 1939 the Battalion was mobilised and by the next day embodiment was completed. The strength of the unit was 31 Officers and 603 Other Ranks. On 4th September it moved to Havant, relieving the 7th Hampshire Regt. and taking over guards on vulnerable points in the Portsmouth area.

On 15th January 1940 it was relieved by 5th/6th Ox and Bucks L.I. and concentrated at Havant and Hayling Island for training. On 13th February Major C. L. Firbank was appointed 2nd-in-Command and Captain R. W. James became Adjutant.

On 18th March the Battalion moved to Tisbury, Wiltshire, and provided detachments at Hindon, East Knowle and Fonthill Gifford. On 24th May it relieved the 11th Royal Fusiliers at Harpenden, remaining part of 129th Infantry Brigade (Brigadier G. E. M. Whittuck, M.C., A.D.C.) of 43rd (Wessex)

Division. The rôle of this Division was to form Southern Command Reserve for the Defence of Great Britain. On 25th May the defences of Hatfield airfield were taken over.

THE 5TH BATTALION (T.A.)

During August 1939 the 5th Battalion was in camp at Exmouth, where it cast off a duplicate unit which became the 7th Battalion. On 2nd September it was embodied at Taunton as part of 135th Infantry Brigade of 45th (West Country) Division T.A. (Commander: Major-General F. V. B. Witts, C.B.E., D.S.O., M.C.). On 7th September this Division, with Headquarters at Exeter, consisted of 134th, 135th and 136th Infantry Brigades.

When embodied, the 5th Battalion had:

Commanding Officer: Lieut.-Colonel J. R. Ware, T.D.
Adjutant: Major J. D. Gage-Brown.
R.S.M.: G. Vickery.
R.Q.M.S.: C. J. Maddocks.

Headquarters was at Taunton, with companies at Taunton, Wellington, Chard, Ilminster, and Minehead. Strength on embodiment was 17 Officers and 605 Other Ranks. On 21st September the Battalion concentrated at Tiverton for Individual Training. On 20th October Major J. D. Gage-Brown was appointed 2nd-in-Command and Captain G. J. Pollard became Adjutant.

On 23rd January 1940 the Battalion moved to the Salisbury Plain area, with headquarters at Warminster. On 3rd February it relieved the 7th Devon Regt. and 5th Wiltshire Regt. at Cosham, Hullavington, Andover and Micheldever. Its rôle was the protection of dumps, airfields and vulnerable points. Headquarters was moved to Trowbridge. In March, Major-General D. F. Anderson, C.B., C.M.G., D.S.O., took command of 45th (Wessex) Division. H.Q. 135th Infantry Brigade moved to Bath. During this period parties were trained in the defence of merchant ships.

On 6th April the Battalion concentrated at Weston-super-Mare for Individual Training, the strength then being 29 Officers and 936 Other Ranks. On 12th May it moved to Crowborough, Sussex, coming under command, temporarily, of 1st (London) Division and D Sub-area, Home Defence. Guards were taken over on bridges and vulnerable points at Ightham, Peasmarsh and Rye. It was then organised as A, B, C, D, X and Z companies, with a strength of 32 Officers and 934 Other Ranks.

THE 6TH BATTALION (T.A.)

On 24th August 1939 the 6th Battalion was formed from the 4th Battalion, with Headquarters at Wells.

Commanding Officer: Colonel G. Flemming, O.B.E., M.C.
2nd-in-Command: Major W. D. C. Trotter.
Adjutant: Captain W. R. F. Ellis.
Quartermaster: Lieut. P. H. Jeffries.

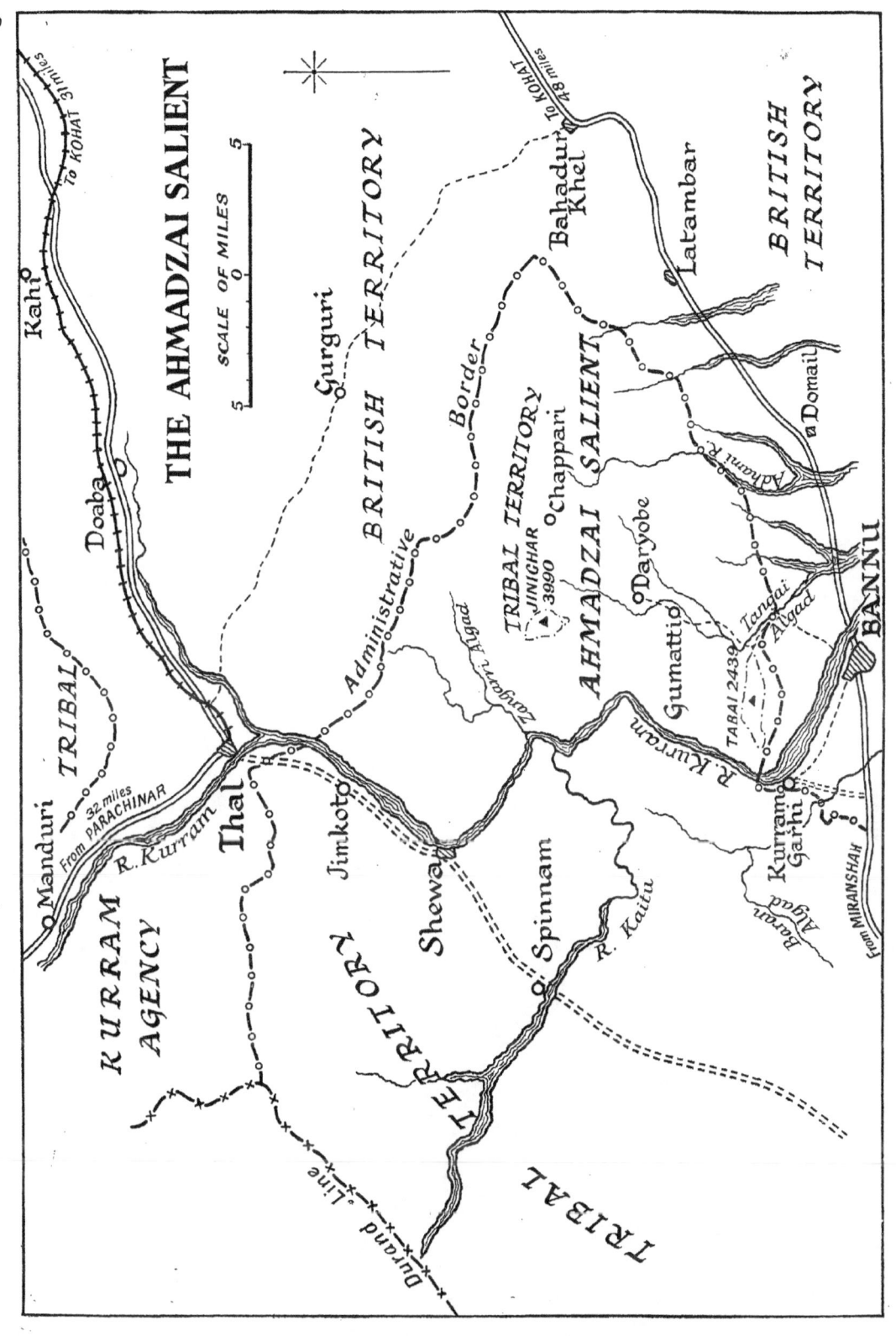

The Officers on the formation of the Battalion were:

Major D. I. L. Beath; Captains R. V. Ridge and J. D. Graham; Lieuts. J. G. Brasier-Creagh, W. G. N. Good, D. D. B. Cook, J. B. Cosens, C. P. Tamlyn, J. Anstey, A. R. B. MacGillicuddy, P. J. Austin, H. J. C. Miles, P. C. Paton, H. Whitefield and S. A. M. Wilmot.

On 27th August C and D companies voluntarily embodied at Barrow Gurney and Weston-super-Mare and were moved to Glastonbury. On 29th August posts were taken over at Burnet, Clevedon and Portishead. On 30th August H.Q. company was embodied at Glastonbury and A and B companies at Castle Cary on 2nd September. On 3rd September the 7th Battalion took over at Portishead and on 5th September A and B companies of the 6th Battalion relieved the 4th Battalion at Bath. The strength was now 20 Officers and 441 Other Ranks. During the latter part of September companies were located at Bath, Locking, Wells and Portishead, A company moving to Glastonbury on 29th September.

THE 7TH BATTALION (T.A.)

This battalion was formed from the 5th Battalion, about 25th August 1939. Headquarters was located at Taunton, with companies at Bridgwater, Highbridge, Yeovil and Crewkerne.

Commanding Officer: Lieut.-Colonel G. P. Clarke, M.C., T.D.
2nd-in-Command: Major R. J. W. Marr.
Adjutant: Major J. Muller, D.S.O., M.C.
Assistant Adjutant: Captain D. W. G. Feaver.
Quartermaster: Captain R. A. Russell.
R.S.M.: C. Dunn.

Company Commanders: Major G. R. Mather; Captains C. M. B. Kite, J. R. A. Courtenay, J. J. D. Duke and B. D. Byers.

The composition was H.Q., A, B, C and D companies, with a strength of 10 Officers and 565 Other Ranks. The Battalion formed part of 135th Infantry Brigade of 45th (Wessex) Division. On 3rd September it took over the defence of Whiteball Tunnel and Dunster Junction railway station. On 8th September Private H. M. Waterworth was killed by a train at Dunster.

On 27th September Battalion Headquarters moved to Bridgwater and the Battalion took over guards at Highbridge, Bridgwater, Washford, Doniford, Burnham, Durston, Portishead and Watchet. Two companies were sent to Bath to act as Command Reserve. On 31st December 1939 the strength was 26 Officers and 617 Other Ranks.

Headquarters moved to Bath early in January 1940 and, after relief by the 6th Battalion, the unit moved to Salisbury Plain. Here it provided guards at Old Sarum, Tidworth, Porton and Boscombe Down airfields. While in this area there was an influenza epidemic.

On 14th February A and B companies returned to Bath for Internal Security duties. About 12th March Headquarters moved to Tiverton and in April the Battalion concentrated there for Individual Training.

On 12th May, with the German invasion of the Low Countries, the Battalion was sent, first, to Sussex, to take over duties near Rutley and Horsted Keynes. On 23rd May it moved to Hatch Park, Ashford, Kent and next day to the Royal Military Canal near Hythe, where it formed part of the Forward Defence Line coming temporarily under command of 1st (London) Division.

At the end of May there were changes in appointments:

> 2nd-in-Command: Major W. S. C. Curtis, M.C.
> Adjutant: Major E. T. Boileau.
> Quartermaster: Lieut. (Q.M.) C. J. Maddocks.
> Intelligence Officer: Lieut. A. Palmer.
> R.S.M.: C. Dunn.
> R.Q.M.S.: J. Durman.

THE 8TH (HOME DEFENCE) BATTALION

In August 1939 a National Defence Company organisation came into being. This was to find static guards. On 23rd August, Colonel J. J. Aitken, C.M.G., D.S.O., O.B.E., was given the rank of Acting Captain A.O.E.R., and appointed to command " A " National Defence Company. His officers were Captain G. W. McFayden, M.C. and A/Lieuts. A. S. B. Roberts, W. E. Nash and J. H. C. Liddon (all A/Lieut. A.O.E.R.).

On 24th August calling up notices were received, C.Q.M.S. J. Kirby being the first Other Rank to be attested. On 29th August the company was re-named " E " National Defence Company, of No. 80 Group, National Defence Companies. On 4th September it relieved the 7th Battalion on the Whiteball Tunnel. The strength was then 5 Officers and 65 Other Ranks.

On 1st November the 8th (Home Defence) Battalion, The Somerset Light Infantry, was formed with D and E companies. A/Captain J. J. Aitken was appointed to command with the rank of Lieut.-Colonel. The Group Commander was Colonel the Duke of Somerset, D.S.O., O.B.E.

> 2nd-in-Command: Lieut.-Colonel C. R. Spear, D.S.O., M.C.
> Adjutant: Lieut. B. D. Collinson-Cox.
> Quartermaster: Lieut. W. A. Thackeray.

Officers with the unit were: Captains G. W. McFayden M.C., and J. E. Portal, D.S.O., Lieuts. A. S. B. Roberts, W. E. Nash, J. H. C. Liddon, E. A. Cuvelier, V. D. Robinson, V. J. Brown, F. F. Francis, O. E. Barnett and C. H. B. Botting.

The Battalion was dispersed on guard duties all over Somerset. On the 14th November three Other Ranks were killed on railway duty at Wellington, being struck by a train. On 20th December guards at Washford Camp were taken over. The strength at the end of the year was 11 Officers and 315 Other Ranks.

On 16th February 1940, C Company was formed and on 6th April the Battalion was organised as three companies in fourteen platoons. The strength had risen to 24 Officers and 418 Other Ranks. At the end of April, Headquarters was at Taunton, with detachments at Washford, Watchet, Seaton, Honiton, Bridgwater, Highbridge, Clevedon and Portishead. Major G. W. McFayden became 2nd-in-Command.

THE 11TH (HOLDING) BATTALION

This unit was raised at Ludlow, in January 1940, by Lieut.-Colonel K. G. G. Dennys. It consisted of four rifle companies formed from the I.T.C.s of the Somerset Light Infantry, South Wales Borderers, Welsh Regt. and Gloucestershire Regt. At first it was employed to receive recruits and to give Primary training.

FORMATION OF A SOMERSET LIGHT INFANTRY BRIGADE

On 16th November the 6th Battalion concentrated at Weston-super-Mare, forming part of 135th Infantry Brigade of 45th (Wessex) Division. This brigade consisted of 5th, 6th and 7th Battalions, Somerset Light Infantry. The following are extracts from correspondence on the subject:

From the Colonel of the Regiment to the Private Secretary to H.M. the King, dated 8th November 1939:

"I shall be grateful if you will give my humble duty to His Majesty the King and place before him the attached letter from the Commanding Officers of the 5th, 6th and 7th Battalions, The Somerset Light Infantry (Prince Albert's). Our Colonel-in-Chief may be interested to know that for the first time in the history of the Regiment a Somerset Light Infantry Brigade is now in being and I am confident that the battalions of which it is composed will worthily uphold the traditions of the Regiment."

From the Rt. Hon. Sir Alexander Hardinge, P.C., K.C.V.O., dated Buckingham Palace, 11th November 1939:

"It is a matter of great interest to your Colonel-in-Chief to know that for the first time in the history of the Regiment a Somerset Light Infantry Brigade is now in being. His Majesty warmly thanks all ranks of the three battalions for the loyal assurances contained in their message and sends them his best wishes. He knows well that the fine traditions of the Regiment will be safe in their hands."

The rôle of the 135th Infantry Brigade was to form South-Western Area Reserve. H.Q. of the Brigade was at Taunton, the commander being Brigadier A. L. W. Newth, C.B.E., D.S.O., M.C., T.D. The Brigade Major was Captain J. P. Eason. A Brigade School was set up at Tiverton.

On 13th January 1940 the 6th Battalion relieved the 7th Battalion at Portishead, the Weston airfield and Burnham wireless station. The weather was very cold and there was an epidemic of German measles.

On 8th January Silver Bugles were presented to the 6th Battalion. These had been subscribed for by the Officers, Old Comrades' Association of Weston-super-Mare, the Bath Territorial, Constitutional and Victoria Bowling Clubs, the Licensed Victuallers Association and others.

On 16th March A and B companies took over duties at Chilmark. On 12th May, following the German invasion of the Low Countries, the Battalion moved by train to Forest Row, in Sussex, the unit transport following by road via Stockbridge.

Headquarters, H.Q. company and A company were located at Chelwood Gate; B company at Forest Row; C company at Wych Cross; D company at Danehill; E (Training) company at Nutley. 135th Infantry Brigade was detailed as reserve to 45th (Wessex) Division in Ashdown Forest area, with a rôle to operate towards Rye, Shoreham, or Chatham as the occasion arose. The 6th Battalion relieved the 2nd London Irish Rifles and took over the rôle of Divisional Mobile Reserve. Two platoons were sent to take over Hastings airfield.

On 22nd May Colonel G. Flemming was appointed Garrison Commander Bulford and Lieut.-Colonel W. D. C. Trotter assumed command; Major D. I. L. Beath became 2nd-in-Command.

On 23rd May the Battalion moved to Kennington, in the 1st (London) Divisional area (Commander: Major-General C. F. Liardet, C.B., D.S.O., T.D.). An area was taken over near Wye Racecourse and Broughton Leas. There were many alarms of parachute landings and road blocks were constructed and manned. On 30th May a motor-cycle platoon was formed.

CHAPTER VI

THE BATTLE OF BRITAIN. JUNE–OCTOBER 1940

German invasion of the Low Countries—Formation of Home Guard—Dunkirk—Battle of France—135th Infantry Brigade in Sussex—Italy enters war—Collapse of France—Inspection by H.M. the Colonel-in-Chief—Battle of Britain—7th September: Code word "Cromwell"—31st October: End of Battle of Britain—4th Battalion—8th (Home Defence) Battalion—9th Battalion raised—50th (Holding) Battalion formed

IN the previous chapter we saw the embodiment of the 4th and 5th Battalions, the raising of the 6th, 7th, 8th (Home Defence) and 11th (Holding) Battalions and the formation of a Somerset Light Infantry Brigade (135th Infantry Brigade, 45th (Wessex) Division). After a period of protective duties in Somerset and other counties of Southern England, events drew many of these units to the Eastern and South-Eastern Defences. At the end of May 1940 the 4th Battalion was in Wiltshire; 135th Infantry Brigade in Kent and Sussex; 8th (H.D.) Battalion in North Somerset. The developments of the war which produced this grouping need some explanation.

On 10th May Germany invaded the Low Countries. Mr. Chamberlain resigned and a Coalition Government was formed with Mr. Churchill as Prime Minister. Affairs in France were obviously extremely serious. On 13th May, Mr. Churchill told the House of Commons: "I have nothing to offer but blood and toil and tears and sweat." The next day the War Office announced the formation of "Local Defence Volunteers", the title of this organisation being changed to "Home Guard" in July.

After the capitulation of the Dutch Army on 15th May, the Germans began to thrust deep into Flanders and took Brussels on 17th May. It was early apparent that the French Heavy Armoured Force, about which much had been heard, was not going to materialise. By 25th May the Germans were surrounding the Belgian and French forces and most of the B.E.F. On 27th May Calais fell and next day the Belgian Army capitulated, leaving the flank of the B.E.F. exposed. The evacuation from Dunkirk began on 28th May and continued until the night of 2nd/3rd June. 224,585 British and 112,546 French and Belgian troops were taken off. But their arms, equipment and stores were left behind.

On 4th June Mr. Churchill made his famous appeal to the Nation: "... We shall fight on the beaches, we shall fight in the fields ... we shall never surrender." The outlook was, indeed, grim.

> " I wis in all the Senate,
> There was no heart so bold,
> But sore it ached, and fast it beat,
> When that ill news was told.

> Forthwith uprose the Consul,
> Uprose the Fathers all,
> In haste they girded up their gowns,
> And hied them to the wall."

On 5th June the Battle of France began. There was little doubt, now, that the Narrow Seas constituted Britain's last obstacle against invasion and that the enemy would make every effort to cross it. Work had already been done on coast defence, as well as on the major plan for the Air Defence of Great Britain, known as "A.D.G.B." The latter included fighter and artillery defences in a deep coastal belt running southwards and westwards from the Wash to the Bristol Channel and taking in London and the Home Counties. With the prospect of early invasion attempts on the South Coast, intensive work on beach defence began, on a line from Yorkshire, through the Thames Estuary, to Cornwall. The coast was sealed off everywhere with concrete pill-boxes, wire entanglements, mine-fields and other obstacles. Inland from the beaches, defences were sited in depth, the defensive belt being divided up into areas, sub-areas and sectors, with formations allotted to the defence of each. Mobile reserves, to operate against landings, either from the sea, or by parachute, were provided and exercised. All this entailed a great deal of manual labour, the provision of vast quantities of material and a serious transportation and accommodation problem. Superimposed on these arrangements was the task of re-equipping the forces evacuated from Dunkirk. The time available for these projects was short.

THE 135TH INFANTRY BRIGADE

This brigade of the 45th (Wessex) Division (Commander: Major-General D. F. Anderson, C.B., C.M.G., D.S.O.), included the 5th, 6th and 7th Battalions. At the end of May 1940 the Division, with the 1st (London) Division (Major-General C. F. Liardet, C.B., D.S.O., T.D.) under command, was responsible for the defence of the Home Counties area of Kent (excluding London and Chatham), Sussex and Surrey.

This area was organised in four sub-areas:

A. 1st (London) Division. C. 136th Infantry Brigade.
B. 134th Infantry Brigade. D. 135th Infantry Brigade.

D sub-area included Farnborough (Kent)—Tonbridge—Tunbridge Wells —Uckfield. 135th Infantry Brigade was disposed as follows:

5 Somerset L.I. on East. 6 Somerset L.I. in Mobile Reserve.
7 Somerset L.I. on West. 7 Devons was also allotted, temporarily, to the Brigade.

The rôle of 135th Infantry Brigade was to form the 45th (Wessex) Division reserve and to be prepared to repel sea, or air landings, within the Divisional area, or to move against a break through by the enemy. This was the original plan and continued in operation. But, in practice, brigades within the Division were switched from one task to another as the situation demanded.

JUNE–OCTOBER 1940

On 1st June 5th Battalion headquarters moved to Rye to take over beach defences. The strength of the Battalion was 32 Officers and 934 Other Ranks. The 6th Battalion remained in the Kennington area and took part in anti-invasion exercises in co-operation with the newly formed "Local Defence Volunteers", later to become the "Home Guard". The 7th Battalion began work on pill-boxes and other defences along the Forward Defence Line of the Royal Military Canal, linking up with the Shorncliffe Garrison area at Hythe. C, B and D companies were in forward localities with A company in Mobile Reserve. Work on actual and dummy defences went on throughout June.

On 10th June Lieut.-Colonel G. P. Clarke left the 7th Battalion and was succeeded in command, on 25th June, by Lieut.-Colonel A. E. Snow. Major W. S. C. Curtis became 2nd-in-Command. On 21st June Major J. D. Gage-Brown left the 5th Battalion to raise the 9th Battalion at Taunton. On the same day parties from the 5th, 6th and 7th Battalions were taken to form the 135th Infantry Brigade Anti-tank company. Towards the end of June the 259th (West Country) Field Company R.E., was co-operating with the 7th Battalion in preparing bridges for demolition.

On 11th June Italy declared war on France and Britain. On 14th June the Germans entered Paris. It was clear that the French front was cracking everywhere. By 23rd June the Germans had reached the Atlantic Coast at St. Nazaire and the French armies in the Vosges capitulated. On 22nd June armistice terms between Germany and France were signed; on 24th June similar terms were signed between France and Italy. The Battle of France was over. Mr. Churchill announced that Britain would fight on and told the House of Commons: "All depends on winning the battle, here in Britain, now, this summer."

On 28th June the 7th Battalion moved to New Romney and took over beach defences in the area Dungeness–Dymchurch. The 6th Battalion moved to a similar task in the Dymchurch–Lydd area. On 1st July the 5th, 6th and 7th Battalions were inspected by H.M. the Colonel-in-Chief, near Rye. Later, commanding officers took luncheon with H.M. at Rye. This was a great inspiration to all ranks.

Early in July the 135th Brigade, under XIII Corps, was disposed on beach defences as follows:

Right: 7th Battalion; Lydd—Greatstone—Littlestone.
Centre: 5th Battalion; Cliff End—Appledore.
Left: 1st (London) Division; in Shorncliffe area.
Reserve: 6th Battalion; in Lydd area.

On 10th July the Battle of Britain began. Extensive defence exercises were carried out in the 135th Infantry Brigade area while work on beach defences continued. On 30th July the brigade was inspected by H.R.H. the Duke of Gloucester. The Germans began to build up invasion forces and collect shipping in the French Channel Ports. German air attacks began and, between 11th July and 25th August were mainly directed against convoys of shipping in the Channel.

On 1st August the 5th Battalion took over "A" sector with headquarters at Dymchurch. Air attacks on this sector began on 18th August. Dymchurch was heavily bombed and damaged on 24th August, but there were no military casualties.

On 2nd August 2/Lieut. G. D. Bond was appointed Adjutant of the 7th Battalion, which was inspected on 7th August by General Sir Alan Brooke, C.-in-C. Home Forces. On 29th August strong formations of German bombers crossed the coast, dropping bombs in the Lydd sector. Air attacks increased in September, particularly on London. On 6th September S. M. Parr, 5th Battalion, shot down a M.E. 109 with a Lewis gun. On 7th September, G.H.Q., Home Forces, issued the code word "Cromwell" (Invasion imminent) to all Eastern and Southern Commands and all London formations.

Dispositions during September were as follows:

H.Q. 45th (Wessex) Division: Hawkhurst, Kent.
H.Q. 135th Infantry Brigade: Orlestone.
5 Somerset L.I.: Lydd-Dungeness.
6 Somerset L.I.: Dymchurch area.
7 Somerset L.I.: New Romney area.

On 27th September 31st Infantry Brigade Group arrived as Divisional reserve.

On 12th September Mr. Churchill, General Sir John Dill and General Sir Alan Brooke passed through the 6th Battalion area and saw the men at work. On the 19th September the V.C.I.G.S. (Lieut.-General R. H. Haining, C.B., D.S.O.) inspected forward defences. Work went on on beach defences and mine-laying. But A company, 7th Battalion, found time to win the Brigade "cross-Marsh" marching championship. On 28th September Private Wild, 7th Battalion, was killed by stepping on a mine near Greatstone and three civilians were injured by the explosion of a booby-trap at Littlestone. On 27th September Lieut.-Colonel E. H. C. Frith, M.B.E., succeeded Lieut.-Colonel J. R. Ware, T.D., in command of the 5th Battalion.

The German invasion of Britain (Operation Sea-Lion) had been fixed for 21st September. On 17th September it was postponed owing to the necessity to disperse concentrations of barges, following British air attacks on French invasion ports. That was the beginning of the end of the invasion.

During October there was no change in the dispositions of 135th Infantry Brigade. German fighter-bomber attacks on R.A.F. fighter airfields and air attacks on London, increased in intensity. There was much enemy air activity; the Lydd, Littlestone and New Romney areas being heavily attacked by M.E. 109's. There were, however, practically no military casualties. On 30th October, in the 7th Battalion area, Mr. Mogg, a fisherman, exploded five beach mines with his bicycle and was killed. Indeed, throughout this period, the civil population suffered far more casualties, from various causes, than the military. In the 6th Battalion, Captain J. B. Cossens was appointed Adjutant

JUNE–OCTOBER 1940

Throughout this period the three battalions of the brigade had much work to do in guarding crashed German aircraft and in the capture and interrogation of enemy airmen. There were a number of "spy scares" and on one occasion enemy agents landed from small boats on the Channel Coast. All these men were intercepted and captured.

By 31st October the Battle of Britain was virtually over. As a result of their failure to gain air superiority, German invasion plans had to be postponed indefinitely and the major threat had passed. During the period the total German losses over Britain were 1,733 aircraft destroyed and 643 damaged.

THE 4TH BATTALION

This Battalion was at Harpenden and Hatfield at the end of May, forming part of 129th Infantry Brigade (Brigadier G. E. M. Whittuck, M.C., A.D.C.) of 43rd (Wessex) Division. On 3rd June it moved by road and rail to Byfleet and, next day, a motor-cycle platoon was formed.

Between 8th June and 28th June, 129th Infantry Brigade was in reserve for the Defence of London. On 29th June the Battalion was relieved by the 2nd Welsh Guards and moved by rail to Aylesbury, where it was accommodated in a tented camp. Its rôle was now Mobile Defence under IV Corps.

On 15th July it moved to the Saffron Walden–Great Chesterfield area. On 17th July Lieut. (Q.M.) Johnson M.C., was appointed Quartermaster. On 12th September Brigadier G. E. M. Whittuck was succeeded by Brigadier W. K. M. Leader, O.B.E., M.C., in command of 129th Infantry Brigade.

8TH (HOME DEFENCE) BATTALION

This Battalion remained in North Somerset. In June the strength was 39 Officers and 837 Other Ranks. The Adjutant was Captain R. J. Barnes.

On 24th July B company proceeded to Aylesbury to take over a Prisoners of War camp. On 12th August one platoon of E company took over Weston Zoyland airfield.

9TH BATTALION

On 1st July 1940 the 9th Battalion was raised at Taunton by Major J. D. Gage-Brown, who had been Adjutant of the 5th Battalion since 1936.

2nd-in-Command: Major J. D. Crosthwaite, D.S.O., M.C.
(posted from Queen's Regt.).
Quartermaster: Lieut. (Q.M.) A. Foster, M.C.
(posted from East Yorks Regt.).
Adjutant: 2/Lieut. H. G. Brummel.
R.S.M.: V. Fudge (posted from 5th Battalion).
R.Q.M.S.: Durnford.
O.R.S.: Fisher.
Signal Officer: Lieut. D. B. M. Durie.
M.O.: Lieut. J. Leslie, R.A.M.C.
Chaplain: Rev. W. J. Stewart-Crump (Vicar of Bicknoller).

The Battalion was raised with a cadre of 11 Officers and 150 Other Ranks from the I.T.C. (3rd Reserve Battalion) Taunton and the 50th (Holding) Battalion. 800 Other Ranks were taken in direct from civil life. The organisation was: H.Q. company (Signals, carriers, mortars, pioneers, transport); four rifle companies. On 4th July the cadre assembled at Taunton and on 8th July moved to St. Audries Holiday Camp, Bicknoller. With the Battalion, at first, were:

Lieuts. G. Baker, H. B. Stewart, B. S. Sparrow, L. Digby, A. G. Kingston, D. B. Pratt; 2/Lieuts. S. H. Cair, H. N. Ingram, J. E. M. Napier, E. R. C. Inge, R. F. Crocombe, F. T. Croker, C. E. Mansfield, C. E. T. Jackson, J. W. Dunning, R. J. R. Catford, L. W. Balch, S. Pavey, A. Young, A. P Tregenna, A. Delafield, J. N. Goodwyn and K. H. Maunder; C.S.M.s: Hall, Somerfield, Duckett and Hodson; C.Q.M.S.s: James, Hill and Barber.

By 18th July 200 recruits had joined. On 20th July an anti-paratroop force (distinct from what was termed "K" Force of the Home Guard) was formed with two civilian coaches as transport. The Battalion was under Bridgwater sub-area (Brigadier J. N. Lumby, M.C.) which formed part of 11th Infantry Group of four battalions.

By the end of July the strength had risen to 21 Officers and 943 Other Ranks. These were mostly Somerset men with an average age of 26 years. At this time the Battalion had only 150 rifles and bayonets, 1 pistol and 150 picks and shovels. Of these 30 service rifles and 85 D.P. rifles were on loan from the Cadet Corps. It was not until 11th August that 800 service rifles were received.

Between 11th and 14th August Williton was bombed and the anti-paratroop force rounded up Germans from two crashed bombers near Highbridge. On 2nd September the Battalion was inspected by Lieut.-General H. E. Franklin, D.S.O., M.C., commanding VIII Corps.

On 7th September code word "Cromwell" (Invasion imminent) was received and the Battalion placed at two hours' notice to move. Its rôle was to block all roads from the Bristol Channel to Exmoor, between Minehead and Bridgwater. The Battalion went into bivouacs until ordered to "Stand down" on 20th September.

On 28th September headquarters moved to Burnham-on-Sea, with B and C companies at Brent Knoll and C company at Highbridge. On 14th October the Battalion relieved the 9th Buffs at Saltash. 11th Infantry Group was renamed 211th Infantry Brigade, forming part of No. 6 Support Group, Devon and Cornwall Division, VIII Corps. At Saltash the Battalion was employed on constructing and wiring defences.

11TH (HOLDING) BATTALION

On 10th June 1940 this unit was broken up. The Somerset Light Infantry Company moved to Weston-super-Mare and formed the nucleus of the 50th (Holding) Battalion, The Somerset Light Infantry.

JUNE–OCTOBER 1940

Commanding: Lieut.-Colonel K. G. G. Dennys.
Adjutant: Captain R. F. Stileman.
Quartermaster: Captain (Q.M.) J. M. Lumbers.

The organisation was H.Q. company and four rifle companies, the personnel being by direct intake from the 26 years of age group. 200 evacuees from the Channel Islands formed the fourth company. At first the only weapons available were Ross Rifles.

The unit was first employed as a Beach Defence Battalion, constructing beach defences at Weston-super-Mare. In August, headquarters moved to Burnham-on-Sea, with rifle companies in the area Burnham–Brean Down. Here it was employed on beach and anti-paratroop defence and the defence of bridges and vital points. Guard duties were extremely heavy and interfered seriously with basic training.

CHAPTER VII

THE BATTLE FOR EXISTENCE—
NOVEMBER 1940–DECEMBER 1941

Situation in Russia—Dominions war effort—Situation in France—Events in Britain 1940—Air attacks—4th Battalion—135th Infantry Brigade—8th and 9th Battalions—50th (Holding) Battalion redesignated 10th Battalion—Britain in 1941—4th Battalion—135th Infantry Brigade—Royal Hamilton Light Infantry—8th Battalion redesignated 30th Battalion—9th Battalion—10th Battalion—2nd Battalion at Gibraltar—1st Battalion in India—The international field in 1941—United States enter war

THE Battle of Britain caused a postponement of immediate German invasion plans, but did not remove the danger of invasion. Western Europe, with the exception of Spain and Portugal, had been overrun by the Axis Powers and, already, the Italians were preparing large-scale attacks on our possessions in North Africa.

Russia was, at the first, on the Axis side, though to what extent this assistance was merely opportunist will be for future historians to decide. She had forestalled German troops in Southern Poland and towards the Carpathians in 1939, and in the same year picked a quarrel with Finland. For this she was expelled from the League of Nations in November 1939. But her war with Finland was short-lived and was settled in March 1940. She began to extend, however, into the Baltic States of Latvia, Estonia and Lithuania. Russian forces, at this time, did not appear to be of any great military value, in the modern sense. She seemed to be relying on her traditional system of masses of men, ill-equipped, ill-trained and ill-led.

The situation in the autumn of 1940 was that Britain and the Commonwealth had their backs to the wall and were left, almost alone, to carry on the fight for democracy and liberty. The initiative had passed to the enemy and the struggle was one for bare existence.

The first contingent of Canadian troops had landed in Britain on 17th December 1939 and further contingents, which played their part in the Battle of Britain, continued to arrive. Anzac troops began to arrive in Egypt from 12th February 1940. Indian troops were already in Egypt and the Red Sea area and further contingents were sent. South Africa sent troops to Uganda and, later, to Egypt. With the collapse of France the Dominions went ahead with the raising of forces, but the situation regarding arms, equipment, vehicles and ammunition was desperate in all areas, following the enormous losses suffered by the B.E.F. Everywhere shortages of essentials delayed expansion and training and, indeed, made the position of forces facing the enemy highly precarious.

NOVEMBER 1940–DECEMBER 1941

In India, after an initial wave of enthusiasm, which could not be turned to full account, the Congress Party, led by M. K. Gandhi, withdrew its support from the war effort. Discussions between the Viceroy and Congress leaders broke down on 30th September 1940 and, thereafter, Congress was non-co-operative. This caused difficulties and anxieties, but did not affect the raising of new forces and their despatch overseas. The Princes and the Independent Kingdom of Nepal gave unstinted help with troops and supplies. Vast quantities of stores and materials were sent overseas from India and these were never replaced. Thus the equipment of new forces and the maintenance of existing forces was a matter of extreme difficulty and improvisation.

After the collapse of France, a Collaborationist government under Marshal Petain and M. Laval was set up at Vichy and caused complications with French overseas possessions. General de Gaulle was recognised, on 26th June 1940, as the "Leader of all Free Frenchmen". He began, forthwith, to organise Free French Resistance movements both in France and outside.

On the High Seas the German submarine campaign took heavy toll of our merchant shipping. Our convoys in the Channel, the Western Approaches, the Bay of Biscay and the Mediterranean were subject to air attack from shore based aircraft. German surface raiders preyed on shipping in the Atlantic, Pacific and Indian Oceans.

Throughout all this period—up to the end of 1941—the United States remained sympathetic, but neutral. Following the close of the Battle of Britain plans for the Invasion of France, when the time came to resume the offensive, were set on foot. This operation became, thenceforth, the major aim of Allied strategy.

EVENTS IN BRITAIN—1940

Following the failure of the Germans to overcome our fighter defences, they turned their attention, during the autumn and winter of 1940–1, to bomber attacks on centres of industry, ports and communications. These attacks continued, with varying severity, to the end of 1941. In November 1940, Birmingham, Southampton, Liverpool and Bristol were heavily attacked. In December 1940 attacks switched to the London area, the greater portion of the City of London being destroyed by fire. Thereafter the main areas under attack were the south coast ports, the Midlands and London.

During November–December 1940 there was a re-shuffle of land forces in Britain, following the removal of the immediate threat of invasion.

4th BATTALION

On 7th/8th November 1940, 129th Infantry Brigade moved from Saffron Walden to the Shorncliffe–Folkestone area. Intense air activity was encountered on the march. On 9th November, the 4th Battalion was disposed as follows:

    H.Q., D and R companies: Shorncliffe.
    A company: Caesar's Camp.
    B company: Dover Hill.

From 24th November 129th Infantry Brigade took over No. 4 Coastal Sector, the 4th Battalion moving to the area.

Battalion H.Q.:	Folkestone.
H.Q., D and R companies:	Radnor Park.
A and B companies:	near Hawkinge.

On 5th December Hawkinge airfield was heavily bombed. By 21st December German guns were in position on the French coast and shells were falling among convoys in the Straits of Dover.

135TH INFANTRY BRIGADE

Early in November the brigade was relieved in the Romney Marsh area by 132nd Infantry Brigade, 44th Division. The 45th (Wessex) Division moved to the north of England, into the Doncaster area, coming under I Corps and Northern Command.

On 7th November the 5th Battalion was disposed at Ackworth—High Ackworth—Badsworth—South Featherstone—Moor Top. The billets were very bad. A Motor Coach Company R.A.S.C. was attached to the Battalion, and the latter was given the rôle of a Mobile Force. On 16th November Captain G. R. Chetwynd-Stapylton was appointed Adjutant. On 16th December R.S.M. G. Vickery was commissioned and posted to the Battalion. C.S.M. H. L. Trebble became R.S.M.

On 6th November the 6th Battalion went into very overcrowded billets at Wakefield where it was engaged in mobile exercises.

On 5th November the 7th Battalion was relieved by the 4th Royal West Kent Regt. and moved to the area Castleford–Allerton Bywater–Swillington. Its rôle was mobile defence. During December it was engaged in exercises and training.

OTHER BATTALIONS IN BRITAIN

The 8th (H.D.) Battalion remained in North Somerset. The strength at the end of 1940 was 49 Officers and 921 Other Ranks. The 9th Battalion remained at Saltash. On 9th October the 50th (Holding) Battalion, at Burnham-on-Sea, was renamed the 10th Battalion, The Somerset Light Infantry. It remained on coastal defences and engaged in exercises and training under 3rd Division and VIII Corps (later under V Corps). When redesignated:

Commanding Officer:	Lieut.-Colonel K. G. G. Dennys.
2nd-in-Command:	Major J. L. Bond.
Adjutant:	Captain R. F. Stileman.
Quartermaster:	Captain (Q.M.) J. M. Lumbers.
M.O.:	Captain T. Russell, R.A.M.C.

BRITAIN IN 1941

Events for units of the British Army in Britain during this year were not spectacular. 1940 had been a period during which units, from force of circumstances, had had to learn by experience and systematic training had gone by the board. The experience gained was valuable. But during 1941 systematic re-equipment of units and collective training was proceeded with. The object was to produce an army mentally and physically fit, and adequately equipped, to undertake a campaign of reconquest.

THE 4TH BATTALION

There was heavy snow and severe weather in the Folkestone area in January. During this month Major (Q.M.) R. W. Stephens, M.B.E., was appointed Quartermaster. 2/Lieut. M. J. G. Hindle became Assistant Adjutant.

On 5th February the Battalion moved to Great Monegham, near Deal, and worked on defences in the area Upper Deal–Ringwould–Sutton.

On 27th February Lieut.-Colonel Bishop vacated command and was succeeded by Lieut.-Colonel R. H. Bakewell from the 2nd Battalion. At this time the R.S.M. was A. Wynne and the R.Q.M.S. F. G. Hale. On 14th March Brigadier Leader was succeeded by Brigadier G. Brunskill, M.C., in command of 129th Infantry Brigade. On 2nd April the Battalion was inspected by H.R.H. the Duke of Gloucester and on 7th April Jellalabad Day was celebrated according to custom.

On 19th May the Battalion was relieved by 4th Royal Sussex Regt. and moved to a tented camp at Chilston Park, near Lenham, Kent. It was disposed, with an anti-paratroop rôle, in the area Wickling–Hogbarn–Warren Street–Stonebridge–Lenham. At this time the commander 43rd (Wessex) Division was Major-General Allfrey, D.S.O. and the Corps Commander, Lieut.-General B. L. Montgomery, C.B., D.S.O. During June the Battalion was engaged in Divisional and Corps Exercises.

On 30th June R.Q.M.S. F. G. Hale was commissioned and appointed Quartermaster; on 11th August Captain E. A. Trotman was appointed Adjutant; on 1st September R.S.M. Holt was posted to the Battalion as R.S.M. In July Lieut.-Colonel W. S. C. Curtis, M.C., assumed command in succession to Lieut.-Colonel Bakewell. During this period Major C. L. Firbank was 2nd-in-Command.

During August assistance was given to farmers to get in the harvest. September saw large scale exercises to practise the Home Guard in street fighting in south-east London. Between 1st/4th October G.H.Q. Exercise "Bumper" practised formations over a wide area of the Home Counties.

On 15th October the Battalion moved into winter quarters at Linton and Loose and the remainder of the year was taken up with Divisional and Corps training.

135TH INFANTRY BRIGADE

January saw very severe weather throughout the Divisional area. During this month individual, company and battalion training was proceeded with. During February the Division moved into Eastern Command.

135th Infantry Brigade was disposed as under in the new area:

    5th Battalion: Aylesbury, with the rôle of Mobile Force.
    6th Battalion: Dropmore, Bucks.
    7th Battalion: Thame, with B and C companies at Great
               Haseley, A and D companies at Kingsley.

Brigade exercises were held in March; Divisional exercises in April. These were followed by Command Exercise, "Bulwark".

On 7th January Lieut.-Colonel Trotter was posted from the 6th Battalion to command the 45th Division Reconnaissance Battalion, formed from units within the Division. He was succeeded, on 24th January, by Lieut.-Colonel B. J. Corballis, M.C., from the 2nd Battalion. On 11th October Lieut. J. H. S. Richards was appointed Adjutant.

During June the brigade took part in Command Exercise "Bulldog", in the area Preston–Barningham–Norwich. During this exercise 2/Lieut. G. F. H. Tredwin, 6th Battalion, late Sergeant 5th Battalion, was killed by a falling tree.

In July the brigade moved into XI Corps area (Commander: Lieut.-General H. R. S. Massey, C.B., C.M.G., D.S.O., M.C.) in the Colchester district. 45th (Wessex) Division was then commanded by Major-General H. de R. Morgan, D.S.O. While here the brigade was initially disposed as follows:

    5th Battalion: Hyderabad Barracks, Colchester, in Brigade Reserve.
    6th Battalion: Abberton.
    7th Battalion: Roman Way Camp.

Duties included defence works on the Stanier Line, coast defence, training exercises, training of the Home Guard and assistance to farmers in lifting the potato and sugar-beet crops.

THE ROYAL HAMILTON LIGHT INFANTRY, CANADIAN ARMY

A small digression is here necessary. This Battalion was mobilised on 2nd September 1939 under the command of Lieut.-Colonel H. G. Wright. It remained at Standard Barracks, Hamilton, until 27th May 1940, when it moved to Camp Borden for eight weeks' intensive training. On 24th July it sailed from Canada in s.s. "Antonia", arriving in England on 1st August 1940. It was employed in various anti-invasion rôles in Southern England during the autumn of 1940 and spring of 1941. On 27th May 1941 it moved to bivouacs at Ibstone Common, near Thame, in the 7th Somerset L.I. area. It was played into camp by the band and bugles of the 7th Battalion. For a week a programme of sports and entertainments was carried out. This was the first meeting during the 1939–45 War of the R.H.L.I. and a unit of the Somerset Light Infantry.

NOVEMBER 1940–DECEMBER 1941

8TH (HOME DEFENCE) BATTALION

On 5th January 1941 Weston-super-Mare was bombed. C company stores, in Stafford Road, were destroyed. During January D company moved to Burnham-on-Sea and automatic weapon training was proceeded with.

In March, H.Q. Western Area took over operational control from H.Q. Southern Area, the area commander being Brigadier J. A. Churchill, D.S.O., M.C., A.D.C. On 24th March, Bridgwater was bombed. During April, VIII Corps commander visited coastal defences. On 18th April, Lieut. F. W. Simkins was appointed Adjutant. The strength of the Battalion had now risen to 46 Officers and 996 Other Ranks.

During July, E company moved to Churchstanton, A company to Bridgwater and Felton airfield, and a platoon of C company took over the defences of the Severn Tunnel. In September there were Area Exercises. By the end of the month the strength was 52 Officers and 1,426 Other Ranks.

On 5th October Lieut.-Colonel C. R. Spear, M.V.O., M.C., assumed command, *vice* Colonel Aitken. On 1st December 2/Lieut. J. Dare was appointed Assistant Adjutant. Lieut. (Q.M.) W. J. Atkins succeeded Lieut. (Q.M.) J. Lucas as Quartermaster, on 19th December.

On 29th December the 8th (H.D.) Battalion was re-designated the 30th Battalion, The Somerset Light Infantry. The strength was then 61 Officers and 1,491 Other Ranks.

THE 9TH BATTALION

During the spring of 1941 the 9th Battalion moved to Seaton Barracks, Crownhill, Plymouth, with one company at Wembury and one company in the area Plymstock–Ernsettle. Its rôle was Mobile Coastal Defence and the protection of Roborough airfield. A.F.V.s, known as "Armadillos", were issued, as well as maxim and Hotchkiss guns. The Devon and Cornwall Division was commanded at this time by Major-General F. E. Morgan.

On 21st/22nd and 28th/29th April, Plymouth was heavily bombed and the Battalion employed in clearing up. On 20th May it relieved the 5th Gloucestershire Regt. at Uffculme and Cullompton and joined the 144th Infantry Brigade (Brigadier J. H. Hamilton, D.S.O.) of 48th Division. It was then engaged in collective training and, on 8th June, was converted from a Beach Defence unit to a Field Force Battalion. This entailed the issue of additional equipment and vehicles.

In August it moved to Penny Gillian Camp, near Launceston, with the rôle of counter-attack force in the Cornwall sector. September was taken up with Divisional training with tanks and with Corps Exercise "Bumper". A period of individual and specialist training followed in October.

On 15th November 48th Division moved to Northern Command. The 9th Battalion was employed on coastal defence in the Skegness area.

Major W. H. F. Routh joined the Battalion in December.

10th BATTALION

Early in 1941 the Battalion moved to Portland. On 15th April a bomb fell on A company headquarters near Chesil Cove. Captain M. J. Watson, company commander, and 8 Other Ranks were killed. 2/Lieuts. E. B. Culverwell, A. F. Searle, M. H. Vincent and G. B. Smith were wounded. Other bombs fell on Portland. During May there were 50 alerts in the area. Bombs were dropped on 30th May, but there were no casualties. June saw 19 alerts on the Island.

On 23rd July the Battalion moved to the Isle of Wight and was disposed as under:

Battalion H.Q.: Golden Hill Fort, Freshwater.
A, B, C companies: Colwell Bay–Totland Bay.
D company: Brook Bay–Compton Bay–Freshwater Bay.

The autumn was spent in exercises and training.

Between 13th and 16th November the Battalion joined the 143rd Infantry Brigade in Lincolnshire and was disposed as under:

Battalion H.Q.: Mareham-Le-Fen.
A and B companies: Woodhall Spa.
B company: Tattershall.
C company: Coningsby.

On 26th November the Battalion marched to Horncastle area, C company being located at West Ashby. During December it was employed assisting farmers to lift the sugar-beet crop. At this duty it demonstrated that, at topping beets, the men of Somerset are second to none.

2nd BATTALION

During the whole period the 2nd Battalion remained at Gibraltar. Duties included providing guards for ships and the manning and construction of defences in Camp Bay, Europa Pass, Rosia, Moorish Tower, Drawbridge and Woodford Battery. During July and August 1940 there were air raids on the Rock, but little damage was done. On 24th/25th September 1940 there was a heavy raid by 100 aircraft and over 300 bombs were dropped. C and D company stores were destroyed by fire. Work continued on defences during the spring of 1941, the 4th Devon Regt. assisting.

During April, work was concentrated in the Southern area, at South Mole, Napier Battery, Europa Tunnel and Monkeys Cave. These works were practically completed. On 25th April Lord Gort became Governor and Commander-in-Chief.

During May, posts at Little Bay Fort were completed and work began on posts on the South Mole. The full manning of posts was brought into operation. During June pill-boxes at the south end of Europa Tunnel, Europa

Pass and Camp Bay were completed. In July O.R.Q.M.S. Chapman received the B.E.M.

During the latter part of 1941 the Battalion was much reduced in strength by the despatch of drafts and there was consequent delay in the construction of defences. On 17th October it was inspected by H.R.H. the Duke of Gloucester.

1st BATTALION

On 3rd June 1940 the Battalion concentrated at Multan for service in the Middle East, but plans were changed and it settled down to summer training, which included the construction of defences against possible air attack. The weather was extremely hot, the temperatures often rising to over 120 degrees by day. Multan is on the verge of the Indian desert and gets very little monsoon rain; the country round is watered by canals and wells. There is therefore little relief from the heat in the late summer and conditions favour the breeding of swarms of malaria mosquitoes. Consequently the sick rate from heat in the summer and from malaria in the autumn was high in both seasons spent there. Great care was taken to reduce casualties by carrying out parades in the shade of trees and adding salt to drinking water.

On 12th March a platoon of thirty picked N.C.O.s and men was sent to Kohat to join a company of the Rajputana Rifles (A.F.I.). This was in connection with possible parachute landings in frontier districts. Major A. Hunt, followed by Captain C. W. S. Satterthwaite, commanded this column until it was broken up in September.

In September 1940 Lieut.-Colonel A. F. Harding left to join the Middle East Staff. Major H. W. Spurrell officiated in command until the arrival of Lieut.-Colonel G. H. Cole in December. Between September 1940 and March 1941 the Battalion was engaged in Frontier Warfare Training.

In October 1941 the Battalion moved to Sialkot and soon afterwards went into camp with Jhelum Brigade for training in preparation for its move to Waziristan.

THE INTERNATIONAL FIELD IN 1940–41

The general course of events has been described in Chapter IV, but certain other happenings require mention, as they lead up to the entry of the United States into the war.

On 27th September 1940 a ten-year pact between Germany, Italy and Japan was signed in Berlin. Thereafter, Japan began to increase her aggressive strategy in the Pacific.

On 6th January 1941 President Roosevelt defined the "Four Freedoms" to Congress and urged the supply of weapons and munitions to the Allies. On 10th January the Lease-Lend Bill was introduced into Congress and, after approval by the House of Representatives, was signed by the President on 11th March. This measure was of the utmost value to the Allied cause.

On 14th August news was published of the meeting of President Roosevelt and Mr. Churchill on H.M.S. "Prince of Wales" and U.S. Cruiser "Augusta", in the Atlantic. At this the Atlantic Charter was formulated. During the year the United States voted vast sums for defence and gradually, guided by the President, public opinion veered towards more active assistance to Britain. Thus, when the final act of aggression by Japan was committed at Pearl Harbour, on 7th December 1941, President Roosevelt had the United States solidly behind him.

War was declared on Japan on 8th December and on Germany and Italy on 11th December. Congress then voted the despatch of United States forces to any part of the world.

CHAPTER VIII

FIGHTING BACK—1942

General situation 1942—1st Battalion in India—Entry of Japan into war—Reversal of military policy in India—Operations in Waziristan—Action at Greenwood's Corner—Datta Khel operations—Situation in Burma and Assam—Insurrection in India—1st Battalion joins 7th Indian Division—2nd Battalion at Gibraltar—4th Battalion at Dover—Royal Hamilton Light Infantry—135th Infantry Brigade—5th Battalion—6th Battalion—7th Battalion leaves 135th Infantry Brigade—9th Battalion—10th Battalion—Conversion to 7th Battalion (L.I.) The Parachute Regt.—30th Battalion

1941 was a disastrous year for the Allied cause. But, during that year, the Axis powers made two vital mistakes which, in the end, were to lead to their defeat. In June Germany invaded Russia; in December Japan attacked the United States. It was the overwhelming resources, in manpower and materials, possessed by these two nations, operating from East and West, which finally resulted in the cracking of the Axis nut.

The first portion of 1942, however, saw further disasters for the Allies. In the East the Japanese drove relentlessly westwards and southwards. The Philippines, Malaya, Siam, Burma and the Netherlands East Indies were quickly overrun. In the West, the Germans swept into Russia through the Ukraine and the Crimea and began to invade the Caucasus. Leningrad and Moscow were seriously endangered. Britain was heavily attacked by air; the threat of invasion from France remained and sea communications were harassed by submarine and air attack. In North Africa the Third German Offensive in Libya was only halted at the gates of Alexandria and Cairo.

It was not until the autumn that the Japanese advance to India was halted on the Indo-Burma frontier and the drive towards Australia checked by the Battle of the Coral Sea. In Russia the Germans were held at Stalingrad and, later, pushed back. In North Africa the Battle of El Alamain resulted in our taking the offensive once more. By the end of the year British-American forces had landed in Algeria.

Throughout the fluctuations of the struggle, the army in Britain continued to prepare for the counter-offensive.

THE 1st BATTALION IN INDIA

The entry of Japan into the war, followed by the invasion of Malaya, Siam and Burma, with a threat to the security of India itself, caused grave reactions on India's war effort.

Already, during the latter part of 1941, the German drive into Russia had caused anxiety in the Middle Eastern countries of Turkey, Iraq and Iran, namely those countries which, with Afghanistan, were loosely knit by the

Saadabad Pact. A German invasion of the Caucasus might well be a prelude to a "Drang nach Osten", which might overrun Iran and Afghanistan and reach the Western Frontier of India. The traditional "Russian Bogey" had, for the time, been replaced by a far more substantial ghost. These anxieties had their repercussions on the fanatical Muslim populations of the tribal areas on both sides of the Durand Line, resulting in an increase of unrest, which was fostered by Axis agents in Kabul and elsewhere.

Plans were put in hand in India to prepare the passes into India from the west—the Bolan and Khyber—for defence against a modern army. In addition tank obstacles were constructed in minor defiles through the North-West Frontier hills, particularly in the Kurram, Tochi and Gomal valleys.

While the German menace was a distant one, the Japanese forces were at the very doors of India. During 1940 and 1941, in spite of non-co-operation by the Indian National Congress, new military formations had been raised, trained, equipped and sent overseas. To the Indian public it was explained, as was true, that under conditions of modern warfare, a frontier could not be defended by sitting on it. If enemies on sea, land and in the air were to be kept at a distance, the Outer Bastions of India—in the Middle East and Malaya—must be secured. The enemy must be prevented from securing land bases from which hostile aircraft could operate against the great cities of the Plains of India.

The attitude of the Indian politicians—a small but vociferous handful of intelligentsia—was that Indian manpower and resources were being used to prosecute a war which was not of India's making and in the direction of which Indians had no say. India, so they maintained, was in a state of servitude and was being exploited to further the ends of an European-made conflict, regarding which Indians had not been consulted. The entry of Japan into the war, her proclaimed policy of a "New Order in Asia" and her immediate victories over European and American forces, not only caused panic among the masses in India, but encouraged political elements to hope that the hour of India's "liberation" was at hand. Subversive elements came out into the open and their activities everywhere increased. The object was to sabotage the defence of India. Their efforts received further encouragement from the operation of a "scorched earth" policy which was set on foot, by government, in eastern areas.

In the defence field there was a complete reversal of policy. Formations, up to December 1941, had been trained and equipped for mobile warfare conditions in Middle East theatres of war. Practically all the available equipment in India had been used up to furnish these formations and despatch them. The demands for equipment in more vital theatres of war—particularly Britain and Egypt—were so pressing that very little of this material and stores was replaced. Just when essential vehicles and weapons became available, they were diverted to Russia. As a result, when Japan declared war, India was almost defenceless. Her arsenals were empty; she had practically no aircraft and no anti-aircraft, or coastal, artillery. Such troops as remained in the country were short of stores of all kinds; recruits were being trained with dummy rifles made of wood.

It must be remembered that all India's main lines of communication led to her major port installations on the west coast. They were designed, together with all base depots, hospitals and reception camps, to embark and maintain forces to the westwards. Her ports on the east coast were undeveloped and the communications to them indifferent. Burma was isolated from India by a stretch of forest-covered hills, through which no roads or railways ran. The only communications with Burma were by sea, or air. On the Indian side of the Burma frontier Assam, Manipur and the Arakan were mainly served by river. Such roads and railways as existed, were sufficient only for the very small amount of traffic between those areas and Bengal.

Thus, when India was threatened from the east, not only had her whole military organisation to be switched from west to east, but she had to construct new base lay-outs, build new airfields and develop new communications to maintain forces in the Eastern Provinces. In addition she had to re-equip and train her troops for jungle warfare, in a terrain and climate to which they were entirely unaccustomed. The army in India had a long tradition of fighting in intense dry heat, in open country, or in scrub covered hills. Damp heat of sub-tropical jungles was almost entirely foreign to both British and Indian troops. They had to be provided with the necessary clothing and equipment for the strange conditions; they had to learn jungle tactics and to cast off the fear engendered by fighting in the sweltering heat beneath dense foliage, with a field of view of only a few yards before them.

All this reversal of policy had to be carried out under an immediate threat of invasion; while the populations of the eastern and southern provinces were panic-stricken; and while subversive elements were doing all they could to tamper with the loyalty of troops, to sabotage communications and to let the Japanese in. That is, briefly, the background against which the later operations of the 1st Battalion in the Arakan must be seen. But in the meantime, in January 1941, while all available forces in India were being sent to Burma, or concentrated in the east and south-east, watch and ward had still to be maintained on the North-West Frontier, where German efforts to foster unrest were intensified. Internal security, also, had to be maintained, in a situation which rapidly began to deteriorate.

OPERATIONS IN WAZIRISTAN

On 18th January the 1st Battalion moved to Gardai, a perimeter camp near Razani, in Waziristan, close to the road from Tal-in-Tochi to Razmak. Here it joined the 3rd Indian Infantry Brigade (Brigadier Quayle) consisting of 1 Somerset L.I.; 1/10 Baluch Regt.; 7/16 Punjab Regt.; 4/3 Gurkha Rifles.

The brigade was engaged in normal road protection duties. The Battalion, in its turn, provided men for permanent piquets and for opening and protecting the road for the movement of convoys to and from Razmak, on

"Road Open" days. The area was disturbed and piquets were frequently sniped at night; mainly by gangs sent out by the Fakir of Ipi, from his cave area at the head of the Tochi Valley. The first casualties occurred in March when one Other Rank was fatally wounded by a sniper and another seriously wounded. This fatal casualty led to an unfortunate incident.

ACTION AT GREENWOOD'S CORNER

It was customary for all fatal casualties occurring on the road to be buried in the British Military Cemetery at Razmak. On this occasion there was not likely to be another "Road Open" day for some time. Therefore, on 7th March, it was decided to send the body in an ambulance to Razmak, with two armoured cars and an escort, commanded by Lieut. Hume, in two three-ton open trucks. The party reached Razmak safely and, perhaps encouraged by this, decided to return in the same manner on the 8th March.

From Razmak to the Razmak Narai, the road runs through open country and is dominated by certain permanent posts. From the Narai it runs down the east side of a deep valley, with a steep, tree-covered spur overhanging it. Where the spur ends, not far from the main valley, near Gardai, there is a sharp hairpin bend in the road, known as Greenwood's Corner. This is overlooked, at short rifle range, by another spur.

As the party approached Greenwood's Corner, at 1100 hours, heavy fire was opened on it from a tribal ambush on the spur. The Indian driver of the leading armoured car stopped, blocking the road so that the remaining vehicles could not pass at speed and get out of range. The enemy fire then came on the escort in the open three-ton trucks and they were hastily emptied. Lieut. Hume was seriously wounded at the first, but at once organised and directed a counter-attack against the spur. The enemy, however, were well concealed in the scrub and their strength was uncertain. Lieut. Hume then crawled to the leading armoured car and induced the driver to start. With the road cleared he withdrew his men to the trucks and the party, with its casualties, got away and returned to Gardai. In this affair 1 Other Rank was killed, 1 Officer and 6 Other Ranks wounded.

On the same day, 8th March, about 1500 hours, the garrison of No. 9 Camp Piquet, furnished by the Battalion, was engaged in clearing scrub from the field of fire, covered by two rifle platoons. It had been arranged that the covering party was to be assisted back from their position by the fire of howitzers located in the camp. When the withdrawal began a shell landed among the retiring troops, four Other Ranks being wounded.

Further casualties occurred during May and June during the course of road protection duties. Snipers were troublesome. One sniper, from the regularity of his activities, was known as "Seven o'clock Charlie" and it was alleged that watches in camp were set by his opening round. During June there were local operations to round up gangs in the neighbourhood of Razani, resulting in a few casualties. One of these was Sergeant Chambers, of the family of that name with long connections with the Regiment. His skull was slightly grazed by a bullet, but the shock caused him to fall on the steep hillside and he died from a broken neck. His body remained in tribal hands for a few days, but was subsequently recovered, unmutilated.

DATTA KHEL OPERATIONS

On 28th July the Razani and Razmak Brigades concentrated at Gardai, under Major-General Deedes, for an operation to relieve pressure against the Datta Khel Scouts Post in the Tochi Valley. For some time this post had been intermittently attacked by followers of the Fakir of Ipi, using a tribal gun, and had been invested.

The advance across the hills began on 8th August and Mami Rogha was reached, after some opposition, on the same evening. B company, under Captain Congreve, were successful in taking hill feature 6001, overlooking the camp site. The next day the force reached Datta Khel and remained in that area for three weeks, sending punitive columns across, and towards, the head of the Tochi Valley. At the end of August it returned to Gardai. R.S.M. C. W. Smart (Officiating Quartermaster) and Sergeant Reed (Sergeant cook) received mentions for Meritorious Service.

In July Major H. W. Spurrell, M.C., was posted to Gauhatti and Major E. C. H. Evered officiated as 2nd-in-Command until the arrival in September of Major C. N. N. Delaforce (R.S.F.). On 10th September the Battalion moved to Delhi to be re-equipped and trained for jungle warfare. The internal situation was disturbed and it was called upon to quell riots in the city. By 1st November the reorganisation had been completed and the Battalion was ready to join the 7th Indian Division.

THE SITUATION IN BURMA AND ASSAM

During the spring and summer of 1942 events had been moving swiftly in the war with Japan. On 10th January Lower Burma and Tennaserim were invaded from Siam. By 9th March our forces had evacuated Lower Burma and Rangoon had fallen. On 1st May communications by road, between Burma and China, were cut at Lashio. Mandalay and Myitkhina fell during the next week and on 4th May the Japanese took Akyab, in the Arakan, by a sea-borne landing. The Andaman Islands had already fallen and the Japanese controlled the Bay of Bengal. By the end of May British-Indian forces from Burma had been withdrawn to the Kalewa–Tamu–Imphal area in Assam and Chinese troops to Ledo in northern Assam.

At this time the organisation on the Indo-Burma frontier was as follows:

In Assam: IV Corps.
In Arakan: XV Corps.
At Ledo: Stillwell's Chinese-U.S. troops.
At Mogaung: 3rd Indian Division (Wingate).

The whole was under 14th Army.

During the autumn of 1942 the administrative "build-up" in Assam began in earnest, being mainly directed towards the establishment and improvement of rail, river and road communications and the move up of stores and supplies. The 14th Indian Division was moved into the Arakan, to check the Japanese advance from Akyab.

INSURRECTION IN INDIA

In India itself the internal situation had deteriorated. This was due to three causes; the fear of invasion, the strain placed on the railway system for military purposes and the consequent dislocation of normal traffic for civilian supplies, and the increase in subversive activities. On 14th July the National Congress Working Committee, now openly hostile, published a resolution demanding the withdrawal of British rule from India and threatening a mass struggle, on non-violent lines, on the widest possible scale. There is no doubt that extremists, led by M. K. Gandhi, intended to take full advantage of the situation and desired the entry of Japan into India as favouring their demands for "liberation". There is no doubt, also, that violent methods of achieving their ends were contemplated and planned and that the leaders, fearing arrest, endeavoured to set up an under-ground organisation to take their place in that event.

On 8th August, the National Congress met in Bombay and confirmed the resolution of the Working Committee. On 9th August, M. K. Gandhi and all members of the Working Committee were arrested and interned. Riots at once broke out in Bombay and Delhi and police and troops were used against the rioters.

Thereafter a definite rebellion began. Fortunately it was ill-co-ordinated and the risings ill-timed. It began in the Bombay and Gujrat areas and spread eastwards across central India. Communications of all kinds were sabotaged and many acts of brutality committed. Great destruction was caused, particularly as regards railways, bridges and signals. On certain sectors of the railways in the east United Provinces, Bengal and Bihar, over 1,000 miles of railway track were torn up and over 100 stations gutted. Disruption of communications made the movement of troops to disturbed areas difficult and, in addition, caused much danger and delay in the preparations for the defence of the eastern frontier. Training had to be suspended everywhere, for some six weeks, and troops used to restore order. Efforts to subvert the troops were widespread, but largely ineffective.

In the middle of November the 1st Battalion moved to the Attock–Campbellpore area and joined 114th Indian Infantry Brigade (Brigadier T. Roberts) of 7th Indian Division (Major-General T. W. Corbett). The brigade consisted of 1 Somerset L.I.; 4/14 Punjab Regt.; 4/5 Gurkha Rifles. The brigade was supposed to be training for jungle warfare. The area was, however, largely tree-less and actual training was for North-West Frontier fighting. At the end of the year the Battalion was in camp near Nowshera, the weather being extremely cold and severe.

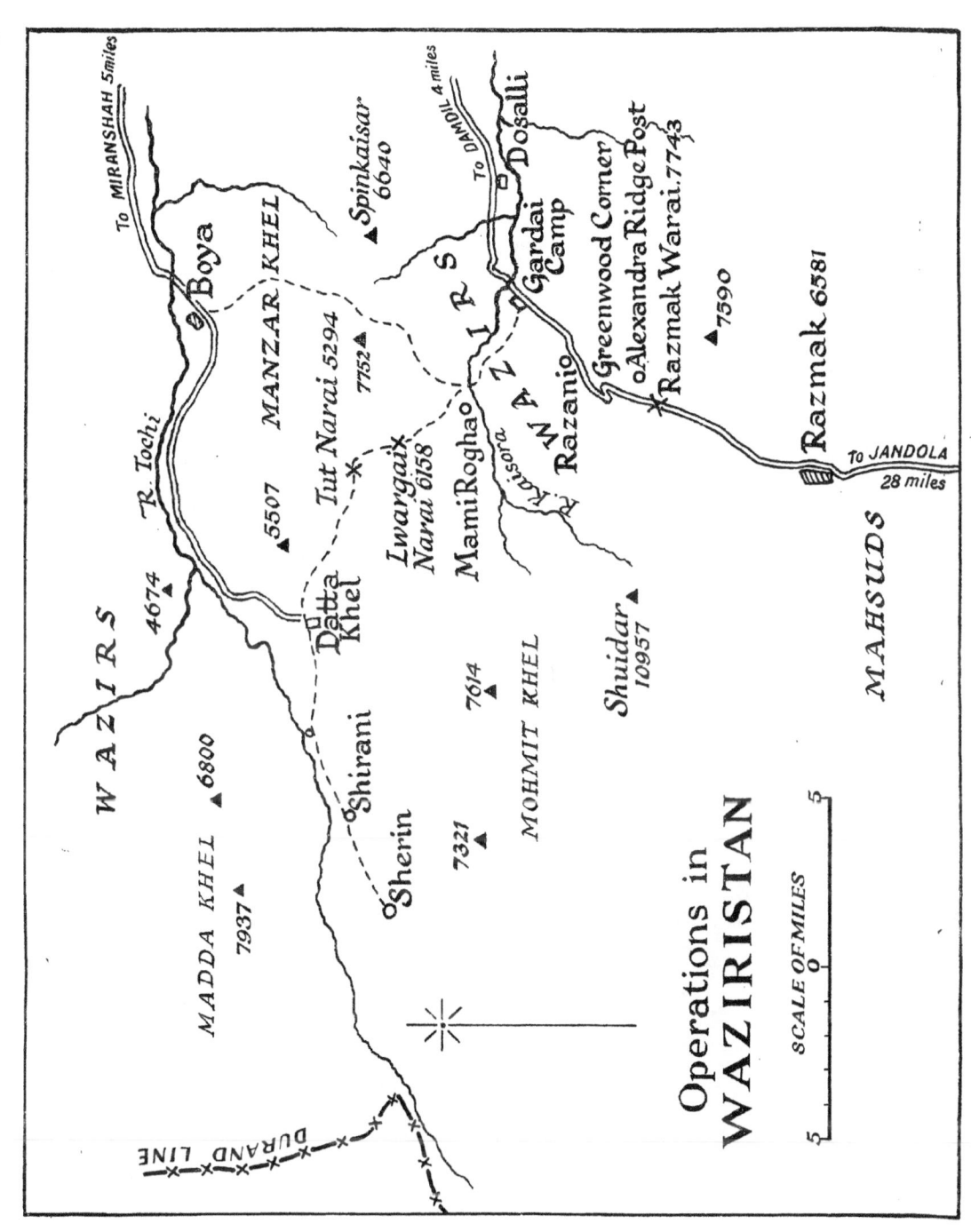

1942

2ND BATTALION—GIBRALTAR

The 2nd Battalion remained at Gibraltar during the whole of 1942 and continued duties and work on defences. There was, naturally, a feeling of great disappointment and frustration. On 4th February Lieut.-Colonel B. J. Corballis, M.C., was appointed to command. On 20th February Captain H. G. M. Bell relieved Captain T. L. Ingram as Adjutant and on 1st May Major F. R. Tubbs became 2nd-in-Command.

4TH BATTALION

On 10th February 1942 the Battalion moved to a new area near Dover, headquarters being at the Duke of York's Royal Military School. At this time Major-General G. I. Thomas had assumed command of 43rd (Wessex) Division.

During the period while the Battalion was at Dover there was continual shelling of the area from German guns on the French coast near Cap Gris Nez. The shelling, in spite of a very efficient warning system, caused great damage and many civilian casualties in the town.

On 12th February the German battleships "Gneisenau", "Scharnhorst" and "Prinz Eugen" were seen moving up Channel and were engaged by our coastal batteries. On 18th March, B and D companies moved to Manston airfield; C company moved to Ramsgate. On 1st April there was a heavy air raid on Dover, civilian casualties being 12 killed, 8 missing and 16 severely injured. On 7th April Jellalabad Day was celebrated according to custom.

On 24th April B and D companies were relieved at Manston by the 7th Buffs and on 15th May the Battalion moved to summer training quarters at Barham, near Canterbury. Here it was engaged on brigade and divisional exercises. On 1st July it returned to Dover, to experience the usual shelling.

In June, Major C. L. Firbank left to take command of the 6th Battalion and was succeeded as 2nd-in-Command by Major C. G. Lipscombe.

On 3rd August it mobilised for a Field Force rôle and, on 20th August, moved to Wooton Court, Barham. Brigadier G. H. L. Mole, D.S.O., M.C., took over command of 129th Infantry Brigade. On 24th August O.R.Q.M.S. J. Willis was awarded a C.-in-C.'s certificate for Meritorious Service. On 23rd September the Battalion was inspected by Lieut.-General J. G. des R. Swayne, C.B., C.B.E., commanding South Eastern Army.

On 3rd October the Battalion returned to Dover. The shelling on 5th October was particularly heavy. 49 shells fell in the town, civilian casualties being 4 killed and 15 severely injured. On 25th October the Colonel of the Regiment (Major-General V. H. B. Majendie, C.B., D.S.O.) visited the Battalion. Shelling continued to the end of the year, being particularly heavy on 9th/11th November (11 civilians killed) and 10th/11th December (1 killed, 7 injured).

In December, Captain T. M. Watson was appointed Adjutant. N.C.O.s with the Battalion included, R.S.M. F. Holt, R.Q.M.S. L. F. Male and C.S.M.s C. E. Scutt, C. E. Sampson, R. G. Cleaves, F. Card and C. Jones.

ROYAL HAMILTON LIGHT INFANTRY

Between 24th and 27th December a party of 4 Officers and 25 Other Ranks of the R.H.L.I., were guests of the 4th Battalion for Christmas. In addition to being introduced to the German shelling, a suitable programme of entertainment was arranged. Among the guests were Captain Carroll and Lieuts. Reekie, Firth and Howard.

135TH INFANTRY BRIGADE

The brigade remained, for most of 1942, in the Colchester area. Higher formations were as follows:

Eastern Army:	Commander, Lieut.-General K. A. N. Anderson, C.B., M.C.
XI Corps:	Commander, Lieut.-General J. T. Crocker, C.B.E., D.S.O.
45th (Wessex) Division:	Commander, Major-General H. de R. Morgan, D.S.O.
135th Infantry Brigade:	Commander, Brigadier A. L. Newth, C.B.E., D.S.O., M.C., T.D.

In September, Lieut.-General J. A. H. Gammell, C.B., D.S.O., M.C., became Eastern Army commander. In August, Brigadier G. McI. S. Bruce, O.B.E., M.C., succeeded Brigadier Newth in command of 135th Infantry Brigade and was relieved by Brigadier J. Vicary, M.C., on 1st October.

During the autumn of 1942, the 7th Battalion left the "Somerset Light Infantry Brigade", moving on 23rd August to Holland-on-Sea and, later, to the Isle of Wight.

In July, H.Q. First Army was formed in Scotland to take command of the British element of the forthcoming invasion of French North Africa. H.Q. First Army Defence Company (Somerset Light Infantry) was formed at the same time, and personnel for the Defence Company were drawn entirely from 135 (Somerset Light Infantry) Brigade. The Defence Company consisted of four officers and 140 other ranks, and was commanded by Captain J. C. Clarke. During its two years' existence, it was always maintained as a regimental unit, and was reinforced, when necessary, with personnel of the Somerset Light Infantry.

5TH BATTALION

This Battalion relieved the 7th Battalion at Clacton-on-Sea, on 12th January 1942, and returned to Colchester on 24th February. On 26th May it relieved 4th D.C.L.I., at Walton-on-Naze.

On 19th January Captain S. Vickery was appointed Adjutant until relieved by Captain The Lord Darling on 1st November. On 4th April, Lieut.-Colonel R. H. Bakewell assumed command and was succeeded by Lieut.-Colonel C. S. Howard on 31st July. On 16th June, Lieut. (Q.M.) E. Thrift was appointed Quartermaster; Major D. D. B. Cook became 2nd-in-Command on 2nd October. The R.S.M. at this time was R.S.M. Lovell.

6TH BATTALION

On 22nd February the Battalion relieved the 7th Battalion at Clacton-on-Sea, following the same battalion to Abberton—Tollesbury—Mersea on 12th May. On 8th September it returned to Colchester and for the remainder of the year was employed in training and agricultural assistance. On 26th January, Lieut.-Colonel S. J. Brice assumed command and was succeeded by Lieut.-Colonel C. L. Firbank in June.

7TH BATTALION

On 12th January the 7th Battalion relieved the 6th Battalion at Colchester and followed the same battalion to Abberton—Tollesbury—St. Osyth on 23rd February. On 12th May it relieved the 6th Battalion on beach defences at Clacton-on-Sea. On 23rd August it moved to Holland-on-Sea and, on 12th September, to Freshwater, Isle of Wight. Here it joined 214th Independent Infantry Brigade (Brigadier H. Essame). This brigade consisted of 7 Somerset L.I.; 5 D.C.L.I.; 12 Devon Regt. It formed part of Hants and Dorset District, commanded by Major-General Sir M. O'Moore-Creagh, K.B.E., M.C. The brigade was employed on beach defences.

On 1st July Lieut.-Colonel P. Lewis relieved Lieut.-Colonel A. E. Snow in command. On 7th August, Lieut.-Colonel R. G. P. Beasley, T.D., was appointed to command, the Adjutant being Captain W. H. Goudie.

9TH BATTALION

In January 1942 the Skegness defences were reorganised into company localities. The 9th Battalion was ordered to find drafts for other units and this caused great disappointment. On 27th January the Battalion was inspected by Lieut.-General B. C. T. Paget, C.B., D.S.O., M.C., C.-in-C. Home Forces.

On 5th March it was withdrawn from coastal defences to a counter-attack rôle at Woodhall Spa, remaining under 144th Infantry Brigade. During May it was engaged in training with 144th Army Tank Battalion and in the use of assault boats and kapok bridging. Towards the end of May it moved to Louth, in the northern coastal sector of 48th Division. Captain C. Mallalieu was appointed Adjutant in June.

In August, 48th Division ceased to have a Field Force rôle and became a draft-finding formation. The 9th Battalion, however, retained its Field Force rôle and was ordered to prepare to move to Northern Ireland. This entailed much handing over of equipment and stores.

During the autumn it moved to Banbridge, joining 72nd Independent Infantry Brigade and taking part in Exercise "Punch". It then moved to Northern Ireland, coming under Northern District, Static Units (Commander, Major-General V. H. B. Majendie, C.B., D.S.O.). Here, under almost peace conditions, it was employed on training with U.S. troops and cutting flax for farmers.

10TH BATTALION

In February 1942 the 10th Battalion moved to Woodhall Spa, with A, B and C companies at Roughton Moor Camp. On 4th March it moved to the Spilsby area, coming under 143rd Infantry Brigade of 48th Division. Headquarters was at Spilsby, with companies at Old Bolingbroke, East Keel, Sausthorpe, Halton Holegate. In April it moved to the Skegness coastal sector, under I Corps, with headquarters at Burgh-le-Marsh and companies at Skegness, Ingold Mills, Wainfleet, Gibraltar Point. In June it returned to Spilsby.

At this time Captain J. N. Taylor was Adjutant, with Major G. W. B. Rooke, 2nd-in-Command and Lieut. (Q.M.) R. Fortnum, Quartermaster.

On 5th September it relieved 8th Suffolk Regt. at Berkhamstead, coming under 223rd Infantry Brigade and Eastern Army. During October it was engaged in an exercise for the relief of the perimeter defences of Chequers.

On 2nd November a letter was received from the Adjutant-General, the War Office, offering conversion into a Parachute Battalion. The only alternative was disbandment. On 6th November the Battalion, less one telephone operator, was paraded in a secure hall. It was in complete ignorance of what was proposed. Lieut.-Colonel G. W. Lathbury, M.B.E. (Oxf. and Bucks L.I.) told the men bluntly that from 7th November the 10th Battalion would cease to exist and the 7th Parachute Battalion would be formed from it. Men were told that there would be no compulsion at all to join the new unit and they were given several days to make up their minds. At the expiry of that time, nearly 450 men volunteered. In some cases, whole platoons volunteered, a notable example being the Signal Platoon. Medical examinations were then carried out and the new unit was left with some 200 officers and men. 14 days were allowed to carry out the conversion. Thus, on 8th November, the 10th Battalion, The Somerset Light Infantry, became the 7th Battalion (Light Infantry) The Parachute Regt., Army Air Corps.

On 20th November Major R. T. O'B. Horsford took command of the "Home" details and on 27th November Lieut.-Colonel K. G. G. Dennys was posted to No. 3 Infantry Depot, Southend-on-Sea. Lieut.-Colonel H. N. Barlow was appointed to command the new unit on 21st December.

On 2nd December the 7th Battalion (L.I.) moved to Ringway airfield, near Manchester, for preliminary training. Non jumping administrative appointments were filled from volunteers who were below the required medical standard. Among them Captain (Q.M.) R. P. H. Fortnum.

Among the officers who went to carry out jumping training were:

Major A. P. Johnson, 2nd-in-Command, Captains R. S. Neale, W. A. Hayball, P. G. H. Mansfield, D. R. Reid, J. N. Taylor, J. J. Webber; Lieuts. J. A. Bowler, W. F. E. Bennett, D. C. Farr and R. A. Penney.

By 18th December 14 Officers and 180 Other Ranks had completed qualifying jumps. On 21st December the Battalion moved to Gordon Barracks, Bulford.

THE 30TH BATTALION

In January 1942 the Battalion was engaged on intensive training at Stapley Camp, under conditions of severe weather and bad accommodation. Much irritation was caused by continual alterations in the siting of airfield defences, necessitating the filling in of old trenches and the digging of new ones.

On 28th February Lieut.-Colonel Spear proceeded overseas and was succeeded, temporarily, by Major E. A. Carse (late Oxf. and Bucks L.I.) 2nd-in-Command, until the arrival, on 13th April of Lieut.-Colonel W. H. F. Routh. In April the strength was 40 Officers and 1,400 Other Ranks.

2nd-in-Command: Major D. L. Gough, M.C., T.D.
Adjutant: Captain A. L. Young.
Quartermaster: Captain (Q.M.) W. J. Atkins.

During May the Battalion was under Somerset and Bristol Area (Brigadier R. P. J. Wyatt, M.C.), with headquarters at Frome, and South Somerset Sub-area (Colonel C. P. S. Layard, M.C.). Headquarters of the Battalion was at Stapley Camp, with detachments at Filton, Whitchurch, Charmy Down, Yeovil, Frome, Church Stanton, Minehead, Hartland Point, Exeter and Severn Tunnel. In July contingents of the U.S. Expeditionary Force arrived in the area at Chard and Stapley. Weston-super-Mare was heavily bombed in June and C company sent to clear up damage.

On 15th August the Battalion was reorganised into three companies of six platoons each and disposed as under:

Battalion H.Q.: Stapley.
A company: Charmy Down—Filton.
B company: Charlton Hawthorne—Exeter.
C company: Churchstanton—Weston—Yeovil—Whitchurch.

In September the Battalion concentrated at Yeovil for reorganisation and intensive training. On 29th October it joined 115th Infantry Brigade (Brigadier S. A. Foster) of 38th Division (Major-General D. C. Butterworth) in Dorset and was disposed, on coast defence, as under:

Battalion H.Q.: Wareham.
A company: Hengistbury—Sopley.
B company: Brandy Bay—Bullbarrow.
C company: Ringstead.
D company: Weymouth.

The strength was then 31 Officers and 1,041 Other Ranks, with Captain R. B. Holder, Adjutant and R.S.M. V. Rogers.

CHAPTER IX

OPERATIONS IN THE ARAKAN—1943 TO APRIL 1944
1st BATTALION

Battalion at Nowshera—Move to Chindwara—Move to Calcutta and Chittagong—The state of the Battalion—The Theatre of Operations—Climate—Topography—Communications—Forces in the Arakan, autumn 1943—Order of Battle, 7th Indian Division—Japanese forces in the Arakan—Plan of Operations, autumn 1943—Battalion moves into Arakan—Patrol actions near Waybin—Task of 7th Indian Division—Operations near Taung Bazar—Operation "Cotton"—Situation at the end of December 1943—Operation "Hook"—The Pyinshe Ridges—Operation "Hook" continued—First action on Pyinshe Kala Ridge, 25th January 1944—Japanese counter-offensive—Plans for advance in Kalapanzin valley—The second action on Pyinshe Kala Ridge, 28th February 1944—1st Battalion leaves the Arakan

1943, in brief, saw the defeat of the Axis armies in North Africa, the invasion of Italy and Russian victories in the Ukraine and elsewhere. It saw the Japanese held in their southward and westward drives. It saw the intensive build-up of the armies in Britain for the Normandy invasion. These events can, however, be dealt with subsequently. It will be convenient, in this chapter, to record the history of the 1st Battalion during the preliminary operations against the Japanese in the Arakan, since these not merely form a separate phase of the war, but a separate part of the history of the Regiment. The period of these preliminary operations, which had a marked bearing on subsequent strategy on the Indo-Burma border, covered 1943 and part of 1944 and are dealt with here as a whole.

Chapter VIII found the 1st Battalion as part of 114th Indian Infantry Brigade of 7th Indian Division at Nowshera. It remained in these formations throughout the period under review. In the Nowshera area the division was supposed to be training for jungle warfare, but few more unsuitable areas could have been found for this purpose. Actually, as has been seen, the major part of the training was for North-West Frontier operations, though such training, in point of fact, would have been useful in the subsequent campaign in the Arakan.

MOVE TO CHINDWARA

On 16th January 1943, 7th Indian Division moved to the Chindwara area of the Central Provinces, where the terrain was more suitable. About this time Major-General T. W. Corbett was succeeded in command of the division by Major-General F. W. Messervy, C.B., D.S.O. There is little record of the actual training which the division received during the spring and early summer of 1943. It is clear, however, that it was carried out under great difficulties and that a common doctrine for jungle tactics had not been fully evolved. Neither the climate, nor the terrain of the Central Provinces approximated very closely to those of the dense forest areas of the Indo-Burma Frontier and the Arakan and it was not possible to introduce a great degree of realism into the training.

MOVE TO CHITTAGONG

During May 1943 orders came for 7th Indian Division to relieve 26th Indian Division in the Arakan and brigades moved, first, to the Calcutta area. 114th Brigade, with the 1st Battalion, moved on 29th May to the neighbourhood of Deula, south of Calcutta, the Battalion being located, in a defence rôle, near Diamond Harbour, at the mouth of the R. Hugli. Lieut.-Colonel Cole left for England and Lieut.-Colonel C. N. N. Delaforce assumed command.

During June and July the division concentrated in the Chittagong area. Advanced parties from the Battalion left by rail on 8th June, reaching Chittagong on 10th June. The main body sailed in H.T. "Melchior" on 13th June, arriving on 16th June, followed by the transport. It was first accommodated in huts. By the first week in September the divisional concentration was complete. On 18th June Lieut. (Q.M.) C. W. Smart was appointed Quartermaster *vice* Captain (Q.M.) G. H. Farmer.

THE STATE OF THE BATTALION

Some mention must here be made of the general conditions prevailing within the Battalion, since these had a marked bearing on subsequent events. During the latter half of 1942 and in 1943 British units in India had been very much under strength. This was due to the operation of various repatriation schemes, by which men were sent back to England. For various reasons, connected with operations elsewhere, the replacement of these men was greatly delayed. During the period between the outbreak of war in September 1939 and the end of 1941, 26 Regular Officers and more than 300 Regular Warrant Officers, N.C.O.s and men, that is to say some 60 per cent. of experienced personnel, were, by War Office orders, drafted to various appointments in the United Kingdom, or to other theatres of war.

It is fair to say, however, that all British units in India were similarly depleted, since they were the only source of supply of trained men for the various operations then in hand elsewhere. At this time Japan had not entered the war.

When the Battalion mobilised for operations against the Japanese these deficiencies had not been made up. For some time, to remedy shortages, the Battalion had been reduced to three rifle companies. The fourth rifle company was only restored in the field, about one month before first contact with the enemy. The Battalion entered the Arakan under strength and so remained for the whole of the operations.

These shortages affected training and promotion of junior leaders. Promotion of Other Ranks was held up pending the arrival of reinforcements. When at last they came, in the field, 120 promotions were made in one day. A few weeks later another 60 promotions were made to replace wastage due to sickness and battle casualties. This had a most serious affect on the continuity of platoon and section leadership. When the Battalion left the Arakan, in April 1944, there had been a turnover of 300 per cent. in N.C.O.s in one year. The intake of N.C.O.s with drafts was very small and those who joined were often lacking in both experience and confidence. Between January and May 1944 the period when the Battalion was continuously in close contact with the Japs and suffering battle casualties, not to mention the high sickness rate, the total reinforcement of full rank N.C.O.s which the unit received was not more than 14. Due to the climate the sickness rate was always high and during one period of 10 days 6 officers and 114 other ranks were evacuated suffering mainly from jaundice and dysentery. Neither of these complaints can be cured quickly which meant men away from the Battalion for months on end.

Drafts to the Arakan were very infrequent and none of the men so received was trained either for war or jungle life. Many who so joined had never thrown a live grenade. None had received any mental or physical training for the jungle tactics required. One draft of 50, which arrived during operations, came from ten different units and had no N.C.O. above the rank of Lance-Corporal. During the period of operations, drafts arriving for the Arakan received three weeks' jungle training at the Reinforcement Centre before joining the unit. This was entirely inadequate for men who really required two to three months' basic training. One draft was received which had been sent from the U.K. to complete basic training in India. A large proportion of this draft had to be sent back from the front to carry out marching and saluting drill, which was the elementary stage of training which the men had reached.

The same applied, to a large extent, to officer reinforcements. The officer strength of the Battalion was only made up in the late autumn of 1943, after arrival in the Arakan. Of 12 officers who joined, only three could be classed as trained leaders capable of commanding platoons. The remainder came from Movement Control, Auxiliary Force (India) and Supply Services. They lacked, through no fault of their own, knowledge, experience and confidence.

The adverse conditions appear to have been allowed to persist for at least one year before the Battalion went on active service. There is no doubt that they had a marked effect on the general efficiency of the Battalion and its preparedness for war. There is no doubt, also, that representations on the subject were made. But it seems surprising that drastic action was not taken. There would appear to have been time to do this during the preliminary training period. As it was, at the last moment, personnel was scraped together from all over India to make good deficiencies. Then, it was too late. Thus the Battalion had a most unfavourable start to operations. It is interesting to note, as will be seen from a subsequent chapter, that no unit was allowed to leave Great Britain for operations unless it was fully up to strength, had been up to strength during the training period and had every officer and man trained and tested for the task ahead. It is true that, during 1943, India was providing troops under great difficulties and that man-power, materials and time were short. Allowance must be made for these difficulties. Later, when more experience had been gained from fighting and training had been organised on sound doctrine, training divisions were formed in India to which whole units were sent and where reinforcements were adequately trained and taught to fight and keep fit under jungle conditions. That excellent policy, however, still lay in the mists of the future.

THE THEATRE OF OPERATIONS

Some general description of the Arakan is necessary, so that difficulties of climate and terrain may be understood.

Climate. The year, in the Arakan, has four seasons. From December to March it is generally dry, pleasantly warm by day and cold at night. From April to May it is hot by day and cool at night. During June to September the south-west monsoon brings heavy rain. It is cool while it is raining, but very sticky and uncomfortable during the fine periods. During October and November it is very sticky and unpleasant. Malaria is endemic, but is at its peak during March, June and October. Leeches are very active during the monsoon and their bites, with those of other insects, as well as cuts and wounds, easily turn septic. Sandfly fever is prevalent in coastal areas in dry weather and intestinal diseases, particularly dysentry, common. It is not a white man's country either for peace, or war.

Topography. The Arakan consists, roughly, of five areas, from west to east:

(*a*) The R. Naf valley, including the Teknaf Peninsula, which reaches the sea near Maungdaw.

(*b*) The Mayu Range, which resembles in form the Arakan Yomas, but is narrower, the average width being some seven miles. Its southern spurs reach the sea near Indin, Donbaik and Foul Point.

(*c*) The R. Mayu valley, known in its upper reaches as the R. Kalapanzin, running roughly north to south, between the Mayu Range and the Arakan Yomas and reaching the sea near Rathedaung.

(*d*) The Arakan Yomas, lying between the R. Kalapanzin and R. Kaladan. This, like the Mayu Range, is a tract of innumerable steep ridges, many of them razor-backed, covered with dense forest and bamboo thickets. At the south of the range is Rathedaung, at the mouth of the R. Mayu. The tract is seamed with a maze of "chaungs", or water-courses, empty in the dry weather, but full during the monsoon. Many of these "chaungs", throughout the Arakan are, near the coast, affected by the tide.

(e) The R. Kaladan valley, flowing from north to south, east of the Arakan Yomas and reaching the sea at Akyab.

The river valleys are generally flat, covered with rice (paddy) fields intersected with small bunds and innumerable streams, which meander through them. The valleys are dotted with villages, mostly of rude bamboo and matting huts and with many small ridges and "pimples" covered with forest and scrub. These form ideal defensive positions. During dry weather the valley floors are passable to wheels almost everywhere. In wet weather they are impassable except to animals, or men on foot. Near the coast, the streams are broader and, like the main rivers, are tidal. They are often fringed with thickets, high grass and mangrove swamps and are serious obstacles.

Communications. The only land route, available for motor vehicles, is the road from Chittagong, southwards, through Ramu and Bawli Bazar to Maungdaw. From it, links run between Ramu and Cox's Bazar and from Maungdaw, across the southern spur of the Mayu Range, to Buthidaung on the R. Mayu. The latter link contains tunnels and was in the hands of the Japanese.

As far as Maungdaw the road is two-way and fair-weather. South of Maungdaw an indifferent fair-weather track ran to Indin, Donbaik and Foul Point. The area contains no stone for road making and the tidal "chaungs", particularly in wet weather, present serious bridging problems.

Inland from the coast are only rough mule tracks over the wooded hills. The main routes into the Kalapanzin valley are over the Goppe and Ngakyedauk Passes. These passes were not high, but the surface was very rough and gradients steep, needing much work to prepare them for motor vehicles. From Taung Bazar, on the Kalapanzin, routes across the Arakan Yomas to the Kaladan valley could only be negotiated by porters. A great deal of the transport for divisions was provided by mule companies.

FORCES IN THE ARAKAN—AUTUMN 1943

Operations in the Arakan were controlled by XV Corps (Lieut.-General Christison) and 14th Army (commanded by Lieut.-General W. J. Slim, from 24th January 1944). North of XV Corps area, was IV Corps, in the Manipur area, with 17th and 23rd Indian Divisions.

During the autumn of 1943, XV Corps had at its disposal 5th and 26th Indian Divisions and 81st (West African) Division (Major-General C. G. Woolner). During May 1943, 26th Indian Division (Major-General C. E. N. Lomax) comprising 4th, 36th and 71st Indian Infantry Brigades, had withdrawn from positions near Indin and Donbaik, on the Mayu Peninsula, to the north of the line Maungdaw–Buthidaung. This was due to the threat of Japanese landings, in rear of the division, from the sea. On withdrawal, the Japanese installed themselves on the Maungdaw–Buthidaung Road in strength, fortifying the tunnels near the junction of that road with the road to Waybin and Bawli Bazar and patrolling northwards in strength.

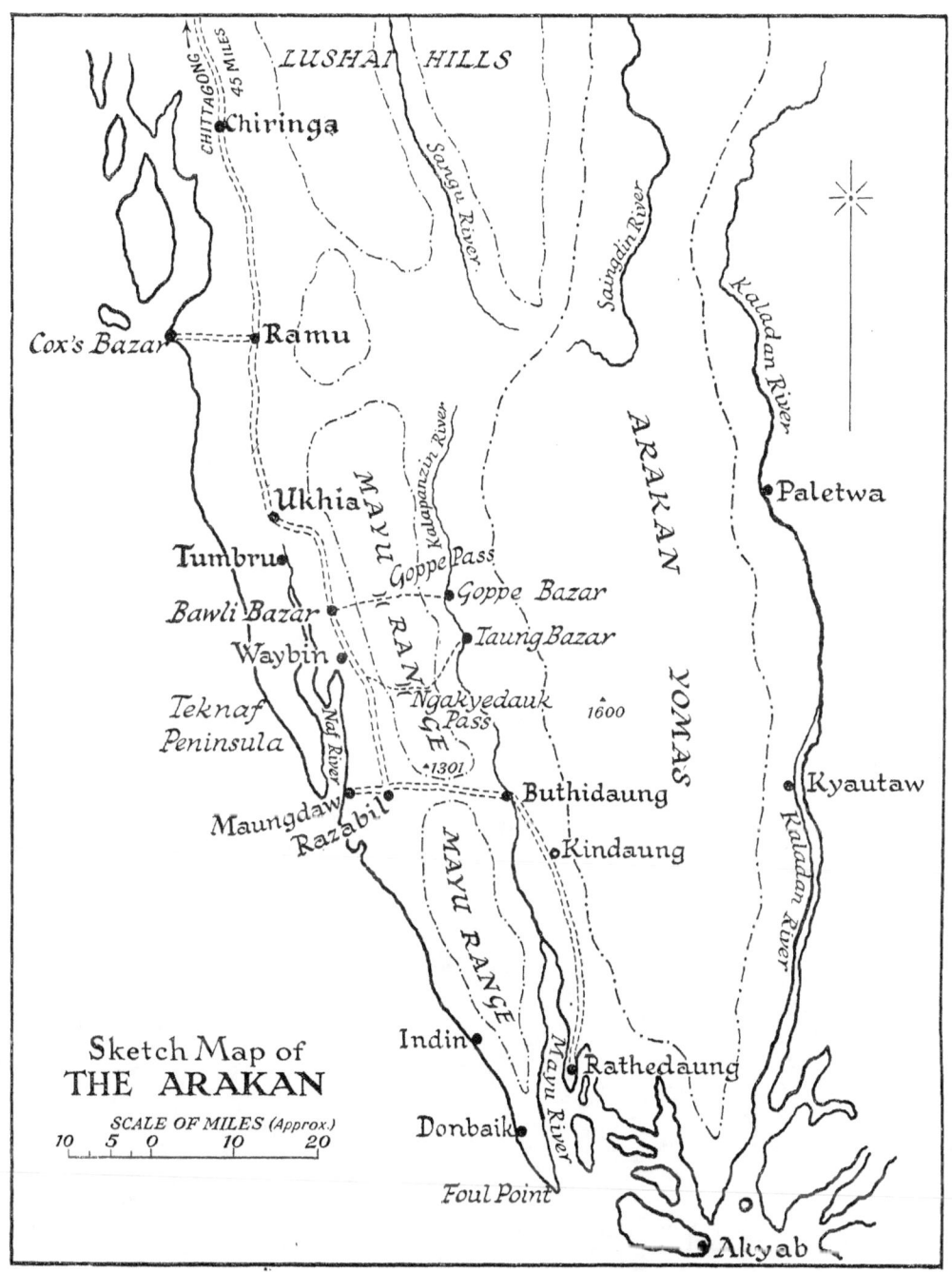

ORDER OF BATTLE OF 7TH (GOLDEN ARROW) INDIAN DIVISION

The Order of Battle of 7th Indian Division included:

33rd Indian Infantry Brigade (Brigadier F. J. Loftus-Tottenham)
    4/15 Punjab Regt.   4/1 Royal Gurkha Rifles.
    1 Queen's Regt.

89th Indian Infantry Brigade (Brigadier J. C. Martin)
    5/1 Punjab Regt.   4/8 Royal Gurkha Rifles.
    1 K.O.S.B.   7/2 Punjab Regt.

114th Indian Infantry Brigade (Brigadier T. Roberts)
    4/14 Punjab Regt.   4/5 Royal Gurkha Rifles.
    1 Somerset L.I.

JAPANESE FORCES IN THE ARAKAN

These, under General Sakurai, were based on Akyab and included:

    H.Q. 55th Division.
    55 Cavalry Regt.
    55 Mountain Artillery Regt. (less one Battery).
    One troop 3 Medium Artillery Regt.
    143 Infantry Regt.
    112 Infantry Regt.
    One battalion of 213 Infantry Regt.
    One battalion of 214 Infantry Regt.
      (both these last were from 33rd Division).

In February 1944, 144 Infantry Regt. from 54th Division arrived.

PLAN OF OPERATIONS—AUTUMN 1943

The tasks laid down by the commander of 11 Army Group for 14th Army for the winter of 1943/44 were as follows:

(A) To secure the frontiers of Bengal and Assam.
(B) To occupy North Burma as far as Myitkhina.
(C) To advance into the Arakan down to and including the road Maungdaw–Buthidaung. This was the task allotted to XV Corps.

The first step by XV Corps was to carry out the relief of 26th Indian Division by 7th Indian Division. When the latter entered the area 26th Indian Division was disposed as under:

        4th Indian Infantry Brigade: Bawli Bazar.
        36th Indian Infantry Brigade: Cox's Bazar.
        71st Indian Infantry Brigade: Tumbru.

These brigades were disposed in a series of defended localities known as "keeps", from which contact was maintained with the enemy by patrolling.

On 7th July a composite company from the 1st Battalion was sent to Cox's Bazar. The remainder of the Battalion left Chittagong on 28th August and marched south, in seven stages, the 82 miles to Tumbru. It reached Bawli Bazar on 3rd September and took over detachments at Waybin on 6th September.

PATROL ACTIONS NEAR WAYBIN

The Japanese, patrolling north from Maungdaw, seem to have relied on strong standing patrols, well concealed and protected by wire and other obstacles. Some of our patrols went out for 24 hours to lie up and form ambushes, but others were small moving patrols. The latter were extremely difficult to operate in country consisting of scrub covered ridges interspersed by valleys with paddy fields and numerous "chaungs" some wadeable, others deep. Such patrols were a task for very highly trained men. As has been said, jungle training was not of a high standard.

On 12th September a small patrol under Major E. T. H. Ubsdell and Major A. M. Cripps, R.A., was sent out to reconnoitre the Rekhat Chaung, towards Maungdaw. The patrol, working in pairs, with the two officers leading, reached the Chaung and crossed it. They thought they saw an enemy position on the forward slopes of a spur across the valley and, on crossing the paddy fields, found concertina wire. It was about 1330 hours and the patrol was fired on by heavy and light automatics concealed in the scrub. Casualties occurred at once. Major Ubsdell and Private F. Lee were wounded, the latter being missing, believed killed. The Japanese came down on the remainder of the patrol, which got back to Waybin, individually, with great difficulty.

On 26th September a patrol under Lieut. J. H. Lloyd was sent out to lay an ambush south of Waybin and, while doing so, was engaged by Japanese, who fired on it, from short range, as it neared the top of a small slope. The Japanese then attacked. A second patrol, under Sergeant C. Filer, working in conjunction with Lieut. Lloyd was also attacked. The Japanese came down to search for casualties and it is believed that they killed the wounded. Survivors of these two patrols had to lie up, and later got back to Waybin with difficulty. As a result of this action Lieut. J. H. Lloyd and Privates Hutchings, Rostrom and Rowlands were posted as "missing, believed wounded". Sergeant C. Filer was also wounded, but escaped.

These first clashes with the enemy were unfortunate. They seem to show that lack of training led patrols into enemy ambushes, where they were attacked at very short range.

On 21st September Lieut.-Colonel Delaforce was admitted to hospital and relieved by Major W. R. Lawson.

THE TASK OF 7TH INDIAN DIVISION

During the monsoon period, between June and September, the gap separating our forces from the Japanese had been some 10 miles wide. When

7th Indian Division entered the Arakan there were some three weeks of rainy weather to go, but the ground remained wet and boggy until November. The division was told that the primary task of XV Corps was to seize the Maungdaw–Buthidaung road and that no operation was to be undertaken which would jeopardise this aim. Subject to this the division was to close up to the Japanese and to hold the ring for the concentration of XV Corps, expected to be complete about mid-November.

To further this "closing up" process, it was necessary for part of the division to cross the Mayu range into the Kalapanzin valley, and thence to close up towards Buthidaung. Accordingly, on 25th September 114th Brigade was relieved by 89th Brigade in the Bawli area and moved round, over the Goppe Pass, into the Kalapanzin valley, directed on Taung Bazar. On 30th September, 1 Somerset L.I. left Waybin and moved over the Goppe Pass. 114th Brigade was then disposed in the Kalapanzin Valley as under:

    1 Somerset L.I.:   Goppe Bazar.
    4/14 Punjab Regt.:   Pringkhaung.
    4/5 Royal Gurkha Rifles: Taung Bazar.

It was about this time that the battalion was reorganised, but had not yet sufficient men to form the fourth rifle company. At the end of September, 7th Indian Division was disposed as under:

    H.Q.:   Bawli Bazar.
    Left: 114th Brigade—Pringkhaung—Taung Bazar—Goppe Bazar.
    Right: 89th Brigade—Teknaf—Waybin—Bawli South—Goppe Pass.
    Reserve: 33rd Brigade—Taungho—Tumbru.

36th Indian Infantry Brigade of 26th Indian Division was at Shalimar, 4 miles east of Cox's Bazar.

During October, 7th Indian Division was engaged in closing on the enemy, improving communications and laying in stores. Two lines of advance to the objective were available:

(*a*) by the fair-weather road, down the coast, from Bawli Bazar on Maungdaw;

(*b*) by the Kalapanzin valley on Buthidaung. This line involved the crossing of the Mayu Range and the preparation of tracks over the Goppe and Ngakyedauk Passes. The Mayu range formed a difficult obstacle between the two lines of advance.

Early in October there were indications that the Japanese had begun to thin out and brigades were ordered to "push the enemy defences and be prepared to take advantage of a withdrawal by a planned follow-up, aiming at isolating and destroying delaying detachments". In the second half of October, 33rd Brigade was taken from reserve and sent into the Kalapanzin valley, being located overlooking Awlanbyin, on the Ngakyedauk Chaung, some five miles south of Taung Bazar. This brigade was, therefore, on the right of 114th Brigade.

OPERATIONS NEAR TAUNG BAZAR

Between 14th and 20th October, B and C companies, 1 Somerset L.I., moved to Pringkhaung and by 1st November the Battalion was concentrated near Linabi, to the south-west of Taung Bazar. This was then headquarters of 114th Brigade, which moved to Taung Bazar on 21st November.

On 11th November, 1 Somerset L.I. relieved 4/5 R. Gurkha Rifles, with A and B companies forward, overlooking enemy positions south of the Ngakyedauk Chaung. This stream, flowing from the south-west, joined the Kalapanzin River some 4 miles south of Taung Bazar. During the move the battalion was shelled by a Japanese regimental gun.

This period (October–November) was one of planning of operations, the issue of orders and their subsequent cancellation. The general plan was to infiltrate southwards, forcing the enemy to retire by manoeuvre and only attacking, when necessary, those positions still held. Much work, also, had to be done on improving tracks over the passes and in the Kalapanzin valley itself. These tasks took up men.

By the middle of November, 5th Indian Division was moving into the Bawli Bazar area. On 14th November 89th Brigade, of 7th Indian Division, crossed the Ngakyedauk Pass and came into position on the right of 114th Brigade along the Ngakyedauk Chaung. No Field Artillery could be brought over the Mayu Range and 89th and 114th Brigades had two artillery groups made up from the Mountain Regiments of 5th and 7th Indian Divisions. H.Q. 7th Indian Division moved to Badana, some two miles south-west of Taung Bazar, early in December. A divisional Administrative Base was formed near Sinzweya at the eastern end of the Ngakyedauk Pass.

The plan, now, was for 5th Indian Division to close up on Maungdaw, while 7th Indian Division operated towards Buthidaung, moving down the Kalapanzin valley. 81st (West African) Division began to move into the upper reaches of the Kaladan Valley, on the north-east flank of 7th Indian Division, but separated from it by the Arakan Yomas. On 1st December, 7th Indian Division was located as under:

Left: 114th Brigade, with H.Q. at Bogigyaung, east of the Kalapanzin and two miles south of Taung Bazar, with 4/14 Punjab Regt. and 4/5 Royal Gurkha Rifles to the south.

Centre: 33rd Brigade on the Ngakyedauk Chaung, facing Awalanbyin. 1 Somerset L.I. was, at this time, attached to this brigade.

Right: 89th Brigade, extending the line south-westwards along the Ngakyedauk Chaung.

OPERATION "COTTON"

The first intention of 7th Indian Division was to push the enemy back from the line of the Ngakyedauk Chaung and to the east of the Kalapanzin. Accordingly 33rd Brigade was ordered to cut off the west of three fingers of the hill feature behind Awlanbyin, which was strongly held. These three fingers ran down to the Chaung and overlooked crossing places. 89th Brigade was to secure the start line for the operation, which entailed crossing the Chaung, and to protect the right flank of the attack. 114th Brigade was ordered to send one battalion to Paledaung, east of the Kalapanzin, and sweep the west bank of that river with fire.

33rd Brigade had four battalions for the operation; 1 Queen's Regt., 4/15 Punjab Regt., 4/5 Royal Gurkha Rifles and 1 Somerset L.I. 4/5 Royal Gurkha Rifles moved into position to cover the main crossing on the night 30th November/1st December. 4/15 Punjab Regt. attacked the northern end of the finger at dawn on 1st December, 4/5 Royal Gurkha Rifles moving forward on the right. Both attacks met little opposition and by 1600 hrs. the bulk of the feature was cleared. In the meantime 1 Somerset L.I. sent patrols to the northern end of the east finger. These patrols crossed the Chaung and searched a spur, known as "Bone", finding it clear of enemy.

At 1320 hours a liaison officer from 33rd Brigade reached battalion headquarters with orders for the battalion to cross the Chaung. No move was possible before 1500 hours, when the order for crossing was C, B, Battalion H.Q. A company was ordered to remain in position, covering the crossing, west of the Chaung. A bridgehead was to be established some 500 yards south of the junction of the Chaung with the R. Kalapanzin. Owing to a high tide and the depth of water in the Chaung, C company was delayed and boats had to be brought down from upstream. By 1800 hours C and B companies were established on "Bone" spur, but Battalion H.Q. remained west of the Chaung for the night. On 2nd December Battalion H.Q. crossed. Active patrolling southwards continued, the enemy being located on a spur some 1,000 yards south-east of "Bone". At 0955 hours B company attacked a spur forward of their position. The leading platoon, under Lieut. Anderson, reached a neatly laid out cook-house in a clearing. It was ominously quiet, but a Bren gunner opened fire on a boot sticking out of a thicket. This was answered by light automatic and rifle fire and grenades from enemy hidden close by. The platoon was forced to withdraw, Privates Morris, Marcquick and Berryman being wounded. Private Berryman died of wounds later.

On 3rd December patrolling continued. A projected attack for 1 Somerset L.I. and 1 Queen's Regt. for 5th December was subsequently cancelled. The enemy still held the centre of the three fingers, overlooking Awlanbyin. During the night 4th/5th December patrols penetrated to Zadebyin and Dabingzaya, east of the Awlanbyin position and on the west bank of the Kalapanzin. These were clear of enemy. During 5th December, A company joined the battalion east of the Ngakyedauk Chaung. Patrolling continued on 6th December, patrols finding Maunggyihtaung clear on 7th December.

It was during this period of patrol activity that an incident took place as the result of which the George Cross was awarded, posthumously, to Private Joseph Henry Silk. The following is the citation in *The London Gazette*:

"On the 4th December 1943, the men of the platoon to which Private Silk belonged were sitting down on a slope in the jungle, cleaning their weapons. The latter included grenades, all of which were fused. Some of Private Silk's comrades were sitting round him. Below him, on the slope, were other soldiers cleaning their weapons and above him was Company Headquarters. Owing to the thickness of the jungle Private Silk would be unable to see anybody except the men immediately round him, although he could hear talking from above and below. For some reason unknown a grenade belonging to Private Silk ignited and the fuse began to hiss. He shouted, 'Look out!', rolled over clutching the grenade to his stomach and placing his body between the grenade and the majority of men immediately around him. The grenade exploded, killing Private Silk instantly and slightly injuring two men.

There is little doubt that Private Silk had appreciated at once that he could not safely throw the grenade away, because of the men above and below him on the slope and that, in order to minimise injury to his comrades sitting round him, his body was the best shield immediately to hand. Private Silk's level-headedness, cool courageous action and self-sacrifice undoubtedly saved many lives."

At 1000 hours on 7th December the battalion was relieved by 4/15 Punjab Regt. and moved to Taung Bazar, reverting to 114th Brigade. Here it was located in village huts for reorganisation and training. While here the fourth rifle company was added and promotions of 120 N.C.O.s were made. The fourth rifle company (D) was mainly composed of a newly arrived draft of only partially trained men. It was commanded by Major M. J. G. Anley. Major Boileau, recently arrived from 53rd Reconnaissance Regt. was 2nd-in-Command, and Major Lawson reverted to command H.Q. company. On 12th December Lieut.-Colonel P. Lewis assumed command of the Battalion.

SITUATION AT THE END OF DECEMBER 1943

Towards the end of December it was noticed that the enemy was not using the Buthidaung–Maungdaw road as a supply route, but carrying out movements by sea round Foul Point. The Japanese made little attempt to stop patrolling down to, and across, the road. XV Corps gave orders for an advance to the general line Indin–Rathedaung, by 5th and 7th Indian Divisions. The advance was to be made with two intermediate bounds and to rely on infiltration and encirclement. Casualties were to be avoided as far as possible, consistent with speed.

On 25th December the intention of 7th Indian Division was to cut off enemy garrisons in the area between the R. Kalapanzin and the Arakan Yomas and to establish a block near Dabragyaung, some three miles east of Buthidaung. The plan, to be put into action during January 1944, was roughly as follows:

Operation Hook: by 114th Brigade, southwards on east of the R. Kalapanzin.

Operation Butt: by 33rd Brigade, in centre, southwards on Buthidaung.
Operation Punch: by 89th Brigade, on right, towards Htindaw.

In accordance with these instructions, 114th Brigade was to move southwards from Bogigyaung area as follows:

4/5 Royal Gurkha Rifles and 4/14 Punjab Regt., forward battalions, to move on Hkamweywa and Taungdaungywa, in the foot-hills of the Arakan Yomas. Thence the next bound was to be Zadidaung and Dabragyaung, astride the road east of Buthidaung.

1 Somerset L.I. was to move on Pyinshe from the north.

A secure Brigade Base was to be formed on the general line Ywetnyudaung–Kayingyaung, to be known as the "Brown Line". From there the advance would continue south to secure a bridgehead over the Saingdin Chaung at the Rathedaung road crossing near Kindaung. This was known as the "Green Line".

At the end of December 1943, before these projected operations began, 114th Brigade was disposed as under:

Brigade H.Q. and Defence Company: Bogigyaung.
1 Somerset L.I. and A.T. Company: Taung Bazar.
4/5 Royal Gurkha Rifles: In contact with the enemy in the area Paledaung–Kwazon and patrolling to Kyuakit and Oktaw.
4/14 Punjab Regt.: East of Bogigyaung on the high ground.

One battery, 24th Mountain Regiment, was in support of the brigade.

OPERATION "HOOK"

During the first week of January 1944, 1 Somerset L.I. remained in the area of Taung Bazar. On 9th January, A company took over defence of brigade H.Q. area at Bogigyaung. On 13th January, C and D companies moved to a bivouac area near Kwazon, in the first phase of the relief of 4/5 Royal Gurkha Rifles. On the same day 4/14 Punjab Regt. and 4/5 Royal Gurkha Rifles began to advance southwards down the east bank of the R. Kalapanzin. On 14th January, 1 Somerset L.I. took over positions on the Pyinshe and Pyinshe Kala ridges, from 4/5 Royal Gurkha Rifles.

On 15th January, 114th Brigade issued orders for Operation Hook. The object was to cut off and destroy enemy garrisons between the Kalapanzin and the Arakan Yomas foot-hills, north of the road Buthidaung–Kindaung. Phase I, already completed, was the concentration of the brigade forward.

Phase II. 4/14 Punjab Regt. to capture Taungdaungwya hill.
1 Somerset L.I. and 1/11 Sikhs (now under command) to exert frontal pressure.
Phase III. 4/5 Royal Gurkha Rifles to capture Pt. 232, lying east of Kyetmauktaung.

	1 Somerset L.I. and 1/11 Sikhs to exert stronger frontal pressure and 1 Somerset L.I. to be prepared to side step to the east if ordered.
Phase IV.	4/14 Punjab Regt. to move east of 4/5 Royal Gurkha Rifles (on Pt. 232) and capture hills south-east of Dabrugyaung, patrolling to Pt. 442, south-west of Zadidaung.
	1/11 Sikhs to clear Kyaukit and occupy Thankrwe.
Phase V.	4/5 Royal Gurkha Rifles to pass through 4/14 Punjab Regt. and occupy Pt. 442.
	1 Somerset L.I. and 1/11 Sikhs to mop up.

This was an ambitious programme. In practice, enemy action did not permit of these operations going according to plan. It must here be noted that from a hill near the Maungdaw-Buthidaung road, known as Pt. 1301, the Japanese had complete observation of all movement in the Kalapanzin valley.

On 15th January 1 Somerset L.I. was disposed on the northern ends of the Pyinshe Ridges. C company, under Major Ogilvie, was on the right at the northern end of Pyinshe Ridge. D company, under Major Anley, was on the northern end of Pyinshe Kala Ridge. Battalion H.Q. was on the Pyinshe Ridge in rear of C company. Brigade H.Q., with A company and the Mountain Battery was east of Oktaw. The Brigade Administrative Base was at Kwazon.

During the 15th January a patrol of C company was fired on at short range at the southern end of Pyinshe Ridge. Privates Fox and Pegden were reported missing. In the afternoon enemy artillery registered the southern end of the ridge.

On the 16th January, 4/14 Punjab Regt. attacked and secured the Windwin feature, meeting stiff opposition. 1 Somerset L.I. was ordered to watch the Pyinshe and Pyinshe Kala positions and establish a post on the Pyinshe Ridge, some 1,000 yards north of the southern end. If the enemy withdrew from the southern end of the ridge, it was not to be occupied (having been registered) but was to be left empty with booby-traps. On 17th January patrols reported the southern end of the Pyinshe Ridge strongly held. The next day these observations were confirmed by patrols under Lieut. Cassels. During the day information was received that 7th Indian Division, west of the Kalapanzin, had failed to contact the enemy. Further progress by units of 114th Brigade was very slow, due to strong opposition. It was clear that the Japanese were very sensitive to any advance down the Kalapanzin valley on Buthidaung.

On 19th January 1 Somerset L.I. harassed the enemy on the Pyinshe Ridges and drew heavy fire. 4/14 Punjab Regt. got on to the hills near Taungdaungywa, but the enemy still held out on the northern end of the spurs.

THE PYINSHE RIDGES

It will here be convenient to give some description of the Pyinshe Ridges, on which 1 Somerset L.I. were engaged during the latter part of January and early February 1944. The Arakan Yomas foothills, reaching into the Kalapanzin valley on the east, were a series of long ridges, rising to about 300–400 feet above the valley floor, some, running from north to south, being as long as three miles without a break. There were, also, in the valley, isolated hills surrounded by paddy fields. In the fields, intersected by small bunds and water channels, heaps of unreaped rice were often set on fire by artillery and mortar fire. The hills and ridges were covered with dense jungle which, in many places, had to be cut to make movement, even in file, possible. The Gurkhas found scrub cutting fairly easy with kukris. But the tools issued to other units had soft blades, the handles came off and the life of a "machete" or "dah" was generally less than one day's work. Replacements were negligible. Much of the work of cutting paths fell on the Pioneer platoon, under Lieut. O'Donnel and Sergeant Hanlon, which was supplied with billhooks.

Some two miles due east of Windwin was a high point (Pt. 1600) which was used by the Japanese as an observation post, giving a clear view over the whole of the valley. Any movement of troops could be seen and men moving in the paddy fields raised clouds of dust. This high point was harassed, from time to time, by A company 1/11 Sikh Regt., known as "Workcol" from the name of Captain Workman, its commander. Supply problems were extremely difficult as all stores and ammunition had to come on mule back over the Ngakyedauk Pass and cross the Kalapanzin by ferry at Paungdawbyin.

The Pyinshe Ridges ran north and south in the valley and were very thickly wooded. The tops of the ridges were razor-backed and somewhat like "switch-backs". A way had to be forced through the jungle and zigzag paths cut to link up sections and platoons. Reconnaissance was extremely difficult in the very thick scrub as it was impossible to see more than a few yards in any direction. Movement with heavy loads in the sticky heat was arduous and many stores had to be dragged up the steep slopes with ropes. Wire was in very short supply and slit trenches were protected by sharpened bamboo stakes (*panjis*) stuck into the ground. Water could only be obtained by digging at the foot of the hills and the flow was very slow. It was extremely difficult to pin point enemy positions. Much of the patrolling was done by sending out parties at night to lie up and observe movement for 24 hours. The Japanese bunkers along the top of the ridges were well dug in and strongly held.

OPERATION "HOOK" CONTINUED

It is clear from examination of the orders issued for this operation that it entailed wide dispersion of units of the brigade in very thick and difficult country. This dispersion, later, had its dangers.

On 20th/21st January a night patrol of 1 Somerset L.I. under Lieut. Bally, ran into an ambush on the Pyinshe Ridge and engaged the enemy at short range with hand grenades. Private Whitcombe was killed and Private Combstock wounded. On 21st January a day patrol was engaged and Lieut. Gillett wounded.

By 22nd January 4/14 Punjab Regt. had secured the hill feature overlooking Taungdaungywa, on the left flank of the brigade. 4/5 Royal Gurkha Rifles, moving on a wide arc, through difficult country, further east, swung round south-westwards and reached the hills above Kyetmauktaung on 23rd January. Both units met strong opposition. During the night 23rd/24th January 4/14 Punjab Regt. was heavily counter-attacked, but drove off the Japanese with heavy losses. 4/5 Royal Gurkha Rifles L.-of-C. was cut, but was subsequently restored after a stiff fight.

Attention was now turned to the capture of the high ground overlooking Kyetmauktaung. For this operation it was intended that 4/14 Punjab Regt. should attack from the direction of Taungdaungywa, while 4/5 Royal Gurkha Rifles moved in an arc to the east and attacked from the south. The crux of the operation was the enemy strong point at the southern end of Pyinshe Kala ridge, which dominated the line of advance of 4/14 Punjab Regt. The enemy, also, still held the ridge south of Windwin, as well as a position at Zadidaung, which was not under pressure at all. On the extreme right "Workcol" was exerting pressure on Kyaukit.

114th Brigade was now very much strung out on a front of some five miles as the crow flies, in country interspersed with Japanese defended localities. Moreover 4/14 Punjab Regt. and 4/5 Royal Gurkha Rifles were drawing further and further away from the L.-of-C. running to Paungdawbyin ferry.

THE ACTION ON THE PYINSHE KALA RIDGE

On 23rd January 1 Somerset L.I. was ordered to prepare to take the strong point on the southern end of Pyinshe Kala Ridge. D company (Major Anley), already in positions on the northern end of the ridge, was detailed for the task. On the night of 23rd/24th January reconnaissance was unsatisfactory owing to thick mist and the operation was, therefore, postponed for 24 hours. A second reconnaissance by Major Anley on the night of 24th/25th January was more successful. The attack was timed to start at 0600 hours on 26th January.

A good deal was known about the enemy position, for a patrol under Lieut. Cassels had lain up close to it for 24 hours. A switch-back track had been cut along the top of the ridge to facilitate patrolling. This ended in an almost perpendicular drop of about 80 feet, followed by a similar rise to the enemy position. On the east the ridge fell, like a cliff, to a stream and was unclimbable without the use of ropes. The southern end of the ridge, around the enemy position, was thick jungle, ending on the north in a razor-backed ridge, not wider than 3 feet at the top. On each side was a perpendicular drop of over 100 feet.

The only way into the enemy position was on the south-west side, a steep convex slope, covered with jungle. From this, a subsidiary spur, with a zigzag path, led to the enemy bunkers. An approach on the west side could not be used as it was under mortar fire from Zadidaung and enemy positions on the southern end of Pyinshe Ridge.

On 25th January Brigade H.Q. moved up close to the northern end of Pyinshe Kala Ridge. At 0600 hours the attack started, D company having one platoon of A company under command. The approach was made through the village to the west of the ridge, the order of march being Nos. 16 and 18 platoons, No. 17 (fire support) platoon, No. 9 platoon and Company H.Q. It was found impossible to give any artillery support.

The leading platoons attacked up the zigzag path leading to the position. On rounding a bend, some 30 yards short of the objective, No. 16 platoon came under heavy automatic and grenade fire at very short range. The platoon commander and his sergeant were wounded at once and there were some ten casualties in the two platoons. The path was littered with fallen men, making advance for the remainder difficult in the narrow space. Seeing that momentum had been lost, Major Anley called on all to follow him and led the assault. He and others almost at once fell wounded.

The 2nd-in-Command, Captain Kennedy, was now aware of the situation and came forward to join Major Anley. The latter gave orders to dig in. The check to the leading platoons had caused the following platoons on the narrow track to "concertina" and there was some confusion. Captain Kennedy found it necessary to withdraw slightly to the bend on the track where the first casualties had occurred. The intermingling of platoons caused men to dig in where they stood and this caused more confusion in command, which was increased by accurate sniping and mortaring. To some extent old enemy trenches were used. The dead and wounded could not be got away, but were pulled under cover as much as possible. Major Anley refused to be moved until all others had been cared for. While lying out, in an exposed position, he was again wounded. This officer showed the greatest gallantry throughout the day and while lying out, shot in the chest and in the thigh, did all he could to try and organise a restart of the attack. In this he was assisted by his C.S.M. (C.S.M. Boucher) who was wounded at the same time as himself with two rifle bullets in his leg.

During the day attempts were made to get up ammunition by sending a party along the east side of the ridge. This was stopped by fire and only one man, Private B. Harwood, who was wounded, got through.

In the meantime a strong section, under Sergeant McMurran, had been placed on the ridge, north of the objective, as a "stop". While this section was working forward, it is thought that Sergeant McMurran was killed, as he was never seen again. During the day this section was reinforced by a platoon from A company under Lieut. Coakley. While trying to work ahead of his platoon, with a Corporal and two men, Lieut. Coakley and the Corporal became casualties and were not seen again. Lieut. Thomas, from B company, was sent to investigate. He put in an attack along the top of the ridge about 1600 hours. This was abortive and he and others were wounded. In all these attacks, including the original attack by D company, there seems to have been no possibility of providing any covering fire. All attempts to work south along the top of the ridge were met by heavy fire, from short range, in the "cup" (already described) which lay close under the enemy position. The casualties in this "cup" were never recovered. The platoon of A company was withdrawn by the platoon sergeant to the old D company position on the north end of the ridge. It was, however, sent forward again under orders from the Commanding officer.

By the evening of 26th January all men on the ridge were dug in. Ammunition for rifles and Bren guns was running very short. One day's rations were still on the man. Captain Kennedy reported that, although the men were very tired, they could hold on for 24 hours if ammunition was brought up.

During the night 26th/27th January an attempt was made to send up ammunition and supplies by carrier. These, however, were bogged, or bellied, in the darkness in the paddy fields. A mule column was then sent, but was fired on and the mules bolted. A platoon from B company was then sent up with stretcher bearers and more ammunition. When near the position this party was told to wait while the commander reconnoitred. He never returned. After about two hours' wait the stretcher-bearers, with some wounded, took cover in some empty huts at the bottom of the ridge. They were never seen to leave these huts. When the position was finally evacuated on 27th January, it is believed that among the wounded there were Major Anley, Lieut. Cassels, Corporal Francis, Sergeant Thomas, Lance-Corporal Parry (who died of wounds), Privates B. Harwood, Banks and Magee.

Throughout the night of 26th/27th January the enemy harassed the position with fire, endeavoured to infiltrate and indulged in a great deal of shouting, from various places on both sides and in rear of the position. This fire was not returned.

On 27th January, soon after first light, a platoon of B company, plus two sections, under Lieut. R. G. Bell, took up a small amount of ammunition and made contact with D company. The platoon came into position on the lower spur, replacing Lieut. Coldrick's platoon, which moved up into the company H.Q. area. A plan was then made for a further attack. Lieut. Bell's platoon was to work up a spur to the north, while D company attacked frontally. Before this plan could be put into operation, the position came under heavy mortar fire. It was then about 1300 hours.

This fire lasted for 10 minutes and was followed by 10 minutes' intense automatic fire. The enemy then attacked down the path, falling on No 17 platoon, under Lieut. G. A. Moon, and company H.Q. The two Bren gunners of No. 17 platoon were knocked out at once, one gun jammed and the other ran out of ammunition. Lieut. Moon ordered his platoon to throw their grenades and withdraw. Company H.Q. was also heavily engaged and, in the thick jungle, it was impossible to see what was happening to No. 17 platoon.

For some reason unknown, it seems that it was thought that a general withdrawal had been ordered, for Lieut. Coldrick's platoon also began to withdraw. It passed through Lieut. Bell's platoon, telling the latter to withdraw. Captain Kennedy, in the thick scrub and on the steep hillside, was unable to stop the withdrawal. The wounded officers and men left in the huts were never again seen alive.

Lieut. Bell took up a position at the bottom of the spur to cover the withdrawal, but by this time there was considerable confusion as the enemy was following up closely in the thick scrub. The withdrawal had to pass across the paddy fields at the base of the ridge and, in the open, came under accurate machine-gun and mortar fire. Here many casualties occurred. Captain Kennedy withdrew company H.Q. to the huts where the wounded were lying. Here he saw Major Anley and explained the situation to him. He then went back to organise the withdrawal. This withdrawal took place during the afternoon and, during the evening of 27th and night of 27th/28th January, the remnants of D company were collected.

The casualties in this action amounted to some 60 per cent. of the total force engaged and were as under:

	Officers	*Other Ranks*
Killed:	Nil	2
Wounded:	Nil	26
Missing, believed killed:	2	7
Wounded, believed killed:	4	3
Missing:	Nil	26

Total: Officers 6, Other Ranks 64.

Details are given in Appendix M.

On 28th January, 1 Somerset L.I. was engaged in intensive patrolling in the area to bring in wounded. D company was sent back to the Brigade Administrative Base to be reorganised.

THE JAPANESE COUNTER-OFFENSIVE

It has already been indicated that the Japanese were extremely sensitive to the thrust which was developing against Buthidaung. At the end of January 1944, 5th Indian Division was west of the Mayu Range, exerting pressure against Maungdaw. 7th Indian Division, east of the Range, had a very precarious L.-of-C. over the Goppe and Ngakyedauk Passes and no comprehensive programme of air supply. Towards the end of January, it seems that General Sakurai began to set a counter-offensive in motion. In this he may have been influenced by the dispersion of 114th Brigade. 81st (West African) Division was making slow progress in the Kaladan Valley, on the left flank. The Japanese plan seems to have included a move to the east, through the Arakan Yomas, and a descent on the rear of 7th Indian Division, with a view to cutting the supply routes and destroying it. The counter-offensive began to make itself felt on the night 3rd/4th February and, undoubtedly, came as a surprise.

1 SOMERSET L.I.

Between 1st and 3rd February the Battalion continued to exert pressure on the southern end of the two Pyinshe ridges. These were still strongly held by the enemy. The progress by other units of 114th Brigade was very slow, if indeed any progress was made at all.

On 4th February at 0400 hours, C company, on the Pyinshe Ridge, reported the sounds of a large column of men and mules, in the paddy fields, between the two ridges, moving north. There was a very thick mist at the time. It was not certain whether this column consisted of villagers escaping to safety, or parties from "Workcol" consisting of detachments from 1/11 Sikh Regt., or enemy. The previous day it was known that "Workcol" had been sent out to harass the enemy near Pt. 1600, but no one had been told which way the column would return, nor the time. It was usual for such patrols to return by daylight, though this rule was sometimes varied. 1 Somerset L.I. could not communicate with Brigade H.Q. as the Battalion wireless set had been withdrawn to enable Brigade to improve communications for the "left hook". Moreover, land lines from Battalion to Brigade had been cut. When the unknown column was detected, the Battalion was ordered to stand to. The situation was very obscure, for noises in the jungle at night are deceptive.

A runner, Private Hyde, was sent back to report to Brigade. In doing so he ran into some Japanese loading a mule. A message from Brigade said that the column were refugees from Dabragyaung, but might have Japanese among them. At 0545 hours a party of Japanese approached the carrier platoon, which was in the paddy, some 50 yards from Battalion H.Q. The carrier position was rushed and Privates R. Curzon and L. Davey killed. But using their rifles and automatics the platoon beat off this assault, killing one Japanese and wounding many more.

At 0400 hours on 4th February noises of mules were heard passing Brigade H.Q. This was situated at the northern end of Pyinshe Ridge, some 1,000 yards south of Kwazon. At 0500 hours further noises of a convoy passing close to Brigade H.Q. were heard and the "Stand to" was ordered.

In the meantime, in 1 Somerset L.I. area, the mist lifted somewhat and the Japanese were engaged with automatic fire and by parties at Brigade H.Q., some 400 yards to the flank, across the paddy fields. By this time, about 0630 hours, the main body of the Japanese column was well past Battalion H.Q. area and firing was heard from the Brigade Administrative Base area, near Octaung Kalawa.

Captain and Quartermaster Smart, quickly got men of the Transport and Administrative Platoons, under C.S.M. White (who was subsequently wounded), into position on a small hill and this party engaged the enemy with much success. Some 60 Japanese bodies were subsequently found there, while our losses were

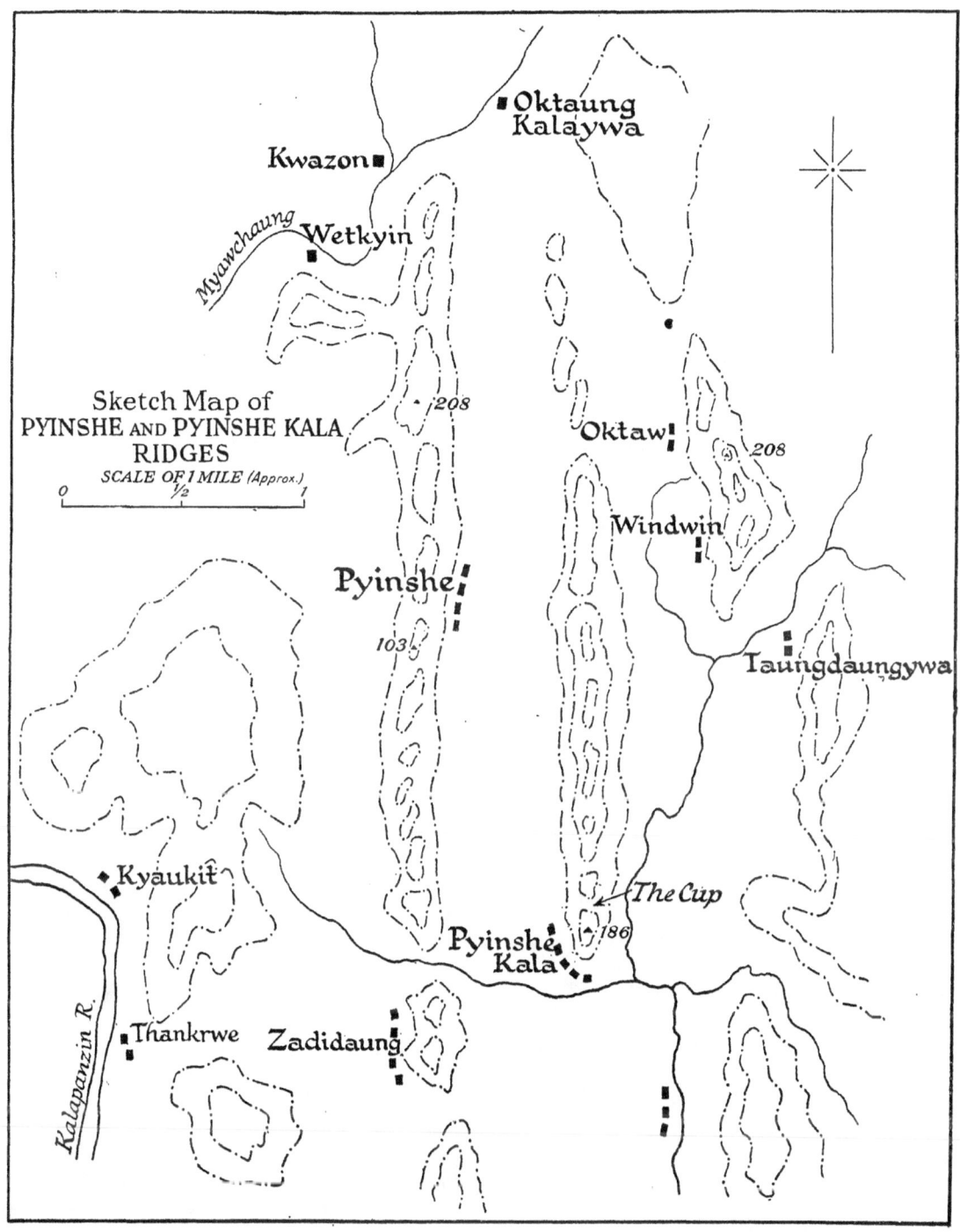

only two wounded. Nearby, the Carrier Platoon of 4/14 Punjab Regt. also did great execution.

The situation was very confused with the coming of first light. The Japanese took up a position on the Kwazon Ridge, between Battalion H.Q. and the Brigade Administrative area. A Mountain Battery opened fire on them and Captain Smart's party had to withdraw to avoid casualties. This was unfortunate as he had shown great initiative in a very successful action. The Japanese now cut all communication between Battalion H.Q. and the Administrative area, except for movement by carrier.

B Company was with Battalion H.Q. and two platoons were formed to furnish a strong fighting patrol, under Lieut. Barnes, accompanied by Lieut. Green. This patrol left Battalion H.Q. at 1045 hours, to clear the Kwazon Ridge and reopen communication to the north. The ridge was a succession of small hills, which were precipitous. During the action both officers were wounded, Lieut. Barnes severely. Lance-Corporal D. Wright stayed with him and both were killed by enemy grenades before a stretcher party could arrive.

114th Brigade was now heavily engaged. At 1900 hours 4/14 Punjab Regt. was ordered to attack and clear the Kwazon Ridge, the attack to go in at first light on 5th February. 1 Somerset L.I. was ordered to put "stops" on this ridge by 2300 hours on 4th February. It became apparent, during the day, that a column of some 800 Japanese had passed through 114th Brigade in the mist and darkness, moving on Taung. It carried supplies for a larger force, moving down the Saingdin Chaung, in the Arakan Yomas, which reached Taung on 4th February. The supply column may have missed its way in the dark, since the route it actually took was extremely hazardous. The bulk of the column got through to Taung Bazar, but the rear, about 300 in all, when engaged took refuge in the ridges on either side of the Pyinshe valley.

In the meantime 7th Indian Division became aware of the danger of the situation. On 4th February 89th Brigade was ordered to move north to Badana, cross the R. Kalapanzin and destroy the enemy in Taung Bazar. 33rd Brigade was to hold west of the Kalapanzin.

Early on 5th February these moves began. 89th Brigade met the enemy moving south-west from Taung Bazar and was soon heavily engaged. In 114th Brigade area 4/14 Punjab Regt. failed to clear the Kwazon ridge.

During the night 5th/6th February, the Japanese infiltrated through 89th Brigade and, in the early hours of 6th February, an attack on 7th Indian Divisional H.Q. began. This was situated in the Administrative Base, at the eastern end of the Ngakyedauk Pass, near Sinzweywa. The only troops available for defence were H.Q. Signals and an Engineer Battalion H.Q. The first attack was repulsed but fighting continued all day. 89th Brigade was ordered to withdraw to positions east and west of Ngakyedauk Chaung and form a "box area". 9th Brigade of 5th Indian Division was ordered to cross the Ngakyedauk Pass from the west and, also, to form a "box area".

During the afternoon of 6th February the Divisional Commander reopened a skeleton H.Q. about 3 miles from the former site, using an armoured vehicle for signal purposes. 33rd and 114th Brigades were ordered to stay where they were and deny any attempts by the enemy to supply their forces at Taung Bazar. All brigades were placed on half rations and all touch between 114th Brigade and division was lost. An armoured regiment was asked for and sent over the Ngakyedauk Pass by XV Corps.

On 7th February the enemy cut the L.-of-C. through the Ngakyedauk Pass and infiltrated in force between 89th and 33rd Brigades. 4/8 Royal Gurkha Rifles and 7/2 Punjab Regt. of 89th Brigade, were forced to withdraw to Linabi after severe fighting. Divisional H.Q. was still heavily beset.

It was now known that the Japanese 112th and part of 213th Regiments had reached Taung Bazar, taking advantage of the dispersion of 114th Brigade and the preoccupations of 4/14 Punjab Regt. and 4/5 Royal Gurkha Rifles in Operation Hook. The plan to destroy 7th Indian Division had nearly succeeded.

On 7th February, in 114th Brigade area, an action began at 0715 hours on the Windwin feature. The enemy began to infiltrate between 4/14 Punjab Regt. and 421 Field Company. Fighting continued all day, but by the evening these two units had linked up, though the enemy were still on the feature. 1 Somerset L.I. and 4/5 Royal Gurkha Rifles searched the north ends of the Pyinshe Ridges, as well as the Kwazon Ridge. 60 Japanese dead were found.

During the night of 7th/8th February a patrol of C Company, 1 Somerset L.I., under Lieut. Davies, encountered an enemy patrol and, without loss to themselves, killed one Japanese and took one prisoner. Lieut. Davies, knowing an identification was required, held his fire and jumped on his man in the dark, overpowering him with difficulty after being bitten in the hand. This officer did consistently good patrol work throughout the campaign and was, subsequently, awarded a M.C. It is believed that this prisoner was the first to be captured by the Division.

On 8th February, 114th Brigade formed a new "box", astride the Mayu Chaung, near Paledaung. 1 Somerset L.I. moved into an area near Wetkyin.

All further ideas of the Brigade plan for a "left hook" had now to be abandoned. In moving into the new "box", Major Lawson did excellent reconnaissance work and was fortunate not to encounter any Japanese. 1 Somerset L.I. moved back into the "box", by companies, during darkness on the night of 7th/8th February. Other units fell into some confusion and suffered casualties owing to difficulties in map reading.

All companies reached their positions with the exception of A company, which was checked by dense jungle. At first light on 8th February, the company was attacked by the enemy with hand grenades, Major Kite, Lieuts. Browning and Walker and two Other Ranks being wounded. Captain Haigh, 2nd-in-Command, sent a platoon to try and shift the Japanese. About the same time Captain Burgess, who was trying to locate A company with a patrol, had one man killed and one wounded by automatic fire. It was not until the next day, after artillery fire and setting the jungle alight, that the enemy was dislodged and A company got into position. Their strength was now only one officer, one C.S.M. and under 40 Other Ranks, with no full rank N.C.O.s.

After this action the "box" was unmolested but life in it was very uncomfortable. Troops were on half-rations and wounded could not be evacuated. Many were kept at the Regimental Aid Post, while serious cases were dealt with by a Company of the Field Ambulance in the "box". Later a landing strip was made and American pilots landed light craft and took off wounded. Supply dropping was also resorted to with success.

By 10th February the general situation was that 5th and 7th Indian Divisions had formed a series of brigade "boxes" from which active patrolling was designed to prevent supplies reaching the enemy. The immediate danger of defeat in detail had passed. But, without a planned operation, no one brigade could contact another. It was now necessary to wipe out the enemy forces which made the original counter-attack, as well as the reinforcements which had since reached them. The problem was complicated by the growing number of wounded who could not be evacuated and by the shortage of supplies. The first essential was to re-open the L.-of-C. over the Ngakyedauk Pass and this was entrusted to 12th Brigade of 5th Indian Division, moving on the Pass from the west. In the meantime 36th British Division, with 29th and 36th Brigades of 26th Indian Division, was arriving in the Bawli Bazar area.

During the night 9th/10th February, units of 114th Brigade heard heavy firing west of the Kalapanzin. Patrolling continued in the brigade area during the next few days. On 12th February, 7th Divisional Administrative Base was heavily attacked. During the next day 5th Indian Division made strenuous efforts to contact 7th Divisional Base. On 14th February troops had got over the Pass and were in sight of the Base. On 15th February, 89th Brigade moved into the Divisional Base "box".

In 114th Brigade area, 1 Somerset L.I. continued intensive patrolling. On 16th February a patrol under Corporal Chiffers searched the north end of Pyinshe Kala Ridge and found it clear. The next day patrols from C and D company reported both Pyinshe ridges clear of enemy. During the night 17th/18th February a patrol under Lieut. Bally penetrated further south, searched the Zadidaung feature and found it clear. Much abandoned material and ammunition was, also, found. Bitter fighting still continued west of the Kalapanzin, but on 18th February, outgoing mail was cleared over the Goppe Pass, for the first time since the enemy counter-offensive began. During the night 18th/19th February a small patrol under Lance-Corporal L. Cousins got as far south as the road leading south-east from Buthidaung, without contacting any enemy.

On 19th February a small patrol of the Gwalior Lancers (7th Division Cavalry Regt.—horsed) with one section of carriers and the mortar carriers of 1 Somerset L.I. moved south with orders to shoot up the jetty at Buthidaung. On the way they met Lance-Corporal Cousins returning with his patrol. The latter then moved south-eastwards and was attacked by an enemy patrol. All three men (Lance-Corporal Cousins and Privates G. Bartram and D. Rush) were wounded, but returned with native help. They had done excellent work and killed two Japanese. Private Bartram received the immediate award of M.M. for his part in this action. He was able to walk, though wounded, and it was largely due to his courage and initiative that his two comrades were brought back safely.

The Gwalior Lancer patrol continued southwards and found the jetty at Buthidaung destroyed. Mortar fire was, therefore, directed on targets in Buthidaung and the patrol returned without further incident. In the meantime 4/14 Punjab Regt. cleared a ridge near Bogigyaung.

On 20th February a patrol of 1 Somerset L.I. found Zadidaung occupied. Later in the day the village was attacked and harassed with mortar fire. During this operation Privates A. Dimmock and F. Otten were wounded. Between 21st and 25th February there were minor patrol incidents, the Zadidaung feature being held strongly by the enemy. Further west operations to clear the Ngakyedauk Pass continued. On 23rd February, 1 K.O.S.B. of 7th Indian Division met parties of 2/1 Punjab and 4/7 Rajput Regts. of 5th Indian Division. On 24th February the Pass was re-opened.

On the night of 27th/28th February, 1 Somerset L.I. positions on the southern end of Pyinshe Kala Ridge were heavily shelled and, later, an attack was put in, which was repulsed. On 29th February, A and D companies moved forward to strengthen the position.

As it was now clear that the Japanese were beginning to give ground after the failure of the counter-offensive, 114th Brigade issued orders on 28th February for a further advance.

ADVANCE IN THE KALAPANZIN VALLEY

The advance was to be made to a general line some two miles south of the road running south-east from Buthidaung, corresponding to the original Green Line. 5/1 Punjab Regt., from 26th Indian Division, came under command for this operation. The deployment of the brigade was to be completed by the 2nd March.

Phase I: 1 Somerset L.I. was to take Zadidaung. 4/5 Royal Gurkha Rifles was to take the Kyetmauktaung hill.
Phase II: 4/14 Punjab Regt. was to seize the Zadidaung hill feature and the hills south of Zadidaung.
Phase III: 1 Somerset L.I. and 4/5 Royal Gurkha Rifles were to pass through 4/14 Punjab Regt. directed on the final objectives.

THE SECOND ACTION ON THE PYINSHE KALA RIDGE

On the evening of 28th February, Captain Hastings, commanding the forward area of two platoons, one under Sergt. Moody on Pyinshe Kala Ridge, reported considerable enemy movement. At 0345 hours on 29th February the enemy launched an attack. This was beaten off, but later under cover of smoke, the enemy penetrated the position and Captain Hastings' platoon withdrew. Seven Other Ranks were wounded and two reported missing. Two mortar detachments were sent to the south end of the Pyinshe Ridge to harass the enemy during the day. No contact could be made with the platoon under Sergeant Moody, which was still in position on the southern end of Pyinshe Kala Ridge. This platoon was well dug in but was now isolated and was heavily sniped and mortared without suffering any casualties. During the evening of 29th February it was withdrawn by Sergeant Moody through Pyinshe Kala Village, where it lay up during the night 29th February/1st March, rejoining the battalion on the morning of 1st March. Sergeant Moody received the immediate award of D.C.M.

At 1500 hours on 29th February, 1 Somerset L.I. was ordered to recapture the lost position on the night of 29th February/1st March. At 2000 hours on 29th February, B company began the attack. By 0100 hours on 1st March the attack had got to within 20 yards of the objective and was then held up by intense automatic fire at close range. Casualties were Captain Webb and Lieut. Price-Stephens wounded; Other Ranks, three killed, thirteen wounded and three missing. During this action Lance-Corporal Pegler, as the result of casualties, took command of his platoon. He showed great bravery and leadership in his efforts to enter the Japanese position and received the immediate award of D.C.M.

On the evening of 1st March, 4/14 Punjab Regt. was ordered to take Zadidaung. Reconnaissance showed that the place was strongly held, so a fresh plan was made on 2nd March. This gave the intention of 114th Brigade as being to infiltrate and mop up Kyaukit and exploit thence to Thankrwe, Nanyagon and towards Thayetkinmanu. 1 Somerset L.I. was to harass the southern point of Pyinshe Kala Ridge and patrol in strength along Pyinshe Ridge.

On 3rd March, 5/1 Punjab Regt. attacked the Kyaukit position. The plan was that, having reached their objective, they should be relieved by 4/5 Gurkha Rifles. The attack was strongly pressed and one company of 5/1 Punjab Regt. had 70 casualties. This company over-ran a few enemy forward positions but could not gain the main feature. Being short of ammunition the battalion had to withdraw before 4/5 Gurkha Rifles could take over.

On 4th March, 4/5 Royal Gurkha Rifles again attacked on the Kyaukit feature, but failed to get a footing. 1 Somerset L.I. maintained pressure on the Pyinshe ridges. Later, D company relieved 4/14 Punjab Regt. on the Pyinshe Ridge, south-east of Wetkyin. On 5th March, C company positions were shelled, Privates J. Robinson and B. Egan being wounded.

On 6th March a further order was issued by 114th Brigade. 1 Somerset L.I. was to continue the task on the Pyinshe ridges, while Kyaukit was captured and exploitation carried out towards Nanyagon. During the night 6th/7th March two platoons of C company, south of Pyinshe Ridge, encountered the enemy in a bunker. Lieuts. P. D. Bally and R. G. Davies and nine Other Ranks were wounded and one Other Rank missing. On 7th March this position was engaged with artillery and mortar fire. Up to 22nd March, 114th Brigade made little progress and patrols were everywhere heavily engaged.

During February, 81st (West African) Division had been making progress in the Kaladan Valley, taking Kyauktaw on 24th February. The Japanese then began to use infiltration tactics and the Division was forced to withdraw northwards. At the end of February the plan of XV Corps was for 26th Indian Division to relieve 7th Indian Division in the Buthidaung sector, the latter to move to join 5th Indian Division west of the Mayu Range. 81st (West African) Division was to remain protecting the left flank in the Kaladan Valley.

114th Brigade issued orders, on 24th March, for the capture of the Zadidaung position. The attack took place on 25th March and was carried out by 4/14 Punjab Regt., and tanks of 25th Dragoons. After initial success it was held up everywhere by 1200 hours. At 1515 hours, C company 1 Somerset L.I. relieved 4/14 Punjab Regt. on the north tip of Zadidaung. Later, a further attack by 4/5 Royal Gurkha Rifles reached its objectives, a feature known as Kidney having been abandoned by the enemy.

At first light on 26th March a patrol of C company found the enemy had withdrawn. D company was moved up to Zadidaung and Battalion H.Q. to the southern end of Pyinshe Ridge. During the night 26th/27th March, patrols found Kyetmauktaung and Thayetkinmanu clear of enemy. The next night 7/2 Punjab Regt. repulsed a strong attack in the Bogigyaung area. During 28th and 29th March shelling and patrolling continued on both sides. On 30th March two platoons of C company were sent to occupy a feature south-west of Zadidaung, known as "Hambone". They encountered opposition and four Other Ranks were wounded. On 31st March, 4/5 Royal Gurkha Rifles again attacked positions south of Kyaukit, with only limited success.

Between 1st and 3rd April patrolling continued. On 4th April 114th Brigade was ordered to prepare to withdraw west of the Kalapanzin.

The official estimate of the number of Japanese employed in the encircling movement which started on 4th February and which, temporarily, isolated 7th Indian Division was 8,000. The counted dead on the Divisional front was 1,500 Japanese; while many more died in the jungle from exhaustion and lack of food.

1st BATTALION LEAVES THE ARAKAN

During 4th and 5th April 1 Somerset L.I. moved northwards along the Pyinshe Ridge towards Kwazon. This movement was observed and shelled by the enemy, one Other Rank being wounded. During the night 5th/6th April, 4/14 Punjab Regt. moved to the west of the R. Kalapanzin. On the evening of 6th April, 1 Somerset L.I. also crossed the river and moved westwards to Sinzweywa, resting there on 7th April (Jellalabad Day). In the evening it embussed and moved over the Ngakyedauk Pass to Bawli Bazar,

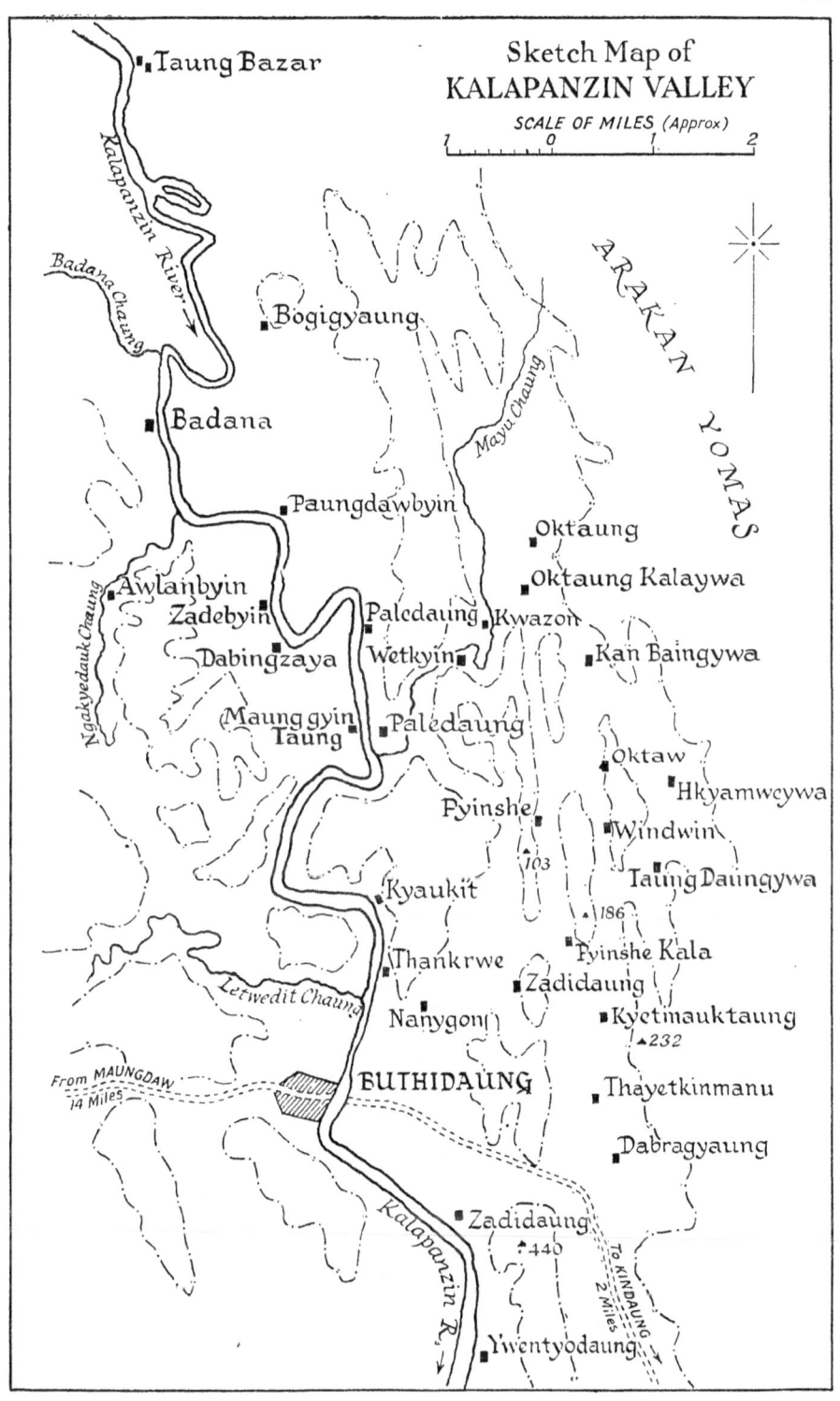

being joined there by B company which provided escort to the mules over the Goppe Pass.

At Bawli Bazar the Battalion was re-organised and, on 10th April, received orders to move to Peshawar. On 16th April it proceeded by M.T. to Dohazari, entraining there on 24th April. It arrived at Ambala on 30th April. It was then destined for North-West Frontier defence.

In a Farewell Message to the Battalion, the commander 7th Indian Division wrote, dated 16th April 1944:

". . . Your Battalion has now been in the 7th Indian Division for one and a half years. . . . It is naturally a matter for regret when a unit which has been so long part of the show has to go elsewhere. On the other hand it is undeniable that you need a period away from a war division so that you can get a chance to absorb the large number of reinforcements which have joined you in the past six months. Do not for a moment imagine that this is the end of fighting for you. . . . I have no doubt that in due course you will be given the chance to prove yourselves in a major theatre of war, as worthy members of the 1st Battalion of a regiment famed throughout history for its loyalty and fighting qualities. Good luck to you all."

CHAPTER X

TEMPERING THE BLADE—JANUARY 1943–MAY 1944

The Casablanca Conference—Training problems, 1939–42—Objects and methods of training—The School of Infantry—The status of infantry—The cutting edge—Weapons and equipment—The avoidance of frustration—The results of infantry training—4th Battalion—Move to France—5th Battalion—6th Battalion—Disbandment—7th Battalion—Move to France—9th Battalion—Preparations for D-day—Disbandment—7th (L.I.) Parachute Battalion—Move to France—30th Battalion —Move to Algiers and Sicily—2nd Battalion—Move to Egypt—Move to Italy

DURING all the troubles and dangers of the fluctuating struggle the Allies never lost sight of the ultimate objective of a landing in France, prior to an assault on Germany. With the entry of the United States into the war, the formulation of plans was simplified. On 14th January 1943, Mr. Churchill, President Roosevelt and the Chiefs of Staff met at Casablanca, North Africa, and laid plans, firstly for the invasion of Sicily in 1943 and, secondly, for the cross-Channel invasion of Normandy in 1944. Thereafter, plans for the latter project and the preparation of the forces required were pressed on. This Chapter deals with those preparations in Britain.

TRAINING PROBLEMS, 1939–42

Some attempt has been made in previous chapters to indicate the trends in the development of infantry and the progress of the training which went on during the early years of the war.

During the years between the wars (Chapter II) it was seen that masses of men on the battlefield were no longer the answer to the problems of modern warfare. The place of the "big battalions" had to be taken by highly mechanised and armoured forces, with lightly armed, but highly "active" infantry to fight in conjunction with armoured vehicles and self-propelled artillery. The rôle of infantry, particularly Light Infantry, had changed little from what it had always been. Infantry required, however, the mechanical vehicles to give it "mobility" in its move to the battlefield, the weapons necessary for attack and defence under modern conditions and the vehicles wanted to develop speed and "activity" of manœuvre in contact with the enemy. Speed of manœuvre was found to be the best form of "armour".

It was seen, also, that training during the period September 1939 to December 1942 was fraught with difficulties. The nucleus of expanded forces existed in the Territorial Army. But that army was not ready to take the field at once, without a considerable period of training and without re-equipping.

During the early part of the period, basic training and the training of specialists was hampered by the necessity for units to take over defensive duties at once. The Battle of Britain and the threat of invasion caused further delays. The disaster at Dunkirk put back, for a long time, the supply of equipment to the units. During 1941–2 there was more opportunity for collective training and the training of all arms and services in co-operation. During that period the weapon which was to destroy the Axis powers was forged. But the blade had still to be tempered and given a cutting edge. This was done during 1943 and the spring of 1944.

During 1941 a combined naval and military force, to study combined operations was assembled in Western Scotland, with H.Q. at Largs. Early in 1942 this force was renamed "The Expeditionary Force". On its staff were Major J. R. I. Platt, Major R. W. Ellis and Major A. K. Cocks. In the summer of 1942, owing to a postponement of plans for an invasion of Europe, the force was renamed "The First Army". Thereafter plans started in earnest for the invasion of French North Africa. Lieut.-Colonel J. R. I. Platt, became A.A.G. The Defence Company for First Army was formed at Largs from battalions of the Somerset Light Infantry as already stated in Chapter VIII.

OBJECTS AND METHODS OF TRAINING

The real planning for, and co-ordination of, training began after Dunkirk in 1940. Home Forces Command set out to achieve certain main objects:

(a) to raise moral to the highest possible level;
(b) to overcome the fear of the unknown by realistic training;
(c) to exploit mobility;
(d) to establish the prestige of infantry as the cutting edge of the battle.

It was essential to raise moral after the disaster of Dunkirk, but it was extremely difficult to maintain it through a long period of training at Home. Success was achieved by insisting on the need for making all training as realistic as possible, for keeping all ranks fully informed of what was expected of them and for explaining the why and wherefore of their tough training. This was the type of training applied, 150 years before, by Sir John Moore, when he trained the incomparable Light Division. It was that Division of Light Infantry which defeated Napoleon's Old Guard at Waterloo, with very little artillery support.

It is interesting to note that the man who, during the early years of the War 1939–45, was mainly responsible for applying this form of training, was himself a Light Infantryman. General Sir Bernard Paget became Chief of Staff of Home Forces in June 1940; C.-in-C. Home Forces in December 1941 and C.-in-C. 21 Army Group in July 1943. It was right and proper that an infantry soldier should train the infantry for the task which lay ahead.

THE SCHOOL OF INFANTRY

To ensure that training was realistic, so that the fear of the unknown could be overcome by experience, the G.H.Q. Home Forces Battle School was established at Barnard Castle in 1942 and, later, developed into the War Office School of Infantry. Here, both senior and junior officers were given an oppotunity of seeing what war was really like so that, later, they could train their men.

This School played a great part in building up a real infantry team spirit and a common doctrine. Thus the status of infantry was maintained and the interests of infantry safeguarded without reducing, in any way, the incalculable values of the regimental system.

THE STATUS OF INFANTRY

One of the objects of this carefully planned and co-ordinated system of training was to ensure the proper recognition of the status of infantry on the modern battlefield. Although the close co-operation of all arms is essential in battle, the infantry, as the cutting edge of the battle, must be as sharp and finely tempered as it is possible to make it. That fact had not been properly appreciated throughout the army.

For some years infantry had been "unpopular", since it lacked the "glamour" of armoured units and other highly mechanised arms. It suffered, also, from the record of the war of 1914–18, when stereotyped methods of attack had resulted in enormous casualties in spite of strong artillery support. It was said of infantry that "their very symmetry became their cemetery" and infantry earned the unenviable title of "the P.B.I.". It was essential that it should resume its proper place on the battlefield.

THE CUTTING EDGE

The cutting edge in battle consists of the infantry rifle companies. Taking an infantry division at a total strength of 18,200—which was an average figure for the war 1939–45—the strength of the rifle companies, including officers, was only 4,500. Assuming a divisional attack on a two brigade front, each brigade with two battalions leading, each on a two-company front, the actual cutting edge, at full strength, is represented by 1,000 riflemen. This is a very small proportion of the divisional strength and emphasises the necessity for sharpening and tempering that edge.

Much of the stereotyped infantry tactics of the period of siege warfare on the Western Front in the war 1914–18, arose from the inadequate training of junior leaders. It was essential to make junior leaders think for themselves and be prepared, at any stage of the battle, to deal with the unexpected and fight forward, by means of fire and movement, using their own available weapons. This demanded flexible team-work and a high standard of initiative. Only thus could the old system of sending infantry slowly forwards in long lines, like dumb sheep to the slaughter, be obviated.

It was emphasised, from the start, that it is the section and platoon commanders, and the men they lead, who win battles and training was built up from this basis. It was laid down that, for effective team-work, the minimum strength of the section should be 10 and of the platoon, 37. It was essential to maintain these strengths for battle, otherwise the cutting edge would be blunted. It was held that it was better for a battalion to go into action with three rifle companies, having platoons at full strength, than with four rifle companies with weak platoons.

There was, however, a dangerous tendency to maintain "specialists" at full strength at the expense of riflemen. This tendency was strongly combatted. It was emphasised that a rifleman was required to display more courage, a higher standard of physical fitness and even more intelligence than any so-called "specialist". The best men should be riflemen and, having picked these, the "specialists" could be selected. With the multiplicity of weapons to be used, the man in the rifle section required more training than the man in the support company.

These, then, were the main lines on which the realistic training was carried out. They have been described in some detail so that a clear picture of the type of infantryman, who landed in Normandy in 1944, may be seen. The response to this training from the rank and file was remarkable. The stimulation of moral throughout the infantry, arising from the system of training, was one of the major lessons of the war. The infantry which was produced for D-day, may not have had the same craft in war as had been learned by the men of the 1st and 8th Armies in Africa. But their moral was of a different character. They came fresh to the fight, with all the enthusiasm and determination which had been poured into them. It may be that they possessed greater dash and keenness than the veterans who had seen the real thing and knew what to expect.

WEAPONS AND EQUIPMENT

In addition to planned training, it was essential that infantry should be supplied with the most suitable weapons, equipment and vehicles, to enable it to undertake its task. At first, such weapons were not available, either in quantity, or quality. A high standard was not achieved during the 1914–18 war, nor during the period 1939–45. Many of the weapons—for example the sniper's rifle and the Piat and Sten guns—were not the best that could be produced. One reason for this was that the design and development of infantry weapons were not entirely in the hands of infantrymen. It is a lesson for the future that infantry should be responsible for developing its own weapons, for the infantryman, alone, can tell under what conditions such weapons will be used and what he requires from them.

THE AVOIDANCE OF FRUSTRATION

Linked closely with tactical and weapon training were realism, endurance, physical fitness and recreation. Realism was developed by reproducing battle conditions with live ammunition and accepting the risk of accidental casualties. Endurance was inculcated by exercises, for long periods, in all kinds of weather and terrain. Recreational training was designed so that all members of a unit could participate in some activity.

It was, however, necessary to maintain interest for all ranks. The combination of higher training—for commanders and staffs—with minor tactical training, often left many with a feeling of frustration, disappointment and boredom. Thus, in large scale exercises, every effort was made to keep the soldier fully in the picture as to the progress of the operations and to carry out tests, during the exercise, of junior commanders and their men. Thus all were kept interested and boredom was largely eliminated.

THE RESULTS OF THE TRAINING OF INFANTRY

The system of training employed in Britain produced units inoculated to withstand battle conditions; men who knew what to expect and were physically and emotionally prepared to take the shock of real war. The success those men achieved, in France and Germany, is now a matter of history.

From their training emerges a lesson for the future. When war broke out in 1939, the army had been sadly neglected for 25 years and was sent into action against an enemy extremely well prepared and efficient. The neglect had resulted in shortages in men and equipment; in inadequate training areas; in great delays in the development of weapons; in peace time safety precautions which rendered realistic training almost impossible. In his History of the British Army, Fortescue wrote:

"At the end of every war the army that has saved us is weakened by the politicians and when the next war breaks out, as usual, we are unprepared and the flower of our army is destroyed while we train our troops. What is the use of sweating one's life out recording past blunders, if no lesson is learnt from bitter experience."

It will be the task of army and infantry leaders of the future to see that that tragic statement no longer applies. But the hope is a forlorn one. The lesson itself is clear; but the malady lingers on.

THE 4TH BATTALION, 1943-4

January 1943 saw the 4th Battalion still at Dover. Air attacks and shelling continued during the spring, being particularly heavy on 2nd March, when 50 shells fell in the town. Training and exercises continued, including exercise "Spartan" in March.

On 3rd May the Battalion moved to summer training quarters at Eythorne, near Canterbury. Here it was engaged in field exercises for D-day. On 6th October it moved to Crowborough and, on 4th November, to Dymchurch, where it was employed on a beach defence rôle. Captain V. A. Reader was appointed Adjutant on 4th January 1943 and Lieut. S. N. Burfield became Assistant Adjutant on 20th July.

On 29th February 1944 the Battalion moved to the South Downs Training Area, returning to Dymchurch on 5th March. Jellalabad Day was celebrated on 11th April. On 12th May the Battalion gave a demonstration of "The

JANUARY 1943–MAY 1944

Wasp" (Flame Thrower) before Mr. Churchill, Field-Marshal Smuts and Mr. Mackenzie King. At this time the Battalion was in 2nd Army, commanded by Lieut.-General K. A. N. Anderson, C.B.

On 29th May a serious accident occurred at Dymchurch, when a dump of No. 75 grenades exploded. Lieut. G. B. S. Wilson and 21 Other Ranks of C company were killed and 5 Other Ranks wounded. During February, R.S.M. Holt received a C.-in-C.'s certificate for Meritorious Service. Major A. W. N. L. Vickers was appointed 2nd-in-Command on 30th March.

On 28th May the warning order for D-day was received and the Battalion placed at 6 hours' notice to move. On 12th June all ranks were confined to billets. The next day orders were received to move to the Marshalling Area. The transport marched to Victoria Docks, London, on 14th June, embarking on 18th June. On 15th June the Battalion moved into the Marshalling Area at Firle Park, Sussex and, on 18th June, at 1130 hours, embarked at Newhaven.

5TH BATTALION, 1943–4

On 25th May, while in the Colchester Area, the 5th Battalion was reorganised as a six-company battalion, with H.Q., Support, A, B, C, and D companies. The strength was then 31 Officers and 872 Other Ranks. The armament included 55 Bren guns and 14 2-inch mortars.

On 10th November it moved to Bally-Na-Hinch, in Northern Ireland, forming part of 45th Division (Major-General J. K. Edwards, D.S.O., M.C).

During the spring of 1944 it was employed in advanced Individual Training and draft finding and had no operational rôle. A publication known as *The Jellalabad Times* was started and ran to 23 monthly editions.

On 20th March 1944 the Battalion returned to England, and relieved 6th Devon Regt. at Seaford. Here it was employed on coast defence. It still continued to find drafts and, as the result of this drain on strength, was reorganised on 15th April into H.Q., S company and C company. By 14th May the strength had fallen to 27 Officers and 272 Other Ranks. On 1st June 1944, Lieut.-Colonel W. Q. Roberts assumed command.

6TH BATTALION, 1943–4

On 3rd February 1943, the 6th Battalion moved from Colchester to Coleraine, in Northern Ireland, forming part of 45th Division. Here it was engaged in training. On 7th April Jellalabad Day was celebrated with a parade for Major-General V. H. B. Majendie, C.B., D.S.O., Colonel of the Regiment and G.O.C. Northern Ireland District. At this time Lieut. (Q.M.) I. C. Guest was Quartermaster.

During May 1943 the Battalion moved to Castle Rock and, in November, to Killyleagh and Shrigley. On 19th December it returned to England, being stationed at Littlehampton, Sussex.

On 3rd January 1944 it moved to Harwich in a coast defence rôle, returning to Peacehaven in March. During May orders were received for disbandment and the dispersal of personnel began. On 21st June Lieut.-Colonel

Firbank assumed command of 135th Infantry Brigade and Major A. B. Rich took command of the Battalion. Drafts began to leave for other units. On 14th July 1944 final disbandment took place and all remaining Other Ranks were posted to the 5th Battalion.

7TH BATTALION, 1943-4

On 8th January 1943 the 7th Battalion took over the South Sector of the Isle of Wight Defences, with H.Q. at Ventnor. At this time appointments were held as under:

> Commanding Officer: Lieut.-Colonel R. G. P. Besley, T.D.
> Adjutant: Captain R. W. Hatch.
> Quartermaster: Lieut. (Q.M.) J. W. Grant.
> R.S.M. W. Durman.

On 1st February the Battalion was reorganised as a five-company battalion. During May, Captain J. L. Denison became Adjutant and was succeeded in June by Captain E. E. Venn.

On 27th May the Battalion moved to Trelowarren, near Helston, Cornwall. Here it was again reorganised, with four rifle companies, as under:

> A company: Captain W. H. Goudie.
> B company: Captain K. J. Whitehead.
> C company: Major G. D. Bond.
> D company: Major C. W. S. Young.
> H.Q. company: Captain C. L. G. Baker.
> Support company: Captain W. D. C. Hedges.
> 2nd-in command: Major E. J. Bruford.
> Adjutant: Captain H. D. Barratt-Lennard. (Succeeded by Captain A. F. Scannell in August).

On 8th June the Battalion was inspected by Major-General Majendie, Colonel of the Regiment, and next day orders were received to mobilise for foreign service. On 25th June it moved to Inveraray, for training in the use of Landing Craft, by day and night. On 15th July it moved to Berwick-on-Tweed, under 43rd Division (Major-General G. I. Thomas) and Northumbrian District. In August, after a spell of Agricultural Assistance at Hartford Bridge, it moved to Uckfield, Sussex, remaining there, engaged in training, between 7th October and 5th November. It then was sent to Hythe, on a coast defence rôle.

On 15th January 1944, the Battalion took over coast defences at Worthing, returning to Hythe in February. There it was inspected by General Sir B. L. Montgomery, K.C.B., D.S.O., commanding 21st Army Group. In March came a move to the Hastings Area, with H.Q. at Battle.

On 31st May orders were received to move overseas and, on 7th June a pamphlet, "France", was issued to all ranks. On 15th June orders came to

JANUARY 1943–MAY 1944

load up and move. The transport proceeded to Silvertown, London, and embarked on v.s.s. "Will Rogers" at Victoria Docks on 17th June, sailing at 1645 hours.

On 15th June the remainder of the Battalion moved to Glynde Camp, Sussex, joining 5/D.C.L.I., and 1st Worcestershire Regt. On 16th June it was split into "craft loads" and, on 19th June, embarked at Newhaven in s.s. "Biarritz". It sailed the same day in adverse weather and had to return and re-enter harbour. s.s. "Biarritz" sailed again at 1610 hours on 21st June, joined s.s. "Princess Maud" and "Canterbury" in convoy and anchored off Ryde, in the Solent. In the meantime the transport from London sailed during 18th/21st June through the Straits of Dover, close to the Isle of Wight and then southwards. On its way this convoy was attacked by cross-channel artillery fire.

9TH BATTALION, 1943–44

On 25th January 1943, the 9th Battalion received a visit from Sir James Grigg, Secretary of State for War. During the spring it was reorganised to include a Support Company. In May 1943, 72nd Infantry Brigade was broken up and the Battalion moved to Perranporth, Cornwall. Here it came under 214th Independent Infantry Brigade (Brigadier H. Essame, D.S.O., M.C.).

On 9th June it was mobilised for a special mission involving an assault on the Azores with a Marine Division. Moral was very high. It then moved for special training to the Combined Operations Training Centre at Inveraray. The operation against the Azores was, however, cancelled and, in July, the Battalion moved to Berwick-on-Tweed. During June it was inspected by the Colonel of the Regiment.

In August there was bitter disappointment when orders were received for disbandment. But, on 11th September, the Battalion was ordered to join 115th Infantry Brigade (Brigadier A. E. Snow) of 38th Division, at Walmer. On 20th October, this move was cancelled. Lieut.-Colonel Gage-Brown fell ill and was succeeded in command by Lieut.-Colonel G. H. Cole. At this time Captain R. E. Southcombe was Adjutant with R.S.M. F. Cook. Major E. C. H. Evered was 2nd-in-Command.

In November the Battalion formed part of 38th Division (Major-General D. C. Butterworth, D.S.O.) in the Berwick-on-Tweed Area. This Division included 113th, 114th and 115th Infantry Brigades. During the autumn the Division was engaged in extensive brigade exercises. In December, from Thropton Camp, the Battalion took part in exercise "Swallow", for which it was commended. At a further exercise on 17th December, in bitter weather, it also received high praise.

On 21st January 1944, 38th Division moved south. The 9th Battalion, under 115th Infantry Brigade, went to Bournemouth and was quartered in two large hotels. Here, Lieut. K. N. Ingham became Adjutant. During February commanding officers of units in the brigade visited Plymouth and

Bideford to inspect types of Landing Craft. This was in connection with a projected operation of 115th Infantry Brigade to capture the Channel Islands. This operation was, subsequently, cancelled. At a much later date, Brigadier A. E. Snow landed on the Islands, with another force, and took the surrender of the German forces.

On 2nd March 1944, the Battalion was inspected by Lieut.-General Sir H. Franklyn, K.C.B., D.S.O., M.C., C.-in-C. Home Forces. On 3rd/4th March it proceeded by march route to Bustard Camp, Salisbury Plain, for exercises. During March, 277 Other Ranks were drafted away from the Battalion.

On 19th March instructions were received for Operation "Overlord", the Invasion of Normandy. 115th Infantry Brigade took over "B" Marshalling Area, at Brockenhurst—Beaulieu—Lymington. The 9th Battalion was located at Fawley and Penerley. H.Q. of the Area was at Balmer Lawn, Brockenhurst.

During April the Battalion took over Nos. 3 and 4 Camps astride the Lyndhurst–Beaulieu road and exercises were carried out to practise handling of arrivals at the camps. 203 Other Ranks were posted to the Durham Light Infantry. During this month, Major J. H. Sydenham, (West York Regt.), was appointed as 2nd-in-Command.

During May, there was close liaison with United States forces, the camps being visited by Generals Thresher, Lee and Littlejohn. Troops began to arrive and, on 26th May, the camps were "sealed". On 3rd/4th June, assault troops from the area assembled on the Landing Craft. On 9th June, United States "follow-up" troops arrived and passed through the area. By 4th July "B" Marshalling Area was closed and handed over to United States forces.

In the meantime, on 29th May, a warning of the break up of 38th (Welsh) Division and 115th Infantry Brigade had been received, together with orders for the disbandment of the 9th Battalion. On 5th July Major-General Butterworth gave a Farewell Address. On 6th July a large draft left the Battalion to be posted to the 4th and 7th Battalions, in 21st Army Group. On 17th July Lieut.-Colonel Cole left the Battalion, which moved to Camp A2 on 5th August. On 23rd August the remnant of the Battalion was sent to Bustard Camp, Salisbury Plain. Here, on 16th September 1944, the 9th Battalion ceased to exist.

7TH BATTALION (L.I.) THE PARACHUTE REGIMENT

In January 1943, the 7th Battalion (L.I.) was at Bulford. Captain R. A. Penney was appointed Adjutant. It began training with 3rd Para Brigade of the Airborne Division, under Major-General F. A. M. Browning, C.B., D.S.O. This Division ultimately became 6th Airborne Division in June 1943, when the 7th Battalion became part of 5th Para Brigade (Brigadier J. H. N. Poett, late Durham Light Infantry). Other brigades of the Division were 3rd and 4th (Brigadier Hackett, D.S.O., O.B.E., M.C.).

During the whole of 1943 and the spring of 1944, intensive training was

JANUARY 1943–MAY 1944

carried out. Early in 1943, Major H. H. Mills, M.C., and Captain B. R. Braithwaite, joined the Battalion. In April H.M. the King inspected the Division at Bulford Fields. On 9th August Captain R. J. N. Bartlett was appointed Adjutant, Major C. A. L. Shipley becoming 2nd-in-Command on 22nd August. On 5th September C.S.M. Johnson, M.B.E., was appointed R.S.M. On 14th October, Major R. G. Pine-Coffin, M.C., was appointed 2nd-in-Command.

1944 saw intensified special training for the invasion of the continent. Brigade drops were carried out by day and night. Early in 1944 the Battalion carried out its first drop as a complete unit. On 25th February Lieut.-Colonel Barlow was appointed Deputy Commander 1st Air Landing Brigade and was succeeded in command of the Battalion by Lieut.-Colonel R. G. Pine-Coffin.

During March, training in street fighting was carried out in bombed areas of south-east London. Here a serious accident occurred in which Sergeant Stenner was killed and Lieuts. J. H. Loch and R. Fleming seriously injured. On 1st April, Major E. H. Steel-Baumme was appointed 2nd-in-Command.

On 13th May preliminary briefing was given for Operation "Overlord", the invasion of Normandy. This was followed by assault boat training at Exeter. On 17th May, the preliminary orders for "Overlord" were issued, the 7th Battalion being directed to work in conjunction with No. 6 Commando. On 20th May there were conferences in connection with the operation. On 30th May the Battalion issued its Operation Order No. 1.

Between 1st and 3rd June the Battalion and companies were briefed at Tilshead and, on 5th June, the Battalion moved to Fairfield Park Airfield, arriving there at 1900 hours. At 2320 hours it took off for France.

30TH BATTALION, 1943–4

In January 1943, the 30th Battalion was on coastal defence in Dorset. During the latter part of 1942, no less than 50 Officers and 3,000 Other Ranks had passed through the Battalion.

On 26th April 1943 it moved to take over the Portland defences from 9th Royal Welch Fusiliers, leaving C company at Weymouth and Ringstead. It was now under 115th Infantry Brigade which, from April 1943, was commanded by Brigadier A. E. Snow. On 27th May it was inspected at tactical exercises by General Sir Bernard Paget, K.C.B., C.-in-C. Home Forces. Its showing at this inspection may have influenced the later decision to send it overseas.

On 6th August orders were received to mobilise for foreign service. The strength was then 27 Officers and 925 Other Ranks. Many of the latter were of low medical category. These were posted to C company at Weymouth and, later, became Home Details under Major R. G. Hyde. 5 Officers and 510 Other Ranks were sent on leave. On 20th August the Battalion was relieved from an operational rôle.

On 3rd September, the strength being 43 Officers and 1,082 Other Ranks, it was inspected by Major-General Majendie, Colonel of the Regiment. On 11th September, advance parties left for Glasgow, followed later by the remainder of the Battalion. On 14th September it embarked on H.T. "Cameronia" at Glasgow. 33 Officers and 732 Other Ranks embarked, the officers including:

> Commanding Officer: Lieut.-Colonel W. H. F. Routh.
> 2nd-in-Command: Major D. L. Gough, M.C., T.D.
> Adjutant: Captain R. B. Holder.
> Quartermaster: Captain (Q.M.) W. J. Atkins.
> Signal Officer: Lieut. A. J. W. Alexander.
> Intelligence: Lieut. A. H. Bennett.
> Transport: Lieut. E. Bateman.
> A Company: Major G. W. Prince, M.C.
> B Company: Major A. V. Denton.
> C Company: Captain T. S. Edney.
> D Company: Major R. Douglas-Bate.
> R.S.M. R.S.M. V. Rogers, D.C.M.
> R.Q.M.S. R.Q.M.S. R. L. Edmunds.

The organisation was H.Q. Company and four rifle companies, each of four platoons, one platoon of each company having bicycles.

On 15th September, after some difficulties due to overcrowding of ships, a convoy of some 14 ships left the Clyde and reached Gibraltar on 22nd September, without incident. On 23rd September the Battalion disembarked at Algiers and moved to a tented camp in "Z" Staging Area, on the road to Cap Matifou. The march was made in torrential rain. On 25th September it entrained at Rouiba for Tunis, arriving there after a journey lasting four days. On 29th September it detrained at La Manouba and moved by bus to Sidi Abdullah, an oasis 12 miles from Tunis, near the ruins of Carthage.

Here it joined 43rd Infantry Brigade (Brigadier G. H. P. Whitfeld, O.B.E., M.C.) consisting of:

> 30 Somerset L.I.   30 Royal Norfolk Regt.
> 30 Green Howards.   30 Dorset Regt.
> 30 Cheshire Regt.   31 Suffolk Regt.

On 9th October it moved to La Manouba and La Marsa, with Battalion H.Q. in the old Palace of the Bey of Tunis. Here it found guards at La Goulette Docks and was much troubled with intestinal sickness. On 25th October, 30th Green Howards and 31st Suffolk Regt. left the brigade. In October 30 Somerset L.I. moved over to Sicily.

2ND BATTALION, 1943-4

January 1943 found the 2nd Battalion still at Gibraltar and working on the construction of defences. In April 1943, B and D companies carried out three weeks' concentrated training at Les Andalouses in North Africa. Here,

Lieut.-Colonel Corballis accidentally sustained a gunshot wound in the head, but returned to duty on 8th July 1943. Major F. R. Tubbs assumed command in his temporary absence. Captain S. Smallwood also received wounds, during this training, from which he died in May 1943. In July, A and C companies followed B and D companies for training at Les Andalouses.

On 4th July the Polish General Sikorski and his Chief of Staff, Major-General Klimecki, were killed in a flying accident at Gibraltar. Before the plane took off and crashed, the 2nd Battalion provided a Guard of Honour for the General. On 5th July the Battalion provided another Guard for the Lying-in-State of the dead General at the Roman Catholic Cathedral and, on 8th July, an escort for the bodies to a Polish destroyer.

A and C companies returned from training in August. In October there was a Fortress Defence exercise. On 30th November, Lieut.-Colonel J. R. I. Platt assumed command of the Battalion. Major G. R. Chetwynd-Stapylton was 2nd-in-Command.

Early in December orders were received for the Gibraltar Brigade, under command of Brigadier Purves, and consisting of Brigade Headquarters, 2nd Battalion The King's Regiment and 2nd Battalion The Somerset L.I. to move to Egypt. On 15th December the Battalion, after five years in Gibraltar, embarked in the troopship "Letitia", and sailed at midnight under naval escort. The voyage through the Mediterranean was uneventful, and on 22nd December the "Letitia" reached Port Said. On 24th December the Battalion disembarked and moved by train to Ataqa Camp, 5 miles from Suez. Here the Gibraltar Brigade was renamed the 28th Infantry Brigade and became part of the 4th Infantry Division which had recently arrived from Algiers under command of Major-General H. J. Hayman Joyce, D.S.O. The 1st Battalion Argyll and Sutherland Highlanders joined the Brigade as the 3rd Battalion.

During January and February 1944 the Brigade carried out intensive training in an endeavour to cram into two months all the battle training missed by five years on The Rock. Intense secrecy surrounded the location of the 4th Division, which, for security reasons, was known as 34th Division. To complete the deception the official address of 28th Infantry Brigade was still Gibraltar and all ranks were warned against giving away the fact that they were in Egypt. As training in combined operations was included in the programme it appeared most probable that an assault landing somewhere in the Eastern Mediterranean was being planned. There was considerable surprise therefore when orders were received in February for the 4th Division to move to Italy. No training had been carried out in fighting in mountainous country, but the Brigade was promised a month's training in Italy before it went into action, a promise which was regarded with some scepticism.

Early in March 28th Infantry Brigade, less 1st Battalion Argyll and Sutherland Highlanders, started to move to Italy. On 7th March the Battalion moved by rail to Port Said where half of it embarked in M.V. "Empire Pride" and the others embarked in H.T. "Devonshire". Both ships sailed in convoy on 11th March, and arrived on 16th March at Naples, where the Battalion disembarked and moved by road to the village of Le Vogie. Here it found itself in steep, mountainous country, and billeted close to the gun area of 4th Division which was already in action. The following day American Flying Fortresses passed overhead and the bombing of Cassino was clearly audible. True to prediction, within four days the Battalion had taken over a sector of the line.

This Chapter has seen the war drawing ever closer. It has seen the disbandment of the 6th and 9th Battalions; the move of the 4th, 7th and 7th (L.I.) Parachute Battalions to France; the arrival of the 2nd Battalion in Italy and the 30th Battalion in Sicily; and the relegation of the 5th Battalion to draft finding in England. Four dates during the period which have been reviewed should be noted.

Landings took place in Sicily on 9th/10th July and in Southern Italy on 3rd September 1943. Airborne troops landed in Normandy on 5th/6th June 1944; D-day was 6th June 1944.

CHAPTER XI

THE CAMPAIGN IN ITALY: I—OPENING GAMBITS, MAY 1943–APRIL 1944

The opening of the Italian Campaign—Landings in Sicily—Resignation of Mussolini—Invasion of Italy—Landing at Salerno—30th Battalion in Sicily—Period of deception—Situation in the autumn 1943 and spring 1944—Landings at Anzio—Arrival of 4th Division in Italy—Orders of Battle of 10 Corps and 4th Division—Operations on R. Garigliano—4th Division transferred to 13 Corps of 8th Army—30th Battalion move to Italy—recreations

CHAPTER X saw the 30th Battalion about to land in Sicily and the 2nd Battalion preparing to disembark at Naples. It is necessary to describe the events affecting the development of the Campaign in Italy in which both these battalions were to be involved.

THE OPENING OF THE ITALIAN CAMPAIGN

On 9th May 1943 the 1st and 8th Armies completed the overthrow of the German-Italian forces in North Africa. There was, then, a general regrouping of British and U.S. forces in the Mediterranean area for the invasion of Italy.

Preliminary operations included the capture of the Islands of Lampedusa and Pantellaria, in the channel between Tunisia and Sicily. On 19th May, Pantellaria was heavily bombed and received a naval bombardment on 31st May. Between 11th and 13th June, Lampedusa, Linosa and Pantellaria Islands were occupied.

On the night of 9th/10th July, U.S. Airborne and British paratroops landed in Sicily and in the early hours of 10th July, U.S. 7th and British 8th Army troops, including Canadian Divisions, landed on Sicilian beaches. The British took Scoglitte, Syracuse and Pachino; the U.S. forces, Gela, Licata and Ragusa.

During July, British and U.S. forces continued to make progress in Sicily. On 19th July, Rome was bombed by 700 U.S. aircraft, from North Africa and Middle East. On the same day Hitler and Mussolini met at Verona to discuss the military situation.

On 25th July, Mussolini resigned and was at once arrested. King Victor Emmanuel assumed command of all Italian forces, with Marshal Badoglio as Prime Minister. The next day the Fascist Party was dissolved and overtures for peace began.

Early in August severe fighting took place in Sicily. This went in our favour and, on 16th August, U.S. forces entered Messina and were followed by 8th Army troops. On 17th August all resistance in Sicily ceased. Preparations were then made for the invasion of Italy.

At 0430 hours on 3rd September, British and Canadian troops of 8th Army landed on the toe of Italy, between Reggio and Catona, establishing a firm beach-head by the evening. They then began to break out inland. On 8th September, Italy surrendered unconditionally. On 9th September, while 8th Army continued to advance northwards from Reggio, Allied forces under General Mark Clark, including U.S. 5th Army, landed at Salerno, south of Naples, and occupied Ventolene Island. On 10th September, German troops occupied Rome, as well as a number of important towns in Northern Italy.

On 14th September severe counter-attacks on the Salerno beach-head began. By 16th September these had been held and U.S. 5th Army resumed the offensive. On the same day patrols of U.S. 5th Army and British 8th Army linked up south of Salerno. 8th Army had been spreading northwards and across Southern Italy. On 22nd September a fresh landing was made on the Adriatic coast at Bari and Foggia was occupied on 27th September.

On 30th September, U.S. 5th Army, operating from the Salerno beach-head, took Avellino and Torre Annunziata on the southern slopes of Mount Vesuvius. They then pressed forward and entered Naples on 1st October.

During the early part of October, progress was made on both army fronts. On 4th October, Free French troops liberated Corsica. On 7th October U.S. 5th Army took Capua, on the R. Volturno, and Caserta, north of Naples. On 13th October the Italian government declared war on Germany. The same day U.S. 5th Army opened an offensive on the R. Volturno, combined with landings from the sea north of the river mouth, towards Mondragone. By the end of the month this offensive had reached Teano. In the meantime, 8th Army had occupied Montefalcone.

It will be seen that two major fronts had now developed. U.S. 5th Army, including British formations, was moving north along the west coast, directed on Rome. 8th Army stretched across the Apennines to the Adriatic coast and was clearing up southern Italy.

30TH BATTALION

On 27th October 1943 the 30th Battalion embarked at La Goulette Docks, Tunis, in four L.C.I.s. The battalion transport moved by road to Bizerta where it awaited embarkation. On 28th October a small convoy was assembled and left Tunisia, escorted by two M.T.B.s.

On 29th October the Battalion, less transport, disembarked at Palermo, Sicily. This was the H.Q. of U.S. 7th Army, in the American Zone of Sicily. The Battalion came under command of H.Q. Island Base Section and went into camp at No. 1 Staging Area, some three miles from Palermo. There was torrential rain and the camp became a quagmire. Here it was employed on guard duties.

On 7th November the battalion transport arrived at Syracuse. Companies

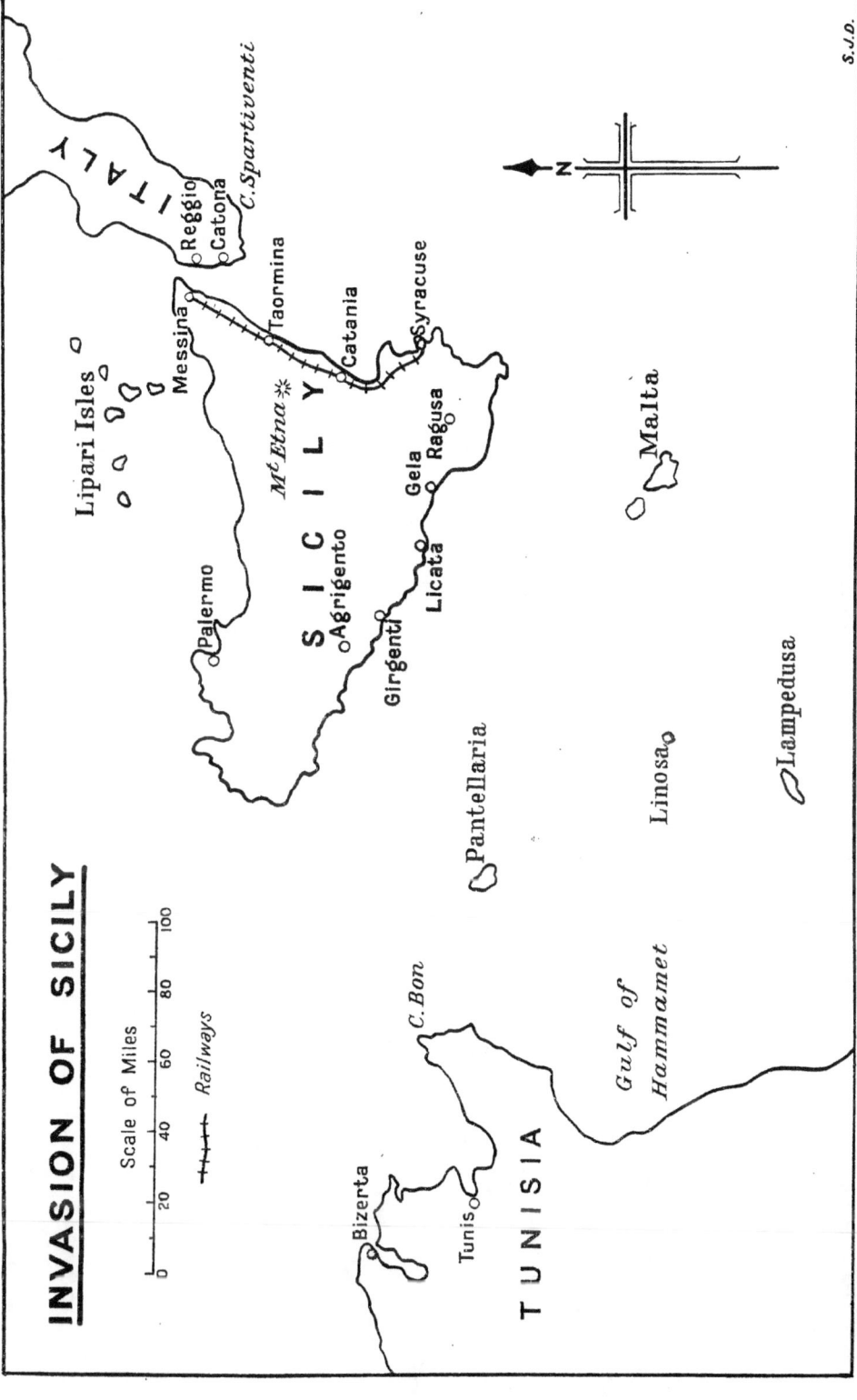

were located at Agrigento, Palmero, and three power stations at Altofonti, Villa Grazia and Lola Piana. On 11th November, 4,000 Canadians arrived in No. 1 Staging Area. Lieut.-Colonel Routh was appointed O.C. British Troops, Palermo.

A PERIOD OF DECEPTION

On 18th November a re-grouping of formations began. 43rd Infantry Brigade, to which 30th Battalion belonged, took over the duties of 40th Division. 30th Battalion was re-designated "119th Infantry Brigade". The C.O. became a Brigadier; the Adjutant, Brigade-Major; and the Quartermaster, Staff Captain. The personnel of the battalion were designated "Divisional Signals" and wore a badge with an Acorn on a White Diamond. This deception was practised to facilitate and conceal the move of 40th and 51st Divisions to Britain, to take part in the invasion of Normandy. The Battalion remained in this rôle until 17th January 1944.

On 25th December 1943, Christmas Day, Lieut.-Colonel Routh lunched with General George Patton at his H.Q. at Palermo. The Battalion was, at this time, being supplied with U.S. Army rations and using American Institutes and Hospitals. After January 1944, A company was employed at No. 3 Staging Area, C and D companies at Palermo and B company at Agrigento.

SITUATION IN THE AUTUMN 1943 AND SPRING 1944

While allied forces in Italy maintained strong pressure, the late autumn of 1943 and the early spring of 1944 saw the build-up of our armies for further advances, when the weather became more suitable for major operations, against a series of well-prepared German lines. In their defence of northern Italy the Germans were helped by the terrain. Inter-communication between the two allied armies was rendered difficult by the central spine of the Apennines, while the many rivers, some flowing in rocky gorges, ran from the hills to the sea and formed obstacles to advances from the south, which were comparatively easy to defend. The central range of the Apennines, also, provided a series of admirable positions and excellent observation for a defender.

On 4th November, U.S. 5th Army captured Isernia, on the upper Volturno and, by occupying Castel Petroso, linked up with 8th Army, advancing on the Adriatic seaboard towards the R. Sangro. On 23rd November, 8th Army crossed the R. Sangro in strength and entered Alfedena. By 1st December the German "Winter Line" in that sector had been shattered. This line, along the R. Sangro, ran, roughly, from the lower spurs of the Apennines to the coast. Bad weather during December and January prevented any large scale operations.

On 5th January 1944, Lieut.-General Sir Oliver Leese took over command of 8th Army. On 15th January, U.S. 5th Army started an offensive on the west, taking Monte Trocchio, overlooking the R. Rapido. On 17th January attacks were launched across the R. Garigliano, British troops of 5th Army being engaged. These made progress in the coastal sector, towards Minturno. Further inland, however, our forces remained on the left bank of the river.

On 22nd January, troops of U.S. 5th Army landed, with little opposition, on the coastal plain at Anzio, south of Rome. By 24th January, the beach-heads had been deepened, Anzio and Nettuno being cleared and occupied. Further inland, on the Garigliano front, the "Gustav Line" was broken into in the hill sector, north of Cassino.

On 3rd and 4th February the Germans launched the First Major Offensive against the Anzio beach-head. This was held after severe fighting. In the meantime operations were developing near Cassino and, on 13th February, the Italians in the Cassino Abbey were warned that it would be bombarded.

ARRIVAL OF 4TH DIVISION IN ITALY (*Map* 18)

Included in General Mark Clark's 5th Army was 10 (British) Corps, under Lieut.-General McCreery, consisting of 5th and 46th Divisions. Towards the end of February it was decided that 46th Division should move to the Middle East and be replaced by 4th Division, from Egypt.

The Order of Battle of 10 Corps, included:

5th Division: 201st Guards Brigade.
 13th, 15th and 17th Infantry Brigades.
46th Division: 1st Guards Brigade.
 128th, 138th and 139th Infantry Brigades.
Attached: 88th U.S. Division, from 2 U.S. Corps.

10 Corps was, at this time, operating on the Garigliano front.

The Order of Battle of 4th Division, included:

Commander: Major-General H. J. Hayman-Joyce, D.S.O.
10th Infantry Brigade: 2 Beds and Herts Regt.
 2 D.C.L.I.
 1/6 Surrey Regt.
12th Infantry Brigade: 2 Royal Fusiliers.
 6 Black Watch.
 1 Royal W. Kent Regt.
28th Infantry Brigade: Brigadier Purves.
 2 King's Regt.
 2 Somerset L.I.
 2/4 Hampshire Regt.

During the latter part of February and early March, 4th Division began to move to Italy and take over from 46th Division. On 21st February, 10th Infantry Brigade landed at Naples, together with H.Q., 4th Division. The latter moved to Sessa. On 7th March, 12th Infantry Brigade arrived and moved into the Galluchio area. On 15th March, 28th Infantry Brigade began to arrive at Naples.

On 15th March, 2 Somerset L.I. landed at Naples and moved to Le Vogie. B. Echelon was sent to Roccamofina. On 17th and 18th March, the Battalion prepared to go into the line in the Garigliano sector.

OPERATIONS ON THE R. GARIGLIANO

10 Corps was holding the line of the R. Garigliano from the sea, eastwards, with N.Z. Corps in the hills on its right. The left, or seaward, flank was thrown forward, across the river. The right flank was drawn back, on the left bank of the river. 4th Division took over from 46th Division from Rocca D'Evando on the right, to the main Naples–Formia road on the left.

Inland, the R. Garigliano runs in a wide level plain. As it nears the sea, it winds through a deep gorge, between the hilly country of Monte Croce on the east and Monte Tuga and Ovinto on the west. Having passed through this hill formation, it floods out into the coastal plain of Minturno. In this area there was a considerable bridgehead, several miles in depth.

4th Division, in taking over from 46th Division, was first disposed as under:

Right Sector: Hermon Force, K.D.G.s., 2/4 Hampshire Regt., reaching north from Masseriola.
Left Sector: across the R. Garigliano.
Right: 201st Guards Brigade (46th Division).
Centre: 10th Infantry Brigade.
Left: 12th Infantry Brigade.
Reserve: 28th Infantry Brigade.

On the right of Hermon Force was 78th Division. On the left of 4th Division, towards the sea, was 88th U.S. Division. 4th Division H.Q. was some 2 miles north of Sessa. The rôle of 4th Division was to simulate attacks, while N.Z. Corps, on the right of 10 Corps, attacked through Cassino when the weather permitted. A partially successful attack in the Cassino sector had developed on 15th March.

On 20th March, 28th Brigade, from reserve, with 2 Somerset L.I. relieved 10th Brigade in the centre of the left sector of the Division. 2 Somerset L.I. moved into what was known as the "Rotondo" sector, some 5 miles south of the junction of the R. Liri and R. Garigliano. Here it relieved 1/6 Surrey Regt. and was disposed as under:

Right forward: D company (Captain W. E. P. Watson)
Left forward: B company (Major H. J. Speed Andrews)
Reserve: C company (Captain C. G. Blackler)
A company (Captain C. D. Hill).

At this time Major C. R. Chetwynd-Stapylton was 2nd-in-Command; Lieut. A. G. Morgan i/c Mortar Platoon; and Captain the Rev. E. M. Hall, Chaplain.

Preparations were now put in hand to resume the offensive in the Garigliano Valley. On 21st March, 2 Somerset L.I. was engaged, under heavy mortar fire, in patrolling. A standing patrol under Lieut. Toms and night patrols under Lieuts. Strickland and R. A. Ostler, clashed with the enemy. The first battle casualties were Sergeant George and Private Tuckfield who were injured by anti-personnel mines. On 22nd March there were further successful actions by patrols under Lieuts. E. D. H. Forman and R. T. Stride.

The enemy was identified as 191st German Infantry Regt. and 71st Infantry Division.

On 25th March, 4th Division was relieved by 4th (Free French) D.M.M. 10th Brigade moved to Alvignano and 12th Brigade to Venafro. 28th Brigade was relieved on 27th March, 2 Somerset L.I. handing over to 1/2nd (Free French) R.T.M. and moving in lorries to the brigade area near Pietra Vaivano.

4th Division now left 10 Corps and was transferred to 13 Corps of 8th Army. On 29th March, 2 Somerset L.I. was visited by the 8th Army Commander, Lieut.-General Sir Oliver Leese, K.C.B., D.S.O.

30TH BATTALION (*Map* 4)

January 1944, in Sicily, was ushered in with heavy snow. During February, the Sabaudia Division of the Italian Liberation forces, from Sardinia, arrived in the Palermo area. The outlying detachments of 30th Battalion were relieved and withdrawn to Palermo itself. On 12th March, C company was relieved at the 10th Port, Palermo, by U.S. troops. On 14th March a warning order was received to prepare to move to Italy.

On 7th April, Jellalabad Day was celebrated according to custom, a special service being conducted by the Bishop of Gibraltar.

On 11th April the Battalion moved to Messina and next day crossed to Reggio by the ferry. Thence it moved to Taranto by train. Here it came under command of No. 6 Base Sub-area (Commander: Brigadier G. V. Palmer, D.S.O.). It now took over railway protection duties and the guarding of freight trains. Its area of responsibility was, Taranto—Brindisi—Bari—Foggia—Termoli—Ortona (railhead). This was the L.-of-C. of 8th Army, operating up the Adriatic coast. The Battalion was first disposed as under:

Battalion H.Q. and C company:	Bari
B company:	Taranto
D company:	Brindisi
A company:	Foggia—Termoli.

The area included responsibility for 22 marshalling yards as well as guards on military trains. Communications were difficult and a pigeon service was opened between Battalion H.Q. and all companies.

The Battalion was employed on train and railway guard duties until its disbandment nearly two years later. These included static guards on marshalling yards, mobile train guards, the prevention of pilfering and so forth.

In spite of heavy duties, there were opportunities for relaxation. A Battalion Dance Orchestra was started under Captain R. B. Holder. This was extremely successful. It broadcast from Bari Radio Station and was in great demand. During July it toured Foggia, Termoli and Vasto, for six days, to entertain the troops. Leave to Rest Camps in Italy was, also, opened. Between May and August, 28 Officers and 650 Other Ranks were granted leave to these camps. The climate on the Adriatic coast was hot during the summer and sea bathing was much appreciated.

CHAPTER XII

THE BATTLES OF NORMANDY—JUNE–AUGUST 1944

Operation Overlord—Plans for invasion of Normandy—Available forces for the initial landings—Enemy forces in France—German forces on the invasion coast—The airborne landings—6th Airborne Division—7th Battalion (L.I.)—First operations in Bois de Bavent area—General situation in Normandy at the end of June—43rd Wessex Division—Sea landings—First contact with the enemy—Crossing of R. Odon—Patrol activities—Operation Jupiter—The attack on Point 112—Operation Greenline—Offensive east of R. Orne—The capture of Maltot—The break-out—The attack on Briquessard—Operation Bluecoat—St. Pierre du Fresne—Plans for August—The attack on Mont Pincon—Crossing of R. Noireau—Battle of the Falaise Pocket—43rd Division front—Advance to R. Seine—Operation Neptune—Enlarging the bridgehead—6th Airborne Division—7th Battalion (L.I.), second operations in Bois de Bavent area—The advance eastwards—Return to England

CHAPTER X saw the 4th and 7th Battalions and 7th Battalion (L.I.) Para. Regt. prepared to leave England for the Normandy Landings. The 4th and 7th Battalions formed part of 43rd Wessex Division; 7th Battalion (L.I.) Para. Regt. formed part of 6th Airborne Division.

OPERATION OVERLORD—INVASION OF NORMANDY (*Map 2*)

The plans of 21st Army Group, consisting of 2nd British Army and 1st Canadian Army, were as follows:

Part I: The assault and breaking of the Atlantic Wall.
Part II: The link-up of the beach-heads and the build-up of the forces for the break-out.

D-day was 6th June 1944. On the night of 5th/6th June airborne landings were carried out by 82nd and 101st U.S. Airborne Divisions in the Cotentin Peninsula, on the west, and by 6th British Airborne Division, north-east of Caen, on the east. The sea landings took place on a 60-mile front on, and east of, the Cotentin (Cherbourg) Peninsula and as far east as Ouistreham, at the mouth of the R. Orne. The landings and beaches were as follows, from west to east:

1st U.S. Army: 7 Corps, Utah, on Cotentin Peninsula.
   5 Corps, Omaha, between Carentan and Port-en-Bessin.
2nd British Army: 30 Corps, Gold, from Port-en-Bessin to La Riviere.
   1 Corps, Juno, from La Riviere to Douvres and Sword, from Douvres to the mouth of the R. Orne.

After the initial landings, primary plans were as under:

1st U.S. Army: To over-run the Cotentin Peninsula, capture Cherbourg, develop operations southwards towards St. Lo, capture Rennes, wheel eastwards and break out across the R. Loire towards the R. Seine.

2nd British Army: To protect the left flank of 1st U.S. Army during the capture of Cherbourg by attacking German armour; to secure airfield sites south-east of Caen; thereafter to pivot on the hinge of the R. Orne, in co-operation with 1 U.S. Army and offer a strong front to any enemy attempt to obtain a lodgement from the east.

The initial beach-heads were to be extended southwards to the general line Carentan–Bayeux–Caen–Cabourg.

AVAILABLE FORCES FOR INITIAL LANDINGS

These were:

1st U.S. Army: 82nd and 101st Airborne Divisions.
7 Corps, 4th U.S. Division.
5 Corps, 1st and 29th U.S. Divisions.

2nd British Army: 6th Airborne Division.
30 Corps, 7th Armd. Division, 49th Infantry Division, 50th Infantry Division.
1 Corps, 3rd British Infantry Division, 3rd Canadian Infantry Division, 51st British Division, 27th, 33rd, 8th and 4th Armd. Brigades, 2nd Canadian Armd. Brigade.

The build-up of 2nd British Army included:

8 Corps: Guards Armd. Division.
11th Armd. Division.
15th Infantry Division.
31 Armd. Brigade.

12 Corps: 43rd Infantry Division.
53rd Infantry Division.
59th Infantry Division.
34 Armd Brigade.

2 Canadian Corps.

ENEMY FORCES IN FRANCE

These included:

XV Army, along the coast from the R. Seine, eastwards to Holland:
Six Field Divisions.
Three Panzer Divisions.
Eleven Lower Establishment Divisions.
One Training Division.

JUNE–AUGUST 1944

VII Army, along coast, from the R. Seine, westwards to Brest:
- Seven Field Divisions.
- Eight Lower Establishment Divisions.
- Three Panzer Divisions.

I Army, on Atlantic coast south of R. Loire:
- One Field Division.
- One Panzer Division.
- One Panzer Grenadier Division.
- One Lower Establishment Division.

XIX Army, on Mediterranean coast:
- Three Field Divisions.
- Two Panzer Divisions.
- Three Lower Establishment Divisions.

GERMAN FORCES ON THE INVASION COAST

On 6th June 1944, the enemy forces in position to oppose the landings included:

Cotentin Peninsula:	243, 709, 91 Infantry Divisions.
	6 Para Regt.
	30 Cyclist Brigade.
Carentan–Bayeux:	352 Infantry Division.
	84 Corps H.Q. (at St. Lo).
Arromanches–Caen:	716 Infantry Division.
South of Caen:	21 Panzer Division.
Caen–Harfleur:	711 Infantry Division.
Le Havre–Escamp:	345 Infantry Division.

Further south and east were:

Lisieux–Evreux:	12 S.S. Panzer Division.
South of Rouen:	116 Panzer Division.
Chartres:	Panzer Lehr Division.

THE AIRBORNE LANDINGS (*Map* 17)

With the story of the initial sea landings, this history is not concerned, since no unit of the Regiment was engaged in them. 6th Airborne Division, however, carried out the initial air landings on the night of 5th/6th June, near the mouth of the R. Orne, roughly in the area Ouistreham–Caen–Troarn–Cabourg.

6th Airborne Division included 5th Para Brigade, composed of 7th (L.I.), 12th and 13th Para Battalions.

At 0030 hours on 6th June a *coup de main* party of six gliders of 6th Airborne Division dropped near Benouville, to seize the bridges over the Canal de Caen and R. Orne. This operation was successful. Between 0100 hours and 0230 hours 3rd and 5th Para Brigades began to drop east of the R. Orne.

Simultaneously, 101st U.S. Airborne Division began to drop near Ste. Marie Eglise, in the Cotentin Peninsula. These two air landings protected the left and right flanks, respectively, of the sea landings.

On 5th June 1944, 7th Battalion (L.I.) reached Fairfield Airfield at 1900 hours. A short service was held by the Chaplain (Captain the Rev. Parry). A few hours later he was killed. At 2320 hours the Battalion took off.

The flight across the Channel was uneventful and, at 0100 hours on 6th June, the Battalion began to drop near Ranville. Shortly afterwards the drop was completed and the companies began to collect. Generally, the whole drop of 6th Airborne Division was more scattered than had been planned, though this misled the enemy as to the area and extent of the landings. In 7th Battalion (L.I.) many loads were dropped in the wrong places and one load was not dropped at all. Thus the Battalion went into action at less than one third strength and without its wireless sets, machine guns, P.I.A.T.S. or mortars.

By 0325 hours the Battalion was on its objectives at Le Port and Benouville, A and B companies being heavily counter-attacked. During these actions Captain the Rev. Parry, Lieuts. Bowyer and Hill and 16 Other Ranks were killed. Major Taylor, Captain Webber, Lieuts. Hunter and Temple and 38 Other Ranks were wounded. 170 Other Ranks were missing, some were dropped in the wrong place and some became casualties in the dropping zone.

In the meantime over 1,100 aircraft of Bomber Command had dropped nearly 6,000 tons of bombs on the coast batteries before dawn. On beach Sword, between Douvres and Ouistreham, in 1 Corps sector, 3rd British and 3rd Canadian Divisions, with 1st Commando Brigade began to come ashore about 0725 hours. The Commando Brigade was directed on Ouistreham and ordered to join 6th Airborne Division. 155th Infantry Brigade of 3rd British Division got ashore about midday and later came into action towards Franceville Plage and Cabourg.

At 1325 hours a battalion of Commandos passed through 7th Battalion (L.I.). In the evening a battalion of Royal Warwicks Regt. arrived and attacked towards Benouville at 2230 hours. During the whole of 6th June, 6th Airborne Division withstood a succession of heavy counter-attacks, but frustrated the enemy attempts to recapture Ranville and wipe out the Benouville bridgehead. During the afternoon 1st Commando Brigade came into action in attempts to extend the bridgehead, but was held on the line Breville–Sallanelles. About 2100 hours gliders of 6th Air Landing Brigade arrived and helped to strengthen the positions gained.

At 0015 hours on 7th June, 7th Battalion (L.I.) was relieved by a battalion of Royal Warwicks Regt. and came into brigade reserve. Odd parties, which had got lost in the landing, rejoined during the day. At 1330 hours a defensive position near the hamlet of Le Hom was occupied. During the 8th June heavy shelling and mortaring continued and, at 2100 hours, the seaborne portion of the Battalion arrived.

JUNE–AUGUST 1944

During the period between 0325 hours and 2230 hours on 6th June, the 7th Para. Battalion (L.I.) beat off with heavy loss eight German counter-attacks on the Benouville bridge-head. Most of these attacks were supported by tanks and self-propelled guns and were delivered by units of the 21st Panzer Division. The Battalion had no anti-tank guns and, as the 3-inch mortars and machine guns had been lost in the night drop, the Battalion had to defend its positions with small arms and P.I.A.T.S.

On 9th June the Battalion continued to hold on to its positions at Le Hom, under heavy shelling and sporadic counter-attacks. At 1111 hours a shell burst on Battalion H.Q., killing 3 Other Ranks and wounding 8. During the morning of 10th June an attack on the woods towards Le Mesnil (north-east of Bois de Bavent) was prepared. This was launched at 1535 hours and, by 1809 hours, had reached Le Mesnil. Major Neale and 10 Other Ranks were wounded. 90 enemy P.O.W. were taken. On 11th June heavy shelling of Le Mesnil continued. Lieut. Thomas was accidentally shot and wounded by a company sentry.

During this period 1 Corps had reached the line of the Caen–Bayeux road near Putot-en-Bessin and Bretteville-L'Orgeuilleuse, but attempts to take Caen had failed. It was evident that the enemy intended to defend the town fiercely. 30 Corps, further west, was engaged in heavy fighting in an attempt to thrust southwards through Tilly-sur-Seulles on Villers Bocage. 3rd British and 3rd Canadian Divisions were directed on Caen. East of the R. Orne, 6th Airborne Division held off all counter-attacks and took heavy toll of the enemy. 1st Commando Brigade secured Franceville Plage, but Cabourg was still strongly held by the enemy.

On 12th June, at 1502 hours, A company, 7th Battalion (L.I.) moved west to support 1st Canadian Infantry Brigade. At 1030 hours on 13th June the Battalion took up a position at Herouvillette, being rejoined by A and C companies from Le Mesnil. Here it was heavily shelled and bombed, losing, between 13th and 15th June, 1 Other Rank killed and 9 wounded. C company was approached by tanks. On 16th June the Battalion position was heavily attacked, but the enemy infantry were contained in a small wood by the accurate fire of C company. They were later wiped out by a counter-attack launched by A company under Captain Parrish. Casualties were 2 Other Ranks killed and 4 wounded. At 0900 hours, C company attacked a small wood near its area, Lieut. Macdonald and 3 Other Ranks being wounded.

FIRST OPERATIONS IN BOIS DE BAVENT AREA

On 17th June, at 0700 hours, the Battalion moved to a defensive position south-east of Le Mesnil in what was known as the Bois de Bavent sector. This was a very unsavoury area for the enemy was very active and shelling intense. Just forward of the position was a group of buildings known as Bob's Farm, so called after Captain "Bob" Keen who commanded C company. At 1440 hours this was successfully raided by B company, who returned at 1630 hours with 6 P.O.W. In this raid Captain Parrish, Lieuts. Farr and Pool and 16 Other Ranks were wounded and 2 Other Ranks killed.

The 18th June saw more heavy shelling. The enemy in the sector was identified as 858 Panzer Grenadier Regt. On 19th and 20th June active patrolling continued in conjunction with an Independent Para Company. 2 Other Ranks were killed and Major Bartlett wounded by mortar-fire. On 21st June 2 Other Ranks were killed and Major Tullis and 6 Other Ranks wounded.

On 22nd June, A and B companies changed over positions. C company was relieved by C company, 12th Para Battalion and withdrawn to rest. Patrolling, shelling and mortaring continued until 25th June, when 7th Battalion (L.I.) was relieved by 8th Para Battalion at 1615 hours and moved to a rest area, west of the hamlet of Ecarde.

Between 25th and 29th June 3 Officers and 100 Other Ranks, without battle experience, were absorbed from the K.S.L.I. On 29th June Lieut. Macdonald died of wounds at No. 86 Base General Hospital and was buried, with Lieut. Hill, at Ranville.

THE GENERAL SITUATION IN NORMANDY AT THE END OF JUNE

Between the 7th and 12th June the *First Phase* of the link-up of the beach-heads was accomplished. On the west, U.S. troops pushed across the R. Vire and R. Aure, reaching Rubercy on 9th June. On 8th June they linked up with 50th British Division near Bayeux.

1 British Corps pressed on to objectives on the Bayeux–Caen road, while 12 Corps advanced in the centre and, by 12th June had reached the line La Belle Épine–Tilly–Cristot–Brouay. East of the R. Orne, 6th Airborne Division and 1st Commando Brigade maintained the bridgehead. By 12th June, 51st Infantry Division was arriving in this area.

Between 13th and 18th June the *Second Phase* of the expansion of the beach-head area took place. On the west 7 and 8 U.S. Corps drove across the Cotentin Peninsula to Barneville, sealing off Cherbourg. Carentan and Isigny were taken and 19 and 5 U.S. Corps began to thrust southwards on St. Lo and Caumont. 7th Armd. Division of 30 British Corps developed an attack towards Villers Bocage, with 50th and 49th Infantry Divisions directed on Tilly-sur-Seulles. This was designed to produce a pincer movement to the south of Caen, where 1 Corps maintained pressure from the north. Operations were slowed by bad weather which delayed unloading of supplies and ammunition on the beaches.

Between 19th and 30th June, the *Third Phase* was carried out. This included the capture of Cherbourg and the establishment of a bridgehead over the R. Odon. In 2nd British Army sector, the main thrust was made by 30 Corps, with 49th Division directed on Tessel Bretteville and Noyers. 8 Corps, further east, was to advance through 3rd Canadian Division (1 Corps) and form a bridgehead over the R. Odon near Gavrus and Baron. 1 Corps was to eliminate the enemy salient north of Caen and then clear the town.

JUNE–AUGUST 1944

On 23rd June, 51st Division of 1 Corps took St. Honorine. 49th Division of 30 Corps advanced on 25th June and took Brettevillette on 28th June. 8 Corps attacked on 26th June and crossed the R. Odon near Baron on 27th June. It is with these operations of 8 Corps that the subsequent narrative is concerned.

43RD WESSEX DIVISION—LANDING IN NORMANDY (*Map* 13)

The emblem of 43 Wessex Division was the Wessex Wyvern. Under this standard the mythical Uther and King Arthur are said to have fought. Alfred the Great is said to have refused to furl it and King Harold fell beneath it at Hastings. It was a most suitable badge for the men of the Western Counties and they maintained and enhanced its reputation.

43rd Infantry Division was commanded by Major-General G. I. Thomas, C.B., D.S.O., M.C., and included:

129th Infantry Brigade (Brigadier Mole, D.S.O.):
    4 Somerset L.I.
    4 Wilts Regt.
    5 Wilts Regt.
130th Infantry Brigade (Brigadier Leslie):
    7 Hampshire Regt.
    4 Dorset Regt.
    5 Dorset Regt.
214th Infantry Brigade (Brigadier H. Essame, M.C.):
    7 Somerset L.I.
    1 Worcs. Regt.
    5 D.C.L.I.

The Division formed part of 12 Corps. But during the early operations it was attached to 8 Corps and, at one period, later, to 30 Corps.

Early in June 1944, 43rd Division was on the Kent and Sussex coast. It concentrated in the area behind Newhaven, from which port the fighting troops sailed. Vehicles and transport sailed from London. On 18th June the 4th and 7th Battalions embarked at Newhaven, but sailing was delayed by bad weather. The convoy proceeded first to the Solent, where it was marshalled and then sailed across the Channel. The wind had gone down but there was a swell. In spite of this few men were seasick. On the voyage many V-1 projectiles were seen and some were shot down. The convoy arrived off beach Juno on 19th June and landings were completed by 24th June. Many troops had to come ashore in water up to their waists.

Divisional H.Q. landed at Courseulles-sur-Mer; the 4th Battalion at Arromanches, where it got ashore dry; the 7th Battalion at La Riviere, the landing being controlled by Major E. J. Bruford.

The march to the concentration area was a hard one, over roads thick with dust and congested by traffic. The 4th Battalion reached Ryes on 19th

June and the 7th Battalion Rucqueville on 25th June. The troops were mainly in bivouacs near the villages and the sounds of heavy fighting drifted across the woods and fields from the direction of Caen. On 23rd June Lieut.-Colonel Curtis, of the 4th Battalion, fell ill and Lieut.-Colonel C. G. Lipscomb assumed command.

FIRST CONTACT WITH THE ENEMY (Map 14)

The Battle for Normandy had by now reached the *Third Phase*, as already described. The task for 2nd British Army was to establish a bridgehead over the R. Odon. 43rd Division, temporarily under 8 Corps, was to take part in this, carrying out Operation Epsom, due to start on 25th June. The plan was to force crossings over the R. Odon and R. Orne, and obtain control of the high ground north-east of Bretteville-sur-Laize, which overlooks the Caen–Falaise road and dominates the exits from Caen to the south. *Phase I* of this operation required 43rd Division to move up in rear of 15th (Scottish) Division to the area Cheux–St. Mauvieu.

15th (S) Division included 44th (Lowland), 46th (Highland) and 227th (Highland) Infantry Brigades. The enemy on 8 Corps front was identified as 1st, 9th and 10th (S.S.) Panzer Divisions.

On 25th June the 4th Battalion (129th Brigade) moved to an area 1 mile west of Brecy, being given a counter-attack rôle. The fields nearby, in the height of summer, were full of ripening corn, the peasants still gathering in hay and tending cattle. On 26th June the Battalion moved over roads and tracks choked with traffic and took over from a reserve battalion of 15th (S) Division, at St. Mauvieu, near Norrey-en-Bessin. Here it was given a counter-attack rôle towards Cheux. On 27th June the whole area was heavily shelled. R.S.M. Holt was wounded and replaced by C.S.M. Smith, who served as R.S.M. for the rest of the campaign. 2 P.O.W. were taken here, both belonging to S.S. Panzer Engineers.

In the meantime the 7th Battalion (214th Brigade) moved, on 27th June, through the Guards Armd. Division, to Cheux. On 28th June it occupied Hill 100, near Cheux, in relief of 7 Seaforths of 15th (S) Division.

During this relief of 15th (S) Division, by 43rd Division, there was great difficulty, owing to the congestion of transport on the roads and the heavy shelling, in locating units, in contact with the enemy, to be relieved. Much of the movement had to be done at night to avoid observation.

When the 7th Battalion reached Cheux it was under heavy shell-fire and threatened by Tiger tanks. During the night, 11th Armd. Division entered the area. 7 Somerset L.I. was, later, relieved by a battalion of the Welsh Guards. During the relief, the combined H.Q. was hit by a shell, resulting in many casualties. It was during this period that the Battalion first encountered the German mortar known as "Moaning Minnie". This threw a very unpleasant bomb.

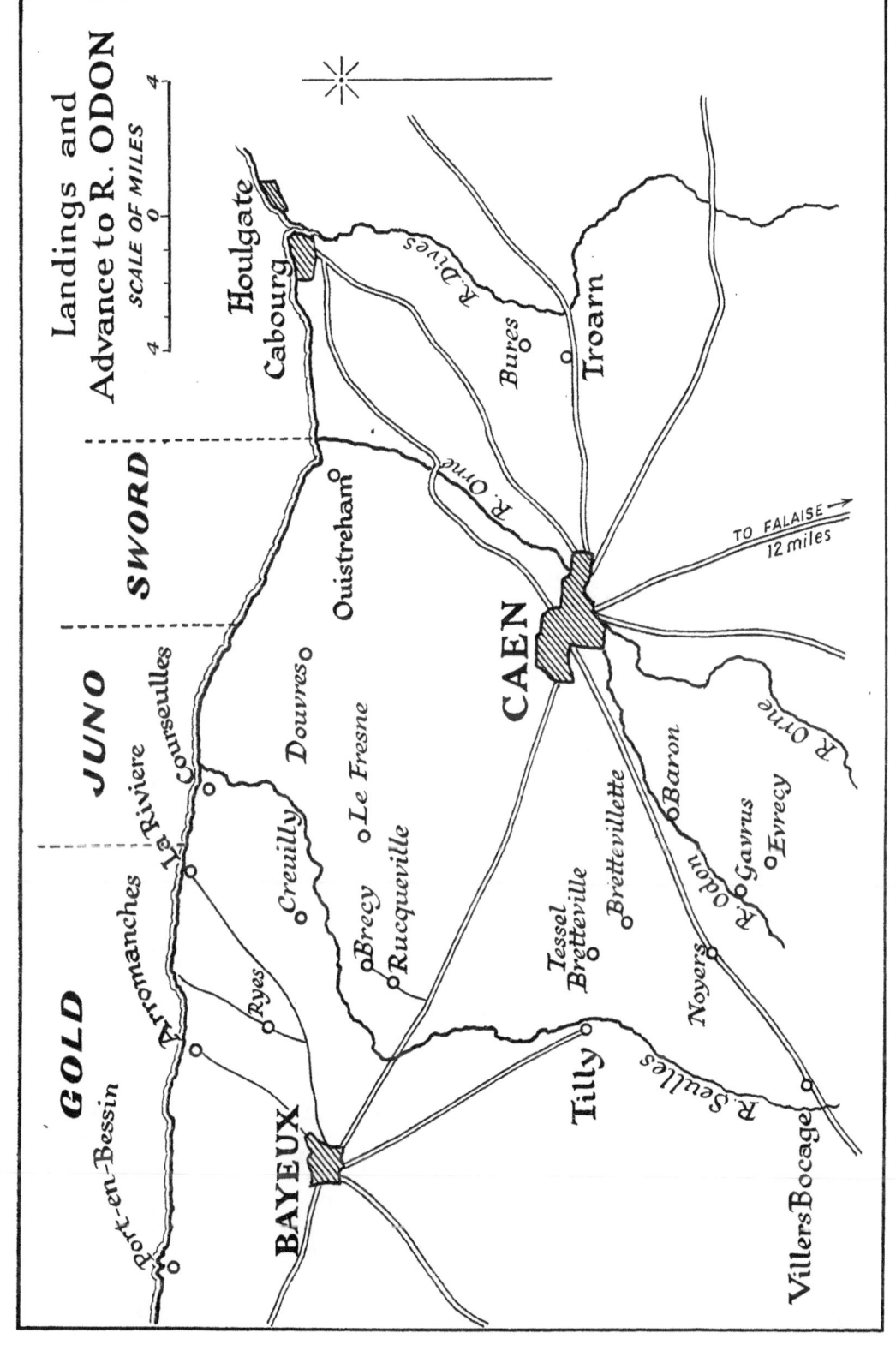

JUNE–AUGUST 1944

CROSSING OF R. ODON BY 4TH BATTALION

During the 28th and 29th June both 4th and 7th Battalions were engaged in patrolling, while enemy shelling continued. On 29th June, 129th Brigade cleared some woods near St. Mauvieu and then crossed the R. Odon. The Brigade advanced on a two-battalion front, with 5 Wilts Regt. on right, 4 Somerset L.I. on left, and 4 Wilts Regt. in reserve.

At 1100 hours the advance started and the Brigade gained some 4,000 yards on the axis Cheux–Mouen–Tourville–Baron. Opposition was slight. The first bridgehead was formed across the R. Odon, with C and D Companies, 4 Somerset L.I. forward on the road Baron–Fontaine Etoupefour. The river here flows through a gorge and the tanks with the Battalion were unable to cross. During this advance the Adjutant, Captain Burfield, was wounded and Captain Reader took his place. 214th Brigade also advanced and by 1700 hours both 4 and 7 Somerset L.I. were in the area Mouen–Tourville. Here defensive positions were occupied under heavy shell-fire.

PATROL ACTIVITIES

Between 1st and 5th July, both Battalions were engaged in patrol activities under heavy shell-fire. In the 4th Battalion area, D company carried out a local attack on 2nd July, but was checked by artillery-fire. Major Vickers was injured by the over-turning of a Jeep. Lieut. Green (Pioneer Officer) was also wounded at this time.

Two gallant patrol actions were carried out by 4 Somerset L.I. at this time. On 3rd July, Lance-Corporal R. Payne and Private W. Blois obtained valuable information about the enemy at Fontaine Etoupefour. 2 S.S. Panzer Grenadier Regt. and the Adolf Hitler Division had already been identified on the Battalion front. On 4th July a patrol under Lieut. R. V. Pinkham reached high ground forward of the Battalion positions and brought back a wounded man and a prisoner—the first taken on the Divisional front for some days. Lieut. Pinkham later received the M.C. for this exploit. On 5th July, 4 Somerset L.I. was relieved by 4 Wilts Regt., withdrawing some 1,500 yards into brigade reserve.

7 Somerset L.I. was heavily mortared in the Tourville–Mouen area and, on 3rd July, Lieut.-Colonel Besley was wounded. His place was taken by Lieut.-Colonel G. C. P. Lance, D.S.O. At this time Captain A. F. Scannall was Adjutant. Lieut. Warner, with the mortar platoon, moved to the vicinity of Verson, firing 500 rounds into the village in three minutes, before withdrawing. Major C. W. S. Young took out a fighting patrol of D company and engaged the enemy before returning. For this he was, later, awarded the M.C. On 7th July the Battalion moved into a position near Verson and dug in on a reverse slope. In this area the Battalion seems to have fed well, for it is recorded that there was abundance of rabbits, chickens, vegetables, currants and raspberries, as well as lump sugar and cider.

OPERATION JUPITER

At the end of June the general position was as follows. The enemy had committed 21 Panzer, 12 S.S. and the Panzer Lehr Divisions. A bridgehead had been established over the R. Odon. 1 Corps had made little progress against Caen. The over-all plan was now to pin and fight the enemy between Villers-Bocage and Caen, while the main U.S. thrust swung southwards and then east to the Le Mans–Alençon area and beyond. The intention was to cut the enemy line of withdrawal from Normandy through the Paris–Orleans gap and force him back against the R. Seine, below Paris.

During the early part of July, 8 Corps Operation Jupiter was planned. This was part of a series of thrusts, delivered by 2nd British Army, with the primary object of making progress southwards towards Thury Harcourt, pressure being maintained on as broad a front as possible.

At this time 2nd British Army was disposed as under:

Right: 30 Corps directed on Hottot and Noyers.
Right Centre: 12 and 8 Corps on line of R. Odon, directed on Evrecy and Maltot.
Left Centre: 2 Canadian Corps directed on Caen.
Left: 1 Corps and 6th Airborne Division, holding ground between Caen and the sea, east of R. Orne.

The task of 8 Corps was to contain the maximum number of enemy divisions and assist in the capture of Caen. 43rd Division, in the left sector of 8 Corps, was directed to secure the high ground between the R. Odon and R. Orne, up to the general line St. Martin Vieux–Feugorolles–Maltot.

On 10th July, 43rd Division, with a tank brigade attached, launched the attack towards Pt. 112, on the Evrecy–Caen road, and Maltot, in the R. Orne valley.

THE ATTACK ON PT. 112

129th Brigade was detailed for this attack. The plan was for 4 Somerset L.I. to attack the hill, while 5 Wilts moved up on the right and 4 Wilts Regt. on the left.

Pt. 112 is a slight rise on the top of a ten-acre plateau, the sides of which slope gently. Apart from a few hedges and a small wood, the whole area was, at the time, covered with standing corn. The plateau is a salient commanding observation over the R. Orne, but is itself under observation from three sides and the approaches afford little cover from view.

During 8th July there had been heavy British artillery fire on Carpiquet and 4 Somerset L.I. awaited the results of a Canadian attack in the Caen sector before advancing. On 9th July, at 1700 hours, the Battalion relieved 4 Wilts Regt. east of the R. Odon.

The Battalion plan for the attack on Pt. 112, supported by a squadron of Sherman tanks, was B and A companies forward and D and C companies in support. Each company had one troop of tanks. It was a "set piece" attack. The assault was covered by the fire of the artillery of two Corps, as well as 3-in. and 4·2-in. mortar concentrations.

At 0350 hours on 10th July the mortar and artillery concentrations opened and at 0500 hours the attack began. An eye-witness has described the attack as follows : ". . . it was more as one imagines a battle to be than any other I have seen. It was just beginning to get light and the whole scene was illuminated by burning carriers and tanks. Flame-throwers were in action. The enemy, using Nebelwerfers, was mortaring the advancing troops. Practically every weapon was in action—rifles, grenades, phosphorous, L.M.G.s and Tanks and the casualties were extremely heavy. Our mortars fired some 5,000 rounds." The first objective was the line of a road from Esquay, eastwards through Pt. 112 to some bushes, 200 yards west of the Croix de Filandrieres on the Evrecy-Eterville road. In spite of the strong artillery support there was much opposition and Pt. 112 was not reached. Casualties were very heavy. Captain K. M. Forward, Lieuts. L. W. Roper and F. Riley and 13 Other Ranks were killed. Majors E. A. Trotman, C. T. Stewart and L. D. Wardle, Lieuts. Deacon, Cherrett, Cox, Thomson, Shuttleworth and Pinkham and 100 Other Ranks were wounded. 67 Other Ranks were missing. 14 P.O.W. were taken and 3 Tiger, 1 Panther and 1 Mark IV tanks were destroyed. A company lost all its officers and was, for some time, commanded by Sergeant Brewster.

It should be noted that the attack was over 1,500 yards of open country and was under observation of the enemy for the whole distance. On reaching the first objective at least 100 S.S. were dead in their slit trenches and two enemy anti-tank guns with their crews accounted for. But the Battalion was now, in the opinion of the Commanding Officer, too weak to attempt any further advance in the face of such fanatical opposition.

For the 4th Battalion this was by far the most unpleasant and bloodiest battle of the whole campaign. The battalion which had sailed from England was virtually destroyed and another created on the battlefield. An intimate and detailed account of the action is given on pp. 19–23 of the Battalion history of the Campaign in North-west Europe, 1944–45. After the war the 43rd Divisional War Memorial was erected on Hill 112 and is sited at the spot, beside the Eterville-Evrecy road, where 4th Battalion O.P. was established in a ditch during the battle.

At 1700 hours 5 D.C.L.I. attacked through 4 Somerset L.I. but failed to reach Pt. 112. This battalion also suffered many casualties, including the C.O., Lieut.-Colonel R. W. James. It only succeeded in reaching what was later known as "Cornwall Wood" and was withdrawn through 4 Somerset L.I. during the night.

At 0200 hours on 11th July, 4 Somerset L.I. forward localities on the line of the Evrecy–Eterville road were over-run by two Tiger tanks. One was hit by a 17-pounder, but got away. During the day the positions were held, though counter-attacked by an infantry battalion with tanks. This attack was broken up by artillery defensive fire. Heavy shelling and mortaring continued all day.

In the meantime the attack of 130th Brigade on Maltot had failed and the forward line of that brigade continued eastwards from the Pt. 112 plateau. 214th Brigade, with 7 Somerset L.I. had been in reserve near Haut Verson and Le Douns. On 10th July the Battalion took up a temporary defensive position near Chateau de Fontaine, coming under command of 130th Brigade. 4 Dorset Regt. had just captured this area and gone on to attack Maltot.

On 11th July, 7 Somerset L.I. area was heavily shelled and mortared and attacked by Tiger tanks. The Commanding Officer and 2nd-in-Command of the 7th Hampshires were visiting Battalion H.Q. 7 Somerset L.I. to liase concerning the relief of 7 Somerset L.I. which was due to take place the same evening. An unlucky shell hit the building in which the conference was taking place and killed the Acting Commanding Officer of 7 Somerset L.I., and the Commanding Officer and 2nd-in-Command of 7th Hampshires. The Intelligence Officer and the entire Intelligence Section, 7 Somerset L.I. were wounded, and there were many other casualties amongst key personnel. Captain W. H. Goudie the Adjutant, assumed temporary command and sent for Major W. M. J. Chalmers (then O.C. B Company) to take over command. Despite the very heavy casualties Major Chalmers with great personal courage and coolness effected the relief successfully within a few hours of the incident. For this he was subsequently awarded a Croix de Guerre (Gilt Star). Major E. J. Bruford took over command. Confused fighting and heavy artillery shelling, causing many casualties, continued during the 11th and 12th July.

On 12th July, 129th Brigade started to move forward. At 0100 hours, 4 Somerset L.I. advanced, D company attempting to infiltrate forward. This attack was met by heavy fire and failed. The casualties during 12th July were 20 Other Ranks killed, 17 Other Ranks missing and 5 Officers and 4 Other Ranks wounded. Several enemy counter-attacks were made, but the ground gained on the plateau was held.

On 13th July, 4 Somerset L.I. was relieved, at 2300 hours, by 4 Wilts Regt. and moved back as Divisional counter-attack battalion.

On the same day, in 130th Brigade area, 7 Somerset L.I. was relieved by 7 Hampshire Regt. and moved back to the neighbourhood of Miebord. During the relief Battalion H.Q. was hit by a shell. Major E. J. Bruford and the C.O. of 7 Hampshire Regt. were killed. On 14th July Lieut.-Colonel J. W. Nicol assumed command of the Battalion from the Oxfs. and Bucks. L.I.

In the meantime, further west, 50th and 49th Divisions had made some progress in 30 Corps sector, advancing towards Hottot. To the east, on 1 Corps front, 51st Division attacked Colombelles, a suburb east of Caen. During 12th and 13th July, 12 Corps took over 8 Corps sector, while 2 Canadian Corps took station between 12 Corps and 1 Corps.

Both 30 Corps and 12 Corps resumed the offensive on 15th July. 30 Corps was directed on the high ground north-east of Villers-Bocage, while 12 Corps was to secure the line Bougy–Evrecy–Maizet. 12 Corps had in view a subsequent advance on Aunay-sur-Odon and Thury Harcourt. These operations were designed to draw off enemy formations from 1st U.S. Army front and gain more depth on the centre and left of 2nd British Army.

OPERATION GREENLINE

43rd Division, now back in 12 Corps, was detailed for Operation Greenline, its task being to cover the left flank of 15th (S) Division. On 15th July, 15th (S) Division passed through 43rd Division and attacked, supported by artillery, and the massed mortars of 129th Brigade. Further east 2 Canadian Corps began to attack towards Caen. During 16th July, 43rd Division was allotted counter-attack rôles.

While leading a deep patrol into the Verson area, Lieut. P. Mercier, a French-Canadian officer with the 7th Battalion, was badly wounded by a German patrol. Private Evers, his escort, promptly shot his assailants and drove off the remainder. He then carried his officer back to safety. Unfortunately Evers was killed a few days later. Lieut. A. C. A. White, on a similar patrol, was very badly wounded. Private Homer carried him back to Verson and then twice returned to his own lines to get assistance. For this act of gallantry he was awarded the Military Medal.

About this time 4 Somerset L.I. received reinforcements of 12 Officers and 394 Other Ranks. Since the start of operations it had received 19 Officers and 479 Other Ranks as reinforcements, which indicates the severity of the fighting. The battalion which landed in France had, virtually, ceased to exist. Indeed, it was said that Colonel Curtis' battalion went up to Pt. 112 and Colonel Lipscomb's battalion returned.

On 17th July, at 2000 hours, 7 Somerset L.I. was relieved by 5 D.C.L.I. near Miebord and moved up to relieve 4 Wilts R. near Pt. 112. 4 Somerset L.I. moved back to the north end of Fontaine Etoupefour, where Major W. Q. Roberts joined as 2nd-in-Command.

On 18th July, 53rd Division delivered an unsuccessful attack on Evrecy. Confused fighting continued over the whole area, 7 Somerset L.I. being near Tournay, with A, B and C companies forward. Up to now, in spite of severe fighting, neither 12, nor 30 Corps had made much progress. The enemy had been forced, however, to pull back three Panzer Divisions into the line. Only one Panzer Division was left in reserve, refitting in the woods north of Falaise. In addition, 1st U.S. Army had been enabled to make ground and had now occupied St. Lo and high ground west of the R. Vire. The stage was set for the break-out.

OFFENSIVE EAST OF R. ORNE

The major plan was now for 8 Corps to cross the R. Orne, west of Caen, through 1 Corps bridgehead, while 2 Canadian Corps crossed, north of Caen, near Colombelles, to open up the suburbs and secure the south-eastern exits from the town. Caen had been taken on 9th July. Attacks began on 18th July and, after making good initial progress, were slowed down by strong opposition and bad weather. By the evening of 20th July the line in this sector ran through Bourgebus–Cagny and the outskirts of Troarn. The enemy had thrown in all available reserves.

In 43rd Division area, 129th Brigade took over from 4th Canadian Brigade in the Eterville area. 4 Somerset L.I. relieved the Canadian Scottish for a further advance on Maltot and came into brigade reserve. In 214th Brigade area, 7 Somerset L.I. was relieved by 5 D.C.L.I. on 22nd July and also came into brigade reserve.

THE CAPTURE OF MALTOT

On 22nd July, 43rd Division launched Operation Express. 129th Brigade attacked Maltot, starting at 1730 hours on 23rd July and occupied the town. On the same day, Operation Pullman to link up 129th and 214th Brigades was only partially successful. On 24th July a patrol of 4 Somerset L.I. under Lieut. P. N. L. Priani and Corporal Ball, went out through the enemy lines and returned on 26th July. Owing to very heavy shelling it was not able to get much information. On 25th July, 4 Somerset L.I. was relieved by 1 R.W.F. (53rd Division) and moved back to Verson. On 26th July, 214th Brigade also moved back, 7 Somerset L.I. going first to Mouen and then to a rest area at Conde-sur-Seulles. This move of 43rd Division westwards was in preparation for further operations towards Mont Pincon.

THE BREAK-OUT (*Map* 15)

The start of the break-out was planned for 24th July, but a false start was made and it was delayed until 25th July. The general plan was for 1st U.S. Army to break out from the St. Lo sector, thereafter swinging east. In the meantime 2 Canadian Corps was to press on towards Falaise, while 30 and 12 Corps maintained pressure in the centre.

In 30 and 12 Corps there was some regrouping of Divisions, 43rd Division moving north-westwards from the Mouen–Tourville area. On 29th July, 7 Somerset L.I., with 214th Brigade, moved up from near Conde-sur-Seulles, to the line near La Poterie. The same day, 4 Somerset L.I. moved from a rest area near Duoy St. Marguerite, to relieve 12 K.R.R.C. (8th Armd. Division) at Livry. Here it came under command of 130th Brigade and, at 0800 hours, on 30th July, attacked Briquessard and a bridge near the village.

THE ATTACK ON BRIQUESSARD

At 0800 hours, 4 Somerset L.I. with one troop of tanks, advanced with D and C companies forward. 5 Dorset Regt. attacked on the right and elements of 50th Division on the left. By 1005 hours the leading companies were within 200 yards of the objective. The advance then became disorganised

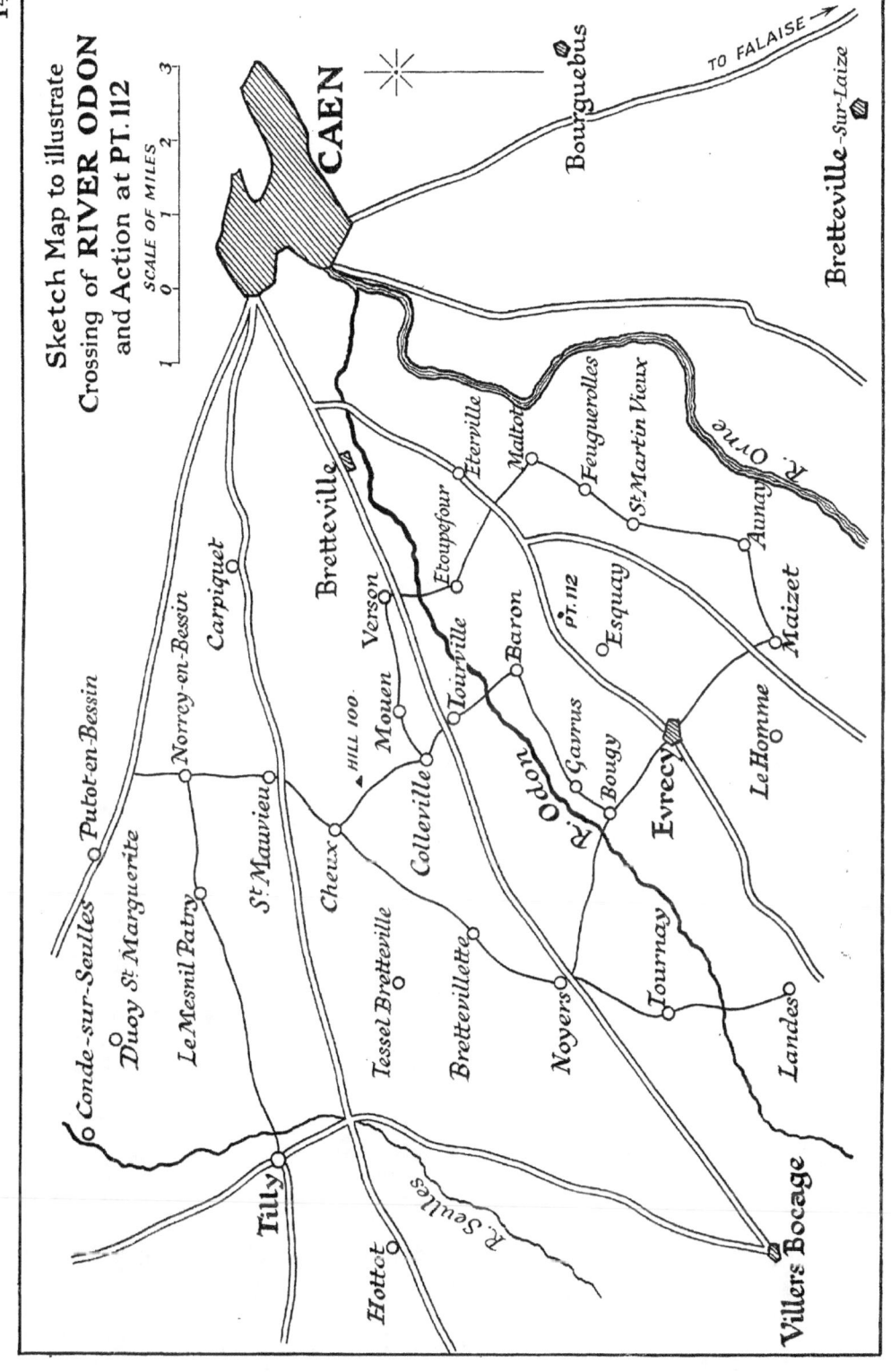

JUNE–AUGUST 1944

owing to the presence of many A.T. and "Schu" mines in the fields and hedges. Sergeant Hayman, with the Pioneers, lifted some 50 mines under fire and was later awarded the M.M. for this exploit. Close support by air kept enemy heads down and by 1300 hours all companies were on their objectives. B company then passed through and secured the bridge at La Trangule, Lieut. Spenser being killed by a sniper while crossing the bridge. In this action Lieut. Gordon Wright and Sergeant Partridge, leading platoons of D company, distinguished themselves. The former received the M.C., the latter the M.M.

Major Braithwaite, the last surviving original Rifle Company Commander, was badly wounded but remained long enough in Command to see his Company on to their objective. He was awarded the M.C. for his conduct of the battle.

On the right of 4 Somerset L.I. 5 Dorset Regt. was checked before reaching its objective. On the left, the attack of 50th Division failed to materialise. Thus 4 Somerset L.I. was thrust forward in a salient, in very close country. Aggressive tactics were adopted to check enemy infiltration and C company staged a local attack on the left, to gain more room. By 2100 hours the situation became easier and the night was quiet. During the action Lieut. Stephens was wounded. Casualties among Other Ranks amounted to over 60, mostly from accurate sniping fire. On 31st July, the Battalion was relieved, at 2100 hours, by two squadrons of 43rd Divisional Reconnaissance Regt. and moved back to Livry. In the meantime, however, at 1300 hours, D company had attacked forward and taken 29 P.O.W. Altogether, 61 P.O.W. were taken during the two day action.

OPERATION BLUECOAT

On 30th July, 43rd Division was concentrating for Operation Bluecoat. The first phase of this had been completed by the capture of Briquessard and the bridge at La Trangule. The second phase entailed the capture of Cahanges.

ST. PIERRE DU FRESNE

On 31st July, 214th Brigade, with 7 Somerset L.I., moved to Caumont, with orders to attack through Les Haies cross-roads on Cahanges. After some last minute changes in the plan, 7 Somerset L.I. crossed the start line at 2230 hours and advanced in the darkness to the cross-roads at Le Bon Homme, later reaching the objective, St. Pierre du Fresne, with little opposition. Here the Battalion dug in, on the morning of 1st August. Very soon, in the growing light, a large body of enemy infantry, with a Tiger tank, was seen, in a valley, forming up for a counter-attack. The tank was fired on by Lieut. Pizzey and Lance-Corporal Johnson and hit, but not disabled. Artillery defensive fire was called for and came down on the enemy causing heavy casualties. But the attack came in and, aided by the Tiger tank, over-ran a forward section post. It was checked by rifle-fire controlled by Corporal MacClernon, while Lance-Corporal Johnson, with a P.I.A.T., got a second shot at the Tiger tank and knocked it out. It was found to be a self-propelled gun, known as a

"Ferdinand". The enemy then withdrew, having been severely mauled. In this action, 7 Somerset L.I. lost 4 Other Ranks killed and 7 wounded.

In the meantime Cahanges had been taken, on 31st July, by 130th Brigade. This completed *Phase Three* of Operation Bluecoat. During July, 43rd Division had taken 886 P.O.W. and destroyed 45 tanks and 14 aircraft.

PLANS FOR AUGUST

The advance by 1st U.S. Army had gone well. 2nd British Army was now regrouped to thrust southwards from the Caumont area. The main attack was to be made by 30 Corps on Villers-Bocage–Aunay-sur-Odon, while 8 Corps was directed on the Vire–Tinchebray–Conde-sur-Noireau triangle. Operations were then to hinge on 12 Corps, operating southwards, east of Villers-Bocage. The line-up, therefore, of 2nd British Army, from west to east was, 8 Corps—30 Corps—12 Corps—2 Canadian Corps.

The advance started on 30 Corps front on 30th July. The Divisions from west to east were 43rd, 7th Armoured and 50th. 43rd Division was directed on the hills west of Jurques, 7th Armoured on Aunay-sur-Odon and 50th Division on the hills west of Villers-Bocage.

On 1st August 43rd Division was ordered to capture Ondefontaine and be prepared to secure Mont Pincon. At 0945 hours 4 Somerset L.I. moved from Livry, through La Landes and in the evening relieved 1 Worcs. Regt. at Canteloupe. Here it was in the assembly area for the attack on Mont Pincon. By the evening of 2nd August, 43rd Division was concentrated in the neighbourhood of Jurques. On 3rd August the attack on Mont Pincon began.

THE ATTACK ON MONT PINCON (*Map* 16)

The Division attacked with 129th Brigade on the right, 214th Brigade in the centre, directed on Mont Pincon and 130th Brigade on the left, directed on Ondefontaine. The order of attack for 214th Brigade was 5 D.C.L.I., 1 Worcs. Regt., 7 Somerset L.I.

At 0200 hours on 3rd August, 5 D.C.L.I. crossed the start line. Progress was very slow and 7 Somerset L.I. remained at St. Pierre du Fresne all day. During the night 3rd/4th August 5 D.C.L.I. attacked Le Mesnes Auzouf and 1 Worcs. Regt. reached La Cabosse.

On 4th August 7 Somerset L.I. moved forward and by 1800 hours had reached Montany. In the meantime 214th Brigade attacked again at 1400 hours, gaining further ground near La Cabosse and Les Maisons. At 1800 hours, 129th Brigade was ordered to capture Mont Pincon.

During 4th August, 4 Somerset L.I. (129th Brigade) concentrated at St. Pierre du Fresne and was joined by the tank squadron of 13th/18th Hussars. At 2100 hours it began to move south, preparations being made for the assault on Mont Pincon, which was timed for 6th August.

On 5th August, 130th Brigade made progress and by 1340 hours had taken Ondefontaine. 129th Brigade was moving up. At 1230 hours

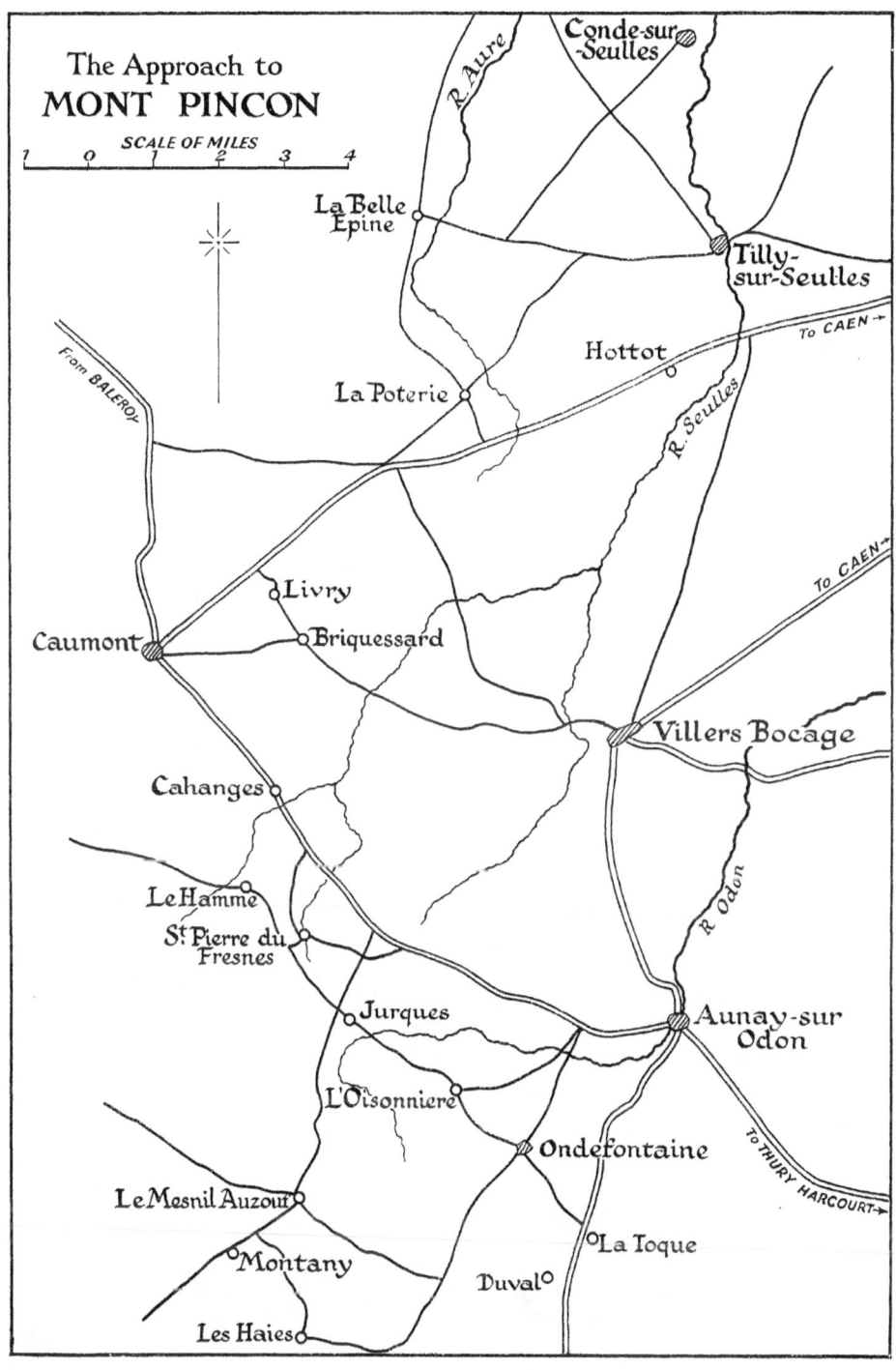

4 Somerset L.I. was checked by a blown bridge at St. Jean Le Blanc. There was heavy shelling and some casualties. By 2100 hours the bridge was repaired and the battalion moved on to Duval.

On 6th August, 129th and 214th Brigades attacked Mont Pincon, assisted by 8th Armd. Brigade. 129th Brigade plan was to attack with 5 Wilts Regt. on right, 4 Somerset L.I. on left and 4 Wilts Regt. in reserve. The axis of the attack was the road La Toque–La Rougerie—Pt. 365.

Mont Pincon completely dominates the surrounding country, much as the Quantock Hills dominate Taunton Vale. The lower slopes are cultivated, but the higher slopes are thickly wooded.

At 1230 hours on 6th July, 4 Somerset L.I. received orders to attack and advanced with A and C companies forward and B and D companies in support. The start line was crossed at 1500 hours. The day was extremely hot and the men fought in their shirt-sleeves. Leading companies were checked, almost at once, by light automatic fire in enfilade. The leading platoon of A company was almost wiped out and B company, also, had serious casualties. The attack was pinned down. Captain J. R. L. Scammel, commanding A company, was wounded. Major R. Thomas, commanding B company, led a handful of men against an enemy post in La Rougerie. He was killed and Lieuts. Wilson and A. Morrison were wounded.

On the right 5 Wilts Regt. had heavy casualties and their C.O. was killed. Major Roberts was sent over to command this battalion.

Towards evening a troop of tanks arrived and 4 Somerset L.I. made a new plan. C and D companies were to pass through and continue the advance. At 2230 hours a few Churchill tanks reached the crest of Mont Pincon on the right. In 4 Somerset L.I. sector, a tank was got into position from where it could fire onto the hillside. This was the turning point of the battle. The Battalion advanced under heavy shell-fire and C and D companies reached the summit as darkness fell. They were followed by A and B companies. About 0100 hours on 7th August, the Battalion dug all-round defences near Pt. 365, just short of the final objective. It was a bitterly cold night, with a driving wet mist and the troops were still in their shirt-sleeves. On the left 4 Wilts Regt. also gained the summit and dug in.

During this battle, on 6th August, 214th Brigade was moving up in rear of 129th Brigade. On the morning of 7th August, Mont Pincon was shrouded in thick mist. At 1000 hours, 4 Somerset L.I. advanced against heavy opposition and secured the final objective. During the day 214th Brigade relieved 129th Brigade. 7 Somerset L.I. was ordered to relieve 4 Somerset L.I. and started to move up the hill at 0800 hours, under heavy shelling and mortaring. At 1430 hours it relieved 4 Somerset L.I. and dug in amidst dense bracken, brambles and small fir trees. 4 Somerset L.I. moved back to Chanterie and, later, to a rest area at Mesnil Auzouf. During the evening, 7 Somerset L.I. relieved 1 Worcs. Regt. at 2130 hours, using B and C companies for this task. At 2130 hours 5 D.C.L.I. (214th Brigade) attacked and captured Le Plessis Grimoult.

The capture of Mont Pincon was a notable event. Lieut.-General Horrocks, commanding 30 Corps, visited 7 Somerset L.I. on 8th August and 4 Somerset L.I. on 9th August, congratulating both battalions and stressing the vital value of the height to the advance of 2 Canadian Corps on the left.

The visit of the Corps Commander and his cheerfulness and cheery personality had a marked effect on the morale of all ranks, for he was never too busy to exchange a word with a private soldier. The action at Mont Pincon is memorable as having been, essentially, a "regimental affair". The 4th Battalion gained the hill and the 7th Battalion held it. It was the first time the two battalions had met on the battlefield, for they were in different brigades. They were very proud of their success and of the manner in which their comrades and rivals had behaved in the face of the enemy.

On 8th August, 50th Division advanced through 43rd Division. 130th Brigade was employed to clear the woods south of Chatepie. 214th Brigade remained on Mont Pincon, under heavy shelling and mortaring.

On 9th August, 214th Brigade continued mopping up. 7 Somerset L.I. was ordered to attack Les Hameaux–Haut Au Roi–Le Saussay, in support of the advance of 50th Division. This attack was successful, the casualties being 7 Officers and 79 Other Ranks, killed and wounded. On 10th August patrols went forward towards La Motiere.

In 129th Brigade, 4 Somerset L.I. relieved 7 Queen's Regt. near La Lande. Major J. L. Brind was posted as 2nd-in-Command in place of Major W. Q. Roberts, who was confirmed as commander of 5 Wilts Regt. On 10th August, 129th Brigade concentrated in the area La Lande–La Mogisiere and on 11th August, 4 Somerset L.I. attacked towards La Planche at 0745 hours, reaching its objectives with slight opposition. On 11th August, 214th Brigade moved down to the R. Druance at Gournay. 7 Somerset L.I. attacked and took La Truladiere.

CROSSING OF R. NOIREAU

On 12th August both 129th and 214th Brigades were again on the move. 4 Somerset L.I. reached St. Pierre La Vielle and spent 13th August mopping up. During this advance the R. Noireau was crossed. On 12th August, 7 Somerset L.I. was relieved on Mont Pincon by 61st Reconnaissance Regt. On 13th August, at 0130 hours it started to advance on Cauville, arriving there at 0800 hours. At 1930 hours it moved on again, exploiting towards St. Lambert. By 2100 hours, B and D companies had reached Pt. 217. Here 987 Panzer Grenadier Regt. was identified.

During 13th August a general enemy withdrawal was noticed. In the evening 7 Somerset L.I. was relieved by 11th Hussars and moved back to Cauville, where it rested on 14th August. Culey-le-Patry had been found clear of enemy.

BATTLE OF THE FALAISE POCKET (*Map 2*)

On 14th August, 30 Corps began the advance to the R. Seine. While the operations described above had been in progress, our forces had every-

JUNE–AUGUST 1944

where been closing in on the Falaise–Argentan pocket, south of Caen. By 4th August, U.S. forces had moved south from the St. Lo area and taken Avranches, on the Atlantic coast, and Mortain. A major enemy counter-attack on Mortain, from the east, between 6th and 10th August, was held. 8 Corps, from the Caumont area had moved south, through Le Beny Bocage and reached the Vire–Conde-sur-Noireau road.

In the eastern sector, 1 Corps and 2 Canadian Corps had taken Caen on 9th July and were pressing south from the town. In the meantime U.S. forces swung eastwards through Laval on Le Mans and Mayenne and by 13 August, 15 U.S. Corps had reached Argentan and Gace, on the south of the Falaise pocket. 12 Corps had closed in towards Thury-Harcourt. Within the pocket lay the remains of the 7th German Army.

43RD DIVISION FRONT (*Map* 16)

On 13th August, 4 Somerset L.I. took over from a battalion of D.L.I. (50th Division) at La Villette. On 15th August, B company entered Clecy. 214th Brigade was ordered to advance south-eastwards across the R. Noireau and R. Orne. 7 Somerset L.I. moved from Cauville on 15th August, at 1730 hours, and on 18th August, at 1100 hours, attacked a hill east of Le Carnet. By 1300 hours, D company was in Le Carnet. 129th Brigade followed 214th Brigade, 4 Somerset L.I. reaching the R. Noireau on 16th August. 129th Brigade then passed through 214th Brigade and found Plum and St. Honorine la Chardonne clear of the enemy on 17th August. In the meantime 4 Somerset L.I. reached La Ferté. 11th Armd. Division was already on the hills near Athis and was relieved by 130th Brigade.

For a time the battle moved forward to the east. Between 17th and 22nd August, 4 Somerset L.I. remained at Plum and 7 Somerset L.I. at Le Carnet. Both battalions rested, free from shelling.

ADVANCE TO THE R. SEINE (*Map* 2)

On 22nd August, 43rd Division began to move eastwards to an area east of Argentan. Our forces were now closing in on the Falaise pocket. The German line of retreat, eastwards, had been closed, on 20th August, by the Polish Armd. Division and shortly afterwards the German forces remaining in the pocket were eliminated.

For the advance to, and crossing of, the R. Seine, our forces from left to right were:

1 Corps, directed on Duclair.
2 Canadian Corps, directed on Elbeuf.
12 Corps directed on Louviers.
30 Corps on Vernon.
U.S. 15, 5, 20 and 12 Corps, further to the south, on Paris, Fontainebleau and Troyes.

The whole of our forces were now on the move.

On 25th August, 43rd Division launched Operation Neptune. The object was to advance to the area of Vernon and secure a bridgehead over the R. Seine. 129th Brigade was to cross at Vernon and 130th Brigade south-west of Conches. 214th Brigade was in reserve.

OPERATION NEPTUNE

On 25th August, at 1500 hours, 4 Somerset L.I. reached 129th Brigade assembly area, west of Vernon. The whole of Vernon was under observation from the east bank of the river, which, here, was some 200 yards wide. Across the river from Vernon, is the village of Vernonnet, which was the battalion objective, at the base of a 300-foot chalk escarpment. Railway and road bridges had been blown, but the road bridge was still passable for a limited crossing on foot, though mined.

129th Brigade plan was for 5 Wilts Regt. to cross on the right, south of the road bridge, with 4 Wilts Regt. in a covering position on the west bank. 4 Somerset L.I. was to cross on the left, north of the road bridge. 1 Worcs. Regt. was under command of 129th Brigade for the operation and was to cross after 4 Somerset L.I. using the damaged road bridge and clear the south end of Vernonnet. Behind the village and the escarpment, lay the Foret de Vernon.

At 1917 hours, on 25th August, 4 Somerset L.I. started to cross, in storm boats and Dukws, covered by all available supporting weapons, using H.E. and smoke. A company, under Major Acock, led the crossing. There was some difficulty in getting the engines of the storm boats, which the battalion had not seen before to start once they were in the water. Opposition, at first, was slight. By 1937 hours, A company had secured a lodgement and was followed by C company, under Major Mallalieu. By 2000 hours, both companies had been held up, for the lodgement had been made on what was, practically, an island, being separated from the east bank by a deep and muddy stream, some 60 yards wide.

Accordingly, B company was sent across in Dukws, at a point some 500 yards upstream, near the road bridge. Once landed, B company cleared the ground up to the village and got a lodgement there in the face of considerable opposition. D company then crossed, but it was almost first light on 26th August before it landed. By 0500 hours all companies and Battalion H.Q were across. Casualties in this action were not heavy, but Sergeant Langley, a notable rifle shot, was killed and Sergeant Partridge wounded. Major Watts, commanding B company, was accidentally injured and Captain Hutchinson took over the company.

In the meantime 214th Brigade, with 7 Somerset L.I., had concentrated at Paly-sur-Eure. On 26th August, it moved forward at 1910 hours, crossed the R. Seine and by 2125 hours had entered the Foret de Vernon, to the north of Vernon, passing through 129th Brigade. 130th Brigade was concentrated in reserve.

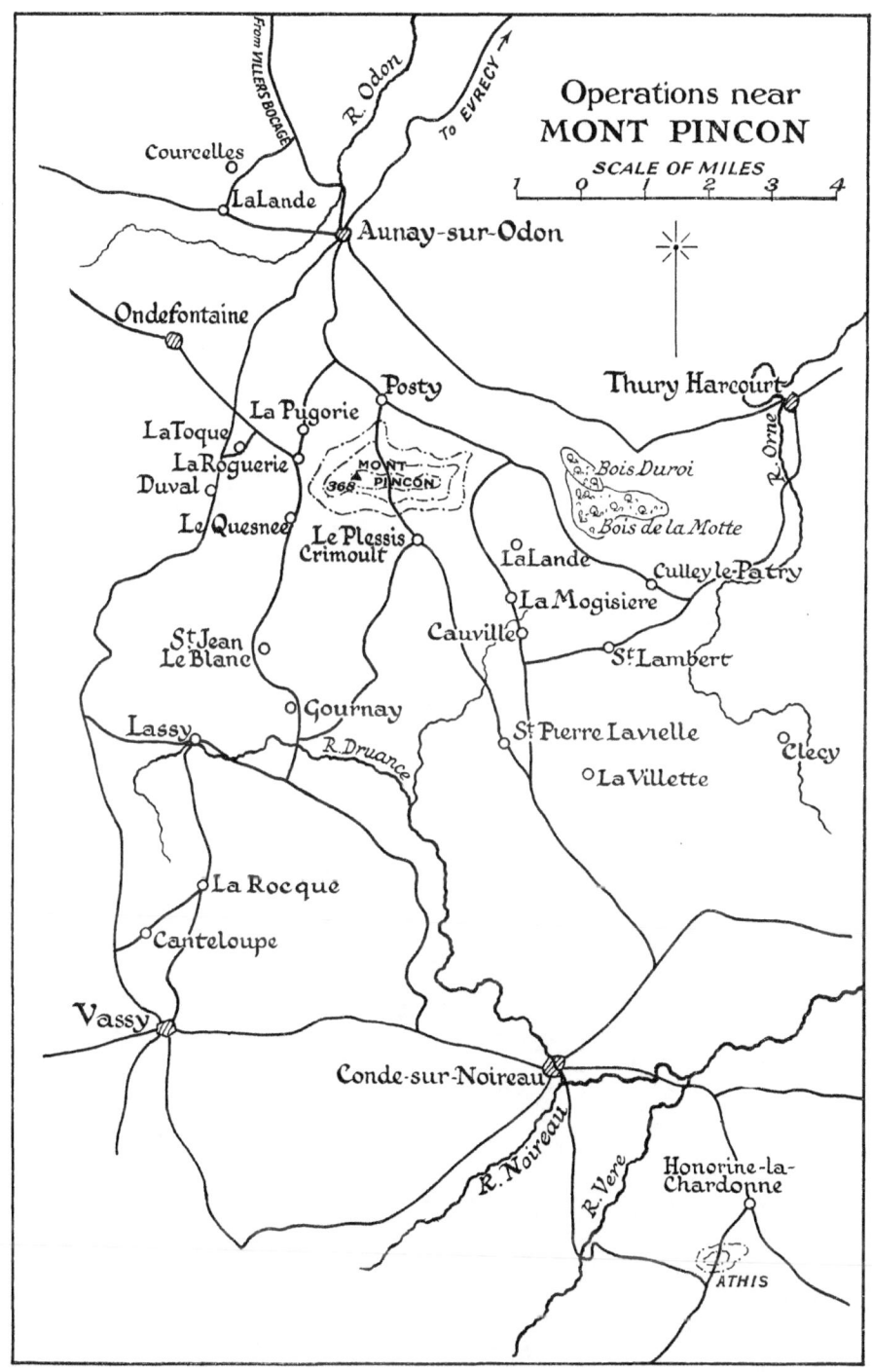

ENLARGING THE BRIDGEHEAD

4 Somerset L.I. was ordered to occupy the village of Bois Jerome St. Ouen, on the edge of the Foret de Vernon. To reach its objective the Battalion had to make its way by unmapped tracks through the forest. B company was leading and reached the Chateau by 1205 hours. Here it was heavily counter-attacked and forced to withdraw. While this action was in progress, on the outskirts of the village, the rear of the Battalion, still in the forest, was attacked by what was afterwards found to be the main German counter-attack force. Confused fighting followed, but the Germans were finally driven off by the arrival of armour during the late afternoon. By nightfall the Battalion was clear of the forest and firmly lodged in the village. B company retook the Chateau at 1600 hours. On the right, 5 Wilts Regt. took Chapelle St. Ouen, after a stiff fight.

On 214th Brigade front, A company 7 Somerset L.I. advanced at 1030 hours on 27th August and was heavily counter-attacked by infantry and tanks. A call for reinforcements was received at Battalion H.Q. At 1600 hours the situation of A company was obscure and there were reports that British P.O.W. had been seen in the area. By 2100 hours no report had been received from the company, but strong patrols moving towards its location were heavily engaged in close fighting. This company was lost in these operations, having been over-run by superior enemy forces.

On 28th August, more troops got across into the bridgehead and the push-out began. An apparent enemy withdrawal was noticed and, at 1930 hours, 7 Somerset L.I. advanced, meeting no opposition. On 29th August, 43rd Division was ordered to hold the bridgehead, while armour and the remainder of 30 and 12 Corps passed through, directed on Amiens and towards the R. Somme. 4 Somerset L.I. moved to Le Mesnil Milon and 7 Somerset L.I to Courville. 43rd Division H.Q. crossed the R. Seine and the Division enjoyed a few days' well earned rest.

The 4th Battalion remained at Le Mesnil Milon for a fortnight. The three-ton lorries were taken away to maintain the armoured thrust into Belgium. This was the first time since June that reorganisation had been possible. The majority of the reinforcements which had been received had to be taught light infantry drill and individual and section training. Much emphasis was placed on drill and turn out. In the evenings there were outdoor cinema shows and parties visited recently liberated Paris.

6TH AIRBORNE DIVISION (*Map* 17)

It will be convenient here to complete the story of 7th Battalion (L.I.) in the Battles of Normandy, though this entails returning to events in July 1944.

On 1st July, 7th Battalion (L.I.) was resting in the area of the bridges over the Canal de Caen and R. Orne, near Benouville and Ranville. The strength of the Battalion was now only 16 officers and 366 Other Ranks.

> A company, two platoons, 90 Other Ranks.
> B company, two platoons, 90 Other Ranks.
> C company, three platoons, 100 Other Ranks.

The rest area was under the muzzles of our artillery, which fired unceasingly, and, consequently, allowed little rest.

1 Corps was now embarking on the capture of Caen, using part of 2 Canadian Corps. 51st Division and 6th Airborne Division, were still on the extreme left flank of 2nd British Army, but 51st Division was used, later, to attack southwards from the Ranville area, on Colombelles, the eastern suburb of Caen.

SECOND VISIT TO THE BOIS DE BAVENT

On 4th July, at 0815 hours, 7th Battalion (L.I.) relieved 8th Para Battalion in the Bois de Bavent sector. The enemy was quieter than before, with less shelling and mortaring. It was thought that he might be pulling out. Plans were made to test this. A night attack by 13th Para Battalion was abandoned and a daylight attack by 7th Battalion (L.I.) considered. The object was to discover if the enemy had thinned out. An attack was abandoned as this would have put the Battalion too far forward of the Divisional perimeter. Vigorous patrolling and "edging forward" was, therefore, ordered.

On 7th July, at 1115 hours, offensives began towards Bob's Farm. B company, on the left, got forward to within 200 yards of the Farm and shot it up with P.I.A.T. bombs. C company, on the right, got very close to the Bois de Bavent. The centre was only 150 yards from the enemy, with small outposts in advance. Along the whole Battalion front, forward defended localities were only one field away from the enemy positions. At 2100 hours, on 8th July, heavy artillery concentrations, announcing the final assault, were heard from the direction of Caen.

During the 9th July—on which day Caen was taken—minor operations continued towards Bob's Farm. On 10th July, a raid was planned, supported by artillery and mortar fire, to occupy enemy positions in rear of the Farm and clear up the forward defended localities. For this B company, under Major Keene, was selected, the main fire support being from eleven automatics on the company front. At 1630 hours the artillery concentrations opened and at 1635 hours, B company passed through A company, under heavy mortar fire.

B company moved up a narrow gully, with two sections on a path to the north. P.I.A.T. guns were used with great effect. The two sections on the path were pinned down at once and the remainder of the company in the gully got into trouble with booby-traps. The gully was waist deep in water and found to be full of anti-personnel mines, Major Keene being wounded by stepping on one. By 1700 hours the raid was held up and authorised to withdraw at 1750 hours. The enemy followed up and brought two automatics to bear on the gully. These were engaged by Sergeant Lucas with a Bren gun, which enabled the company to withdraw. In this raid, which gained valuable information, Major Keene, Lieut. Patterson and 20 Other Ranks were wounded and 3 Other Ranks killed. The latter were Lance-Corporals Coulthard and Price and Private Evans. They were buried at Ranville on 11th July.

On 11th July, Captain N. S. Coppin took over command of B company. During the day, 152nd Infantry Brigade came into position on the right. On 12th July, at 0830 hours, the Battalion was relieved by 8th Para Battalion and moved to a rest area north of Amfreville.

On 21st July, at 1530 hours, 7th Battalion (L.I.) moved into the old positions in the Bois de Bavent sector, south-east of Le Mesnil. 6th Airborne Division was now protecting the left flank of 8 Corps, advancing east of Caen, on Troarn—Bourgebus—Cormelles. Between 21st and 29th July, 7th Battalion (L.I.) maintained its positions under heavy shelling and mortaring. On 30th July, at 1015 hours, it was relieved by 13th Para Battalion and moved to rest area north west of Amfreville.

During the early part of August the drive against the Falaise–Argentan pocket was in progress. On 1st August, 7th Battalion (L.I.) moved into Divisional reserve at Le Bas de Ranville. On 7th August it took up a new position in the Hauger area. Here, under heavy shell and mortar fire, it was engaged in patrolling. On 11th August, at 0330 hours, a patrol was machine gunned at close range. Lieut. Howard and 4 Other Ranks were missing. On 13th August, the Battalion was relieved by 1st Belgian Independent Company and returned to Ranville.

On 14th August, preparations were made to attack the lock gates at Ouistreham, where a small German garrison was still holding out. At 2100 hours, A company took up a defensive position on the west of the gates. This attack did not materialise. On 16th August, A company was relieved by a company of 12th Para Battalion.

THE ADVANCE EASTWARDS (*Map 2*)

On 17th August came news that the enemy was withdrawing on the divisional front and a follow-up was ordered. By 1100 hours, 3rd Para Brigade had reached Troarn and Bures and crossed the R. Muance. On 18th August, 7th Battalion (L.I) marched at 0735 hours and crossed the river at Troarn, thence moving north-east. At 2200 hours, after receipt of an order for a brigade attack, the Battalion moved off, over a road which was being heavily shelled. 2 Other Ranks were killed and 2 wounded.

At 0120 hours, on 19th August, the plan was changed and the Battalion directed on Putot-sur-Auge. The railway was crossed and, at 0550 hours, contact was made with the enemy. The advance continued into Putot-sur-Auge, the enemy losing 14 killed and 50 P.O.W. At 0945 hours, 13th Para Battalion passed through. Heavy shelling and mortaring continued during the day and into the night.

On 20th August, C company attacked and cleared Bonnemont, meeting little opposition. Next day the Battalion joined this company at the Chateau de Bonnemont. On 22nd August the Battalion moved by M.T., to high ground near Pont L'Eveque, relieving 12th Para Battalion, at 1500 hours, in positions near the R. Touques. On 23rd August, C company moved into Pont L'Eveque in Jeeps and cleared the town up to the railway station. Opposition increased. 1 Other Rank was killed and several wounded and the company was ordered to withdraw.

On 24th August, C company patrols reported the town clear and the Battalion moved in and advanced eastwards by march route, contacting the enemy at St. Benoit. A and B companies crossed the railway and seized the high ground beyond the town. On 25th August these positions were consolidated.

On 26th August, starting at 0445 hours, the Battalion marched to Pont Audemer, on the R. Lisle. At 1130 hours the town was occupied, the bridges being found to be destroyed. A defensive position was taken up, with A and B companies on the river bank. At 1600 hours the Battalion came under command of 56th Infantry Brigade of 59th Division. On 27th August it moved to a rest area, south of Honfleur.

On 1st September a patrol was sent to search the woods west of Beuzeville, and found them clear of enemy. Orders had now come for 6th Airborne Division to return to England. On 2nd September, 7th Battalion (L.I.) marched to an assembly area and thence, moved by M.T., through Troarn, Douvres and Ferriers to Arromanches, where it arrived at 1800 hours. On 3rd September, at 1615 hours, it embarked in s.s. "Empire Javelin", reaching Southampton at 1220 hours on 5th September. At 1515 hours it arrived by train at Bulford and the men were sent on leave.

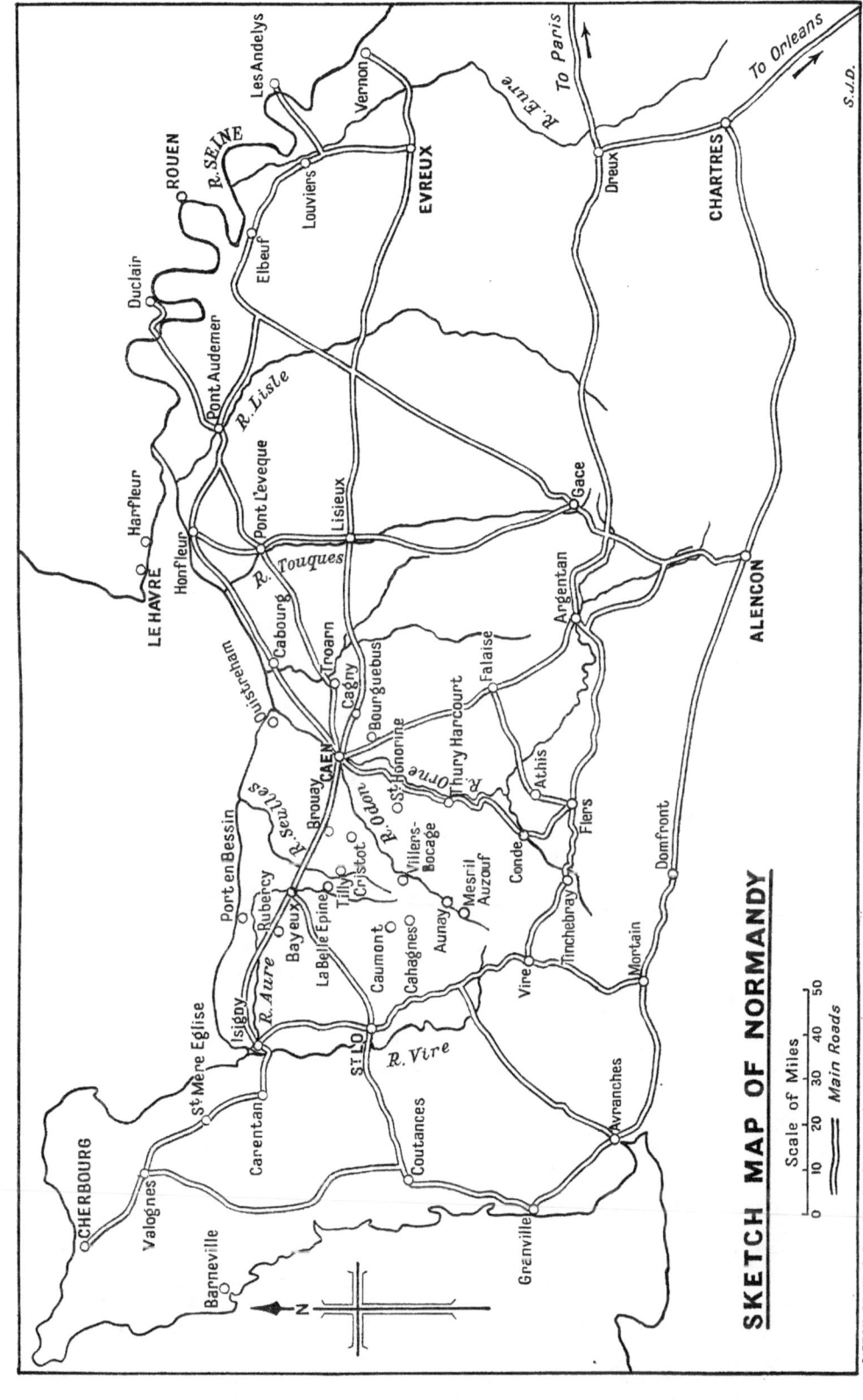

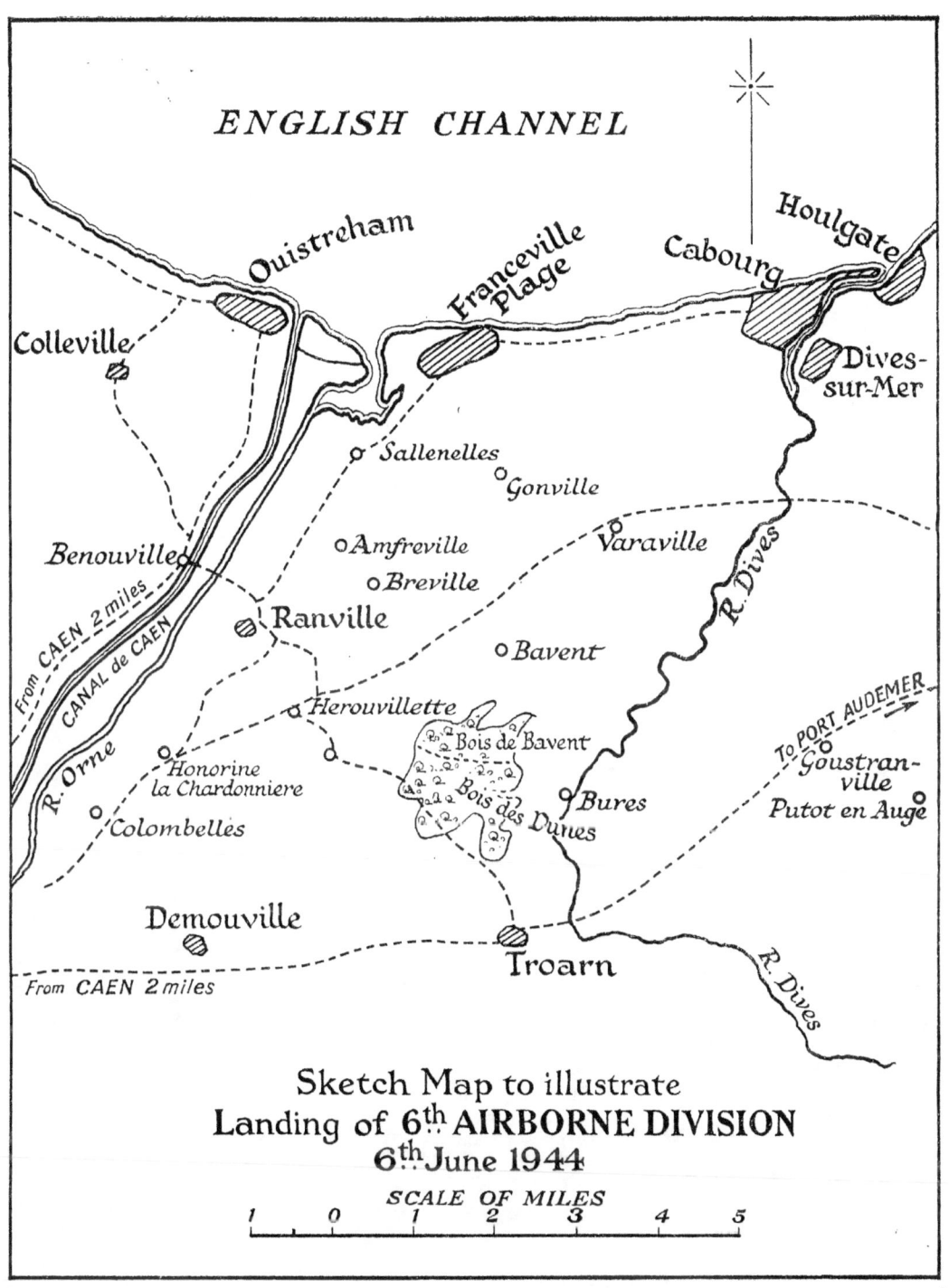

CHAPTER XIII

THE CAMPAIGN IN ITALY: II—THE CROSSING OF THE R. LIRI AND THE FALL OF ROME

Situation in March 1944—Operations in the Valvori sector—Operations in the Belvedere sector—The spring offensive—Operation Honker—The Battle of the Garigliano—The advance to Rome

CHAPTER XI described the arrival of the 2nd Battalion in Italy and its first clashes with the enemy, while part of 5th Army, in the valley of the R. Garigliano. It then formed part of 28th Brigade of 4th British Division. At the end of March 1944, this formation was transferred to 13 Corps of 8th Army. The latter was advancing northwards, with its main forces on the Adriatic sector, but with 13 Corps in touch with the right of 5th Army, which was still building up strength to break out of the Anzio beach-head and advance towards Rome. The junction of 5th and 8th Armies was in the neighbourhood of Cassino and the Monastery, both of which were still in German hands. On the east, 8th Army was across the R. Sangro and building up for a further advance. Generally speaking, the weather during the winter and early spring had been too bad for large-scale operations.

Towards the end of March 1944, preparations were made for 4th Division to take over a sector, on the left of 13 Corps. 2 Somerset L.I. was ordered to join a detachment consisting of 56 Recce Regt. and known as Preston's Force, from the name of the commander. This detachment was responsible for holding a very long front, known as the "Valvori" sector, between 4th Division on the left and the Polish Corps on the right. On 29th March the Battalion had reached Pietra Vairano, a mountain village some 10 miles south of the sector, where it lay up in bivouacs while reconnaissances were carried out. About this time Major-General Ward took over command of 4th Division.

OPERATIONS IN THE VALVORI SECTOR

Pietra Vairano and the road forward were both under observation and enemy shell-fire. The improvised track, onward from the village, was known as the "Inferno" and was only usable at night by a limited number of vehicles. Much of the supply in the sector itself, was by pack-mule. Free French forces were in the area and the Battalion made its first acquaintance with Moroccan "Goums" as well as with the Algerian wine which was part of the French ration.

On 2nd April, advance parties from the Battalion began to filter forward, meeting with heavy shelling near Aqua Fondata, where Lieuts. R. A. Ostler and C. G. Barfoot were wounded. During the night 2nd/3rd April, the

Battalion moved up and by 0315 hours relieved the Free French 7th R.T.M., taking over the sector Cicurro–Valvori. These reliefs are described as being "highly international".

The positions occupied were on the summit of a high ridge which fell steeply to the R. Rapido in the rear and less steeply to the valley of a small stream on the front. Beyond the latter stream, some 1,000 yards distant, were the enemy positions. The Battalion position was based on the village of Valvori, a mountain retreat for rich people, which had been effectively looted by the Free French and their predecessors. It was empty of inhabitants. B and D companies were forward on the right and left respectively, with A company further left in Valvori and C company echeloned back in the centre. The enemy was mainly Austrian, of doubtful value and with little artillery support. There were, however, many well handled mortars and plenty of ammunition for them, as well as expert patrollers, probably men picked for the work. Between the two positions there was a wide "no man's land", with which the enemy was extremely familiar. The weather was now clear and warmer, with starlight nights.

During 3rd and 4th April ambush patrols were led by Lieuts. T. A. Harris and E. D. A. Forman. On 5th April, Captain W. E. P. Watson, with Sergeant Perry and two runners, was visiting one of his platoons at 2130 hours, when they ran into a German patrol which had penetrated between our forward posts. The Germans fired, killing Captain Watson and Sergeant Perry. Later during the night a further patrol under Lieut. Bearman engaged the same enemy patrol and exchanged hand grenades, without apparent casualties on either side. Other patrols under Lieuts. H. Toms and A. Heaps did useful work and the enemy made no further attempts to penetrate this part of the position.

Patrolling in the sector continued until 9th April, Lieuts. E. A. Sutton-Pryce and R. A. Thick doing useful work. There was much mortaring, shelling and sniping, resulting in the loss of 5 Other Ranks killed and 2 wounded. On 7th April, in spite of difficulties, Jellalabad Day was celebrated. On 9th April the Battalion was relieved by part of 4 Recce Regt. and the Italian Baffile Regt. and moved into Divisional reserve.

Between the 10th and 14th April it was engaged, near Il Trevore, in training with tanks, with 11th Royal Canadian Tank Regt. The weather had now improved greatly and the bivouac area was comparatively dry. It is recorded that "the song of the nightingales, by the river, both by day and night was almost deafening".

About this time some 800-odd reinforcements for the Somerset Light Infantry arrived at the reinforcement camps in Italy. They were men of the 5th and 6th Battalions, who, as mentioned in Chapter X, found many drafts in 1944. They were magnificent material and very well trained. Many of them, however, were never to serve with the Somerset Light Infantry. Large numbers of them were drafted to other Regiments, where they acquitted themselves with distinction. It is said that the London Irish had a whole company of them and called them the "Somerset Irish".

THE CAMPAIGN IN ITALY: II

OPERATIONS IN THE BELVEDERE SECTOR

On 15th April the Battalion moved from Il Trevore, by night, to the Belvedere Sector, some two miles south-west of Belmonte Castello, where it relieved 2 King's Regt., also in 28th Brigade. At this time Brigadier Montagu-Douglas-Scott, late Irish Guards, was Brigade Commander, having relieved Brigadier Purves.

The new position was on the top of a razor-backed ridge with a close view of the Monastery Hill, at Cassino. On the left was a higher feature held by 2/4 Hampshire Regt. of 10th Brigade. The ground to the right was very precipitous and was only held lightly. At some points the enemy positions were only a few yards distant and nowhere were they further than 150 yards away. Little patrolling was possible, but there was considerable shelling and mortaring.

While the Battalion was in this sector, the enemy raided 2/4 Hampshire Regt. on the left, entirely eliminating one platoon. During the night 21st/22nd April, 2 Somerset L.I. was relieved by 23rd N.Z. Battalion of the New Zealand Division. At 0700 hours on 22nd April it reached a rest area near Pratella. During the relief there was heavy shelling, as a result of which pack-mules bolted and some wireless sets and other gear were lost. The move took place over the "Inferno" track, where the shelling was so bad that the Battalion had to lie up until it slackened.

SUMMARY OF OPERATIONS UP TO 22ND APRIL

In Chapter XI it was seen that, four days after arrival in Italy, after only two months training in the deserts of Egypt, the 2nd Battalion found itself in action under unusual operational conditions. At this time the opposing forces were facing each other, on wide fronts, in mountainous country. The peaks were very precipitous and on the rocky ground digging was impossible. Two-men "sangars" had to be made from stones. These were difficult to conceal. No movement was possible by day and all supply was by night.

Roads and jeep tracks could only reach the base of the mountains, so supply from there was by pack mule. Mule leaders included Indians, Arabs, Basutos and Italians. Food was issued in ten-man packs, largely tinned meat and biscuits, and cooked on "tommy cookers". There was no threat from tanks and carriers could not operate, so the Support Company, except from the Mortar Platoon, remained with B Echelon.

Offensive operations were limited to small scale patrolling and Mortar, or Artillery fire on observed enemy movement. The weather was very cold and continued inactivity was inclined to cramp the initiative of all ranks. This lack of opportunity for training and leadership was, later, a severe handicap when more mobile operations developed.

THE SPRING OFFENSIVE

Preparations now began for a spring offensive to link up 5th and 8th Armies near the Anzio beach-head, before a large-scale advance on Rome. These preparations included intensive training in the crossing of rivers and the use of assault boats and rafts. On 26th April the Battalion moved to Barracone on the R. Volturno and carried out exercises there until 2nd May. About this time, the Battalion was joined by Majors T. P. Luckock, P. Nation and H. Platt, who took command, respectively of C, D and A companies. About this time the Battalion received a visit from Lieut.-General John Harding.

Early in May, 28th Brigade relieved 21st Indian Infantry Brigade in the sector southwards from Cassino station to La Pieta. On 3rd May, 2 Somerset L.I. relieved 3/15 Punjab Regt. in the area Une Belle Ascensione–La Pieta, in the Monte Trocchio area of the R. Liri Valley. This was a quiet sector. B company remained in the B echelon area near Quatro Venti.

The object of this move was to give the Battalion an opportunity to see part of the river over which it would, later, have to attack. From the Battalion positions, fields ran down to the R. Garigliano on the front, with fields and farms on the far bank. Some miles to the east the ruins of Cassino Monastery stood up on a hill. While here, the Pioneer Platoon was engaged in cutting lanes through an extensive U.S. minefield which covered the front. On the night of the 5th/6th May the Battalion was relieved by 2/4 Hampshire Regt. of 28th Brigade and moved to bivouac at Alife, where it was engaged in tank training with 17/21 Lancers.

OPERATION HONKER

The overall operation preparatory to the break through for the advance on Rome was known as Honker. Plans began to take shape early in April and preliminary discussions had reached brigade level by 17th April. This operation is variously described as the crossing of the R. Rapido, or R. Liri, or R. Garigliano. This was probably due to the fact that all three rivers had to be crossed and lower formations were only concerned with their own particular part of the operation.

On 6th May a conference was held at which Lieut.-General Sir Oliver Leese, Lieut.-General S. C. Kirkman, C.B.E., M.C. (13 Corps), the Commander 4th British Division, Brigade and Battalion commanders were present. Plans for the operation were given out and explained with the aid of scale models of the country. All ranks were briefed on the models later.

On 9th May 4th British Division received final orders for the crossing of the R. Garigliano. The crossing was to be made, west of Cassino, to establish a bridgehead through which other forces could pass, to attack the Gustav and Hitler Lines and, in conjunction with 5th Army from the Anzio beach-head, advance on Rome by Highways 6 and 7.

On the Garigliano sector of the attack, the Polish Corps was to attack Cassino Monastery Hill on the right; 4th British Division was to cross in the centre; 5th Indian Division was to cross on the left of 4th British Division. The attack by 4th British Division was the key to the whole operation, since the sector allotted to it included, on the right, Highway 6 from Cassino to Rome. This was the route for the main advance.

4th British Division plan was as follows:

> *Right:* 10th Brigade.
> *Left:* 28th Brigade.
> *Reserve:* 12th Brigade.

2/4 Hampshire Regt. was already on the frontage of the river. This battalion was, therefore, made responsible for the approaches to the river, the launching sites and the arrangements for ferrying assault troops.

On 28th Brigade front there were two crossing places; X on the right and Y on the left, separated by about 300 yards. The brigade plan was for 2 King's Regt. to carry out the initial crossing, securing an objective some 400 yards from the far bank of the river, known as the Brown Line. 2 Somerset L.I., was to follow 2 King's Regt., pass through and secure a further objective known as the Blue Line. 2/4 Hampshire Regt., after completing its task for the initial crossings, was to cross to the right and secure a position known as the Red Line.

The whole operation was to be supported by a creeping artillery barrage starting on the far bank of the river. It was believed that the opposition in the Gustav Line, close to the river, would be light and that the main enemy forces would be encountered in the Hitler Line, some miles to the north. It was hoped that surprise would enable the Gustav Line to be penetrated rapidly and, thereafter, the Hitler Line stormed before it could be adequately manned. The operation was timed for the night of 11th/12th May.

THE BATTLE OF THE GARIGLIANO

On the night of 10th/11th May 2 Somerset L.I. moved in M.T. to the assembly area south of Monte Trocchio. Here, with 2 King's Regt., it lay up preparatory to the assault. Zero hour was fixed for 2345 hours on 11th May. When the time came, there was a thick mist over the valley, accentuated by smoke.

2 Somerset L.I. was to follow 2 King's Regt. The Battalion plan was for A company, followed by B company to move down to crossing X, on the right. C company, followed by D company was to move to crossing Y, on the left. The approaches were by somewhat narrow tracks cut through the minefields. After crossing, the Battalion was to form up behind 2 King's Regt., pass through and advance to the Blue Line. These movements were to be in conformity with the creeping barrage time-table.

At 2300 hours the artillery programme opened with a tremendous roar. It was probably the largest artillery concentration assembled, up to this time, during the war. 2 King's Regt. moved forward by the marked tracks to start crossing, in assault boats, at 2345 hours. The battalion was 30 minutes late at the crossing places, owing to delays. At 2345 hours, 2 Somerset L.I. passed the start line and at once ran into the tail of 2 King's Regt. The valley was now filled with thick smoke, though it is uncertain whether this was put down by the enemy, or our own artillery. Enemy shelling and mortaring added to the confusion of the mist and smoke.

Shortly after midnight, 2 Somerset L.I. reached the boat assembly position, some 200 yards from the bank of the river. Here the guides from 2/4 Hampshire Regt. could not be found to lead the companies to the crossings. After a search the respective routes were located and the leading companies moved down to the crossing places. It was now apparent that the crossing by 2 King's Regt. had not gone well. The current was stronger than had been estimated and, though the bulk of the leading company had crossed, many boats had been swept downstream. A wire rope had been got across by the Engineers, but accurate mortar fire had knocked out many of the boats.

The tracks through the minefields were now congested by Engineer vehicles moving down to the river with rafts and ferrying equipment. The infantry had to move off the tracks, in the darkness, into ground uncleared of mines. Men were sent back to bring up reserve assault boats and some were obtained after much difficulty and delay.

Lieut.-Colonel Platt now reached crossing Y and found that little was going on. The crossings were now two hours late and the timed artillery programme had ceased. Four boats were collected and the remaining company of 2 King's Regt. sent across, followed by C company, 2 Somerset L.I. under Major Luckock. It was now 0300 hours on 12th May.

By 0400 hours C company had completed crossing. It was re-organised and, after passing through 2 King's Regt., went forward and reached the line of a road, parallel to and some 400 yards from the river bank. Here it came under heavy fire from spandaus firing on fixed lines and consolidated.

In the meantime things were going equally badly at X crossing on the right. There had already been many casualties from enemy shelling and most of the Battalion wireless sets were out of action. A company had managed to get one platoon, under Lieut. F. A. Sutton-Pryce, across under heavy fire. This party succeeded in linking up with elements of C company on the left. Major H. Platt, however, who had also crossed, while trying with a small party to deal with an enemy post, was wounded and taken prisoner. Lieut.-Colonel Platt, at crossing Y, sent Captain Winlove-Smith to X crossing to bring B company round to Y crossing. This was accomplished successfully and the company disposed in a supporting position on the near bank of the river.

By this time, the Engineers, with great gallantry, had got a second wire rope across, upstream from crossing Y. D company was ordered to cross here, under Major P. Nation. Using an assault boat as a ferry, after considerable trouble due to casualties, the company reached the far bank. One platoon had already lost touch in the smoke and darkness and had crossed with C company. Lieut.-Colonel Platt also crossed and D company was sent forward some 200 yards to the left of the bridge-head, to link up with C company.

Forward Company wireless sets were now out of action. Lieut.-Colonel Platt, therefore, recrossed the river and was able to report the situation to Brigade on the No. 22 set of the supporting battery commander. He also met

THE CAMPAIGN IN ITALY: II

Lieut.-Colonel Garnons-Williams of 2 King's Regt. Mortar fire was now increasing and, owing to some mistaken order, B company withdrew from the river bank to the boat assembly position. Battalion H.Q., with Lieut.-Colonels Platt and Garnons-Williams now crossed and the two commanders went forward to reconnoitre. Lieut.-Colonel Garnons-Williams was almost at once seriously wounded by a mortar bomb and died from his wounds two days later.

It was now daylight, but the thick mist and smoke still made some movement possible. As the smoke cleared, Lieut.-Colonel Platt decided that no further advance was possible without considerable artillery support. As he was crawling back from the front towards Battalion H.Q. he was wounded in three places by a mortar bomb. He was forced to lie where he was for the rest of the day and the following night.

During the day, the 12th May, no movement was possible owing to intense mortar, spandau and sniping fire. On the evening of the 12th May, the parties of 2 King's Regt. and 2 Somerset L.I. across the river were formed into a composite force under Major Odling-Smee, 2 King's Regt. This was known as Smee Force. When darkness fell Lieut. A. G. Morgan was able to work forward and contact Lieut.-Colonel Platt. The latter could not be moved without stretcher bearers. There was no movement now across the river and orders to 2/4 Hampshire Regt. to cross were cancelled. The only way to cross the river was to swim and by this means a verbal message was sent back to Brigade H.Q., giving the position of forwards troops and saying that no further advance was possible without artillery support. It was also stated that many wounded required collecting.

During the night 12th/13th May no further troops crossed the river and the enemy seemed to be closing in on the small bridgehead. In the meantime, however, 10th Brigade, on the right, had effected a lodgement. On the morning of the 13th May, this had been sufficiently enlarged to enable the Engineers to construct a bridge to take tanks. About noon, 2/4 Hampshire Regt. was ordered to cross supported by tanks. As this attack progressed, the fire on 28th Brigade bridgehead began to slacken. About 1400 hours, the enemy started to surrender. C and D companies then went forward to the Blue Line and were joined by 2/4 Hampshire Regt.

It was now possible to collect the wounded. Lieut.-Colonel Platt, who had lain out for 30 hours, was carried in by four P.O.W. The prisoners were rounded up by R.S.M. Lander and Provost Sergeant Axe. The enemy had not been able to evacuate Major H. Platt to the rear and he was released by 2 Hampshire Regt. Owing to the delay in treatment of his wound he lost his leg.

The casualties for the action were:

Killed: 12 Other Ranks.
Missing: Lieut. E. R. Thomas, 2/Lieut. A. Heaps and 38 Other Ranks.
Wounded: Lieut.-Colonel J. R. I. Platt, Major H. Platt, Captain J. B. Winlove-Smith, Lieuts. T. E. O. Scrope-Howe, D. G. Strickland, J. C. Gleason, 2/Lieut. P. A. Thick and 94 Other Ranks.   Total 153.

4th British Division was now pulled out to rest. On 14th May, 2 Somerset L.I. rested in the assembly area and was joined by the companies from Smee Force. On 15th May it moved by M.T. to Piedmonte D'Alife to rest, while the advance on Rome continued. On 16th May, Lieut. Colonel A. D. McChechnie, D.S.O., from the Honourable Artillery Company (Infantry) T.A., was appointed to command the Battalion. On 20th May the Battalion was visited by Lieut.-General Sir Oliver Leese, the Army Commander. The Brigade Commander sent the following message to the Battalion:

"I congratulate you on your extremely gallant performance during the battle. You had a really tough task but at no time did you waver in your determination to see it through. Your brave action, I fear, cost lives, but to gain supremacy of the river was essential to the whole battle and this you achieved. Next time, with your great fighting spirit and the experiences you have gained, there will be no limit to your successes."

The Battalion continued to rest and train until the end of May. In the meantime our forces overran the whole of the R. Liri valley, piercing the Gustav Line. On 18th May, the town of Cassino was taken by British troops and the Monastery stormed by troops of the Polish Corps. The same day Highway 6 was cut, while U.S. forces took Formia, nearer the coast. On 23rd May the offensive from the Anzio beach-head was launched, while Canadian troops of 8th Army broke through the Hitler Line. The capture of Monte Cairo, Atina and Ceprano followed.

On 2nd June, U.S. troops entered Valmontone on Highway 6 and Velletri on Highway 7. At 1930 hours, on 4th June, Allied troops of 5th Army entered Rome and the Germans withdrew northwards.

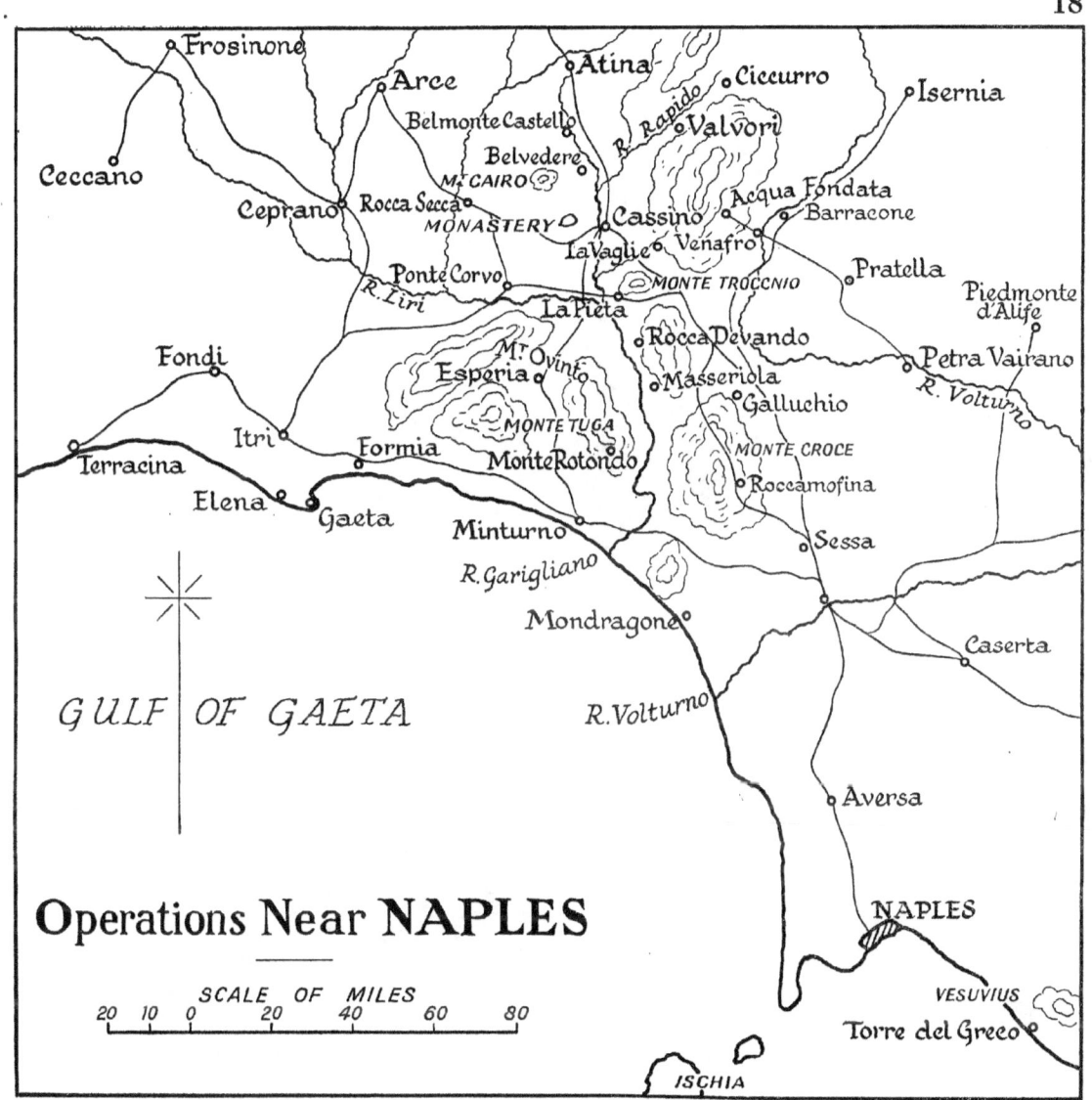

CHAPTER XIV

NORTHERN EUROPE—SEPTEMBER–DECEMBER 1944

The grouping of forces for the Pursuit—The advance into Belgium—Plans for 2nd British Army—The problem for 30 Corps—The advance of 43rd Division from the R. Seine—129th Brigade—214th Brigade—The Battle for Arnhem—The advance of 30 Corps—43rd Division, Operation Garden—Situation at the end of September 1944—43rd Division operations—Regrouping of 2nd British Army—General situation at the end of October—Operation Clipper—Operations near Geilenkirchen—General situation at the end of November—Operations in early December—The Battle of the Ardennes—43rd Division operations. (Map 3)

THE Crossing of the R. Seine, as described in Chapter XII, so far as the Vernon crossing was concerned, was not an easy operation. The intention had been for 30 Corps to cross near Vernon and 12 Corps between Les Andelys and Louviers. The concentration of these two Corps had been delayed because two U.S. Corps had driven northwards across the axis of advance from the Dreux area to Elbeuf.

By 1st September, 2 Canadian Corps was advancing, on the left flank, on Boos and Rouen. 30 Corps, with 43rd Division under command, had crossed the R. Seine near Vernon and, with the Guards Armd. Division and 11th Armd. Division, was advancing on Lens–Douai–Lille. 12 Corps had crossed near Louviers and was moving through Les Andelys. 1 Corps crossed last, near Duclair.

Further south, 1st U.S. Army crossed the R. Seine between Mante-Grassicourt and Melun, directed on the line Laon–Peronne. On the extreme right, 12th U.S. Army swept forward on Troyes, Chalons-sur-Marne and Reims.

In brief the formations in the pursuit of the Germans were grouped as follows:

Left: 1st Canadian Army, along the Channel coast.
Left centre: 2nd British Army, directed on Brussels and Antwerp.
Right centre: 12th U.S. Army Group, directed on Peronne and Reims.
Right: 1st and 3rd U.S. Armies, directed on Troyes and St. Dizier.

THE ADVANCE INTO BELGIUM

After their defeat in the Normandy battles and the elimination of the Falaise–Argentan pocket, the Germans retreated rapidly, leaving behind much material and equipment. They left garrisons in the Channel Ports. On 1st September, 1st Canadian Army reached the area Le Treport–Dieppe–Rouen, while 3rd U.S. Army liberated Verdun and Commercy and then crossed the R. Meuse. 2nd British Army took Amiens on 31st August and on 3rd September, entered Brussels and Tournai. The next day Antwerp, Lille, Louvain and Malines, as well as other important places were liberated. On 6th September, 1st Canadian Army isolated Calais.

On 7th September, 2nd British Army crossed the Albert Canal, in Belgium, reaching Ypres, Wavre and Huy, while 3rd U.S. Army, having crossed the R. Meuse in strength, began to cross the R. Moselle. By 8th September, 1st Canadian Army had taken Nieuport and Ostend and 1st U.S. Army was in Liége. Le Havre surrendered on 11th September.

Between 12th and 15th September, German forces on 2nd British Army front began to withdraw from the area of the Albert and Escaut Canals. 1st U.S. Army breached the Siegfried Line east of Aachen and entered Germany near Prum and Malmedy.

PLANS FOR THE 2ND BRITISH ARMY (*Map* 19)

2nd British Army was now confronted with the problem of crossing five major obstacles. These were:

(i) the Neder Rijn at Arnhem.
(ii) the R. Waal at Nijmegen.
(iii) the R. Maas at Grave.
(iv) the Wilhelmina Canal, north of Eindhoven.
(v) the Zud Willemsvaart Canal linking Helmond and S'Hertogenbosch.

Road and rail bridges over these obstacles at Nijmegen, Arnhem and Grave were believed to be intact. The main feature of the plan to surmount these obstacles was to use airborne troops to drop, as a "carpet", across them, on the general axis of the road Eindhoven–Uden–Grave–Nijmegen–Arnhem. A bridgehead was to be formed north of Arnhem.

For this operation, 1st Airborne Division was to be employed, together with the Polish Para Brigade. This force was to capture the Arnhem bridge intact. 82nd U.S. Airborne Division was to drop and secure the bridges at Nijmegen and Grave and obtain a lodgement on the high ground between Nijmegen and Groesbeek. From 2nd British Army, 30 Corps was directed on Arnhem, with 8 Corps on its right and 12 Corps on its left. The corridor through which 30 Corps was to advance, with all speed, was a very narrow one.

THE PROBLEM FOR 30 CORPS

43rd Division was now in 30 Corps. The intention of 30 Corps was to thrust forward from the R. Meuse–Escaut Canal bridgehead, directed on the general line Arnhem–Nunspect, with Guards Armd. Division as the spearhead. 43rd and 50th Divisions were to follow, in that order. If the bridges were found to have been destroyed, 43rd Division was to undertake bridging operations and, later, to advance through Appeldoorn and secure crossings over the R. Ijssel at Deventer and Zutphen. 50th Division was to be in 30 Corps

SEPTEMBER–DECEMBER 1944

reserve and was, ultimately, to secure the high ground north of Arnhem and then cross the R. Ijssel at Doesburg.

The above is the general account of the Pursuit to Belgium and the German Frontier and the setting of the stage for the operations culminating in the Battle for Arnhem. It is now necessary to return to the details of the move of 43rd Division to the area from which the advance on Arnhem was made.

THE ADVANCE OF 43RD DIVISION FROM THE R. SEINE (*Map* 3)

During the first days of September, 43rd Division remained near the Vernon bridgehead, on the R. Seine, while other formations passed through to take up the pursuit of the enemy. During this period it came under 8 Corps.

129th Brigade, with 4 Somerset L.I., was in the area of Le Mesnil Milon and Gasny, with brigade H.Q. at St. Genevieve. 214th Brigade, with 7 Somerset L.I. was in the Foret de Vernon. A fortnight was taken up with recreation, re-equipping and individual training.

Lieut.-Colonel Nichol, of 7 Somerset L.I., was ordered to report to 8 Corps for posting. Major T. B. Elliott was temporarily in command, until relieved, on 8th September, by Lieut.-Colonel H. A. Borradaile (Devon Regt.). It will be remembered that A company was lost during operations near the Chateau de Vernon on 27th August. This company was now replaced by a company from the South Staffordshire Regt. under Major L. Roberts who served with the Battalion for the rest of the Campaign.

129TH BRIGADE

About 8th September, 43rd Division received orders to advance to Belgium, leaving 130th Brigade, temporarily, behind. On 14th September, 129th Brigade began the move. At 1115 hours, 4 Somerset L.I. left Le Mesnil Milon in M.T. and arrived at Canteau, Belgium, at 0330 hours, on 15th September. During the move a Lloyd carrier, which had broken down and been left behind the column, mistook the words *tout droit*, in reply to a request for road direction, and interpreted them as "first right". The carrier took this turning and found itself liberating village after village of grateful Belgians. Otherwise the Battalion transport ran through, 176 miles, without a hitch; a very creditable performance.

The route lay through Gasny—Gisors—Beauvais—Amiens—Albert—Cambrai—Valenciennes—Mons—Malines, to Diest. On the way the column passed the Waterloo memorial. At 1115 hours, on 15th September, the Battalion moved on to Linkhout, the marching personnel being moved in Dukws. Thence it moved to De Groot Heile ("The Blasted Heath"). Here it remained until 20th September.

214TH BRIGADE

On 15th September, 7 Somerset L.I. concentrated at Braine le Comte and moved by M.T., following the same route as 4 Somerset L.I., to Diest.

43rd Division was now assembled in the area north of Diest, coming under command of 30 Corps. In the meantime 50th Division had relieved Guards Armd. Division in the De Groot bridgehead. 30 Corps was now assembled for the advance on Arnhem.

THE BATTLE FOR ARNHEM (*Map* 19)

On 17th September the airborne troops began to drop on their objectives, the first landings starting about 1300 hours. 1st Airborne Division dropped near the Arnhem bridge. Paratroops of 101st U.S. Airborne Division secured the bridge at Veghel, but the bridges over the Wilhelmina Canal at Son were blown. 82nd U.S. Airborne Division seized the bridge over the R. Maas at Grave intact, as well as the bridges over the Maas–Waal Canal, between Grave and Nijmegen.

THE ADVANCE OF 30 CORPS

At 1425 hours on 17th September, 30 Corps ordered Guards Armd. Division to advance on Eindhoven. The weather was misty with intermittent rain. Guards Armd. Division pushed forward, with 50th Division mopping up in rear. U.S. paratroops got into Eindhoven and, at 1700 hours, our armour broke the enemy resistance. 50th Division ensured the security of the De Groot bridgehead and then passed to command of 8 Corps, on the right. At Arnhem itself the situation of 1st Airborne Division was obscure.

At 0615 hours on 19th September, Guards Armd. Division started to cross the Wilhelmina Canal at Son and, by 0900 hours, linked up with 82nd U.S. Airborne Division at Grave. On the right, in 8 Corps sector, 3rd Division secured a bridgehead at Lille–St. Hubert, while on the left of 30 Corps, 12 Corps was pushing on west of Eindhoven.

During the 19th September, heavy fighting continued, with the situation of 1st Airborne Division at Arnhem becoming acute. Plans were now made by 30 Corps to push on with all speed to Arnhem on 20th September, with 43rd Division moving up rapidly from the south. The object now was to concentrate all efforts to relieve the Arnhem bridgehead.

43RD DIVISION—OPERATION MARKET GARDEN

On 21st September, 43rd Division completed its move to the transit area, following in the wake of Guards Armd. Division. In the meantime, on the 20th September, 214th Brigade was ordered to advance, directed on Arnhem. At 1630 hours, 7 Somerset L.I. moved off and, at 1900 hours, crossed the Escaut Canal. At 1925 hours the frontier into Holland was crossed and at 2330 hours the Battalion passed through Eindhoven. On 21st September, after crossing the R. Maas at Neder Hasselt, the Battalion moved off at 1530 hours for Arnhem and, at 1830 hours, harboured near Nijmegen, south of the river. Here it was employed getting up ammunition for a further advance of Guards Armd. Division. The Battalion had been ordered to attack Oosterhout on the evening of the 21st, but this was later countermanded and the approach march stopped. During the 21st September only 130th Brigade of 43rd Division was actually in the Nijmegen bridgehead.

In the meantime, 129th Brigade, with 4 Somerset L.I., followed in rear of 214th Brigade and moved into a harbour area north of Grave.

At 2330 hours on 21st September, 43rd Division was ordered by 30 Corps to capture the Arnhem road bridge intact and to contact 1st Airborne Division, with all speed, in the area of the Oosterbeek ferry, subsequently passing one brigade over the Neder Rijn. The two brigades of 43rd Division were now concentrated in the Nijmegen bridgehead.

43rd Division plan, for the 22nd September, was to advance at first light, through Guards Armd. Division, with 214th Brigade on the left and 129th Brigade on the right. 214th Brigade was to advance through Oosterhout and 129th Brigade was directed on Nijmegen–Arnhem. The object was to secure the Arnhem bridge intact and contact 1st Airborne Division.

The 22nd September dawned dull and cloudy, with intermittent rain. At 0400 hours, having marched all night, 4 Somerset L.I. reached 129th Brigade harbour area near Grave. During this march a Dukw overturned. Lieut. A. A. Barker and 6 Other Ranks of C company were killed and many others injured. At 1200 hours the Battalion reached Nijmegen. Here it stayed for the night 22nd/23rd September.

214th Brigade began to advance at 0700 hours. At 0930 hours, D company, 7 Somerset L.I. was fired on south of Oosterhout and deployed. The Company Commander, Major C. W. S. Young, was severely wounded and died in hospital that night. C company, supported by one troop of tanks, was then sent round on the right to try to capture Oosterhout from that flank. This attack was held up. A plan was now made to attack with A and B companies supported by the remainder of a squadron of tanks. This attack was launched at 1500 hours, from the south, after forming up under cover of the high dyke on which the roadway ran. By 1800 hours all companies were on their objectives. The enemy was identified as 64th Panzer Grenadiers and one Mark IV tank was captured by B company. The Battalion was established for the night 22nd/23rd September in Oosterhout and 5 D.C.L.I. passed through.

At 0630 hours, on 23rd September, 214th Brigade continued the advance. 7 Somerset L.I. moved out of Oosterhout directed on the south-east part of Elst. At 1400 hours the Battalion passed through Valburg. The starting line for the attack on Elst was just east of Valburg and the objective was the main road running from Nijmegen to Arnhem. Apart from some shelling, which caused casualties in C company, there was no opposition until the last stage. As it grew dark D company reached the main road and captured some 30 prisoners from a small post. By 1830 hours the Battalion had dug in on its objectives.

129th Brigade moved up in rear of 214th Brigade. At 1200 hours, 4 Somerset L.I. left Nijmegen and crossed the R. Waal.

During 24th September, fighting to secure the whole of Elst continued. At 0840 hours, B company, 7 Somerset L.I., cleared the cross-roads in Elst and close fighting continued in Elst and the area throughout the day.

Enemy resistance had stiffened and the advance of 43rd Division was now definitely checked on the line Bemmel–Bessem–Elst. Early on 25th September, 7 Somerset L.I., in Elst, was heavily shelled and mortared. At 1620 hours, B company, with one company of 1 Worcs Regt., gained further ground near the cross-roads in Elst and consolidated. Close fighting continued during the night 25th/26th September and during the morning of the 26th September. At 1630 hours, 7 Somerset L.I. was relieved by 4 Wilts Regt. and moved back to Herveld and occupied local farm houses and barns.

During 26th September, 129th Brigade was moving up to relieve 214th Brigade. 4 Somerset L.I. moved up into the Elst area, by march route, and relieved 1 Worcs Regt. 129th Brigade H.Q. was moved up across the R. Waal.

It had now become clear that the relief of 1st Airborne Division in the Arnhem bridgehead was not possible. A decision had, therefore, been taken to withdraw the remnants of the Division from Arnhem. This was timed for the night of 25th/26th September. 43rd Division was ordered to assist this withdrawal. For this task 130th (which had now rejoined the Division) and 214th Brigades were selected. 4 Dorset Regt. of 130th Brigade had been sent forward and had already secured, by 2330 hours on 25th September, a small bridgehead over the Neder Rijn, on the left of 1st Airborne Division. During the night 25th/26th September the withdrawal began.

On 27th September, 214th Brigade advanced. At 1230 hours, 7 Somerset L.I. was ordered to move forward and drive back the enemy over the Neder Rijn, downstream from the Arnhem bridge. At 1530 hours the attack was launched, with A and C companies leading. At 1630 hours the enemy was encountered north of Zetten and the advance held up though A company reached the outskirts of Randwijk after stiff opposition. Later in the evening this company continued the attack and captured Randwijk. This action cleared the way for C company. At 2200 hours C company attacked the dyke bank and reached the objective without further opposition, consolidating the position at 2230 hours.

During 27th September, 129th Brigade remained holding positions in the Elst area, with 5 Wilts Regt. on the left and 4 Somerset L.I. on the right. 4 Somerset L.I. held the line of the railway running through Elst, with B and A companies forward on the left, D company on the right and C company in reserve. A spirited patrol action was fought at Rijkeswaard.

On 28th September, 7 Somerset L.I. mopped up in the river area on the Neder Rijn, taking 145 P.O.W. At 1600 hours the Battalion was relieved by 1 Worcs Regt., and moved back to the area Zetten–Andelst to rest. On 29th September it moved up again to relieve 1 Worcs Regt., leaving Battalion H.Q. at Zetten. The 30th September was filled up with active patrolling. There was no further move in 129th Brigade area.

SEPTEMBER–DECEMBER 1944

SITUATION AT THE END OF SEPTEMBER 1944

The gamble at Arnhem, with the object of gaining rapidly a bridgehead over the Neder Rijn, had failed, but it had been a glorious failure. On the credit side the Nijmegen bridgehead over the Rhine was a valuable strategic acquisition. By the end of September 8 Corps, on the right, had made contact with 30 Corps in the centre and was on the general line Weert–Deurne–Boxmeer–Cuijk, where it had contacted 82nd U.S. Airborne Division, 12 Corps was on the left of 30 Corps in the Schijndel area, on the line of the Oss–S'Hertogenbosch railway.

1st Canadian Army, with 1 British Corps, had relieved 12 Corps in the Antwerp area. During the latter part of September, Boulogne and Calais had been stormed and preparations made to clear the Scheldt estuary, so as to open Antwerp as a supply port.

The object of 21st Army Group was now to secure the Ruhr, striking south-eastwards from the Nijmegen bridgehead, between the R. Rhine and R. Meuse. This thrust was to be combined with U.S. Army operations directed against Cologne and Dusseldorf.

Plans for this operation were delayed for certain reasons. Antwerp was not yet opened as a port and supply problems, from the Channel ports, presented serious difficulties. The enemy resistance had stiffened and 2nd British Army had not sufficient resources available to begin the assault on the Ruhr.

43RD DIVISION

On 1st October, 43rd Division was employed in securing the eastern flank of 30 Corps, between the R. Waal and R. Neder Rijn. During the first week the Germans made heavy and repeated counter-attacks.

214th Brigade, with 7 Somerset L.I., continued to patrol forward in the Zetten area. On 3rd October, the brigade was relieved by U.S. forces. 7 Somerset L.I. handed over to 506th U.S. Regt. and, at 2330 hours, moved back to rest at Ewijk. Here it stayed until 7th October.

129th Brigade remained in close contact with the enemy near Elst. Between 1st and 4th October, 4 Somerset L.I. was counter-attacked on several occasions and heavily shelled and mortared. The Battalion was short of ammunition and defensive fire had to be strictly controlled. Guards Armd. Division, on the right of 4 Somerset L.I., was also heavily engaged. Casualties during this period were heavy. Lieuts. D. R. Stuart and H. F. A. Barnes were killed; Majors J. R. Acock and B. A. Watts and Lieut. Mylchrest wounded by shell-fire and in beating off attacks. On 4th October the Battalion took P.O.W. of 1st Panzer Grenadiers. On 5th October, the Battalion was relieved, at 1930 hours, by a U.S. Airborne Regt. and moved to an area west of Nijmegen to rest.

On 7th October, 214th Brigade moved up again. 7 Somerset L.I. moved into the area Diest–Afferden to protect the left flank of the Corps artillery area and to block the Druten–Nijmegen road.

REGROUPING OF 2ND BRITISH ARMY

Orders now came for 30 Corps to take over responsibility for 2nd British Army front between the R. Waal and R. Maas, facing east. Included in the operation of taking over this front were:

Phase I: 129th Brigade of 43rd Division, to relieve 9th Brigade of 3rd Division and come under 3rd Division on arrival in the new area.

Phase II: 43rd Division to take over from 3rd Division (8 Corps) on 9th October.

Phase III: 130th Brigade of 43rd Division to relieve 505th R.C.T. (82nd U.S. Airborne Division) by first light on 11th October.

On completion of this operation, 43rd Division would be on the right of 30 Corps, with 8th Armd. Brigade under command. Its rôle was to be responsible for 30 Corps front from the R. Maas to the Corps junction with 82nd U.S. Airborne Division. This rôle was to be carried out by active patrolling.

On 8th October, 129th Brigade relieved 9th Infantry Brigade of 3rd Division in the area Malden–Mook. 4 Somerset L.I. relieved 2 E. Yorks Regt. at Malden, to the east of Nijmegen. This was in the brigade reserve area and was quiet.

On 9th October, 214th Brigade moved into an area near Malden. 7 Somerset L.I. relieved 1 Royal Norfolk Regt., with A and B companies forward, and started active patrolling. On 11th October the Battalion was relieved by 5 D.C.L.I. and moved into reserve, where it rested.

On 13th October, 129th Brigade relieved 214th Brigade, near Malden. 4 Somerset L.I. relieved 7 Somerset L.I., in an area of sandy hills and small fir trees. This was the brigade reserve area, 4 and 5 Wilts Regt. being forward battalions. While here, 4 Somerset L.I. was heavily shelled and mortared, but carried out some excellent patrol work. Deep penetration patrols towards the Reichwald Forest were led by Lieuts. P. N. L. Priani and J. B. Alliban. The latter, who was accompanied by Corpl. McQuillan, later received the M.C. for this work. Other patrols were led by Lieuts. S. W. Jary, Bull, Potter and Bullock. A patrol under Lieut. Jary attempted to cross the R. Maas, but failed owing to flood waters.

On 23rd October, 130th Brigade relieved 129th Brigade and 4 Somerset L.I. moved back to a rest area. Here the Adjutant, Captain Reader, contracted appendicitis and was succeeded by Captain T. M. Watson.

In 214th Brigade area, 7 Somerset L.I. had moved back to a rest area west of Malden and, on 16th October, was addressed by the Corps commander, Lieut.-General B. G. Horrocks, C.B., D.S.O., M.C. On 18th October, 214th Brigade took over from 130th Brigade, 7 Somerset L.I. relieving 5 Dorset R. in the Groesbeek area, where it was engaged in active patrolling. On 22nd October it was relieved by 5 D.C.L.I. and went into brigade reserve.

On 25th October, it moved up to relieve 1 Worcs Regt., near Knapheide, west of Groesbeek, where it was in close contact with the enemy. On 27th October, D company, in a position near the Monastery, was heavily shelled.

On 28th October, 129th Brigade relieved 214th Brigade. 4 Somerset L.I. took over the Knapheide sector from 7 Somerset L.I. The latter moved back to a concentration area near Mook, 214th Brigade being in Divisional reserve.

129th Brigade was disposed in the Groesbeek area with 4 Somerset L.I. on the right, 5 Wilts Regt. on the left and 4 Wilts Regt. in reserve. On the right of 4 Somerset L.I. was 4 Dorset Regt., of 130th Brigade. Knapheide was at the bottom of a forward slope, overlooked from ground sloping up to the Reichwald and from the Forest itself. The area was the scene of the drop by 82nd U.S. Airborne Division and was strewn with broken gliders.

At 0220 hours, on 31st October, A company H.Q.—the left forward company of 4 Somerset L.I.—was raided by a party of about 25 enemy. The H.Q. was in a house and the wall was blown in by a pole charge. The house was then attacked from the rear and the raiders attempted to rush the back entrance. Those who got in were shot down by Captain Bullock and C.S.M. Davis. The house, however, was set on fire by the explosion and had to be evacuated. 2 Other Ranks were killed by the explosion and 2 reported missing. The raiders lost 5 killed.

The Battalion front in this sector was in very flat country, with no cover except for scattered houses and farms. All movement had to be made by night. Several good patrols were, however, carried out, particularly by Lieut. S. W. Jary (who was awarded the M.C.), Sergeant Brown and Lieut. Alliban. The latter, while on patrol, was temporarily blinded by an "egg" grenade. On 5th November, 130th Brigade relieved 129th Brigade, 4 Somerset L.I. was relieved, and crossed the R. Maas to a rest area at Cuijk.

214th Brigade had relieved 130th Brigade, in the Katerbosch area on 2nd November, 7 Somerset L.I. taking over a sector from 5 Dorset Regt. Here it was engaged in active patrolling. On 6th November the Battalion was relieved by 5 D.C.L.I. and moved into brigade reserve at Mook.

GENERAL SITUATION

During the latter part of October, 2 Canadian Corps was clearing the Scheldt estuary, penetrating into South Beveland. The dykes on Walcheren Island had already been broken, early in October, by R.A.F. bombing. After a landing by commandos, followed by 52nd Division, near Flushing and a naval bombardment on 1st November, Flushing was taken on 2nd November. By 8th November, Walcheren had been mopped up. The Port of Antwerp was not, however, opened until 28th November.

OPERATION CLIPPER (*Map* 21)

Between 12th October and 3rd December operations by 2nd British Army were undertaken, (*a*) to clear the west bank of the R. Maas and (*b*) to make ground up to the R. Roer. The dispositions of 2nd British Army were, roughly:

- *Left:* 8 Corps, from Boxmeer in the north, to the road Weert–Meijel–Venlo.
- *Centre:* 12 Corps, south of 8 Corps, to the line Maeseyck–Wessem–Roermond.
- *Right:* 30 Corps, south of 12 Corps to the line of the R. Wurm.

9th U.S. Army lay to the south of 30 Corps. 43rd Division was on the right of 30 Corps, opposite Geilenkirchen, with 84th U.S. Division on its right.

Between 10th and 12th November, 30 Corps began to prepare for Operation Clipper. This operation was to be carried out in conjunction with large scale operations of 9th U.S. Army, further south. The object of 30 Corps was to capture Geilenkirchen, so that U.S forces could use the main road running through that town.

The plan for 43rd Division, as part of Operation Clipper, was for 214th Brigade to break through north of Geilenkirchen and cut the road leaving that town in a north-easterly direction. 130th Brigade was to capture Bauchem and, subsequently, Waldenrath and Straeten.

In accordance with this plan, 43rd Division began to move to the Maastricht area on the 10th/11th November. On 10th November, 129th Brigade moved to the Rumpen area, 4 Somerset L.I. reaching Kling, near Brunssum, at 0800 hours, after a very cold drive, in convoy, all night. Here 129th Brigade relieved 407th R.C.T. of 102nd U.S. Division and was disposed with 4 Somerset L.I. on right, 4 Wilts Regt. in the centre and 5 Wilts Regt. on the left. The brigade, on this day, crossed into Germany for the first time.

The sector occupied by 4 Somerset L.I. was a large one, for U.S. battalions had a much larger over-all strength than British battalions. It stretched from Teveren on the right, to Gillrath on the left—some 4,000 yards of front. The main position was some 1,000 yards from the enemy. Between 12th and 17th November, the Battalion was engaged in patrolling between Waldenrath and Schierwal, where there were extensive minefields.

214th Brigade was relieved by a Canadian Brigade near Katerbosch. 7 Somerset L.I. handed over to 1st South Saskatchewan Regt. on the night 9th/10th November. At 0725 hours on 10th November, it moved back to Schinnen and, on 12th November, to Kling.

On 15th November, Brigadier G. H. L. Mole, D.S.O., M.C., commanding 129th Brigade, was fatally injured by the explosion of some mines, which were being off-loaded from transport near his H.Q. He was buried at Brunssum and succeeded by Brigadier J. O. E. Vandeleur, D.S.O., late Irish Guards.

OPERATIONS NEAR GEILENKIRCHEN

43rd Division now had 8th Armd. Brigade under command. 18th November was D-day for Operation Clipper, the object being to clear the country up to the R. Roer. Geilenkirchen was one of the intermediate objectives of

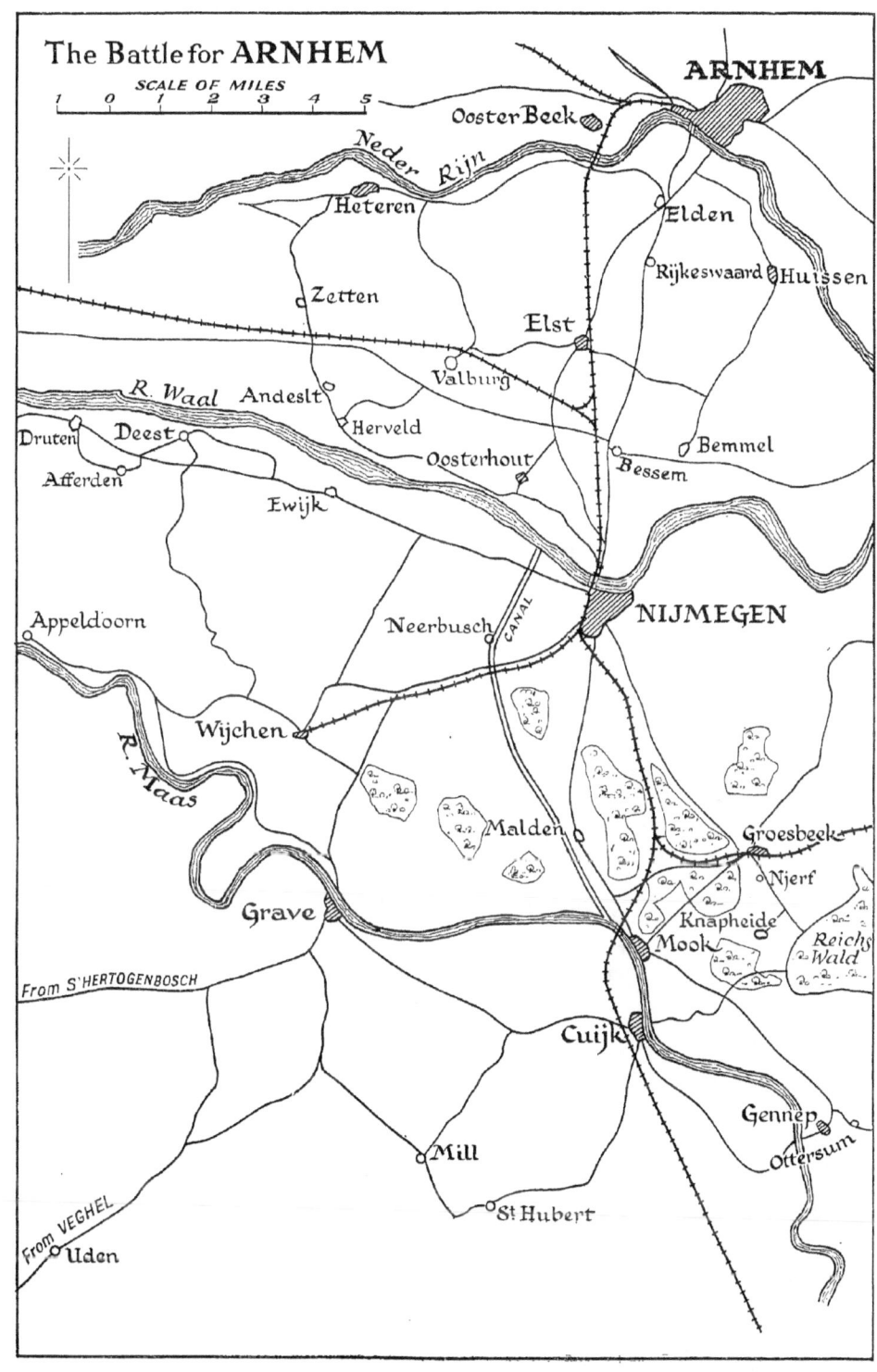

84th U.S. Division supported by the Sherwood Rangers. Gillrath was the starting point for the attack. At 0700 hours, 84th U.S. Division, on the right of 43rd Division, started an attack on Prummern. At 1000 hours 214th Brigade began to advance, with 1 Worcs Regt. on left and 7 Somerset L.I. on right.

At 1230 hours, B and D companies, 7 Somerset L.I. attacked Niederheide and, by 1430 hours, the Battalion had captured their objective. At 1350 hours, 1 Worcs Regt. attacked Tripsrath and Rischden. At 1600 hours 4 D.C.L.I. passed through 7 Somerset L.I. and attacked Hocheid and Bruggerhof. By 1410 hours, 84th U.S. Division, on the right, was in Prummern.

The attack of 130th Brigade started at 1530 hours. 5 Dorset Regt., under 214th Brigade, attacked Bauchem and obtained a lodgement in the village by 1830 hours. By 2000 hours, 214th and 130th Brigades had gained all objectives, having taken 300 P.O.W. The captured area was heavily shelled and mortared.

During the day 129th Brigade was in reserve and used its mortars to stiffen the artillery fire plan. The attacks of the two leading brigades were covered by very heavy concentrations of artillery fire, which dazed the enemy.

On 19th November (D plus 1 for Clipper) the projected attack of 130th Brigade on Waldenrath and Straeten was postponed owing to a heavy counter-attack which came in on 84th U.S. Division south of Prummern. This was held and the Division then took Geilenkirchen and cleared up the valley of the R. Wurm to Suggerath. 5 Dorset Regt. passed through 7 Somerset L.I. and attacked a wood, south-west of Tripsrath, which was still held by the enemy. The maps were extremely inaccurate and 7 Somerset L.I. were able to point out the correct objectives. A further attack was then launched by 130th Brigade to clear up Bauchem. This was successful. While this was in progress a stray shell killed Captain C. A. Humphries and 2/Lieut. K. G. Oxland of 4 Somerset L.I.

In 214th Brigade sector, 7 Somerset L.I. attacked at 1330 hours, passing through 5 D.C.L.I. at Hocheide, to clear the woods towards Hoven. By 1630 hours all companies were on their objectives. P.O.W. from 330th Volks Grenadier Regt. were taken. The Battalion maintained its positions all night under heavy shell-fire.

In the evening, C company 4 Somerset L.I. was moved up to strengthen 5 Dorset Regt. of 130th Brigade in Bauchem.

On 20th November (D plus 2) 214th Brigade was engaged in active patrolling. On 21st November (D plus 3) 5 D.C.L.I. with D company 7 Somerset L.I. launched an attack from the woods east of Hocheide and captured Hoven. It was now clear that the enemy was strongly opposing the advance to the R. Roer. On the 22nd November (D plus 4), the enemy counter-attacked Hoven and 5 D.C.L.I., was forced to withdraw from the village. 7 Somerset L.I. less B company, was also withdrawn southwards into the area Geilenkirchen-Suggerath. 129th Brigade with 4 Somerset L.I. was drawn back to a rest area near Cuijk. Heavy shelling of the whole area continued.

On 23rd November (D plus 5) C company, 4 Somerset L.I., was moved up to the Geilenkirchen area and, later on the same day, 129th Brigade moved up and relieved 214th Brigade. 4 Somerset L.I. took over from 7 Somerset L.I., the latter moving back to rest in the area Nierstras–Gotenrath–Teveren. Active patrolling under heavy shelling continued in the Geilenkirchen sector.

On 28th November, 214th Brigade relieved 130th Brigade, 4 Somerset L.I. relieving 7 Hampshire Regt. at Gillrath and being engaged in active patrolling.

During November, 43rd Division took 679 P.O.W.

GENERAL SITUATION (Map 7)

By the end of November the supply problem had been eased by the opening of the Port of Antwerp. By the end of November 30 Corps was disposed between the R. Wurm and R. Meuse with 43rd Division on the right and Guards Armd. Division on the left. On the right of 43rd Division was 84th U.S. Division. Geilenkirchen had been taken and this had aided the main U.S. thrust, further south, on Cologne. The advance of 30 Corps had been parallel to and not through the Siegfried Line, the reduction of which was a laborious task.

Operations, generally, had been hampered by bad weather and it was not until 16th November that the main U.S. advance on the axis Aachen–Cologne started. Still further south, 3rd U.S. Army had advanced on 8th November and taken Metz, thereafter reaching the line of the R. Moselle.

It should be noted that, on 1st August, Allied forces had landed in the south of France, between Toulon and Nice, and had pressed northwards. This advance developed into operations in which 6th U.S. Army and 1st French Army were engaged. Alsace–Loraine was entered and the R. Rhine reached between the Swiss frontier and Mulhouse. Further north, 7th U.S. Army took Strasbourg and turned north towards Karlsruhe.

OPERATIONS IN EARLY DECEMBER (Map 21)

In December, the whole countryside on 2nd British Army front was saturated and waterlogged, partly from heavy rains and partly from enemy inundations. Thus movement of any kind was difficult. A re-grouping now began in preparation for the Battle of the Rhineland. U.S. forces were directed to take over the right sector of 30 Corps area, so as to release that Corps for an assault on the Reichwald Forest. Certain other commitments of 30 Corps were taken over by 12 Corps.

For the assault on the Reichwald, 30 Corps was allotted the Guards Armd., 15th, 43rd and 53rd Divisions and was ordered to concentrate in the Nijmegen bridgehead, with a view to a drive towards Krefeld. This was timed to start on 12th January 1945. These plans were, however, frustrated by the German counter-offensive in the Ardennes, which started on 16th December.

43RD DIVISION

Early in December moves in connection with the re-grouping of 30 Corps began. On 1st December, 214th Brigade, near Gillrath, was relieved by Corps troops and moved to the Kling–Merkelbeek area. On 2nd December, 129th Brigade was relieved in the Geilenkirchen sector by 130th Brigade and, also, moved back to reserve near Merkelbeek. 4 Somerset L.I. moved to a rest area near Teveren–Gothenrath.

On 3rd December, 214th Brigade again moved up into the line, 7 Somerset L.I. relieving 5 D.C.L.I. in the Rishden sector. Contact patrolling continued. On 6th December, 129th Brigade relieved 214th Brigade, 7 Somerset L.I. moving to a concentration area at Teveren and 4 Somerset L.I. being in 129th Brigade reserve near Niederbusch.

On 8th December, 129th Brigade was relieved by 156th Brigade of 52nd Division and moved back to the Merkelbeek area. 4 Somerset L.I. moved to rest at Treebeek, where it began reorganising and training.

On 12th December, 43rd Division passed from the command of 30 Corps, temporarily, to 12 Corps and, on 16th December, was relieved by 52nd (L) Division of 12 Corps. 214th Brigade, with 7 Somerset L.I. now moved to Meersen.

THE BATTLE OF THE ARDENNES (*Map 3*)

The slowness of the advance of 2nd British Army in October and November, due to bad weather and administrative difficulties, had given the enemy time to refit his strategic reserves. By mid-December he had increased his available field force to some seventy divisions. He now planned a major, and desperate, counter-stroke to restore the situation. His object was to surprise the Allies, cross the R. Meuse and drive through to Antwerp.

He concentrated his striking force with great skill and secrecy. His intention was to cross the R. Meuse between Liége and Givet, with 6th S.S. Panzer Army on the right and 5th Panzer Army on the left. Each of these armies contained four divisions. Seventeen infantry, paratroop and Panzer Grenadier divisions were available to follow behind the Panzer and S.S. spearheads.

The counter-stroke started on 16th December and the surprise was complete. By 18th December the attack had reached Stavelot–Trois Points–Vielsalm. In 21st Army Group the process of transferring the bulk of available troops to the north, prior to the drive through the Rhineland, was stopped. It was decided to move 43rd and Guards Armd. Divisions from the area southeast of Maeseyck, to the west and move 53rd Division from Roermond to Turnhout.

On 19th December, the move of 30 Corps to the north was cancelled and the Corps was ordered to assemble in the area Louvain–St. Trond. 30 Corps was now allotted the Guards Armd., 43rd, 51st and 53rd Divisions, with three Armd. Brigades.

By 19th December, enemy armour had reached the line Hotton–Marche–

Laroche and the gap in the Allied line extended from Durbuy to Bastogne. 30 Corps was, therefore, ordered to move with all speed to the new concentration area.

43RD DIVISION

On 19th December, 43rd Division was on the move. 129th Brigade moved to a concentration area near Neerglasbeek, east of the Asch–Bree road. 4 Somerset L.I. was located at Opoeteren. On 20th December the brigade moved on to Weert and, on 21st December, to Tongres.

214th Brigade left the Meersen area on 19th December for Tilburg, but, while on the move, was diverted to a new area, 7 Somerset L.I. reaching Bilsen at 1600 hours. 43rd Division was now placed at one hour's notice for further action. It was now, again, under 30 Corps, with 34th Armd. Brigade under command. Its tasks were as follows:

(*a*) to concentrate in the area Hasselt–Bilsen–Tongres;
(*b*) to hold the concentration area firmly;
(*c*) to be prepared to develop a reconnaissance screen along the R. Meuse, from Huy to Vise, delaying any enemy attempt to cross in this sector;
(*d*) to prepare to garrison and hold the bridges over the R. Meuse from, both exclusive, Namur to Liége;
(*e*) in the event of an enemy thrust on Brussels from the south, or south-west, to be ready to move to an assembly area east, or west of Brussels, preparatory to taking offensive action.

In pursuance of this plan, 130th Brigade, on 23rd December, was sent to an area north and north-west of Wareme. By 25th December, 43rd Division was established on the crossings of the R. Meuse and ready for a counter-attack rôle.

While these moves were taking place, 21st Army Group had taken over command of 1st and 9th U.S. Armies, north of the salient in the Ardennes created by the German advance. These armies had become separated from 12th U.S. Army Group by the deep German penetration.

The German counter-stroke continued to press forward, but the main enemy plan had miscarried. 6th S.S. Panzer Army failed to break the U.S. line in the Malmedy–Stavelot sector. Finally, on 22nd December, having failed to find any soft spot, 2 S.S. Corps of 6th S.S. Panzer Army was swung westwards to try and break through to Liége, from the south, via Durbuy. By 25th December, the enemy offensive had been sealed off within the area Elsenhorn–Hotton–St. Hubert–Bastogne and all routes to the R. Meuse effectively blocked.

30 Corps was now ordered to take over the sector Givet–Hotton, on the right of 1st U.S. Army, to enable 7th U.S. Corps to be available to attack towards Houffalise.

In accordance with these orders, 43rd Division, with 6th Guards Armd. Brigade under command, was moved to an area east of Maastricht and there came under 12 Corps.

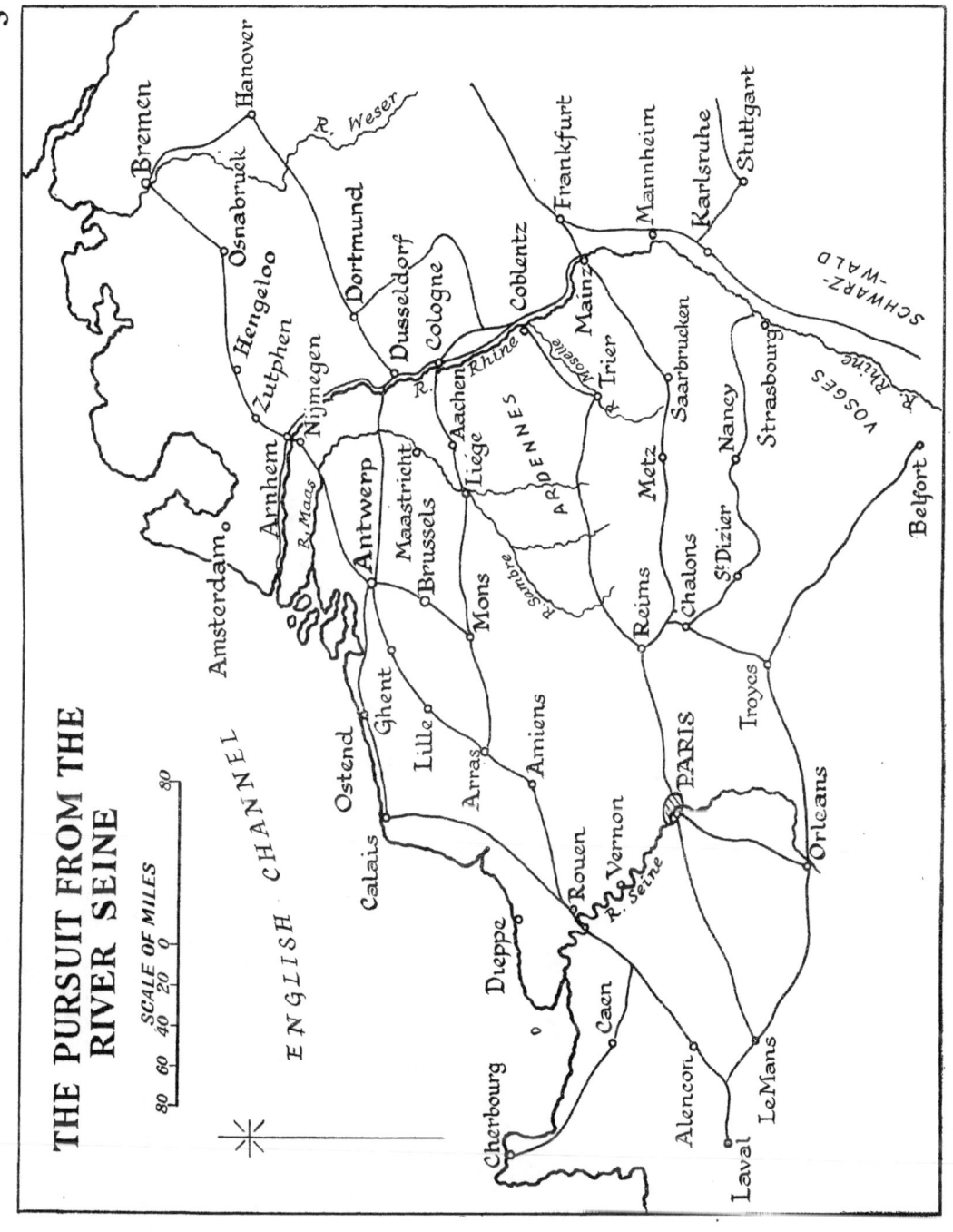

129th Brigade, with 4 Somerset L.I., moved to the Hulsbeek sector. 214th Brigade, with 7 Somerset L.I., moved to the sector Moorvelo–Hulsen–Hassenberg–Snijdersburg. The whole division was placed at three hours' notice to be prepared to repel paratroop landings to the south-east of Aachen.

The situation, however, was very much easier and the major danger of the threat to Brussels had been removed. That this was so, is evidenced by the fact that, on 31st December, the first leave parties left the division for the U.K. The task now ahead was to eliminate the German pocket in the Ardennes.

CHAPTER XV

THE CAMPAIGN IN ITALY. III—ROME TO FLORENCE, 1944

2ND BATTALION

The general situation—The situation in June 1944—The battle for Vaiano—The clearing of the Lake Trasimene position—The advance to Arezzo—The action at Ricasoli—The advance to Florence —The capture of Florence

CHAPTER XIII dealt with the fortunes of the 2nd Battalion in the Battle of the Garigliano, which was followed by the advance of 5th and 8th Armies on Rome and the capture of the City on 4th June, 1944.

THE GENERAL SITUATION

The story of the campaign in Italy is one of disappointments and the course of events, influenced by world strategy, must have caused great irritation to the Higher Command in the Mediterranean theatre.

The terrain over which the allied armies had to advance against strong and determined opposition was admirably suited to a skilled defender. On either side of the "leg" of Italy, the sea restricts wide turning movements and efforts to overcome this disadvantage by sea-borne landings in rear of enemy positions were rendered difficult owing to shortages of craft, material and man-power. Movement along the coastal plains, on either side of the central mountain spine, was hampered by the many rivers running at right angles to the lines of advance. These had to be crossed in the face of determined opposition and, since the Germans were past-masters of delaying tactics, inundations and demolitions, they all had to be bridged. The mountains in the centre, not only provided excellent defensive positions, with adequate observation for a defender, but complicated supply problems and rendered lateral communication between the two armies extremely difficult.

It was not until the country began to broaden out, north of Lake Trasimene, towards the plains of Lombardy, that there was more scope for manœuvre and the possibility of advancing on a broad, co-ordinated front.

A further and even more serious difficulty arose. Whenever the stage seemed set for a break through and rigorous exploitation of success, forces were drawn away from Italy to meet the pressing needs of other theatres of war. In the autumn and winter of 1943–4, formations were sent to England to stiffen the forces available for the invasion of Normandy. During the summer of 1944, further formations were withdrawn to provide for the landings in Southern France on 15th August. Still later in the year, divisions had to be found to

THE CAMPAIGN IN ITALY: III

meet the serious situation arising in Greece. And still later, further Canadian formations were taken to provide weight for the crossing of the Rhine and the advance into Germany. Thus the Higher Command in Italy never had quite enough men, or tanks, or guns at their disposal to finish off the Germans and ensure an early and decisive settlement of the campaign.

THE SITUATION IN JUNE 1944

Early in June 1944, 4th British Division formed part of 13 Corps of 8th Army, operating on the right flank of 5th Army, which was advancing northwards between Rome and the western seaboard.

8th Army plan was for 13 Corps to advance north, in conjunction with 5th Army on its left and other formations of 8th Army on the Adriatic coastal plain on its right, to secure the area Terni–Narni. In this movement 10 Corps was on the right and 13 Corps on the left. 13 Corps, at this time, included:

6th British Armd. Division. 78th British Division.
6th S.A. Armd. Division.   9th Armd. Brigade.
4th British Division.   25th Tank Brigade.

The advance of 13 Corps was on three routes:

Joker: Polombara–Morrilone (4th Division).
Spade: Palestrina–Rome–Monterondo–Confini–Terni (6th Armd. Division).
Heart: Highway 6–Rome–Narni (6th S.A. Armd. Division).

On the left of 13 Corps, 5th Army advanced on a two corps front, with 2 U.S. Corps on the right and 6 U.S. Corps on the left. The advance of 13 Corps began on 7th June, directed on Arezzo–R. Bibiena–Florence.

On 1st June, 28th Brigade of 4th British Division, with 2 Somerset L.I. was near Piedmonte D'Alife, resting. On 5th June, 4th Division took over from 78th Division and a Free French Division, between Arce and Frosinone, with 10th and 12th Brigades forward and 28th Brigade in reserve. 2 Somerset L.I. moved up to Valmontone, south of Palestrina.

On 9th June, 5th Army troops took Viterbo and by 14th June 78th Division of 13 Corps entered Orvieto. In the meantime 4th Division was moved up, passing east of Rome. 28th Brigade, with 2 Somerset L.I. passed through Tivoli and after concentrating 12 miles north of Rome, reached a concentration area at Grotte San Stefano, north of Viterbo, on 16th June. Here it began training for a mobile armoured advance.

The enemy was now holding ground on either side of Lake Trasimene, 13 Corps being directed to the West of the Lake, on Trasimene–Chiusi. The advance on this position began on 21st June, 4th Division moving up to relieve 78th Division. 28th Brigade was leading and relieved 36th Brigade of 78th Division near Strada. 2 King's Regt. was on the right and 2 Somerset L.I. on the left. Here Major C. G. C. Fox and 1 Other Rank were killed by shell-fire.

THE BATTLE FOR VAIANO

During 23rd June, 2 Somerset L.I. patrolled towards Vaiano. Preparations were made for an attack, with 78th Division on the left and 4th Division on the right. At 0800 hours on 24th June, 2 Somerset L.I. joined up with tanks from B Squadron 12 Canadian Tank Regt. and crossed the start line at 0945 hours. C company was on the right and B company on the left, with A company patrolling on the left flank and D company in close support of the leading companies. The object was to clear the divisional axis of advance, Vaiano–Lavilla–Lopi–Gioiella. 78th Division on the right was attacking along the edge of Lake Trasimene.

The advance was strongly opposed. At 1000 hours the tanks with 2 Somerset L.I. crossed a stream at the foot of the first objective, but heavy spandau fire sent C and B companies to ground in high standing corn. Major P. J. Nation and Lieuts. D. G. Bearman, W. O. Goldsworthy, A. H. Smith and C. G. Barfoot were wounded and the tank commander killed. Contact with B company was lost. Heavy shelling and mortaring continued until 1800 hours, when the enemy began to withdraw. A company then advanced but was held up by spandau fire from Vaiano on the left. At 1900 hours a small party under Lieut. P. A. Thick crossed the stream and broke into a house, destroying a spandau crew. Lieut. Thick was killed and Lance-Corporal Collingwood wounded. The remainder had to withdraw. Heavy rain came on and the positions gained were consolidated for the night. The casualties for the day were 1 Officer killed and 3 Officers and 26 Other Ranks wounded.

At 0830 hours on 25th June contact had been made with all companies. A projected attack by 2 King's Regt. was cancelled. C company 2 Somerset L.I. attempted to get forward, Lieut. E. D. H. Firman being wounded. C and D companies managed to reach the first objective and, by 1230 hours, D company had gained the second objective. Here it consolidated, having taken 6 P.O.W. of a German Para Regt.

At 1330 hours, C company again advanced under strong opposition. B company was then ordered to pass through. A company was sent up to assist D company, engaging the enemy in houses. 12 Other Ranks were wounded. At 1430 hours 2/4 Hampshire Regt. moved up on the left and was heavily counter-attacked but drove off the enemy. The position on the right flank was obscure and all companies of 2 Somerset L.I. dug in for the night. On this day Vaiano had been taken.

At 0200 hours on 26th June, 2/4 Hampshire Regt. was again counter-attacked and all troops on the front "stood to". A fresh plan was made for 2 King's Regt. to pass through 2 Somerset L.I. and 2/4 Hampshire Regt., but this was cancelled. At 1245 hours B and D companies, 2 Somerset L.I., with two troops of tanks, the whole under Major T. P. Luckock, advanced to a ridge in front of and to the right of the previous positions, patrolling forward to a small hamlet which was found unoccupied. Plans for a further advance were cancelled. The tanks were withdrawn from the forward companies and four A/T guns sent up. On this day Chiusi was taken.

During the night 26th/27th June, D.C.L.I. of 10th Brigade came into the area and attacked through 2 Somerset L.I. with artillery support. By 1400 hours on 27th June, the whole of 10th Brigade had passed through and 2 Somerset L.I. consolidated and improved the position. On 28th June, 28th Brigade was rested near Poggio de Papa.

THE CLEARING OF THE LAKE TRASIMENE POSITION

On 29th June, 10th Brigade reached Martelli and Pozzuolo, while on the left, 78th Division was nearing Castiglione. On 30th June, 10th Brigade attacked and took Petrignano and in the evening the enemy began to withdraw. The next day contact was lost on the whole front of 13 Corps. 28th Brigade moved up to relieve 10th Brigade near Pozzuolo and at 0830 hours began to advance towards San Marguerita, on a broad front, with 2 Somerset L.I. and 2 King's Regt. leading. 2 Somerset L.I. had C and B companies forward, each supported by two troops of tanks. 4 Recce Regt. formed a screen in front. By 1040 hours San Marguerita was entered without opposition and by 1340 hours C company, with 2/4 Hampshire Regt. on its left, had reached the fourth objective unopposed. The advance had gained $3\frac{1}{4}$ miles.

C company now reported stiffening resistance and much artillery and spandau fire. Battalion H.Q. was moved up to Poderi Stella. By 1630 hours, C company, with 2/4 Hampshire Regt. on the left, took the final objective and consolidated. The enemy was surprised and retreated hastily, leaving 6 P.O.W., two infantry guns, one 88 mm. mortar and much equipment. About 1800 hours, Battalion H.Q. was shelled and the enemy tried to infiltrate into D company area but was beaten off, leaving 5 P.O.W. D company was withdrawn slightly.

On 2nd July, at 1040 hours, D company, on the right flank, was heavily counter-attacked by enemy tanks. A confused fight followed, but by 1355 hours, the company had successfully withdrawn and linked up with A company. In these operations we lost 3 Other Ranks killed and Lieut. A. H. Smith and 12 Other Ranks wounded.

THE ADVANCE TO AREZZO

On the night 2nd/3rd July, the enemy withdrew and 12th Brigade passed through 28th Brigade. 28th Brigade moved up in rear of 12th Brigade, advancing at 0415 hours, on 3rd July, supported by tanks. At 1030 hours, Capazzano was reached without opposition and a further 3 miles gained. The troops were now very tired and mines and demolitions were encountered. In the afternoon 2 King's Regt. passed through 2 Somerset L.I. and the latter rested near Capazzano for the night. During the day 2/4 Hampshire Regt. took Colonna.

On 3rd July, the Battalion embussed and moved to a concentration area north of Foiano, the plan being to follow 2 King's Regt. and, later, to advance on the left of that battalion. At 1300 hours 2 Somerset L.I. advanced and, after covering 3 miles, met opposition on the first objective, north of Badicorte, from spandaus and mortars. 2 King's Regt., on the right, continued to advance slowly. 12th Brigade, on the left, was held up. The position gained was consolidated, with Battalion H.Q. at Gesa.

During the night 3rd/4th July, A and D companies relieved C and B companies and, at 0830 hours on 4th July, the advance continued with little opposition. By 1700 hours, the objective was reached. A company, on the left, was at Dorna. D company, on the right, was north of Badia Al Pino. Battalion H.Q. was at Matroia. This village was overlooked by the enemy. 12th Brigade, on the left, was held up south of Civitella di Caiana and 6th Armd. Division, on the right, was checked south of Arezzo. While bringing up rations, Colour-Sergeant Keyes, of A company, was killed by a shell.

On 5th July there was no move. The plan for 28th Brigade was for 2 Somerset L.I. to advance, on 6th July, supported by tanks and pass through 2 King's Regt. During the day 2/4 Hampshire Regt. worked forward to a position 6,000 yards west of Arezzo. The weather was very hot and dry. On this day Major Lord Darling and Major J. H. Small took command, respectively, of A and D companies.

Early on 6th July, A and B companies moved up to the start line. By first light B company was in 2 King's Regt. area and A company moving on the lower slopes of the first objective. The whole area was under enemy observation, with heavy shelling and mortaring. The tanks were unable to get up as the tracks had been heavily cratered. Both companies were held up and unable to get forward. So they remained during the day. But at 2100 hours an artillery barrage enabled C company to pass through D company and, by 2225 hours, both companies attacked and gained the objective, taking 4 P.O.W. D company consolidated at Tuori and the V.M.G. and Mortar sections were sent up to C company. 1/6 Surrey Regt., of 10th Brigade, was now ordered to pass through. Shelling was still heavy and one company managed to reach C company, after suffering heavy casualties.

During the night 6th/7th July, A and B companies attacked and, after a stiff fight, took part of a wooded hill. B company relieved a company of 2 King's Regt. which had been badly mauled. On 7th July, 4th Division was in close contact with the enemy on the whole front. 2 Somerset L.I. positions were heavily shelled and mortared, several tanks being hit. Rations could not be brought up and the men were short of food. Rations were, however, got up during the night, though there was much confusion and loss of contact with companies.

On 8th July shelling and mortaring continued and the men were now very tired. A patrol under Lieut. Kirkwood encountered enemy who had infiltrated between forward companies and Battalion H.Q. and beat them off. C company was heavily counter-attacked, but held its ground. It came, however, under our own artillery defensive fire and suffered 12 casualties.

A and D companies were, also, counter-attacked but drove off the enemy. In the meantime, 6th British Armd. Division had advanced to the east of Castiglione Florentino, while 10th Brigade began to take over from 28th Brigade on the right of 4th Division. 13 Corps decided to put in an attack on the right flank of the Corps. At 0330 hours, on 9th July, 2 Somerset L.I. was relieved by 2 Beds and Herts Regt., of 10th Brigade, and moved back to rest.

On 9th July, 13 Corps plan was for 6th British Armd. Division to secure the high ground Anastasio–Agazzi, secure crossings over the R. Arno and then occupy Arezzo. This attack was to be made in daylight, supported by 4th Division. 6th S.A. Armd. and 2nd N.Z. Divisions were held in reserve. The attack was timed for 10th July, but was postponed for 3 days to allow 2nd N.Z. Division to come into position. On 11th July, 13 Corps front was extended to include Siena–Pistoia and on 12th July, 8th Indian Division came under Corps command.

On 15th July, 13 Corps attack was launched at 0100 hours, south of Arezzo, with 6th British Armd. and 2nd N.Z. Divisions. 12th Brigade of 4th Division supported the attack with fire. 8th Indian Division attacked Palazzo del Pero. 28th Brigade of 4th Division took over from 12th S.A. Motor Brigade of 6th S.A. Armd. Division. On 16th July the enemy broke contact on the whole front. 13 Corps ordered a general advance and Arezzo was cleared by 0945 hours. 28th Brigade advanced with 2 King's Regt. on the right and 2/4 Hampshire Regt. on the left, with 2 Somerset L.I. following in M.T. On 17th July, 2 Somerset L.I. reached the neighbourhood of Cennina.

THE ACTION AT RICASOLI

At 1100 hours on 17th July, the advance continued, with 2 Somerset L.I. on the right of 2 King's Regt. A company was on the left, without tanks, and B company on the right with tanks. Progress was slow owing to difficult country and demolitions but there was no opposition. By the evening Mercatale and Rendola had been reached. At 0500 hours on 18th July, 4th Division continued the advance with 12th and 28th Brigades leading. 10 Corps was advancing on the right of 4th Division. On 12th Brigade front, 2 D.C.L.I. took Montevarrchi, but on 28th Brigade front, 2 Somerset L.I., at 1315 hours, ran into stiff opposition south of Ricasoli. At 1545 hours, B company attacked Ricasoli from the west, but was checked and had to withdraw slightly. It was clear that the place was strongly held and no progress was made during the night.

On 19th July, 6th Armd. Division was established along the south bank of the R. Arno. On 28th Brigade front, D company 2 Somerset L.I. was sent up, at 0700 hours, to help B company. At 1045 hours, these companies called for artillery support and fire on Ricasoli. They then attacked, but by 1300 hours had been held up by heavy mortaring. Major J. H. Small and Lieuts. L. V. Whitehead, P. J. Bell and Rampton were wounded. 2 Other Ranks were killed and 2 wounded. D company was forced to withdraw southwards and by 2100 hours all forward movement had ceased. Captains A. F.

Searle and A. H. C. Morle were sent up to D company. At 2200 hours patrols were sent out towards Ricasoli and to contact 2/4 Hampshire Regt. on the right. The latter was ordered to pass through and attack.

At 0400 hours on 20th July, Ricasoli was reported evacuated and C company moved up to Tumme. At 0520 hours, B and D companies advanced and entered Ricasoli, taking 5 P.O.W. Here these companies were joined by C company and 2/4 Hampshire Regt. then passed through towards Cavriglia. 2 Somerset L.I. consolidated in Ricasoli under shell-fire. In the meantime 6th Armd. Division had taken Querciabella.

THE ADVANCE TO FLORENCE

On 20th July, 13 Corps intention was to seize crossings over the R. Arno, east and west of Florence, the Corps axis of advance being Castellina–Casciano–Signa. The enemy had once again broken contact. Corps tasks were: 2nd N.Z. Division on the left and 6th S.A. Armd. Division on the right to gain crossings over the R. Arno, west of Florence; 8th Indian Division to protect the left of 2nd N.Z. Division; 4th British Division to protect the right of 6th S.A. Armd. Division; 6th British Armd. Division to protect the right of 4th British Division.

On 21st July, 28th Brigade, of 4th Division, took Cavriglia without opposition. 10th Brigade then passed through and 28th Brigade was rested. On 23rd July, the enemy having broken contact, it was thought that a race would develop for the first formation to reach Florence. But these hopes were short-lived. During the day 2 Somerset L.I. relieved 2/4 Hampshire Regt. near Meleto. Lieut.-Colonel McKechnie took over temporary command of 28th Brigade and Major G. R. Chetwynd-Stapylton assumed command of the Battalion.

On 24th July the advance continued but on the next day opposition began to stiffen on 4th Division front, near Ponte. It was clear that the enemy intended to hold strongly to the line San Giovanni–Loro. At 0200 hours on 25th July, 2 Somerset L.I. began to advance, with A and C companies, to Pian Fiancesse and thence through Camporeggi, on a mountain track, towards Ponte. The advance was supported by tanks and by 1200 hours A company was well ahead, with D company in possession of the high ground west of Gaville. 14 P.O.W. of 735th Panzer Grenadier Regt. were taken. Battalion H.Q. came under shell-fire, 3 Other Ranks being killed and 3 wounded. At 2300 hours the Battalion went into tank harbour for the night.

On 26th July patrols found Ponte unoccupied, but the road badly cratered. Enemy were reported in Pavelli, Poggerina and San Andrea, but during the afternoon 2 King's Regt. entered Pavelli. During the night 26th/27th July the enemy thinned out on 13 Corps front. On 27th July, 6th S.A. Armd. Division gained Mercatale and 8th Indian Division, on the extreme left, reached Montespertoli. At 0600 hours, A and C companies, 2 Somerset L.I., attacked Poggerina and by the evening B company had occupied the ridge S.E. of San Lucia. There was heavy shelling and mortaring during the day.

On 28th July, 6th British Armd. Division, on the right, entered Loro and 8th Indian Division on the left reached San Donato. The three divisions in the centre, however, were strongly opposed and fighting hard. On 4th Division front, 28th Brigade could make little progress, but 2/4 Hampshire Regt. took San Lucia while 4th Recce Regt. moved slowly towards Figline.

On 29th July it became clear that the enemy had five divisions south of Florence on the general line Figline–Fuecchio and along the R. Greve. 13 Corps decided to break through and continue the advance. Tasks allotted were: 2nd N.Z. Division to capture Laromola and Torri; 6th S.A. Armd. Division to attack Casa Vecchia; 8th Indian Division to contain the enemy on the line of the R. Pesa; 4th British and 6th Armd. Divisions to continue their present rôles on the right.

On 29th July, patrols of 2 Somerset L.I. reported San Martino and Cappacini occupied. Little movement was made all day and there was heavy enemy mortaring. On 30th July, 28th Brigade plan was for 2/4 Hampshire Regt. to attack west of San Martino, while 2 Somerset L.I. patrolled to the village. If it was unoccupied, 2 King's Regt. was to pass through 2 Somerset L.I. Alternatively, 2 King's Regt. was to stiffen the attack of 2/4 Hampshire Regt. should this be necessary.

At 0615 hours, the attack of 2/4 Hampshire Regt. near San Martino was successful, while 4th Recce Regt. pressed forward to the high ground north of Figline. At 0920 hours, 2 King's Regt. passed through 2/4 Hampshire Regt. and made further progress on the left flank of the Brigade. 4th Recce Regt. was held up at San Martino, but in the meantime 10th Brigade attacked and took Figline. On the left, 2nd N.Z. Division occupied San Andrea and San Michele. Lieut.-Colonel McKechnie resumed command of the Battalion.

On 31st July, after a heavy artillery bombardment, C company, 2 Somerset L.I., took San Martino at 0720 hours, the enemy having withdrawn at first light. D company then passed through to Tipercoli and reached an objective near San Pietro del Torreno, consolidating there about 1230 hours. Tanks were moved up and 4th Recce Regt. made progress on the right. But by 1700 hours, further advance had been checked by artillery and spandau fire. On the left, 2nd N.Z. Division, after beating off several fierce counter-attacks, entered Romola.

On 1st August the enemy began to withdraw. At 0550 hours patrols of 2 Somerset L.I. reported no contact. At 1250 hours, 2 King's Regt. advanced, with 12th Brigade moving forward on the left. By 1610 hours, 2 King's Regt. had reached Poggio Alla Croce. 2 Somerset L.I. followed in the wake of 2 King's Regt.

On 2nd August, 2 King's Regt. was checked, but in the afternoon patrols of C company, 2 Somerset L.I. reported Linari and San Polo clear. On the extreme left, 8th Indian Division had taken Castiglioni. A general advance of 13 Corps began in the evening, with 6th S.A. Armd. Division crossing the R. Greve. On 3rd August the advance became a pursuit, with the enemy in full retreat. 28th Brigade, on 4th Division front, moved on and in the evening

2 Somerset L.I. reached the area San Donatino. 2/4 Hampshire Regt. passed through San Bartolomeo. On the extreme left, 8th Indian Division crossed the R. Pesa.

On 4th August, troops of 13 Corps entered the southern outskirts of Florence, south of the R. Arno. All bridges across the river were found demolished. The Corps was now regrouped, with 2nd N.Z. Division on the left, 1st Canadian Division in the centre and 4th British Division on the right. 8th Indian Division was ordered to consolidate on the line of the R. Greve.

By 1400 hours, on 4th Division front, 2 Somerset L.I. reached Peruzzi, while 2/4 Hampshire Regt. was nearing the R. Arno. On 5th August, 4th British and 1st Canadian Divisions were ordered to clear the ground up to the R. Arno. 1st British Division was now placed at the disposal of 13 Corps and was ordered to concentrate at Figline between 6th and 9th August and then pass through 4th British Division, which was to withdraw to Corps reserve. The intention of 13 Corps was now to gain bridgeheads over the R. Arno, prior to the liberation of Florence and a further advance northwards. On the right, 10 Corps was directed on Pontasieve, while on the left, 2 U.S. Corps of 5th Army, was to pass through 2nd N.Z. Division and attack Monte Albano, 2nd N.Z. Division being withdrawn into 13 Corps reserve.

At 0600 hours on 5th August, C company 2 Somerset L.I. attacked Mt. Pilli, reaching the objective and coming under heavy shell-fire. A plan was then made for A and B companies to attack Incontro and the Monastery. At 2359 hours the attack started, but by 0230 hours on 6th August, had been held up by spandau fire and had to withdraw to Terzano. No progress could be made when daylight came and by 1420 hours both companies had been withdrawn with a loss of 2 killed, 4 missing and 3 wounded, including Lieut. A. L. Dinham. During the day patrols from 4th Division crossed the R. Arno, east and west of Florence.

On 7th August, 28th Brigade remained held up near Incontro and preparations were made for 10th Brigade to pass through and attack. The attack started at 0300 hours on 8th August and by 1800 hours, 2 D.C.L.I. were firmly established in the town, the enemy withdrawing on Pontasieve. During the day 2 Somerset L.I. lost 2 killed and 1 wounded from shell-fire and at 2130 hours all companies had been concentrated preparatory to moving out of the line. On 9th August, at 0530 hours, the Battalion moved by M.T. to a rest area south of Assisi. Here it remained until 17th August, when it was visited and complimented by Lieut.-General Sir Oliver Leese.

On 10th August, parts of 10th Brigade of 4th Division crossed the R. Arno east of Florence and the Division was then relieved by 1st British Division. On 11th August the Germans evacuated Florence, being unable to feed the population. During the next few days the occupation of the city was carried out and on 18th August, 13 Corps passed to command of 5th Army. By 24th August, the Germans began to withdraw northwards, followed up by 6th British Armd. and 8th Indian Divisions. Plans were now begun for the assault on the Gothic Line.

CHAPTER XVI

THE BATTLES OF THE ROER AND THE RHINELAND

The European situation in January 1945—Situation in other theatres of war—43rd Division—Clearing the Ardennes Pocket—7th Battalion (L.I.)—Reduction of the Ardennes salient—The advance to Bure–Grimbiermont—The advance to the R. Ourthe—The clearance of the Roermond triangle—Operation Blacklock—43rd Division—Plans for the Battle of the Rhineland—The concentration—Operation Veritable—The Battle of the Rhineland (First Phase)—The action at Cleve—The action at Bedburg—The battle of the Rhineland (Second Phase)—Operations near Goch—Operation Blockbuster—Operations of 214th Brigade towards Xanten—The capture of Xanten—7th Battalion (L.I.) in Holland—The Royal Hamilton Light Infantry

THE EUROPEAN SITUATION IN JANUARY 1945

BY the end of December 1944, the German salient in the Ardennes had been sealed off and the great counter-stroke had failed. It remained only to clear up the pocket which had been created, before further advance to the Rhineland and into Germany.

U.S. forces to the south of the pocket had not yet sufficient resources in hand for a major offensive. It was decided, therefore, to employ 2nd British Army, south and east of the R. Meuse, to release 7 U.S. Corps for further operations. For this purpose, 30 Corps was selected and directed to take over the sector Givet–Hotton on the right flank of 1st U.S. Army. In the meantime, 3rd U.S. Army continued operations towards Bastogne and Houffalise.

SITUATION IN OTHER THEATRES OF WAR

While 21st Army Group and U.S. Armies had been pressing on towards the German frontier in Northern Europe, other forces had been making progress in the encirclement of the Germans. The latter were now being compressed, into the central German fortress, from all sides.

During 1944, U.S.S.R. forces had been advancing steadily, if slowly and, at the same time, with allied aid, building up a striking force. During June 1944, the First Russian Offensive against Finland was staged. In July, Minsk was taken by the 1st and 3rd White Russian Armies. This was followed by large-scale operations on the R. Bug and in the Ukraine. In August, Roumania was eliminated and Bucharest, on the 2nd Ukrainian Front, entered. Progress was also made in the Lake Peipus area and by the capture of Sandomierz.

In September an armistice was signed with Finland and operations cleared Bulgaria. Towards the end of October, the 1st Baltic Army, working down the coast, entered East Prussia. By the end of the year U.S.S.R. forces were fighting in Budapesth.

In Italy, September saw the crossing of the R. Arno by 5th Army troops, and the breaking of the Gothic Line by the 8th Army. The latter continued to advance in the Adriatic sector and, by the end of the year, had reached Faenza and Ravenna. Everywhere the Germans were being forced back. Their difficulties were added to by the disruptive effect, in Germany itself, of allied bombing of communications and production areas.

43rd DIVISION (Map 21)

On 1st January 1945, 43rd Division was concentrated in an area east of Maastrict, under command of 12 Corps. Its rôle was to destroy all enemy formations penetrating to vital areas of 12 Corps, or of 13 and 19 U.S. Corps.

During the first fortnight of January there was heavy snow and very severe frost in the area. 129th Brigade was near Hulsbeek and engaged in training until 10th January. This brigade, with 4 Somerset L.I., had counter-attack rôles for the Aachen, Geilenkirchen and Gillrath areas, on the south of the Roer triangle.

214th Brigade was near Moorveld. 7 Somerset L.I. was engaged in reconnoitring defensive positions at Eynatten and making preparations for the defence of Maastrict, in the event of an enemy break through from the Ardennes.

On 11th January, 43rd Division began the relief of 52nd (L) Division. This was completed by 12th January, by which time the right sector of 12 Corps had passed to 43rd Division from 52nd (L) Division. 12 Corps was now disposed as follows:

Right: 43rd Division (Kogenbroich–Hastenrath).
Centre: 52nd (L) Division (Nuth).
Left: 7th Armd. Division.

43rd Division sector was allotted as follows:

Right: 214th Brigade (Teveren).
Left: 129th Brigade (Niederbusch).
Reserve: 130th Brigade.

The Divisional area included, roughly, Geilenkirchen–Gillrath–Teveren–Brunssum–Schinvelt–Gangelt. These dispositions, together with those of 12 Corps as a whole, are important in view of the subsequent operations for the attack on the Roer triangle.

In 214th Brigade, 7 Somerset L.I. relieved 6 Cameronians of 52nd (L) Division, in the line, at Bruggerhof. On its right was 17th U.S. Cavalry Regt. and on the left, 1 Worcs. Regt.

In 129th Brigade area, 4 Somerset L.I. moved up to Gangelt on 11th January, where it took over from a battalion of 157th Brigade of 52nd (L)

BATTLES OF THE ROER AND THE RHINELAND

Division. 129th Brigade area lay between Kreuzrath and Gillrath, covering Sittard from the east. 4 Somerset L.I. was disposed as under:

A company: Vinterlin, C company: Hastenrath,
B company: Kievelberg, D company: Gangelt.

The Battalion remained in this area until 19th January. It was noticed here that the Germans were using dogs for sentry work and patrolling. All companies were in full view of the enemy and each was wired in and protected by minefields. The weather was bitter, with snow and severe frost up to 20 to 30 degrees at night. The Battalion now had white snow clothing. On the whole, however, the sector was a quiet one at this time.

CLEARING THE ARDENNES POCKET

On 3rd January, having been freed by the handing over of the Hotton–Givet sector to 30 Corps of 2nd British Army, 7 U.S. Corps attacked, in bitter weather, and, by 7th January, cut the enemy supply route on the Laroche–Vielsalm road, south of Grandmenil.

On 4th January, 30 Corps also attacked on a front of two divisions. 53rd Division went forward in touch with 7 U.S. Corps and took Grimbiermont on 7th January. 6th Airborne Division which, in the emergency which had arisen from the German thrust towards Brussels, had been brought over from England, had some stiff fighting, further south, around Bure, which it took on 5th January. It is now necessary to follow the fortunes of 7th Battalion (L.I.) with 6th Airborne Division.

7TH BATTALION (L.I.) PARA REGT.

After the end of the Battles of Normandy, 7th Battalion (L.I.) had been sent back to Bulford on 5th September 1944, as already described in Chapter XII. After a period of leave and reorganisation, it was ordered to mobilise on 12th September and complete this by 30th September. During October, training continued. Between 8th and 12th October, street fighting was practised in bombed areas of south-east London. On 30th October, a "battalion drop" was practised at Winterbourne Stokes.

On 21st December, orders came to prepare to move. The German counter-stroke in the Ardennes was now well under way. On 22nd December, the Battalion moved to a transit camp near Southampton and, at 0930 hours on 24th December, embarked on T.S. "Princess Astrid". The ship anchored in convoy off Cowes. At 0400 hours, on 25th December, the convoy sailed to an anchorage off Deal and thence proceeded to Calais, where the Battalion disembarked. At 2130 hours on 25th December, it left Calais in M.T., reaching Menin at 0930 hours on 26th December and Namur at 1915 hours the same day.

THE REDUCTION OF THE ARDENNES SALIENT

The operations which followed were under 30 Corps. This Corps had been in an area between Brussels and Maastricht, but now moved south to the line of the R. Meuse, between Namur and Givet. From here it struck eastwards, passing to the south of 7 U.S. Corps of 1st U.S. Army. The latter was in the area Durbuy–Ciney. 30 Corps was directed on Laroche–Champlon and thence to the line of the R. Ourthe, which runs southwards from the R. Meuse at Liége. For this thrust, 51st, 53rd and 6th Airborne Divisions, with 29th Armd. Brigade were available.

At 1415 hours on 27th January, having marched from Namur, 7th Battalion (L.I.) reached Erpent and at 1530 hours took up a defensive position. At 1430 hours on 28th December, it was relieved by a battalion of H.L.I. of 71st Infantry Brigade and moved back out of the line. On 29th December it moved by march route, at 1600 hours, to the Stave area, with A and B companies at Corenne. On 30th December the Battalion concentrated at Corenne at 0730 hours and, at 1030 hours, moved in Kangaroos to Celles, where it took up a defensive position.

On 2nd January 1945, the battalion set off at 1545 hours, by march route, directed on Wellin. While on the way it was re-directed to Hour, where it arrived at 1850 hours.

THE ADVANCE TO BURE–GRIMBIERMONT

30 Corps now began to advance with 53rd Division on the left, in touch with 7 U.S. Corps on its left, and 6th Airborne Division on the right. On 3rd January, at 0700 hours, 7th Battalion (L.I.) concentrated at Belvaux and, at 1430 hours, launched an attack on Wavreille. At 1445 hours contact was made with the enemy and, after a stiff fight, the village was cleared at 1730 hours. 3 P.O.W. of 9th Panzer Division were taken. At 2345 hours, forward patrols found Forrieres strongly held.

The positions in Wavreille were held during the 4th and 5th January under heavy shell-fire. On 6th January the Battalion was relieved by 12 Para Battalion and marched to Eprave, where it arrived at 1830 hours. This was also in the line and the Battalion was engaged in patrolling. On 7th January, 53rd Division took Grimbiermont.

THE ADVANCE TO THE R. OURTHE

30 Corps now ordered 51st Division to pass through 53rd Division and move forwards, directed on Laroche–Champlon, while 6th Airborne Division continued to advance on the right.

On 8th January, at 1515 hours, 7th Battalion (L.I.) marched to Jemelle, which was reported clear of enemy. It occupied the village at 2030 hours. The next day, at 1250 hours, the village of On was occupied and, by 1600 hours, A company had entered Hargimont. The weather was bitter, with frost and snow and, on 10th January the Battalion was equipped with white snow suits. On the same day patrols of 6th Airborne Division reached St. Hubert and made contact with 3rd U.S. Army to the south. 7th Battalion (L.I.) remained at Hargimont until 17th January, when it marched back to Eprave, arriving there at 1330 hours.

By 13th January, 51st Division was on the line of the R. Ourthe, southwards from Laroche, while 17 U.S. Airborne Corps, to the north, was attacking south-wards from Malmedy, on St. Vith, and threatening the base of the German communications in the salient. By 16th January, the salient had been reduced to a bulge.

It was now decided to withdraw all British formations from the Ardennes as soon as possible, so as to re-group for the Battle of the Rhineland. On 22nd January, at 0530 hours, 7th Battalion (L.I.). embussed at Eprave for Holland, A and C companies reaching Panningen (Holland) at 1900 hours. The Battle of the Ardennes was over.

THE CLEARANCE OF THE ROERMOND TRIANGLE (*Map 21*)

North of the Ardennes, the enemy was still holding out, west of the R. Roer, in the triangular area Roermond–Dremmen–Bocket–the Juliana Canal, which runs roughly parallel with the R. Meuse, east of Maeseyck. The centre of this strongly defended area was Heinsberg.

The task of clearing this area, which had to be reduced before the Battle of the Rhineland could be staged, fell to 12 Corps. This Corps employed 7th Armd. Division on the left, along the line of the Juliana Canal, directed through Susteren, on Roermond; 52nd (L) Division in the centre, to advance from Sittard through Bocket, on Heinsberg; 43rd Division on the right, to advance through Waldenrath on Dremmen and thence south-westwards towards Lindern. On the right of 43rd Division, 102nd U.S. Division was to attack east of the R. Wurm, through Lindern and thence northwards between the R. Wurm and R. Roer. The plan, therefore, was to reduce this pocket, by attacks from the south-west, south and, ultimately, the rear.

12 CORPS OPERATION BLACKCOCK

12 Corps task was known as Operation Blackcock. The object was to eliminate the enemy in the area between the R. Meuse, R. Wurm, R. Roer. 13 U.S. Corps was to co-operate with artillery support on the right of 12 Corps and to attack a spur north-east of Randerath. The operation was to take place in a series of Phases, known, respectively, as Angel, Bear, Crown, Hart, Jug I and Jug II and Kettle.

Phase I (Angel) started at 0730 hours on 16th January, with the advance of 7 Armd. Division on the left. The weather was very bad, with a thaw, sleet and fog. On 18th January, Phase II (Bear) began, with the advance of 52nd (L) Division from near Sittard. This advance was intended to link up with the progress made by 7 Armd. Division on the left. The latter was now swinging eastwards, north of Susteren, some 7 miles north of Sittard. The going was very bad, the weather worse and the armour could do little to help the infantry.

On 19th January, Phase III (Crown) began and 52nd (L) Division advanced towards Bocket.

43RD DIVISION

On 20th January, in sleet and snow, 43rd Division began Phase IV (Hart), with 129th Brigade leading. 129th Brigade was in the area, Vinterlin–Hastenrath–Neiderbusch–Gangelt. At 0815 hours the advance began, with 5 Wilts Regt. on the left and 4 Somerset L.I. on the right. C company, 4 Somerset L.I., found Schummerquartier unoccupied and A company entered Langbroich without opposition at 1330 hours. Mines made of wood, to resist detectors, were encountered for the first time. In the meanwhile 5 Wilts Regt. entered Breberen.

On the extreme left, 7 Armd. Division took the high ground near Bocket, while in the centre, 52nd (L) Division was directed on Heinsberg.

On 21st January, Phase IV (Hart) continued. In 43rd Division, 130th Brigade relieved 129th Brigade and the latter moved back to Schinveld. 4 Dorset Regt. of 130th Brigade then took Waldenrath. 214th Brigade now came up on the right of 130th Brigade, with 7 Somerset L.I. patrolling, under heavy shell-fire, towards Hoven.

On 22nd January, Phase IV (Hart) was completed by an attack of 130th Brigade, in which 7 Hampshire Regt. took Putt. On 23rd January, Phase V (Jug I) began. 129th Brigade moved up from Schinveld in M.T. to an assembly area at Waldenrath. The brigade then attacked, with 4 Wilts Regt. on the right, directed on Straeten, and 4 Somerset L.I. on the left. 4 Somerset L.I. plan was to attack in four phases, as follows:

(*a*) B and D companies to form in Putt and attack Schiefendahl;
(*b*) A company to form up in Schiefendahl after capture and attack Erpen;
(*c*) C company was then to attack Schlieden and
(*d*) D company was to attack Donseln.

These villages were some 1,000 yards from each other and the ground between them was flat and devoid of any cover. The countryside was frozen, with a light covering of snow and filled with unknown minefields. Each company was carried to the attack in Kangaroos and supported by Churchill tanks of 6th Guards Armd. Brigade. Very heavy concentrations of artillery and mortar fire were arranged for the attack.

At 1230 hours B and D companies crossed the start line. Owing to some hitch only sufficient Kangaroos arrived to carry B company. Consequently, D company had to advance on foot. Unfortunately, almost at the start, D company lost its commander, Major Garner, who was injured by the explosion of a mine under a Kangaroo. As B company advanced, seven of the eleven

Kangaroos were blown up by mines, causing many casualties, in full view and under the fire of the enemy. Captain J. M. F. Hutchinson dismounted the company and reformed to attack on foot through the minefield. The artillery concentrations were very effective and the village of Schiefendahl was stormed and taken at 1500 hours, together with many P.O.W. Captain Hutchinson received the M.C. for this action. In the meantime, on the right, 4 Wilts Regt. took Straeten, with 400 P.O.W.

At 1600 hours, A company 4 Somerset L.I. formed up in Schiefendahl and launched an attack on Erpen, 1,500 yards distant over open country. This attack was successful, taking 150 P.O.W., four infantry guns, two mortars and two 88 mm. guns. By 1800 hours the village was cleared and the company dug in. In the meantime, 5 Wilts Regt. passed through 4 Wilts Regt. and took Uetterath and the neighbouring hamlets of Baumen and Berg.

During the night of 23rd/24th January, 4 Somerset L.I. was disposed as under:

    A company: Erpen.
    B and D companies: Schiefendahl.
    C company: near Waldenrath.

The whole area was full of mines, making the supply problem extremely difficult and hazardous. During the night two Mark IV tanks attacked A company, supported by a company of infantry. Captain T. M. Bullock directed the fire of Churchill tanks on the enemy, while his batman, Private E. Cross, although badly wounded, seized a 2-in. mortar and fired on the enemy until his ammunition was expended. The attack was beaten off. For this exploit Private Cross received the M.M.

During the 22nd and 23rd January, 214th Brigade, with 7 Somerset L.I., was in reserve. Lieut.-Colonel Borrodaile was appointed G.S.O. I (Operations), 30 Corps and was succeeded in command, temporarily, by Major J. B. Elliott. The latter was relieved on 26th January by Lieut.-Colonel I. L. Reeves, D.S.O., M.C. (K.S.L.I.).

On 24th January, at 1525 hours, C company 4 Somerset L.I. attacked Schlieden and occupied it, without difficulty, about 1700 hours, taking 50 P.O.W. At 1600 hours, 5 Wilts Regt. on the right sector of 129th Brigade, attacked and took Donseln, with 101 P.O.W. This village was then taken over by D company, 4 Somerset L.I. On the same day 52nd (L) Division took Heinsberg.

On 25th January, 43rd Division began Phase VI (Jug II and Kettle), with 130th Brigade attacking on the left of 129th Brigade towards Heinsberg. At 1000 hours, 5 Dorset Regt. had taken Schalhausen and contacted 52nd (L) Division in Heinsberg. 214th Brigade moved up on the right of 129th Brigade. 1 Worcs Regt. occupied Hoven and 7 Somerset L.I. the neighbouring hamlets of Kouenbosch and Zurndahl. By nightfall, 130th Brigade had reached the R. Wurm at Porselen and were in Dremmen and the neighbouring villages of Grebben, Hulhoven and Eschweiler.

On 26th January, 12 Corps operation Blackcock was completed. 129th Brigade remained in the area Schiefendahl–Erpen–Schlieden, with 4 Somerset L.I. in reserve. 214th Brigade was near Randerath, with 7 Somerset L.I. close by in the hamlet of Bruggerhof. 130th Brigade was forward, towards the R. Wurm, at Oberbruch and Horst and, on 27th January, passed to command of 52nd (L) Division in Heinsberg. On the same day 43rd Division less 130th Brigade, concentrated in an area south of the Geilenkirchen–Sittard road. 129th Brigade moved back to Schinveld, with 4 Somerset L.I. at Treebeek. 214th Brigade moved to the Schimmert area, into billets. The clearance of the Roermond triangle by 12 Corps had ended and the area was now handed over to 9th U.S. Army.

During the January battles, 43rd Division had taken 847 P.O.W.

PLANS FOR THE BATTLE OF THE RHINELAND

It was now decided to move 30 Corps and 12 Corps, northwards, to the Nijmegen bridgehead, to join 1st Canadian Army for the thrust towards the R. Rhine. The main features in the new battle area were the Reichwald Forest, the flood plains of the R. Meuse, R. Niers and R. Rhine and the undulating, wooded country which lay between them. There was a great deal of inundation and flood water over the whole area.

After the concentration of the two Corps had been completed, the plan was for 30 Corps, with six infantry and one armoured divisions and three armoured brigades, to break through the Siegfried Line near Kranenberg and open the road to the high ground near Cleve. This task was allotted to 15th (S) Division. 43rd Division was then to pass through the Materborn area, swing round the Reichwald Forest and capture Goch, in conjunction with an attack by 51st Division from the west. Guards Armd. Division was to move in rear of 43rd Division and, later, turn south to seize the high ground north of Sonsbeck. A strong column was to secure the bridge at Wesel. The whole of this plan was known as Operation Veritable.

THE CONCENTRATION

On 30th January, 43rd Division was ordered to concentrate near Heerenthals, coming under 30 Corps which, itself, was now under 1st Canadian Army. On 31st January, 129th Brigade began to move to the Hallaar area, with 4 Somerset L.I. at Boischot (Belgium). 214th Brigade moved up to the Turnhout area, with 7 Somerset L.I. at Wortel and, later, at Geldorp. Until 8th February both brigades were engaged in training and planning for Operation Veritable.

OPERATION VERITABLE

The detailed plan for this operation was as follows; 1st Canadian Army was to break out from the Nijmegen bridgehead, in the north, moving southeast between the R. Meuse and R. Rhine. The object was to capture Wesel

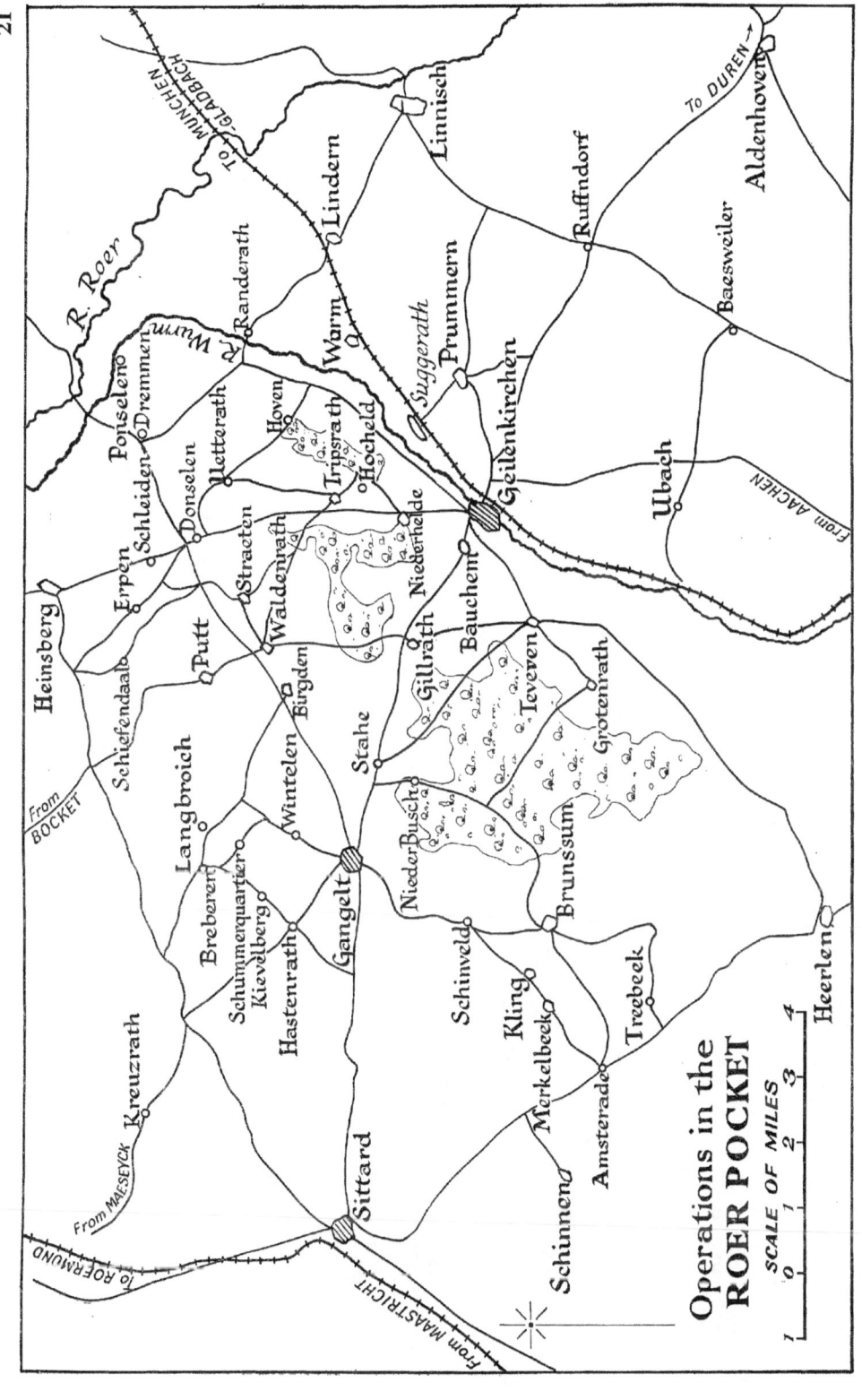

bridge and establish a line Wesel–Geldern, cutting off the Germans on the line of the R. Meuse.

On D *plus* 3 day, U.S. forces were to thrust across the R. Roer at Linnich and Julich and strike north on Duisberg.

The troops available to 30 Corps were 51st (H) Division, 53rd (W) Division, 15th (S) Division, 2nd and 3rd Canadian Divisions.

43rd (W) Division and Guards Armd. Division were in Corps reserve. The tasks of formations were as follows:

(*a*) 51st (H) Division to seize high ground on the Reichwald;
(*b*) 53rd (W) Division to break out from Groesbeek; 15th (S) Division to attack Kranenberg, in the Siegfried Line and the high ground south-east of Cleve;
(*c*) 2nd Canadian Division was directed on Wyler and Kranenberg;
(*d*) 3rd Canadian Division was directed on the canal running north from Cleve;
(*e*) 43rd (W) Division, with 8th Armd. Brigade, was to pass through 15th (S) Division and capture Goch, Weeze, Kevelaer and Geldern.

There were three preliminary phases.

> Phase   I: the move to the concentration area near Eindhoven.
> Phase II: the move to the assembly area near Nijmegen.
> Phase III: the Advance.

THE BATTLE OF THE RHINELAND—FIRST PHASE (*Maps* 19 *and* 22)

D day for Operation Veritable was 7th February, 1945. The actual advance of the infantry did not start until 1000 hours on D *plus* 1 day. On 8th February an artillery programme opened at 0800 hours. According to plan the attack was launched at 1000 hours, with 15th Division on the left, 53rd Division in the centre and 51st Division on the right. 2nd Canadian Division was echeloned on the left rear of 15th Division. By the evening Wyler and Kranenberg had been taken. In the meantime, 43rd Division moved up into the assembly area near Nijmegen. There was heavy rain all day. 129th Brigade had moved to Aarle–Helmond on 7th January and reached the area east of Nijmegen on 8th February.

On 9th February, 43rd Division, with 129th Brigade leading, began to move forward to exploit the break through. 4 Somerset L.I. only reached the assembly area on this day and, at 1800 hours, moved off, following 4 Wilts Regt. 214th Brigade moved up in rear of 129th Brigade and later in the evening advanced down the Nijmegen–Kranenberg road, with 5 D.C.L.I. leading, followed by 7 Somerset L.I. riding on tanks. During the day, 53rd Division had cleared the Stuppelberg feature in the Reichwald Forest, while 15th Division had pierced the Siegfried Line at Nutterden and reached the high ground at Materborn, overlooking Cleve.

During the night 9th/10th February, 43 Division begin to come forward, passed through Kranenberg and reached Nutterden about midnight. The leading companies of 4 Somerset L.I. were riding on tanks. The country was flooded and the roads blocked by craters. During the night 43rd Division passed through 15th Division and took the lead.

THE ACTION AT CLEVE

On 10th February there was rain, sleet and snow. During the early hours of the morning, 129th Brigade advanced on Cleve, with 4 Wilts Regt. leading and 4 Somerset L.I. still riding on tanks, following closely. An hour before dawn the column approached the town, which was believed to have been evacuated by the enemy. This was not so. 4 Wilts Regt. ran into a road block in the darkness and was fired on, several carriers being knocked out at once. The obstruction was cleared and a defensive flank formed to the left. 4 Somerset L.I. then passed through towards the southern outskirts of the town. At 0700 hours, the Battalion reached the centre of the town.

Cleve had been almost totally destroyed by "crater" bombing and the roads were blocked by fallen masonry and trees. A German counter-attack, by troops of 7th German Para Division, now came in from the south and very confused fighting followed. German self-propelled guns picked off carrier after carrier and the advance of the Battalion was finally checked by huge craters, which required bull-dozers to fill them in. The Battalion gradually worked forward until B company was able to secure a road junction, east of the town, where a road led, south-east, through the woods to Bedburg. In this fighting the Battalion was split up into small parties and many acts of herosim were done. Private J. Stephens, a stretcher bearer, and Private H. A. Tipple, later received the M.M. for distinguished services. The latter dealt with an attack by a self-propelled gun, a Panther tank and an infantry party. By the evening the Battalion was established east of Cleve.

During the day, Lieut.-Colonel Lipscomb, entering a house, was confronted by a copy of the picture depicting Doctor Bryden arriving at the Gates of Jellalabad. This picture is now in the Regimental Museum at Taunton.

Later on the 10th February, 214th Brigade moved up on the right of 129th Brigade, passing through Materborn, and relieved pressure on the southern flank of Cleve. 5 D.C.L.I. was the leading battalion, followed by 7 Somerset L.I. Progress was slow owing to strong enemy opposition.

On 11th February there was more snow and rain and the Nijmegen–Cleve road was under two foot of water in some places. 129th Brigade was engaged in consolidation and repelling counter-attacks by tanks and self-propelled guns. In 214th Brigade section, 5 D.C.L.I. was held up near the Reichwald Forest. A brigade attack was staged and launched at 1500 hours. 5 D.C.L.I., on the right, was engaged in the clearance of part of Materborn, with 7 Somerset L.I. on the left, directed on Hau. 1 Worcs Regt. attacked on the right of 7 Somerset L.I. By the evening C company had penetrated to the Cleve–Goch road and was held up there.

BATTLES OF THE ROER AND THE RHINELAND

At 0215 hours on 12th February C company 7 Somerset L.I. launched an attack on the village of Hau and by 0320 hours had obtained a lodgement in the village. Shortly afterwards all companies gained their objectives. P.O.W. were taken and identified as 104th and 105th Panzer Grenadiers, 19th Para Regt. and elements of 116th Panzer Division.

This wild night of snow and sleet was the scene of great gallantry by Major D. B. M. Durie and C.S.M. Evans of C company. In the confusion of the night's fighting, both were involved in hand-to-hand fighting with Germans while clearing houses. Despite this Major Durie's leadership brought his exhausted company through to their objective. Major Durie received the award of the M.C. and C.S.M. Evans the M.M. for this night's work.

THE ACTION AT BEDBURG

On 12th February 129th Brigade continued to advance southwards from Cleve. 4 Somerset L.I. led the advance, with D company as vanguard, supported by a troop of Sherman tanks. The objective was Bedburg and "Hospital Wood" near the village.

D company was ordered to secure the western tip of the wood, so as to enable the Battalion to have a strong point from which to complete its task. D company, under Major F. J. Cooke-Hurle, pressed its attack home and, having crossed the railway embankment, which was strongly held, gained its objective. 57 P.O.W. were taken. During the attack Major Cooke-Hurle was wounded in the leg, but was later able to rejoin his men.

The other companies now launched attacks and by 1700 hours the Battalion was concentrated near Hospital Wood, with the whole Bedburg area secured. Among those taken at Bedburg were 500 lunatics in the Hospital. These caused some embarrassment.

Elements of 15th (S) Division were now level with 129th Brigade to the east of Bedburg, while on the right, 214th Brigade was on the edge of the Reichwald Forest, to the west and rear. In the meantime 51st Division, on the right of 43rd Division, had taken Gennep and joined elements of 53rd Division at Hekkens.

On 13th February, 5 and 4 Wilts Regt. of 129th Brigade passed through 4 Somerset L.I. directed on high ground level with the Stadt Forest Cleve. 7 Somerset L.I., with 214th Brigade, held on to its positions, patrolling near Hau. For his part in these operations, Lieut.-Colonel Lipscomb, 4 Somerset L.I., received a bar to his D.S.O.

THE BATTLE OF THE RHINELAND—SECOND PHASE

By 13th February, the Reichwald Forest had been taken and the further advance to Goch–Udem was developing. On 14th February, 129th Brigade advanced down the road towards Goch, with 5 Wilts Regt. leading. The advance was held up almost at once by a heavy artillery barrage and mortaring and the brigade dug in. In 214th Brigade area, 7 Somerset L.I. near Hau was heavily counter-attacked, but the attack was broken up by defensive artillery fire. At 1530 hours, A company attacked towards Stadt Forest Cleve but, after gaining the objective, was forced to withdraw.

On 15th February there was a pause in the advance. Enemy opposition was still very strong, the weather was bad and the country waterlogged. 129th Brigade held on to its positions and 130th Brigade was sent through to continue the attack. In 214th Brigade area, 7 Somerset L.I. was in close contact with the enemy near Stadt Forest Cleve.

Much of the opposition now being encountered was due to unavoidable delays in launching 9th U.S. Army Operation Grenade. This had been timed to start across the R. Roer, between Linnich and Julich and strike northwards between the R. Meuse and R. Rhine. Floods in the Roer valley, however, had made any advance impossible. Thus 30 Corps, in the north, had to continue the attack alone.

OPERATIONS NEAR GOCH

On 16th February, 4 Somerset L.I., from 129th Brigade, came temporarily under command of 214th Brigade, for a further advance, west of the Cleve–Goch road. The brigade objective was the high ground on the southern edge of the Reichwald Forest, overlooking the road to Goch. At 1300 hours an attack was put in, with 1 Worcs Regt. on the left—in touch with 129th Brigade—and 7 Somerset L.I. on the right. By 1720 hours, after meeting heavy opposition, A and D companies, 7 Somerset L.I. reached the objective and 1 Worcs Regt. shortly afterwards. The positions were then consolidated. Early on the morning of 17th February, the attack was continued. 4 Somerset L.I. was ordered to advance from Bedburg, moving forward over some 6,000 yards of very difficult and waterlogged country, to form up in rear of 7 Somerset L.I. The latter was still closely engaged with the enemy. The approach march was successful, but Major B. A. Watts, commanding C company, was wounded and his place taken by Captain J. M. Hutchinson.

The Battalion attack was to be a silent one, the objective being some 2,000 yards in advance of 7 Somerset L.I. positions. A and C companies led the attack and crossed the start line, through 7 Somerset L.I. at 0300 hours. By 0340 hours, C company had reached its objective, without much difficulty, taking 41 P.O.W. A company was, however, pinned down for a time by spandau fire. This spandau was silenced by Sergeant Weston, using a P.I.A.T. gun. A "Wasp" flame-thrower was then brought into action. But owing to some defect the flame only went a few yards and the burning oil merely served to illuminate the company, lying out on exposed ground. An artillery concentration was called for and this came down about 0400 hours, silencing the enemy weapons.

A company then assaulted, with No. 7 Platoon (Lieut. Walker) on the left and No. 9 Platoon (Sergeant Weston) on the right. No. 7 Platoon was held up by wire, but No. 9, brilliantly led, swung round and raked the enemy

BATTLES OF THE ROER AND THE RHINELAND

position with fire. No. 7 then got through the wire and took the objective. 68 P.O.W. were taken.

4 Somerset L.I. then consolidated in the Pfaidorf area at 0500 hours, having taken 250 P.O.W. For this action, Major V. W. Beckhurst, commanding A company, received the M.C. The action was described by the Divisional Commander as a "model night attack".

At 1100 hours on 17th February, 214th Brigade continued the advance, with 7 Somerset L.I. on the right and 1 Worcs Regt. on the left, directed towards Goch. C and D companies, 4 Somerset L.I., patrolled on the right flank of the attack. 7 Somerset L.I. advanced with B company on the right and C company on the left. B company gained its objectives at 1430 hours and C company, after a stiff fight, at 1700 hours.

On 18th February, 15th Division began to move up through 43rd Division, for the main assault on Goch. At 1450 hours, 44th Brigade passed through 214th Brigade, to the accompaniment of heavy shelling. On 19th February, the attack began to be felt in Goch and the German Commander surrendered. But it was 48 hours before 15th Division, with elements of 51st Division, which had closed in on Goch from the west, cleared the town.

The value set on the fierce fighting for Hau and Goch is well reflected in the awards that the 7th Battalion share: Lieut.-Colonel I. L. Reeves, D.S.O.; Major L. Roberts and Major D. B. M. Durie, M.C.; C.S.M. Evans, Sgt. Chinnock, Private Bond, M.M.

On the left flank of 30 Corps, 2 Canadian Corps had taken the line Udem–Calcar, and the spur beyond. 30 Corps was now ordered to move from the Goch area, through Kevelaer, to Geldern, while 2 Canadian Corps drove through the Hochwald Forest, from Udem–Calcar, on Xanten.

On 20th February, 4 Somerset L.I. attacked on a limited objective near Halverboom. During the 19th February the Battalion had been protecting the right flank of 214th Brigade. The object of this attack was to close the gap which had formed between 5 D.C.L.I. on the right of 4 Somerset L.I. and Canadian troops further east.

C and D companies, using Kangaroos and a troop of tanks, carried out the attack. C company crossed the start line at 1100 hours, going very slowly in the deep mud. During the advance the company commander, Major G. Mallalieu, was killed and there were 25 other casualties. Captain A. G. Hoale took command. C company gained its objectives at 1215 hours and D company was successful at 1238 hours. By 1447 hours, the whole village, which was the objective, had been cleared and 80 P.O.W. taken. For his part in this action Sergeant Burgess received the M.M.

The loss of Major Geoffrey Mallalieu, 4th Battalion, was a grievous loss to all ranks. He had led C company since the early days in Normandy and was much beloved by his men. All the operations for which he was responsible were most carefully planned in every detail; so that his men believed that no attack led by him could ever fail. He possessed a store of unfailing good humour, shrewd common sense, dash, initiative and great personal courage.

His untimely death, after many miraculous escapes, was a great shock to the whole battalion.

At 2050 hours, 4 Somerset L.I. took over from 5 D.C.L.I. and during the 21st February maintained its positions under heavy shell- and mortar-fire. On the evening of 21st February, 7 Somerset L.I. relieved 4 Somerset L.I. and the latter went back to rest near Donsbruggen, remaining there until 27th February. The remainder of 129th Brigade was relieved by 6th Canadian Brigade and moved back to an area near Rosendaal. 214th Brigade passed, temporarily, to the command of 15th (S) Division, but returned to 43rd Division on 23rd February.

On 22nd February the Canadians had taken Brunshof. 7 Somerset L.I., in 214th Brigade, patrolled towards Felemannshof, which was still held by the enemy. On the night 23rd/24th February, 214th Brigade was relieved by 1 Grenadier Guards of Guards Armd. Division and moved back to a concentration area near Cleve.

In the meantime, 9th U.S. Army crossed the R. Roer on 23rd February and, after clearing Julich, began to move northwards on a broad front towards Munchen Gladbach. Further south, 1st U.S. Army took Duren and advanced on Cologne.

On 25th February, B company 4 Somerset L.I. was sent up to Moyland, for left flank protection of 6th Canadian Brigade. On 26th February, 129th Brigade sent 4 Somerset L.I. and 4 Wilts Regt. to take over from 6th Canadian Brigade in positions overlooking Calcar. This area presented a scene of indescribable devastation. 4 Somerset L.I. was employed in mopping up. On 28th February a patrol led by Lieut. M. F. Skittery found that Calcar was unoccupied. 5 Wilts R. was at once moved up and at 1730 hours entered the town. In the evening 4 Somerset L.I. moved to Till to watch the left flank.

214th Brigade also moved up, 7 Somerset L.I. relieving the Canadian Fusiliers Mount Royale, near Kehrum. Further north, 2 Canadian Corps advanced on 26th February, directed on Xanten. During February, 43rd Division had taken 2,725 P.O.W.

OPERATION BLOCKBUSTER

On 1st March, 43rd Division passed to the command of 2 Canadian Corps for Operation Blockbuster. This involved the capture of Xanten. 43rd Division was detailed to clear the left flank of 2 Canadian Corps, to the eastwards. 129th Brigade was now near Calcar, with 214th Brigade in the area Delsendorf–Schmachdarm.

On 1st March, at 2000 hours, 4 Somerset L.I. moved to Tootenhugel and relieved the Royal Hamilton Light Infantry. Thus the Somerset Light Infantry met the affiliated Canadian Regiment on the battlefield. The R.H.L.I. had been ordered to make a night attack on the Hochwald Forest and went off to its task in great fettle. 5 Wilts Regt. came up on the left of 4 Somerset L.I.

On 2nd March, 43rd Division was ordered to extend responsibility for

BATTLES OF THE ROER AND THE RHINELAND

the Corps left flank, northwards towards the Hochwald Forest. 129th Brigade patrolled towards the Hochwald. In 214th Brigade, 7 Somerset L.I. made plans to attack near Kehrum and found Spierhof lightly held by the enemy.

On 3rd March, 43rd Division was ordered to continue the sweep of the Corps left flank to Marienbaum. The intention of 43rd Division was:

(*a*) 214th Brigade to occupy Niedershof–Kehrum and thence move on Marienbaum–Vynen;

(*b*) 129th Brigade to secure the area Till–Calcar.

129th Brigade, therefore, moved back to Till–Calcar to refit, while 214th Brigade prepared to attack towards Xanten.

OPERATION OF 214TH BRIGADE TOWARDS XANTEN (*Map* 24)

At 0900 hours, on 3rd March, 7 Somerset L.I. launched an attack on Kehrum and gained all objectives by 1300 hours. At 1435 hours, D company had cleared Niedershof. 5 D.C.L.I. now formed up in rear of Niedershof and at 1530 hours passed through to attack Marienbaum. At 1800 hours a counter-attack came in on Niedershof and D company 7 Somerset L.I. was forced back.

On 4th March the attack continued. 7 Somerset L.I. contacted Canadian troops on the right. Stiff fighting continued all day.

43rd Division was now advancing astride the road Kehrum–Xanten. 214th Brigade led, with 1 Worcs Regt. on Wardt and 5 D.C.L.I. towards Xanten. At 1135 hours, 7 Somerset L.I. moved forward into Marienbaum. By 1600 hours, 1 Worcs Regt. had taken Wardt.

On the night of 4th/5th March, the right and centre Corps of 9th U.S. Army had reached the line of the R. Rhine between Neuss and Orsoy. 16 U.S. Corps, on the left, was moving towards Rheinberg and Wesel, while further north, 30 British Corps was turning east towards Wesel. The key to the enemy defensive system was Xanten.

On 6th March, 43rd Division was ordered to co-operate with 2nd Canadian Division in the capture of Xanten. 10th Canadian Brigade attacked Xanten, but was checked short of the objective. 7 Somerset L.I. of 214th Brigade, carried out reconnaissances towards the R. Rhine to prevent German patrolling across the river.

On 7th March, 43rd Division and 2nd Canadian Division were ordered to "contain" Xanten and to prepare to attack and capture the Xanten area. D company, 7 Somerset L.I., was moved forwards to facilitate reconnaissances and patrolling.

THE CAPTURE OF XANTEN

On 8th March, 43rd Division was ordered to capture Xanten and the high ground to the south. 2nd Canadian Division was to attack the town from the south-west. 129th Brigade, with a Canadian brigade from Marienbaum, was selected for the attack.

129th Brigade plan was for the attack to be led by 4 Somerset L.I. on the right and 5 Wilts Regt. on the left, conforming with the Canadian Brigade of 2nd Canadian Division on the right of 4 Somerset L.I. 5 Wilts Regt. was directed on Luttingen, a village to the north of Xanten. A company, 4 Wilts was attached to 4 Somerset L.I. for the operations.

The approach to the objective from Marienbaum was astride a long straight road, under observation for its entire length. On either side the ground was water-logged, but when nearing Xanten, an avenue of trees and a few scattered buildings gave some cover for infantry. An anti-tank ditch crossed the road about 500 yards short of the town and the road here was heavily cratered. This obstacle was strongly defended. Xanten, itself, was a heap of rubble, affording excellent cover for a defender.

4 Somerset L.I. plan was for B company, under Major Hutchinson, to attack the anti-tank ditch by night. When this had been taken, A and C companies were to pass through, with Avres and Crocodiles and seize the centre of the town.

At 0500 hours, on 8th March, B company advanced, passing through 5 D.C.L.I. The company was supported by armour and a heavy artillery barrage. Just short of the objective the company was pinned down by spandau fire. The aid of the barrage and the armour had now been lost. A new plan was made and the company fought forward, section by section, into and over the ditch. Four Crocodiles also, got across. In this action Corporal Grant greatly distinguished himself by throwing grenades at the spandau crew and then charging in single-handed. He was twice wounded, but killed the entire crew of the spandau. For this exploit he was awarded the D.C.M.

By 0810 hours the ditch was taken, together with 39 P.O.W. Major J. M. F. Hutchinson received a bar to the M.C. and Lieut. B. D. C. Innes the M.C. Casualties in B company were 13 Other Ranks.

At 1000 hours, A and C companies passed through B company and assaulted the town. Confused fighting followed, with snipers and panzerfaust teams. By 1230 hours both companies were on their objectives, searching houses and dealing with snipers. 27 P.O.W. of 16th Para Regt. were taken.

In the meantime the attack of 5 Wilts Regt. had gone in on Luttingen and, at 1142 hours, was held up short of the objective. The Canadian brigade on the right of 4 Somerset L.I. was also in difficulties. At 1640 hours, D and E companies, 4 Somerset L.I., passed through A and C companies and reached objectives on the east and south outskirts of Xanten.

The positions gained were held all night under heavy shelling. At 0715 hours, on 9th March, 4 Wilts Regt. passed through 4 Somerset L.I. and attacked and captured Luttingen from the south. 43rd Division was ordered to continue the operation of clearing Xanten and the area south of the R. Rhine. 214th Brigade was sent up to relieve 129th Brigade. At 1630 hours, 7 Somerset L.I. moved into Xanten and relieved 4 Somerset L.I. The latter moved back to Till and spent the next two days refitting. 7 Somerset L.I. continued patrolling from Xanten, under heavy shell-fire, until 12th March.

BATTLES OF THE ROER AND THE RHINELAND

On 10th March, 43rd Division was ordered to defend the left bank of the R. Rhine, but the next day received orders that it was to be relieved by elements of 52nd (L) Division and 3rd Division and was to move back into 2nd British Army reserve. On 12th March, 214th Brigade was relieved by a brigade of 52nd (L) Division. 7 Somerset L.I. moved back through Udem to a concentration area at Afferden. 129th Brigade also moved back, 4 Somerset L.I. going to Gennep. Both battalions now began to refit, rest and train for Operation Plunder—the Battle of the Rhine Crossings. The Battle of the Rhineland had been won. While training near Gennep, Major J. L. Brind, of 4 Somerset L.I., left to command 5 Wilts Regt. and was succeeded as 2nd-in-Command by Major A. D. W. Hunter.

7TH BATTALION (L.I.) PARA REGT.

It is necessary now to return to follow the fortunes of 6th Airborne Division.

On 23rd January, after completing its task in the Ardennes salient, 6th Airborne Division was moved northwards to Holland. 7th Battalion (L.I.) went to Panningen. At 1630 hours, on the same day, it moved by M.T. to the vicinity of Kessel and took up a defensive position in contact with the enemy. Here it engaged in patrolling, with slight enemy activity, up to 28th January.

On 29th January it was relieved by 13th Para Battalion and moved to Eschelhoek–Helden, where it rested in brigade reserve. While here the first edition of a Battalion News Sheet, entitled "The Seventh", was issued. On 4th February the Battalion relieved 12th Para Battalion near Baarlo, in the line. On the night of 5th/6th February, a patrol under Lieut. G. Simpson crossed the R. Maas, but made no contact with the enemy. Patrolling continued till the 8th February, with some mortar fire.

On the night of 9th/10th February, Lieut. Simpson again tried to cross the R. Maas, but his boat capsized on some wire. A patrol under Lieut. Nelson was more successful. The object was to take prisoners for identification. None was taken. On 11th February the R. Maas began to rise. On 12th February, however, Lieut. Nelson again crossed the river and secured two prisoners. On this day the Germans fired propaganda leaflets into the Battalion lines.

Between 13th and 14th February the river continued to rise and patrols failed to cross owing to the mud. On 15th February, B company's outposts were flooded out and had to be evacuated, but the next day the river subsided and they were reoccupied.

The employment of an Airborne Division, which is comparatively weak in man-power and fire-power and comprises men trained for a particular task, as infantry, is wasteful and uneconomical. The emergency which necessitated the move to the continent from England had long passed. It was, therefore, decided to return 6th Airborne Division until it should again be required.

On 20th February 7th Battalion (L.I.) was relieved by 290th U.S. Infantry Regt. and moved by road to Mierre. On 23rd February, after a flight of two hours, it arrived in England at 1550 hours and returned by road to Bulford. Here, after a period of leave, it recommenced training. It was not required again until it took part, on 24th March, in the Battle for the Rhine crossings.

THE ROYAL HAMILTON LIGHT INFANTRY

Mention has been made in this Chapter of the meeting, in the field, near Tootenhugel, of 4 Somerset L.I. and The Royal Hamilton Light Infantry. It will therefore be convenient to give some account of the record of the latter. Meetings of the R.H.L.I. had already taken place in England with other battalions of the Somerset Light Infantry, as previously described.

Under the command of Lieut.-Colonel R. R. Labatt, R.H.L.I. landed on Dieppe Beach at dawn on 19th August 1942 as part of the commando raid on that town. The force consisted almost entirely of Canadian units and the raid lasted nine hours. R.H.L.I. captured the Casino and part of the town itself. The casualties in this raid were extremely heavy. 91 enemy aircraft were destroyed, but we lost 98 aircraft, the destroyer "Berkeley" and some 3,350 out of 5,000 troops engaged. In R.H.L.I. only 7 Officers and 150 Other Ranks returned to England, out of a landing strength of 35 Officers and 500 Other Ranks. Fortunately a large proportion of those left behind were taken prisoner. Among those were Lieut.-Colonel Labatt and three company commanders.

As a result of these heavy losses in the Dieppe Raid, the Regiment had to undergo a lengthy period of reinforcement, reorganisation and training. It was first commanded by Lieut.-Colonel J. J. Hurley and, after his appointment as Chief Instructor at Kingston, R.M.C., by Lieut.-Colonel (later Brigadier) J. M. Rockingham, D.S.O.

At the time of the Normandy Landings, Lieut.-Colonel D. Whitaker, D.S.O., was in command. It landed with 3rd Canadian Division, early in July 1944 and first came into action, on 10th July, at Bretteville-sur-Odon, near Verson. Here it relieved 7 Seaforths of 52nd (L) Division. Here, for ten days, under heavy shell- and mortar-fire, it maintained its positions.

On 25th July, 2 Canadian Corps began an attack southwards along the Falaise road. This Corps had taken station, early in July, between 12 Corps in the Eterville–Evrecy area and 1 Corps, north-east of Caen, and had been responsible for the attack on Caen, which fell on 9th July. On 27th July, R.H.L.I. attacked Verrieres, south of Caen, and fought its hardest battle in the campaign, the capture of the village costing 250 casualties. For the next two days it repelled numerous heavy counter-attacks.

Between 5th and 6th August, 1st Canadian Army was preparing for a drive south to eliminate the Falaise–Argentan pocket. R.H.L.I., mounted in armoured troop carriers, headed the armoured thrust. It captured its

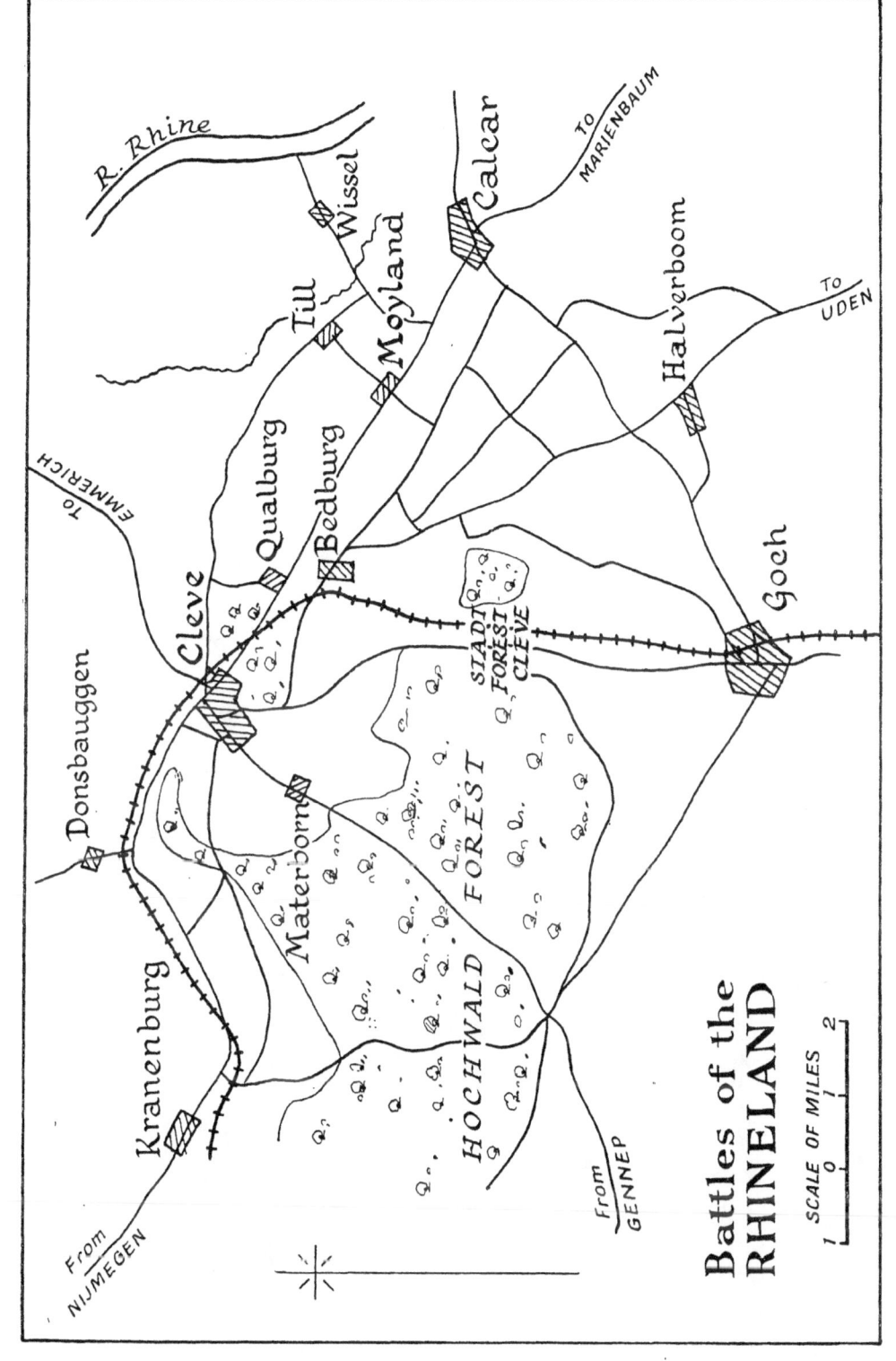

BATTLES OF THE ROER AND THE RHINELAND

objective, the airfield south of Roquancourt, and pressed on, four days later, to take an objective near Barberie. During the attack and subsequent counter-attack, the Regiment suffered 200 casualties. Following the elimination of the Falaise pocket, the R.H.L.I. moved north, to the coast near Dieppe, crossing the R. Seine near Rouen. Towards the end of August, during the Pursuit, it took part in the capture of Bruges.

For a short time the Regiment was employed on the outskirts of Dunkirk and then took over the defences of the harbour area of Antwerp. Later it took part in the drive to the mouth of the Scheldt Estuary and sealed off the entrance to the Scheldt by the capture of Woensdrecht, after a five day battle during which the enemy frequently counter-attacked with tanks and infantry. The final task of the clearance of the Scheldt Estuary was the capture of the town of Heinkensand near the causeway to Walcheren.

The Estuary was cleared early in November, 1944, though the Port of Antwerp was not opened until 28th November. During the next three months, the Regiment was employed in several holding rôles in the Nijmegen bridge-head and then took part, in February 1945, in the Battle of the Rhineland. On 19th February, the Regiment attacked towards Goch from the direction of Calcar, being engaged heavily for four days and beating off many enemy counter-attacks. It was then employed in the Hochwald Forest and in the drive on Xanten, suffering heavy casualties.

The Regiment took part later in the Battle of the Rhine Crossings, crossing the R. Rhine on 28th March 1945. Later it moved to Holland, prior to returning to Canada. The casualties suffered by the Regiment in this campaign, so far as is known, were 119 Officers and 1,947 Other Ranks. 32 Officers were killed.

Lieut.-Colonel D. Whitaker, D.S.O., was wounded while in command and was succeeded by Lieut.-Colonel J. M. Rockingham, D.S.O. Later, at various times, Lieut.-Colonels G. MacLachlan and B. R. Ritchie commanded, followed by Lieut.-Colonel Whitaker when he had recovered from his wounds. He was succeeded by Lieut.-Colonel H. Arrel, who took the Regiment back to Canada.

CHAPTER XVII

8TH ARMY OPERATIONS IN THE ADRIATIC SECTOR: ITALY—AUTUMN 1944

The general situation in August 1944—2 Somerset L.I. moves to Adriatic sector to join 1 Canadian Corps—Corps plans for attack and crossing of R. Marano—Advance to R. Ausa—Advance to R. Marecchia—Operations near San Giustina—The crossing of the R. Savio—The crossing of the R. Ronco—Operations under 5 Corps—Operations on R. Montone—The crossing of the R. Cosina—Move of 2 Somerset L.I. to Taranto en route for Greece—30th Battalion—Move to area in western Italy—List of officers with battalion in April 1945—Surrender of German armies in Italy

THE main fighting in Italy during the spring and summer of 1944, was west of the Apennines, on the front of 5th Army, advancing on the western seaboard, and on the left of 8th Army, where it linked up with 5th Army, west of the mountain chain. Early in the year, 8th Army forces on the Adriatic coast had crossed the R. Sangro and were working slowly northwards. On 18th July, the Polish Corps, which had been transferred eastwards following the capture of Cassino, took Ancona on the east coast. On the next day 5th Army took Leghorn, on the west coast, so that the allied line across Italy ran fairly straight from west to east.

THE GENERAL SITUATION IN AUGUST 1944

The fall of Florence had been a serious blow to the German armies in Italy. But Florence, and the R. Arno valley, lie to the south of the northern portion of the Apennines which still formed a serious obstacle to a northward advance. The Germans now fell back on the Gothic Line, stretching along the Apennines in the west, where they overlooked the Florentine plain, eastwards across the coastal plain towards Pesaro. Thus it covered the approaches from the south to Parma, Bologna and the valley of the R. Po.

The new situation required a considerable re-grouping of available forces, already weakened by the withdrawal of formations to provide for the landings in southern France. 5th Army, on the west, now had to undertake the difficult assault of the positions in the Apennines, while 8th Army had an equally imposing task in the eastern coastal plain, where many river crossings had to be fought for and demolitions and inundations were comparatively easy for a defender to contrive.

On 8th Army front, northwards from Ancona, a series of formidable rivers run across the plain, from the mountains to the sea. Among these, from south to north, were: the R. Esino, with Falconara at its mouth; the R. Conca, reaching the sea at Senigaglia; the R. Metauro, with Fano on the coast; the R. Foglia, running down to Pesaro; and the R. Marecchia, reaching the sea at Rimini. Between Rimini and Ravenna, the Rivers Uso (or Rubicone), Savio (on which is Cesena), Montone (on which is Forli) and Lamone (on which is Faenza) crossed the line of advance northwards. All these rivers had various tributaries and all, together with the towns on them, had to be fought for. Thus the operations in this sector were divided into battles for the crossings of these streams and the reduction of the towns on them.

After the fall of Florence, 4th British Division was moved south some 130 miles, to a new area near Foligno, with Headquarters between Assisi and Spella, in the valley east of Perugia. Here, for some time, prior to transfer to the Adriatic sector, it was engaged in resting, refitting and training. While in this area it came under 5th Army. But on 3rd September, it again reverted to 8th Army, coming into Army reserve. 28th Brigade, with 2 Somerset L.I., was at Foligno. Here, the Anti-tank platoon, less one section, was abolished and a counter-mortar section formed. This is an indication of the great use made by the Germans of mortars for defensive fire. Reinforcements brought the strength of the Battalion to 41 Officers and 807 Other Ranks.

8th Army assault on the Gothic Line began on 31st August, on a 20-mile front in the Adriatic sector. By 2nd September a break through had been accomplished and the Polish Corps took Pesaro, on the coast, on 3rd September. On 5th September, 4th Division was moved over to the Adriatic coast, to an area near Senigaglia, south of Fano. Here it came under 1 Canadian Corps. 2 Somerset L.I. left Foligno on the night 4th/5th September, reaching an area south-west of Fano and moving up on 7th September. 12th Brigade moved in on the same day, but was held up by rain and floods on the R. Conca, west of Pesaro.

28th Brigade, with 2 Somerset L.I., continued to move forward until 9th September, when there was further heavy rain. Bridges over the R. Metauro and R. Arzilla were swept away by floods and for some time the Battalion was marooned between the two streams. On 9th September it reached San Giovanni. Here Lieut.-Colonel McKechnie took over temporary command of 12th Brigade and the command of the Battalion devolved on Major G. R. Chetwynd-Stapylton. 4th Division was now concentrating in the area Tomba di Pesaro, prior to an attack on the enemy positions to the north.

On 12th September, 1 Canadian Corps intention was to break through and destroy the enemy between Rimini, on the coast, and the general line Coriano–Ospedaletto–San Martino. The initial attacks were to be made by 1st Canadian Division on the right and 4th British Division on the left. The programme was a complicated one, involving the following phases:

Phase I: 5th Canadian Armd. Division to attack the ridge near Coriano.
Phase II: 4th British Division, on the left, to pass through 5th Canadian Armd. Division and occupy high ground north of Coriano.
Phase III: 4th British Division was to advance and cross the R. Marano.

Phase IV: 1st Canadian Division, on the right, was to secure the bridgehead over the R. Marano and attack San Lorenzo.
Phase V: 4th British Division was then to advance to the R. Ausa.
Phase VI: 1st Canadian Division was to swing eastwards towards the sea.
Phase VII: both divisions were to attack San Fortunato.
Phase VIII: both divisions were then to advance to the line of the road Rimini–Lavilla and cross the R. Marecchia.

While these extended operations were in progress, 5 Corps was to protect the left flank of 1 Canadian Corps, in the mountain tracts flanking the coastal plain.

In accordance with these orders, 4th British Division plan was for 12th Brigade to pass through 5th Canadian Armd. Division and, in Phase II, attack north of Coriano. Thereafter, 10th, 12th and 28th Brigades were allotted alternative rôles as the situation might develop.

THE ADVANCE TO THE R. AUSA

On the night 11th/12th September, 4th British Division moved up to a new concentration area near San Giovanni. On the night 12th/13th September, 5th Canadian Armd. Division launched its attack and reached its objectives on the high ground near Coriano by 0900 hours on 13th September. 12th Brigade of 4th British Division then moved up and attacked northwards from Coriano, crossing the start line at 0630 hours on 14th September.

At 0530 hours, on 14th September, 28th Brigade began to move forward, following 12th Brigade. 2/4 Hampshire Regt. and 2 King's Regt. were leading with 2 Somerset L.I. in reserve. At 1430 hours 28th Brigade was ordered to start Phase III and advance towards the R. Marano. The two leading battalions attacked across the river, directed on a hill feature near Patrignano. 2 Somerset L.I. moved up east of Coriano.

By the early morning of 15th September, 2/4 Hampshire Regt. and 2 King's Regt. had gained their objectives and consolidated under heavy shell-fire. At 1245 hours, C and D companies, 2 Somerset L.I., moved up to an assembly area west of Ospedaletto, reaching there about 1500 hours. Here they were joined by Battalion H.Q. During the evening C company lost 6 Other Ranks killed and 2 wounded from shell-fire. By this time 12th Brigade had got troops across the R. Marano and 10th Brigade was moving up in rear. At 2000 hours, C and D companies 2 Somerset L.I. attacked through 2 King's Regt. and, after making further ground, dug in for the night.

At 0100 hours on 16th September, the situation looked more favourable and C and D companies were ordered to press home the attack towards Cerasolo. They reached the objective at 0030 hours, but were then held up by armed small arms fire in the glare of burning haystacks. In this limited attack, Lieuts. D. G. Strickland and A. C. Green were wounded, while 13 Other Ranks were killed or wounded.

At 0600 hours, D company, under Major A. V. Ridge, continued the attack and captured Monte Pirolo taking 10 P.O.W. At 0710 hours the

AUTUMN 1944

enemy counter-attacked with tanks and infantry. D company was surprised and the position was over-run and lost. Major A. V. Ridge, Lieuts. T. E. Scrope-Howe and P. T. Attfield, with 30 Other Ranks were captured. One platoon of the company, under Lieut. A. G. Morle, with 27 Other Ranks, was in Reserve in the area of C company.

At 1600 hours, 28th Brigade made a fresh plan to take Cerasolo. A and B companies, 2 Somerset L.I., were to relieve 2 King's Regt. 2/4 Hampshire Regt. was to attack Cerasolo and 2 King's Regt. to attack the feature where D company 2 Somerset L.I. had been lost. 56th Division was to attack simultaneously on the left.

At 0600 hours on 17th September the attack of 2/4 Hampshire Regt. on Cerasolo began. By 0630 hours it was making good progress. 2 King's Regt. cleared Monte Pirolo, but was then held up. Heavy shelling continued during the day, Lieut. A. R. McGillycuddy being killed by a mortar splinter. By the evening Cerasolo was taken.

4th British Division now issued new orders:

(a) 28th Brigade and 6 Black Watch were to clear the ground north-east of Cerasolo;
(b) 9 K.O.Y.L.I. was to relieve 2/4 Hampshire Regt. in Cerasolo;
(c) 18th Lorried Infantry Brigade was to relieve 28th Brigade;
(d) 4th Division was then to advance with 10th Brigade on the right and 12th Brigade on the left.

On the 18th September, 2 Somerset L.I. remained in its positions, but was relieved at 2230 hours by 1 Buffs of 18th Brigade. It then moved back to the original concentration area. Here it rested on 19th September and Lieut.-Colonel McKechnie returned from 12th Brigade to command.

In the meantime, on 18th September, 1 R.W.K. got across the R. Ausa at 0400 hours. 28th Brigade came into divisional reserve after relief by 18th Brigade. During the 19th September, 10th Brigade continued the advance, while 12th Brigade mopped up near San Aquilina.

On 20th September, 28th Brigade, having rested, was placed at 2 hours' notice to pass through 10th Brigade and continue the advance. The key to further progress was now the high ground near Fortunato which was on 1st Canadian Division front. 28th Brigade now began plans for the crossing of the R. Marecchia, depending on the progress made by 12th Brigade advancing on the left. At 1800 hours, in heavy rain, 2 Somerset L.I. moved up to a concentration area north-west of the R. Ausa. During the day 1st Canadian Division attacked and took Fortunato.

THE ADVANCE TO THE R. MARECCHIA

With the capture of Fortunato the Germans fell back and the way was clear for a further advance. 28th Brigade was ordered to move up and at 0100 hours on 21st September, 2 Somerset L.I. moved forward with orders to cross the

R. Ausa. This was successfully accomplished and Battalion H.Q. was established across the river by first light. At 1130 hours A company advanced and by 1415 hours had reached a ridge 3,000 yards south of the R. Marecchia. Very heavy rain came on and the roads soon became impassable, with heavy going in the fields. No opposition was encountered and patrols were sent out to Ospedale. 10th Brigade was now sent up on the left and 28th Brigade ordered to work forward on the right and establish a bridgehead over the R. Mavone.

At 1400 hours, C and B companies 2 Somerset L.I. passed through A company, directed on Spadarolo and Vergiano. At 1630 hours the objectives were gained and at 1715 hours, Battalion H.Q. moved up to San Bertozzi. At 2000 hours, A company passed through C company and crossed the Canale dei Molini. Later in the evening forward elements of the Battalion reached the R. Mavone but were much hampered by mud and water-logged ground. At 2315 hours, 2/4 Hampshire Regt. got troops across the R. Mavone and patrols across the R. Marecchia. In the meantime, 1st Canadian Division had crossed the R. Marecchia further east, while a Greek Brigade attacked and took Rimini.

On 22nd September, 28th Brigade was patrolling south of the R. Marecchia. There was more heavy rain. At 1030 hours, Lieut. E. H. Lane, wearing a civilian jacket and cap, crossed the river and reported San Giustina clear of enemy. At 1315 hours, C company, 2 Somerset L.I., passed through B company, crossed the river and occupied San Giustina, which is on the road from Rimini to Sant Archangelo, by 1536 hours. On the left, 2/4 Hampshire Regt. got across the river about the same time. No opposition was encountered, but 5 Other Ranks were killed and 3 wounded by shell-fire. Captain R. A. Hoey, R.A.M.C., crossed the river and brought the wounded back. At 1600 hours, 4 Recce Regt. also got across on the right.

During the day 1st Canadian Division was sent up to the area of Vergiano, where Battalion H.Q., 2 Somerset L.I., was already established.

At 0400 hours on 23rd September, 5th Canadian Armd. Division passed through Vergiano to San Giustina and the command of the sector passed to this division. At 0900 hours, heavy shelling began on C company area near San Giustina and at 1015 hours a platoon of this company, on patrol, was held up west of the town. 2/4 Hampshire Regt. was now advancing on the right and at 1320 hours was held up south of the Rimini–Sant Archangelo road. On the left, 5th Canadian Armd. Division and 4 Recce Regt. were also checked. The whole area was under heavy shell-fire.

At 1545 hours a platoon of A company 2 Somerset L.I. gained an objective west of San Giustina, but no further advance was possible. The night was fairly quiet, with Canadian troops moving up into the Battalion area. It was clear, however, that the enemy intended to make a stand.

On 24th September, 2 Somerset L.I. maintained its positions, but the platoon west of San Giustina was withdrawn. The night was quieter, with less shelling. Between 25th and 26th September, 28th Brigade was concentrated south of the R. Marecchia, while further east other formations of 8th Army crossed the R. Uso (Rubicone). 4th Division was then withdrawn from the line to rest, 2 Somerset L.I. being located, between the 26th and 30th September near Vergiano.

The Battalion remained near Vergiano carrying out training in street fighting until 23rd October. On the coast, troops of 8th Army worked forward and took San Lorenzo, south of Rimini, where a pocket of enemy had been holding out, on 12th October. On 6th October, Lieut.-Colonel McKechnie was appointed to command 18th Lorried Infantry Brigade and the command of the Battalion fell to Lieut.-Colonel G. R. Chetwynd-Stapylton, with Major T. P. Luckock as 2nd-in-Command.

THE CROSSING OF THE R. SAVIO

During September, 5th Army troops, in the west, had been pressing forward, slowly, against the German defences in the mountains north and north-east of Florence. Early in October an offensive was started towards Bologna and, on 12th October, Livergnano, 11 miles south of Bologna, was reached.

On 7th October, 4th British Division passed to command of 5 Corps and plans were made for 46th and 10th Divisions to attack on the left sector of the Corps. Rain, however, came on and the operations were postponed until the weather improved. 4th Division was placed at 24 hours' notice to move.

The attack of these two divisions was finally launched on 13th October and, on 15th October, 4th Division was ordered to prepare to pass through 46th Division. On 16th October, 4th Division H.Q. was moved up to Longiano and preparations were made for the division to attack, with 10th Brigade leading, to cross the R. Savio south of Cesena. Both 10th and 12th Brigades moved up to the line of the river and on 21st October both brigades got troops across, in spite of heavy enemy barrages on the bridges thrown near Cesena. Further east, Cervia, on the coast south of Ravenna, was taken on 23rd October. The same day, 10th and 12th Brigades of 4th Division assaulted and took Cesena. During this operation, 28th Brigade was in reserve.

The weather was now very bad, with heavy rain, and the R. Ronco, a tributary of the R. Montone, was impassable owing to floods. On the 25th October, however, orders were issued for 4th Division to cross the R. Ronco. The roads on the flat plain were quagmires and the plains themselves waterlogged. No movement was possible on the divisional front and 2 Somerset L.I. remained in the concentration area.

On 29th October, Major T. P. Luckock was appointed G.S.O. II of 4th Division and Major J. A. Pritchard (from the Lancashire Fusiliers of 78th Division) was sent to the Battalion as 2nd-in-Command. Lieut. A. A. Breton received the M.C. for courage and devotion to duty at Ricasoli (mentioned in a previous chapter). Private J. James received the M.M. also for courage at Ricasoli. At 2000 hours on 31st October, the Battalion moved up to Forlimpopoli, north-west of Cesena. Here 28th Brigade again came into the line.

THE CROSSING OF THE R. RONCO

On 3rd November, Lieut.-General Sir R. L. McCreery assumed command of 8th Army. Between 1st and 4th November bad weather continued and some bridges which had been thrown over the R. Ronco, preparatory to crossing, were washed away. There was some spasmodic enemy shelling. 2 Somerset L.I. was employed in improving roads and tracks towards the river. On 6th November the weather improved and preparations were made for 4th Division to continue the advance beyond the river, with 28th Brigade leading. The plan for 5 Corps was to attack with 4th Division on the right and 46th Division on the higher ground on the left. 56th Division was in reserve.

During the afternoon of 7th November, 28th Brigade of 4th Division moved up to a concentration area preparatory to crossing the anti-tank ditch running west from Forli Airfield. At 0240 hours on 8th November, A and B companies 2 Somerset L.I. advanced to the start line and the attack began. A Bailey Bridge forward of the assembly area collapsed under a Churchill tank but there was no delay to the infantry attack. On reaching the anti-tank ditch B company achieved a crossing with the right forward platoon capturing 15 P.O.W. but was checked on the left. At first light Major A. R. Ellis made a fresh plan and by 1030 hours B company had captured its objective with 44 P.O.W. On the right A company encountered considerable opposition which had also checked 2 King's Regt. Lieut. D. G. Bearman was reported missing and probably wounded.

There was now a pause while a tank crossing was constructed behind B company. This took some time owing to the anti-tank and anti-personnel mines and enemy shell fire in the area. By 1500 hours, however C company with tanks in support was passed through B company directed on to A company's original objective. This was taken at 1615 hours and patrols sent out to contact 2 King's Regt. on the right.

At 0400 hours on 9th November, 28th Brigade continued the advance. 2 Somerset L.I. moved forward with B and C companies leading. 2/4 Hampshire Regt. had now come up on the right and, with 2 King's Regt. was directed on Forli. The Brigade was now approaching the R. Montone. By 0800 hours, B and C companies, 2 Somerset L.I., reached the line of the river, with A company in support. At 1200 hours patrols began to reconnoitre for crossing places. The sector was, however, unsuitable for tanks, with water-logged ground and mud, near the river, five feet deep. During the afternoon the enemy was attacked by dive bombers and M.G. fire from the air and replied by heavy shelling on our forward areas. On the next day, formations on the right attacked and took Forli.

OPERATIONS ON THE R. MONTONE

During the 10th and 11th November no movement was possible on 4th Division front. There was deep mud everywhere and the R. Montone was swollen with flood water. Spasmodic shelling and harassing attacks continued,

AUTUMN 1944

the enemy positions being attended to by rocket-firing Typhoons. On the left, however, 46th Division found suitable places for crossings.

On 12th November, 4th Division was relieved by 56th Division, 2 Somerset L.I. being relieved at 1000 hours by the London Irish Rifles. On 13th November the Battalion moved to the outskirts of Forli, where it was visited by Lieut.-General Sir A. F. Harding, K.C.B., C.B.E., D.S.O., M.C.

The enemy had now thinned out and withdrawn beyond the R. Montone. 28th Brigade was ordered to advance and at 2030 hours 2 Somerset L.I. moved north of Forli, preparatory to attacking at first light the next day.

At 0730 hours on 14th November, 2 Somerset L.I. advanced towards the R. Montone, directed on the sector between San Martino and Villa Franca and passing through 4 Recce Regt. and 12 Lancers. 2/4 Hampshire Regt. was advancing on the right. C company, 2 Somerset L.I., was ordered to occupy an area north-east of San Martino. At 0930 hours this advance was stopped by orders from Brigade, but continued later and, by 1200 hours, the company had reached the line of the R. Montone unopposed. Here it patrolled to find crossings. By 2115 hours, crossings known as Nos. 4 and 5 had been reconnoitred, but the enemy on the far bank was alarmed and alert. A company reconnoitred crossing No. 6 without incident, but found it unfavourable. The banks of the river here were 20 feet high, the stream 25 yards wide and 5 feet deep. To the east, on the coastal sector, Santome was taken on this day, while north-east of Forli the R. Montone was crossed at several points.

On the afternoon of 15th November, C company, 2 Somerset L. I., moved a platoon forward towards the river, to forestall the enemy occupation of some houses on the south bank. 4 Recce Regt. was now on the left and 2/4 Hampshire Regt. on the right. At 2330 hours, crossings Nos. 4 and 5 were again reconnoitred without incident. Reports were, however, very unfavourable as the river was here a very formidable obstacle and strongly defended. On 16th November, as a result of these reports, plans for a crossing in this sector were abandoned and, on 17th November, B company was sent back to the R. Ronco to practise assault boat training. At 2200 hours on the same day, the Battalion was relieved by 4 Recce Regt. and on 18th November moved into billets at Forli, where it rested on 20th November.

THE CROSSING OF THE R. COSINA

Plans were now made for 4th Division to cross the R. Cosina and exploit towards Faenza. 10th Brigade was to lead with 28th Brigade following. On 21st November, the attack of 10th Brigade was launched, but failed to establish a bridgehead, though one company was got across the river. There was strong opposition and casualties were heavy.

5 Corps now issued fresh orders. In 4th Division sector, 28th Brigade was to assault and cross the river on the left of 10th Brigade. 46th Division was to attack on the left of 4th Division. In 28th Brigade, the attack was to be made with 2/4 Hampshire Regt. on the right and 2 Somerset L.I. on the left.

2 King's Regt. was already on the line of the river and the attack of 2 Somerset L.I. was to pass through this battalion.

At 2100 hours on 21st November, a patrol of 2 Somerset L.I. under Lieut. E. Middleton, passed through 2 King's Regt. and reconnoitred crossing places, returning with 3 P.O.W. 28th Brigade plan for the crossing was now as follows:

> Phase I: 2 Somerset L.I. was to secure a bridgehead across the R. Cosina, with B company on the left and A company on the right, directed on Caracasone; each company was supported by a troop of tanks.
>
> Phase II: 2 Somerset L.I. was to swing north, with C company on the right, preceded by an artillery barrage.

For each Phase, 2/4 Hampshire Regt., on the right of 2 Somerset L.I. was to conform. Elements of 46th Division were attacking, simultaneously, on the left.

At 1030 hours, on 22nd November, 2 Somerset L.I. moved up to the assembly area. At 2015 hours the attack was launched. The enemy brought down heavy defensive fire on the crossing places. Lieut. A Toms was wounded, but remained with his men. By 2140 hours, B company on the left had got two platoons over the river. Company H.Q. also crossed and reached a point near Casa Caseltina. On the right, A company was held up on the river bank by spandau fire at point blank range, Major E. A. Sutton-Pryce being wounded. The right platoon, led by Lieut. R. W. Strickland however, contacted 2/4 Hampshire Regt. and got across near Casetto.

At 2235 hours, B company platoons across the river were counter-attacked and called for defensive fire, which enabled them to hold on to their positions. It was now clear that the initial crossings had only been partially successful. At 0130 hours on 23rd November the C.O. prepared a fresh plan. C company was to cross the river in rear of B company and moving through the left flank platoon of B company was to attack A company's objective and the village of Casone. Thereafter, B and C companies were to advance to the original first objective.

At 0300 hours on 23rd November, C company having crossed the river began to advance with one platoon directed on Casone. The platoon on the left was held up by spandau fire. Progress was very slow, owing to strong opposition and obstacles encountered in the darkness. By 0745 hours, however, C company had gained its objectives and taken 15 P.O.W. By now it had been possible to throw a bridge over the river and supporting tanks crossed and came forward. 2/4 Hampshire Regt. began to make progress on the right.

At 1015 hours, B and C companies were established on the original first objectives and ready to start Phase II of the operation. On the left, B company was directed on Mezza Strada, Teolagata and Cosina, while C company on the right was ordered to close up and make contact with advanced elements of 2/4 Hampshire Regt.

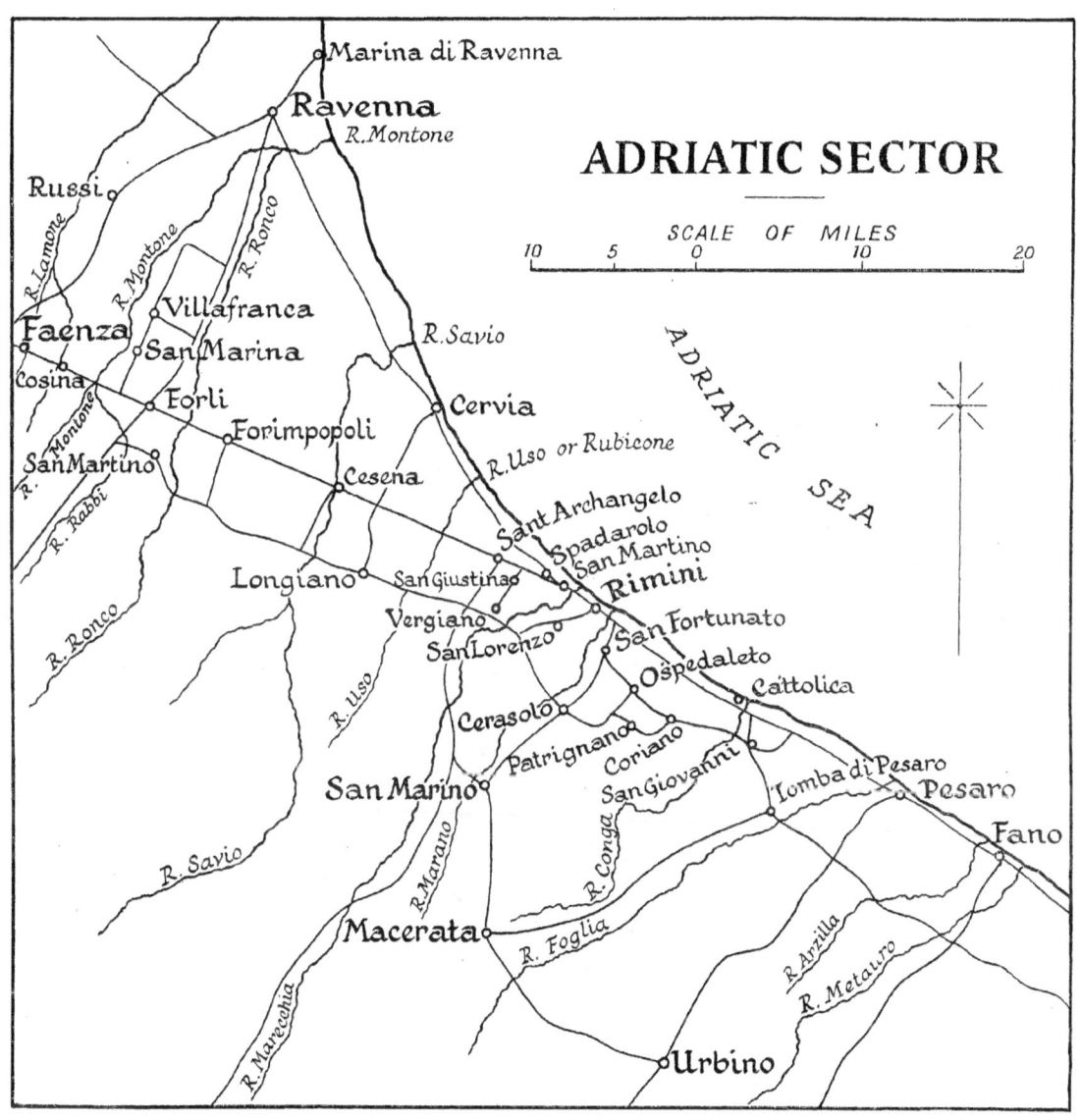

AUTUMN 1944

There were delays in arranging the artillery barrage and in getting the tanks into their forming up position. But at 1530 hours, B and C company advanced supported by tanks. B company, on the left, assaulted and took Mezza Strada, but a further advance was precluded by fire from enemy tanks emplaced in houses. C company on the right made good progress and captured its objective. Capt. J. E. C. Clarke was wounded. B company then passed round by the right and captured its objective through C company. Major A. R. Ellis was wounded and Lieut. A. Toms wounded for the second time. A company was now sent forward and by 2200 hours was established in Mezza Strada. C and B companies maintained their positions under heavy shell-fire, which continued over the whole area during the night. The day had seen some fierce fighting and the casualties were 10 Other Ranks killed and 5 Officers and 42 Other Ranks wounded.

On the morning of 24th November, 2 Somerset L.I. maintained its positions, while 2 King's Regt., followed by 10th Brigade, passed through, moving northwards. At 1500 hours, 2 Somerset L.I. was withdrawn and moved back in M.T. to billets in Forli.

This was the last battle in which the 2nd Battalion took part in Italy. The situation in Greece had now become serious and plans were already on foot to transfer 4th Division to that theatre. On 26th November, 2 Somerset L.I. embussed at Forli and moved south on the first stage of a journey to Taranto, where it was to embark for Greece.

30th BATTALION

The last mention of this battalion was in Chapter XI. The part it played in the Italian Campaign was unspectacular but important. In August it was employed on railway protection duties in southern Italy, between, roughly, Taranto and Termoli. In August, Lieut.-Colonel Routh was appointed O.C. Train and Railway Guards for the L of C Area south of Rome and Ortona. During September arrangements were made for the relief of the Battalion by 512 Battalion, 4th Guards Regt. of the Italian Army (later designated 510 Italian Guard Battalion). 30th Battalion was to move over to railway duties in Western Italy with H.Q. at Torre Annunziata.

On 9th October the relief began, B company sailing from Brindisi to Ancona and moving westwards to Terni, 65 miles north-east of Rome. Between 17th and 22nd October, the rest of the Battalion moved by train and was located in the new area as follows:

- A company: Salerno–Nolere–San Giovanni.
- B company: Terni.
- C company: Caserta–Naples–Aversa.
- D company: Rome and Littoria.

The organisation of Southern Italy Railway Protection was now as under:

- Eastern Italy: 510 Italian Guard Battalion.
- Reggio–Calabria: 550 Italian Guard Battalion.

Potenza–Salerno: 138 Ind. Inf. Company.
Salerno–Naples: A company 30 Somerset L.I.
Caserta–Cerrazo: 136 Ind. Inf. Company.
Naples–Rome: C company 30 Somerset L.I.
Rome–Terni: D company 30 Somerset L.I.
Orti–Arezzo: B company 30 Somerset L.I.

During the whole time the Battalion was employed on train and railway guard duties it was directly under the operational command of Allied Forces Headquarters, but under the administrative command of the various local headquarters in whose areas the companies were located.

On 19th December, Lieut.-Colonel Routh assumed command of all units on trains and static guards on British operated railways, including the L. of C. Area and Operational Zones. At the end of 1944, the strength of the Battalion was 29 Officers and 752 Other Ranks.

In February 1945, the establishment of the Battalion was changed to that of a Garrison Battalion Overseas, with H.Q., and four rifle companies, each of three platoons. The authorised strength was 29 Officers and 699 Other Ranks. On 4th March, 200 Other Ranks, surplus to establishment, were sent, under Major O. C. Noble, to form "O" Garrison Battalion at Naples. Later, this unit moved to Mondolfo.

LIST OF OFFICERS IN APRIL 1945

On 7th April 1945, 30 Somerset L.I. celebrated Jellalabad Day. The Officers and senior N.C.O. then present were:

Commanding: Lieut.-Colonel W. H. F. Routh.
2nd-in-Command: Major D. L. Gough, M.C., T.D.
Adjutant: Captain D. L. P. Rees.
Quartermaster: Captain (Q.M.) W. J. Atkins.
R.S.M.: V. Rogers, D.C.M.

On 2nd May 1945, the German Armies in Italy surrendered unconditionally. There was great jubilation among the allied forces. The campaign in Italy was over.

4

CHAPTER XVIII

THE RHINE TO THE ELBE

The general situation in March 1945—Outline Plan for Operation Plunder—Forces available—The Plan in detail—30 Corps Operation Turnscrew—6th Airborne Division—7th Battalion (L.I.) —The "drop" near Wesel—43rd Division—The crossing of the Rhine—7th Battalion (L.I.)— The expansion of the Rhine bridgeheads—7th Battalion (L.I.) advance on Erle—The Break Out —2nd British Army plans—30 Corps Operation Forrard On—43rd Division—Attack on Varsseveld —Capture of Lochem—7th Battalion (L.I.)—Advance to Osnabruch—43rd Division—Hengeloo— 30 Corps advance on Bremen—7th Battalion (L.I.)—Dash to R. Leine—43rd Division—Advance to Cloppenburg—The general situation—30 Corps closing in on Bremen—The attack on Bremen— The clearance of Bremen—7th Battalion (L.I.)—Advance to R. Elbe—43rd Division—Advance east of Bremen—The closing scene—7th Battalion (L.I.)—Advance to Baltic—The Surrender

THE GENERAL SITUATION IN MARCH 1945 (*Map* 7)

WHILE the Battle of the Rhineland was in progress, allied forces were, everywhere, closing up on the German fortress. From the east U.S.S.R. troops were pressing into East Prussia, Poland and along the line of the Carpathians. Warsaw was taken on 11th January and by 22nd January, U.S.S.R. armies had reached the R. Oder on a 35-mile front. In the Baltic area, Memel fell on 27th January and Lithuania was completely liberated. Early in February the R. Oder was crossed, south of Breslau. In the latter part of February, Poznan was taken and further advances made in East Prussia, towards Danzig and in Silesia.

In Italy, operations were slowed down by bad weather. In the latter part of February, 5th Army opened an offensive west of the Bologna–Pistoia road and took important heights in the Upper Reno valley.

In north-west Europe, Allied forces were, everywhere, moving up to the R. Rhine. From north to south, early in March, the situation was as follows:

1st Canadian Army, directed on Wesel.
2nd British Army, re-organising on the line of the R. Meuse.
9th U.S. Army, driving towards Wesel and Dusseldorf.
1st U.S. Army, attacking Cologne, Bonn and Remagen.
3rd U.S. Army, closing up on Coblentz and driving south-east of the R. Moselle, on Mainz, Worms and Mannheim.
7th U.S. Army, moving north-eastwards from the Vosges, on Mannheim and Karlsruhe.
1st French Army, directed on the Rhine crossings east of Colmar and Mulhouse. This army had already eliminated the "Colmar pocket".

By the third week in March, Allied forces were on the line of the R. Rhine, throughout its length. It was a formidable obstacle. On 7th March, 1st

U.S. Army found a bridge undestroyed at Remagen, crossed the R. Rhine and established a bridgehead on the east bank. At the same time the clearance of Cologne was completed.

During the spring of 1945, Allied air attacks on central Germany had increased in number and intensity. Apart from the disruption of production areas, the strain on the German forces as the result of the destruction of communications was beginning to have effect. German moral, also, was shaken.

The object now was to cross the R. Rhine and penetrate into the central German fortress.

OUTLINE PLAN FOR OPERATION PLUNDER

The plan, in brief, was to cross the R. Rhine, north of the Ruhr, between Rheinberg and Rees, on a two-army front. 2nd British Army was to cross on the left, 9th U.S. Army on the right. The initial bridgehead was to extend to include Emmerich on the north and Wesel on the south. Sufficient depth was required in the bridgehead, to allow large scale forces to form up for a break-out to the east and north-east. The Battle of the Rhineland ended on 10th March. Since speed was the essence of the new operations, 24th March was fixed as D-day for Operation Plunder.

FORCES AVAILABLE

In order to increase the weight available for the crossing and the break-out, 1 Canadian Corps, of one armoured and three infantry divisions, was brought to North Europe from Italy. The move and concentration of this Corps was completed by 15th April.

Exclusive of this reinforcement, the following forces were available for the initial stages of the operation:

2nd British Army: 8, 12 and 30 Corps; 2 Canadian Corps; 6th Airborne Division; 17th U.S. Airborne Division (total: four armoured, two airborne and eight infantry divisions, one commando brigade and one independent infantry brigade).

9th U.S. Army: 13, 16 and 19 U.S. Corps (total: three armoured and nine infantry divisions).

In addition to the land forces, a large Allied Tactical Air Force was made available.

THE PLAN IN DETAIL

The Operation entailed two initial stages.

Stage I was to secure a bridgehead over the R. Rhine from Emmerich on the north to Duisberg on the south. 2nd British Army was on the left (north) and 9th U.S. Army on the right (south). The dividing line between the two armies was the R. Lippe.

The tasks of 2nd British Army were:

(a) to capture Wesel and secure an initial bridgehead there, so as to allow 9th U.S. Army to bridge at that place;

(b) to secure bridgeheads at Wesel, Xanten and Rees.

To the north of 2nd British Army was 1st Canadian Army, roughly in the Nijmegen bridgehead. 2 Canadian Corps, of 1st Canadian Army, under command of 2nd British Army, was to cross and bridge at Emmerich, later reverting to 1st Canadian Army. Thereafter, the latter was responsible for the security of the left flank of 2nd British Army, from Nijmegen to the sea.

Stage II was to expand the bridgeheads to the general line Renkum–Deventer–Rheine–Munster–Hamm. The dividing line between 2nd British and 9th U.S. Armies, inclusive to the latter, ran from the R. Rhine at Wesel, through Raesfeld–Coesfeld–Munster. The dividing line between 2nd British and 1st Canadian Armies, inclusive to the latter, was Emmerich–Doetingham–Ruurlo–Bocurlo–Borne.

2nd British Army task was to secure a general line from Hengeloo–Rheine—exclusive Munster. 1st Canadian Army, after regaining command of 2 Canadian Corps at Emmerich, was to operate to the north and attack the defences of the R. Ijssel from the rear, directed on Deventer and Zutphen.

For the initial crossings 2nd British Army was disposed as under:

Left: 30 Corps; with 3rd Division on the line of the R. Rhine and 3rd Canadian, 51st and 43rd Divisions for the crossing;

Right: 12 Corps; with 52nd (L) Division on the line of the river and 15th Division and 1st Commando Brigade to cross.

Reserve: 8 Corps and 11th Armd. Division.

18th U.S. Airborne Corps, with 6th British and 17th U.S. Airborne Divisions, was to drop on 12 Corps front, east of the R. Rhine, after the crossings had taken place, to disrupt enemy defences north of Wesel.

D-day for the operation was 23rd March, for 2nd British Army, and 24th March for 9th U.S. Army and 18th U.S. Airborne Corps.

30 CORPS OPERATION TURNSCREW (*Map* 24)

Following the conclusion of the Battle of the Rhineland, 43rd Division had moved back into Corps and Army reserve. Planning and training began for the Rhine crossing. The general plan for 30 Corps was that 51st (H) Division should make the assault, while 43rd Division should follow for the build-up.

At 1530 hours on 23rd March, 21st Army Group gave the orders to launch the operation and the artillery programme opened shortly afterwards. A great weight of guns of all calibres had been assembled. At 2100 hours, 51st (H) Division launched the assault in amphibious craft, in the neighbourhood of Rees. All crossings were successful. At 2200 hours, 1st Commando Brigade began to cross on 12 Corps front, landing two miles west of Wesel.

At 0300 hours, aided by an intense aerial bombardment, the Brigade entered the town. At 0200 hours, 15th Division started to cross on 12 Corps front. Further south, 30th and 79th U.S. Divisions crossed the river.

In the meantime, on 30 Corps sector, 43rd Division began to move up to the concentration and assembly areas on 24th March.

During the early hours of 24th March, the airborne forces were forming up. 17th U.S. Airborne Division took off from bases in France, while 6th Airborne Division came from England. The two air fleets, covered by fighters, converged near Brussels and headed for the Rhine.

6TH AIRBORNE DIVISION

7th Battalion (L.I.) had returned to Bulford, from Holland, on 23rd February. Between 7th and 18th March, after a period of leave and refitting, it was engaged in training. On 20th March, it moved to a transit camp at Wimbush and was briefed for 6th Airborne Division operation Varsity. As already stated, 6th Airborne Division had been selected to join 17th U.S. Airborne Division, to form 18th U.S. Airborne Corps, for the Battle of the Rhine.

The airborne landings were timed to follow the initial land attacks, instead of preceding them. The reasons for this were (*a*) daylight had been found desirable for the operation of airborne troops and (*b*) it would be impossible to make full use of the whole of the artillery available to support the land attacks, if airborne troops had been dropped in the target area before the assault began.

The object of the airborne landings—in an area on 12 Corps front, east of the R. Rhine and north of Wesel—was to increase the build-up and intercept the movements of enemy reinforcements into the battle area. The area of the drop corresponded to the known area of the enemy artillery positions.

The plan was for 5th Para Brigade of 6th Airborne Division to drop at 1020 hours on 24th March; that is, 3 to 4 hours after the crossing of the Rhine by land forces in assault boats. 12th and 13th Para Battalions were to seize a certain spur in the area, while 7th Battalion (L.I.) dealt with opposition interfering with this task. 7th Battalion (L.I.), therefore, dropped "looking for a fight"—an ideal rôle for a Para Battalion.

7TH BATTALION (L.I.) PARA REGT.

At 0300 hours on 24th March, 7th Battalion (L.I.) moved to Boreham airfield. 5th Para Brigade took off at 0740 hours and headed for Brussels, thence towards Wesel. At 1018 hours the drop began, according to plan, north-west of Hamminkeln. The drop was rather high—800–1,000 feet—and the men were in the air for some time. There were casualties from A.A. shells bursting among the parachutists. Visibility, generally, was poor. Positions were occupied at 30 per cent. of strength, within 30 minutes of the drop starting. A company was in, complete, about one hour later. All positions were gained by 1200 hours.

THE RHINE TO THE ELBE

There was heavy shelling and mortaring all the morning and Lieut.-Colonel Pine-Coffin was slightly wounded. The enemy had been surprised and no determined counter-attack was made during the day. Prisoners came in in considerable numbers. At 1500 hours the Battalion was ordered to thin out and withdraw to brigade reserve. The casualties for the day were Lieut. Woodburn and 16 Other Ranks killed; Lieut. Nelson and 52 Other Ranks wounded; Lieut. Simpson and 21 Other Ranks missing. Total, 93.

During the day 6th Airborne Division had taken Hamminkeln and bridges near there, over the R. Ijssel, while 17th U.S. Airborne Division took Diersfordt, the high ground to the east and further crossings over the river. Altogether 3,500 P.O.W. were taken. On 25th March there was considerable light automatic and mortar fire. At 0930 hours contact was made with troops of 15th Division and 1st Commando Brigade.

43RD DIVISION

During 24th March, 15th Division, on 12 Corps front, had taken Mehr and Haffen, on the north of the sector. 51st Division of 30 Corps, had stiff opposition near Rees, but took Esserden and Speldorp and reached the outskirts of Bienen. By nightfall, the whole of 30th and 79th Divisions, on 9th U.S. Army front, were across the Rhine between Ossenburg and Orsoy.

On 25th March, 43rd Division and 3rd Canadian Division were ordered to cross the R. Rhine. 129th Brigade, of 43rd Division, with 4 Somerset L.I., moved up into the Marshalling Area (or "Sausage machine") at Marienbaum, the Battalion being split into four echelons (F1—4). At 1600 hours, 43rd Division took over command on the left sector of 30 Corps from 51st (H) Division. The intention was to cross the river and attack and capture Millingen and Hueth, using 9th Canadian Brigade to lead and 130th Brigade to pass through.

During 25th March, while 9th Canadian Brigade took Millingen and Hueth, 130th Brigade was passed over the Rhine into the bridgehead. Rees was finally cleared by 51st Division while, further south, on 12 Corps front, 15th Division took Bislich, being reinforced by a brigade from 42nd Division. 53rd Division then began to cross the river.

THE CROSSING OF THE RHINE

On 26th March, 43rd Division was ordered to clear up Bienen. At 0245 hours, 4 Somerset L.I., with 129th Brigade, began to cross in Buffaloes, without incident. Part of the Battalion crossed by a newly constructed bridge and the whole concentrated east of the river and just north of Rees. The "Beach Landing Organisation" was controlled by Captain R. W. Drewett.

214th Brigade, with 7 Somerset L.I., followed. At 1500 hours the Battalion moved into the Marshalling Area and by 1800 hours had completed all preparations. At 0010 hours on 27th March, the Battalion crossed by the "Lambeth Bridge" and moved to a concentration area at Esserden, arriving there at 0300 hours.

7TH BATTALION (L.I.) PARA REGT.

In the meantime 7th Battalion (L.I.) crossed the R. Ijssel, near Haminkeln, at 1400 hours on 26th March and, by 2000 hours, had occupied its objectives in the new bridgehead. On 27th March, the Battalion, preceded by armoured reconnaissance from 6th Airborne Division, led the advance eastwards, starting at 1100 hours and moving via Brunen towards Erle.

The advance was led by tanks which were held up by flak guns used in a ground rôle and some self-propelled guns. It was decided that infantry could deal with the situation better than tanks and the 7th Battalion was detailed for the task. At 1700 hours, moving by the right flank of the armour, a strong fighting patrol of two companies, led by Lieut.-Colonel Pine-Coffin, got round the enemy. C company, under Major Keane, attacked frontally, while B company, under Major Reid, was held in readiness. C company had a stiff fight but B company got round behind the enemy. At 1800 hours there was a further hold up from light flak guns. These were attacked and, before midnight had been destroyed. 16 P.O.W. were taken. A platoon of B company, under Lieut. Hinman, then was sent forward with a P.I.A.T. gun, to destroy an enemy gun. It returned after two hours with one P.O.W. and news of other enemy guns.

During the night 27/28th March, the advance continued, C company reporting stiff opposition. The company was caught by concentrated fire from flak guns while assaulting the garden of a cottage. Lieut. Kierney and 4 other Ranks were killed and 16 Other Ranks wounded. The company had to withdraw. Lieut. Hinman, with eight men, went out to investigate the position to the north. He returned at 0120 hours, having routed three enemy platoons and taken prisoners. A patrol under Lieut. Pape cleared an area to the south.

THE EXPANSION OF THE BRIDGEHEAD

On 27th March, 43rd Division was ordered, by 30 Corps, to clear the area between Millingen Mer and the Rees–Ijsselburg road and capture Megchelen, or Anholt. The ultimate intention was for 130th Brigade to move on Landport and Anholt, 9th Canadian Brigade now reverted to 3rd Canadian Division.

129th Brigade was now in the Bienen area (on the left) with 214th Brigade near Esserden. At 0900 hours 129th Brigade attacked Millingen Mer, with 5 Wilts Regt. on the left and 4 Wilts Regt. on the right. 4 Somerset L.I. was in reserve near Bienen. The objectives were soon taken with slight opposition. The next phase was for 214th Brigade to attack through 129th Brigade, with 7 Somerset L.I. on the left and 1 Worcs Regt. on the right. The objective was the high ground north of the autobahn, towards Anholt. At 1330 hours the leading battalions reached the start line near Millingen.

7 Somerset L.I. crossed the start line at 1415 hours, with A and B companies forward. At 1600 hours the attack was held up. Lieut.-Colonel Reeves was

wounded and Major C. Brooke Smith (K.S.L.I.) took command. During this battle Corporal Comm gained the immediate award of the D.C.M. for gallantly leading his section forward, when his company was held up under a hail of fire, to turn the whole enemy position. At 1715 hours, opposition slackened and A and B companies went forward to the objectives, followed by C and D companies. During the night, patrols worked forward.

On 28th March, 43rd Division was ordered to make an assault crossing of the R. Ijssel, near Landport, and assault and capture Anholt from the north-west. During this day 214th Brigade was working slowly forward, while 129th Brigade was preparing to attack either Anholt, or Dinxperlo.

On 29th March, the intention of 43rd Division was to capture Landport and construct a bridge over the R. Ijssel at Anholt. There was now considerable congestion on the roads, owing to 2nd Canadian Division having come into 30 Corps bridgehead. 130th Brigade, together with a brigade from 51st Division, was moved up to attack and 4 Dorset Regt. took Anholt. Guards Armd. Division then went through on the left, while 4 Wilts Regt. of 129th Brigade, was sent up to enlarge the bridgehead won by 130th Brigade. 129th Brigade then, with 4 Somerset L.I., moved up to a concentration area in some woods near Anholt, in positions some 400 yards from the enemy. At 1430 hours, 7 Hants Regt. of 130th Brigade, came under command of 129th Brigade, and attacked. By 2200 hours this battalion had secured a further bridgehead over the R. Ijssel, the bridges themselves being blown. 4 Wilts Regt. was then ordered to cross. During the night, 129th Brigade H.Q. moved up to Anholt and was joined by 8th Armd. Brigade.

7TH BATTALION (L.I.) PARA REGT.

On 28th March, 7th Battalion (L.I.) was west of Erle. At 0700 hours, C company attacked and, by 0900 hours, had cleared the enemy from a road block, taking 63 P.O.W. On 29th March it marched at 0900 hours directed on Coesfeld and by 2330 hours had occupied positions west of the town, as far east as the railway. The Coesfeld area was cleared on 30th March.

SITUATION ON THE EVENING OF 29TH MARCH

Expansion of the bridgeheads had gone well everywhere. Enemy opposition had begun to disintegrate. 9th U.S. Army had reached Gladbach, while 6th Guards Armd. Brigade, carrying men of 17th U.S. Airborne Division had reached Dorsten and Haltern. 6th Airborne Division was in Erle and Lembeck. 12 Corps had taken Rhede and was attacking Bocholt. 30 Corps was on the line Haldern–Ijesselburg–Anholt. On the extreme north, 3rd Canadian Division was closing in on Emmerich. 8 Corps, with 11th Armd. Division, was starting to move up on the right of 2nd British Army. All was now set for the break out into Germany.

THE BREAK OUT

21st Army Group intention now was to advance to the line of the R. Elbe. 9th U.S. Army was directed on the line Magdeburg–Wittenberge; 2nd British Army on the line Wittenberge–Hamburg. To the south of 9th U.S. Army, 1st U.S. Army was advancing northwards from Remagen, through Marburg.

To facilitate the advance of 9th U.S. Army, it was allotted the sole use of the bridge at Wesel, primarily shared with 2nd British Army. 2nd British Army was given, as a first objective, the line of the R. Elbe, southwards from Hamburg, the left flank of the advance to rest on Hengeloo–Lingen–Bremen–Hamburg. Subsequent events, however, dictated modifications in this plan.

2nd BRITISH ARMY (*Map* 5)

1st Canadian Army was operating on the left of 2nd British Army, between the left boundary mentioned above and the sea. 2nd British Army advanced as follows:

Left: 30 Corps, on Enschede–Bremen–Hamburg.
Centre: 12 Corps, on Rheine–Nienburg–Luneburg.
Right: 8 Corps, on Osnabruch–Celle–Uelzen.

It was originally intended that 18th U.S. Airborne Corps, on the right of 8 Corps, should take Munster. This Corps, however, ceased to be operational on 30th March and the task of taking Munster fell to 9th U.S. Army. 6th Airborne Division passed to command of 8 Corps on 29th March and 6th Guards Armd. Brigade (from 17th U.S. Airborne Division) on 4th April.

30 CORPS

30 Corps task in the break out was known as Operation Forrard On. This name is an indication of the state of moral and the spirit of all ranks in the subsequent actions. The intention was to penetrate deeply into Germany, using Guards Armd. Division on the right and 43rd Division on the left, for the break out. D-day for this operation was 30th March.

43RD DIVISION (*Map* 25)

On 30th March, 8th Armd. Brigade and 4/7th D.G.s, joined up with 129th Brigade, near Anholt, for the advance. At 1000 hours the brigade started with 4 Somerset L.I. leading and D company as vanguard. The column was an impressive sight, with tanks, kangaroos, carriers, self-propelled guns and a scissors bridge. No limit to the advance was laid down. Guards Armd. Division advanced simultaneously on a parallel road to the south,

There was slight opposition, first at Sinderen, where spandau and panzerfaust teams came to life and knocked out a tank. By 1830 hours D company

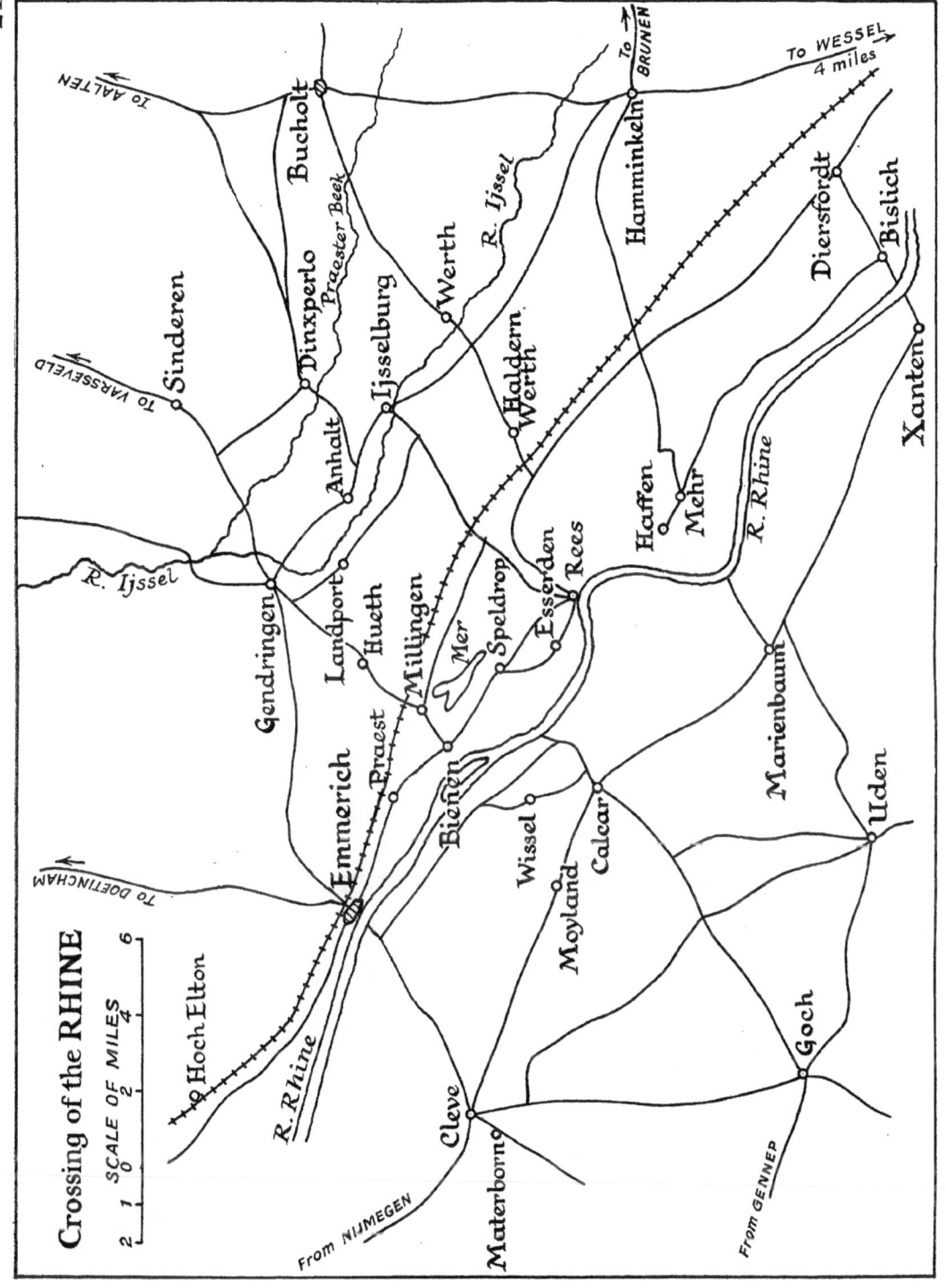

had taken Sinderen and, with A company leading, the advance continued towards Varsseveld. At 1900 hours, A company was held up by self-propelled guns, just short of the town. By 2100 hours, the Battalion had lagered in for the night. There was considerable shelling and at 2215 hours a carrier was hit, killing 2 Other Ranks and wounding 3. In the meantime 5 Wilts Regt. had moved up to Sinderen. During the day 214th Brigade remained in reserve at Anholt.

On 31st March, at 0115 hours, A and B companies, 4 Somerset L.I. launched a silent attack on Varsseveld. Prior to this attack, Lieut. W. R. B. May, with the Dutch interpreter, Sergeant Adriaanse, entered the town to locate the self-propelled guns. On the way back he was challenged by a small enemy post and, firing a Sten gun from the hip, killed or wounded all five occupants.

The attack on Varsseveld was carried out in three stages:

(*a*) A and B companies cleared the southern outskirts of the town;
(*b*) C company passed through to the northern outskirts;
(*c*) D company made for the Slingerbeek, north-east of the town, to secure a crossing.

The attack was entirely successful and by 0600 hours the town was cleared and many P.O.W. taken. D company had some trouble with flak guns and Major Cooke-Hurle was, again, slightly wounded. Lieuts. Potter, W. R. B. May and C. K. Lockerby, distinguished themselves in close fighting in the darkness, the two latter receiving the M.C.

During the 31st March, 5 Wilts Regt. passed through 4 Somerset L.I. in Kangaroos, followed by 4 Wilts Regt. They found blown bridges, but secured a crossing and a bridgehead by the evening.

43rd Division now issued orders for an advance to Lochem, 13 miles north of Varsseveld. The Division was now operating as an armoured division, with armour from 8th Armd. Brigade and infantry brigades in Kangaroos and T.C.V.s. At 2215 hours, on 31st March, 4 Somerset L.I. again took the lead in 129th Brigade, with C company (Major Watts) as vanguard, riding on tanks. During the day 7 Somerset L.I., with 214th Brigade, had moved to Diepenheim.

On 1st April, at 0330 hours, in pitch darkness, C company, 4 Somerset L.I., ran into opposition at Rietache. Fire was coming from near a small bridge and a large cylindrical object was seen on the road-way on the bridge. This was a large mine. Sergeant R. Hayman, of the Pioneer Platoon, went forward and cut the wires connecting the mine as the Germans were running forward to the plungers to detonate it. For this act of gallantry he was awarded a bar to his M.M.

At 0600 hours further opposition was met at Rurrlo and the leading tank was hit by a panzer-faust. It was still pitch dark. A large house, with a moat and a garden, was rushed and by 0930 hours had been cleared, 60 P.O.W. being taken. During this attack Lieut. E. B. Wright was wounded.

THE CAPTURE OF LOCHEM

During the early hours of 1st April, 4 and 5 Wilts Regt. were relieved by 130th Brigade near Varsseveld and moved up in rear of 4 Somerset L.I. At 1030 hours, B company was leading on foot, with tanks, directed on Lochem, which was strongly held. A detour was made and the town attacked from the east. By 1300 hours, B company had been held up, with the loss of 8 Other Ranks killed. A company was then put in and was, also, pinned down by 1400 hours. C and D companies were passed round the right flank and were also held up.

As darkness fell, however, the enemy fire slackened and, pressing forward, C and D companies obtained a lodgement in the eastern part of the town. 72 P.O.W. were taken. Our casualties were 10 Other Ranks killed and 20 wounded. During the night, 4 Wilts Regt. attacked from south to north and completed the capture of Lochem by 0500 hours on 2nd April.

On 2nd April, 43rd Division intention was to direct 8th Armd. Brigade on Delden, with 129th Brigade moving through Lochem to concentrate near Bocurlo. 130th Brigade was to move in rear of 8th Armd. Brigade through Spade–Borculo–Gesteren, while 214th Brigade moved up to concentrate in rear of 130th Brigade.

On the morning of 2nd April, 4 Somerset L.I. was relieved by a Canadian Battalion and moved to Haarlo (Holland) where it rested until 4th April. 7 Somerset L.I. moved up to Diepenham and thence to concentrate with 214th Brigade near Neide. On 3rd April it moved on to Beckum and rested there until 5th April.

7TH BATTALION (L.I.) (*Map 5*)

While 30 Corps had been advancing in the north, 6th Airborne Division, under 8 Corps, on the right of 2nd British Army, continued to advance from Lembeck. At 0200 hours, on 31st March, 7th Battalion (L.I.) advanced in T.C.V.s to an area west of Greven and occupied a position there at 1030 hours. Here it remained until 0900 hours on 2nd April, when it moved on in M.T. to Lengerich. From there, at 2000 hours it marched on towards Osnabruch. There was heavy shelling during the advance. At 1100 hours on 3rd April, the Battalion again moved on towards Osnabruch, reaching objectives on the high ground, west of the town, at 2100 hours. There was no contact with the enemy and patrols entered Osnabruch.

This advance had been part of 8 Corps plan to capture Osnabruch. German resistance on this front was rapidly disintegrating, but the enemy showed much skill in delaying tactics, by the use of demolitions, and made much use of the many waterways to slow up the advance.

43RD DIVISION

On 3rd April, 43rd Division had been ordered to capture Hengeloo and concentrate in the area Goor–Enschede–Borculo and bridge the Twente Canal.

THE RHINE TO THE ELBE

On 4th April the Division was ordered to hold Hengelo and Borne, after capture, and rest the remainder of the Division.

At 0600 hours, on 4th April, 129th Brigade was ordered to be ready to move on Hengelo at one hour's notice. At 1845 hours, 4 Somerset L.I. advanced and moved into Hengelo without opposition, remaining there until 6th April, when it moved to Oldenzaal. This was in rear of 130th Brigade, whose advance to Oldenzaal had been slowed by blown bridges.

On 5th April 214th Brigade moved forward, 7 Somerset L.I. occupying Nordhorn and remaining there until 7th April, on the morning of which Jellalabad Day was duly celebrated.

30 CORPS ADVANCE TO BREMEN

In the meantime regrouping had been taking place in 30 Corps, so that 43rd Division could advance on two axes, preceded, at first, by Guards Armd. Division. The objective, now, was Bremen. 30 Corps plan was for 43rd Division to advance on the left and Guards Armd. Division on the right. Initially, 43rd Division was to act as left flank screen to the operations of 3rd Division, further north, across the R. Ems, in the Lingen area. It was then to break through at Lingen and reach Bremen before Guards Armd. Division.

It was now that the "chase to Bremen" began. An indication of the high moral of the troops—and possibly of the deterioration of the enemy defence—is shown by the spirit of rivalry between formations of 30 Corps. In a 43rd Division Operation Instruction, issued at this time, the following occurs:

"INTENTION. (Not clear as to whether the statement, 'We'll beat the . . .' referred to the enemy, or the Guards Armd. Division)."

On the other hand, on 9th April, a note in 129th Brigade War Diary states, "NOT to be a race with Guards Armd. Division".

6TH AIRBORNE DIVISION—THE DASH TO THE R. LEINE

In 8 Corps, also, the spirit of the "chase" was predominant. On this sector, 6th Airborne Division led the dash from the R. Weser to the R. Leine.

On 6th April, 7th Battalion (L.I.) moved to Petershagen and spent the night there. Here it received orders to advance to the R. Leine. The plan for 5th Para Brigade was:

(*a*) 12 Para Battalion to seize a spur west of the R. Weser;
(*b*) 7th Battalion (L.I.) to seize the crossings over the R. Weser at Bordenau;
(*c*) 13 Para Battalion to move north from Bordenau and seize the crossing at Neustadt.

At 0945 hours on 7th April, 7th Battalion (L.I.) moved eastwards from Petershagen in T.C.V.s. At 1030 hours, 5th Para Brigade H.Q. crossed the R. Weser near Petershagen, 7th Battalion (L.I.) concentrating just east of the river. The advance then began and went more rapidly than was expected.

At 1430 hours, after an advance of some 25 miles, the Battalion reached Altenhagen. From there, still on wheels, it was ordered to seize Neustadt, moving on at 1545 hours, led by the C.O. in a scout car. The route lay across Wunstorf airfield which was held by the enemy. On the way many Germans were encountered and surrendered, giving up their arms.

Near Wunstorf, the Battalion was held up by fire from the airfield. Several lorries were hit by automatic and mortar fire. Lieut. Pape and 5 Other Ranks were killed and 11 wounded. The C.O.'s scout car was fired on by a panzer-faust and the wireless knocked out. Private Strudwick ran back, under fire, with orders to the Battalion. In the meantime Captains Beckingham (Chaplain) and Wagstaff (R.A.M.C.) showed great gallantry in attending to the wounded under fire.

B company was sent forward on the right to work up the river to the bridge, while the rest of the Battalion continued along the road, which entered Neustadt at the opposite end to the bridge. The main objective was the bridge itself.

B company advanced under cover of smoke and supported by the fire of tanks on a small wood near the airfield. In the meantime 13 Para Battalion, which had reached Grosserheidorn, attacked the airfield hangars. This situation was cleared up by 2000 hours.

When B company reached the outskirts of Neustadt, it worked along the left fork of the river—which divided there—and reached a bridge which was not occupied by the enemy. Major Reid realised that there must be two bridges, so moved on cautiously towards the second. This was about 100 yards away and appeared to be unguarded, though aerial bombs could be seen laid on the roadway half-way across the bridge. Since his orders were to seize the bridge intact and secure a bridgehead, he decided to rush the bridge at once, with two platoons under Lieuts. Woodman and Gush leading and the third platoon to follow.

Lieuts. Woodman and Gush were first across at the head of their platoons which took the aerial bombs like hurdlers. Lieut. Woodman noticed that the bombs were connected by electrical wires, so he snapped one of these wires, as he passed, hoping to break the connection. As the third platoon followed the bombs exploded, causing very heavy casualties among the men on the bridge. A large section of the bridge was also destroyed. The two officers and some ten men, some grievously wounded, were the only ones who reached the far bank. Both officers were wounded. Despite their weakness, this party overpowered the Germans and routed them; later, beating off two counter-attacks.

All energies were now directed to getting more men across the river and evacuating the wounded. Much gallant work was done by men with ropes and the only available boat. Captain Wagstaff, Medical Officer, and two men swam the river twice.

A and C companies had already cleared the town. The casualties during this action were 19 Other Ranks killed, 19 wounded and 6 missing believed

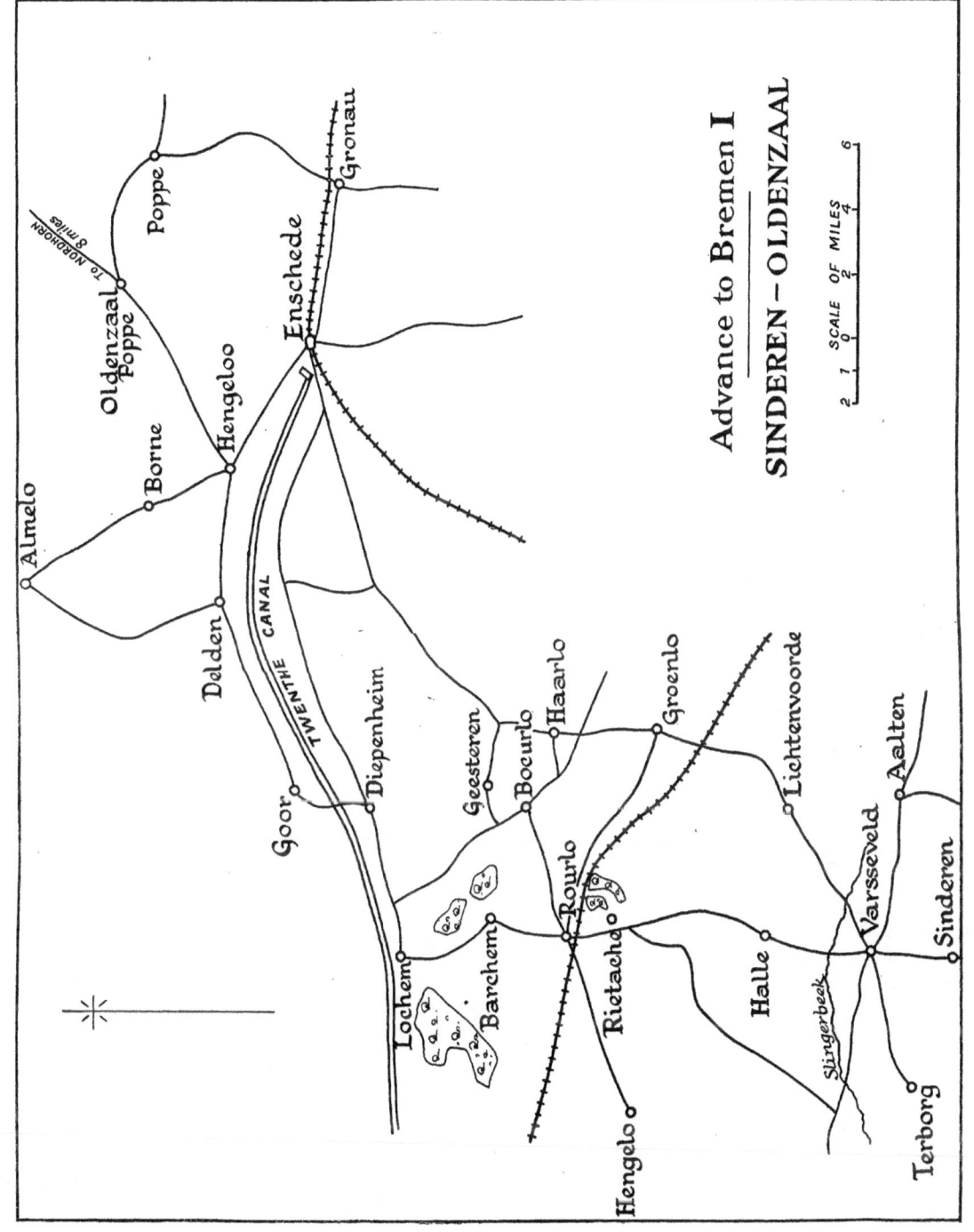

killed. The total casualties for the day were 1 Officer and 26 Other Ranks killed, 3 Officers and 30 Other Ranks wounded. The bodies of 6 Other Ranks were never found.

Next morning, 8th April, A company, with one platoon of C company (Lieut. Archdale) and the M.M.G. Platoon (Lieut. Norton) crossed the R. Leine in boats. B company was pulled out to rest. Many P.O.W. were brought in. Between 9th and 12th April the Battalion remained at Neustadt bringing in more P.O.W. On 13th April it moved to a rest area at Celle, where it stayed until 16th April.

43RD DIVISION (*Maps 26 and 27*)

On 7th April, 43rd Division, while protecting the left flank of 30 Corps, west of Lingen, was advancing on Bremen.

At 1430 hours, 214th Brigade moved forward from the Nordhorn area, along the Bremen road, directed on Lingen. At 1635 hours, 7 Somerset L.I. reached Lingen and the brigade pushed on through 3rd Division. 7 Somerset L.I., supported by 3rd Division artillery, was then ordered to attack Haselunne. C company led the attack and, after some opposition, D company passed through, directed on Plankworth.

During the day 129th Brigade remained at Oldezaal with orders for no move before 0530 hours on 8th April.

On 8th April, at 0930 hours, 7 Somerset L.I. formed up to attack Buckelte. At 1030 hours D company had cleared Baunkel without opposition. By 1730 hours A and D companies had entered and cleared Buckelte, but found the bridges over the R. Hase blown. The assault crossing was lead by A company, who crossed undetected until on the outskirts of the village of Hamm. B company and the remainder of the battalion then crossed: the former securing the bridging site. After some delay in the dark, C and D companies were launched to clear the village which was effected by dawn.

Meanwhile, the sappers working devotedly in the water up to their waists, had constructed a light bridge, hastily christened "Jellalabad", over which the battalion was able to cross at dawn.

In the meantime, 129th Brigade advanced at 0915 hours, directed on an area north of Lingen, preparatory to passing through 214th Brigade. On the way, owing to heavy congestion of traffic on the roads, the brigade was diverted and ordered to concentrate north-east of Lingen.

On 9th April, 43rd Division was ordered to contact 4th Canadian Armd. Division, which was advancing on the axis Meppen–Sogel. In 214th Brigade area, 7 Somerset L.I. stormed and took the village of Hamm and, by 0800 hours, the Battalion transport had crossed the bridge there.

At 0830 hours, 1 Worcs Regt. also crossed the R. Hase and attacked through 7 Somerset L.I. directed on the western half of Haselunne. By 1200 hours the objective was taken with slight opposition. At 1330 hours, 7 Somerset L.I. attacked the eastern half of the town and passed through, at

1415 hours, with no opposition beyond some shelling. The positions in Haselunne were then consolidated.

129th Brigade was now moved up in rear of 214th Brigade. 5 Wilts Regt. passed through 5 D.C.L.I., crossed the R. Hase and, at 1700 hours cleared some woods south of Haselunne. The construction of a bridge over the river was begun. 129th Brigade was now ordered to lead the Division, on the northern route, towards Bremen, with 130th Brigade on the main route through Loningen–Cloppenburg.

On 10th April, 43rd Division was directed on Delmenhorst, being responsible for clearing the area between the road to Spade and the left boundary of 30 Corps. 129th Brigade passed through 214th Brigade, with 5 Wilts Regt. leading, followed by 4 Wilts Regt. After a short check near Elbergen, that town was cleared by 1815 hours and the advance continued until held up by a road block at 2010 hours. 4 Somerset L.I. had reached Eltern at 0915 hours.

129th Brigade was now ordered to advance all night, with 5 Wilts Regt. directed on Hulte and 4 Wilts Regt. on Wachtum. 4 Somerset L.I. was to continue the advance to Loningen, if required.

On 11th April, the advance continued in contact with the retreating enemy. At 0500 hours, B company, 4 Somerset L.I. was sent up to relieve a company of 5 Wilts Regt. By 2045 hours, 4 Wilts Regt. had taken Wachtum and 4 Somerset L.I. had reached Herrsum. 214th Brigade, with 7 Somerset L.I., was rested and made plans to follow up 130th Brigade towards Cloppenburg.

On 12th April, 43rd Division was ordered to press on and keep touch with 4th Canadian Armd. Division on the left. 129th Brigade continued to advance. At 0800 hours, 4 Somerset L.I. moved up to pass through 4 Wilts Regt., with D company leading in Kangaroos, accompanied by tanks. After moving through some woods, under shell-fire, Marren was cleared at 1100 hours, after some opposition. Keiengening was then taken and the Battalion moved north. At 1450 hours it passed through Lindern and was held up near Oster Lindern. C company cleared the road, taking 48 P.O.W. The Battalion was then directed on Peheim, but was diverted to the right on Gronheim. Some opposition was encountered 900 yards short of the village. This was dealt with and 13 P.O.W. taken. By 1900 hours, 4 Wilts Regt. had taken Leiner and 5 Wilts Regt. had moved up into Lindern.

On 13th April, at 0130 hours, 4 Somerset L.I. was established in Gronheim. It then moved on and entered Peheim at 0215 hours. During the day it consolidated at Peheim, with C company at Gronheim. 4 Wilts Regt. remained in Leiner and, later, moved to Morbergen.

On 14th April, 43rd Division stood fast, while Canadian troops moved across the divisional front.

THE GENERAL SITUATION (*Map* 7)

During the first half of April, Allied forces had been closing in everywhere on central Germany. At the end of March, U.S.S.R. troops took

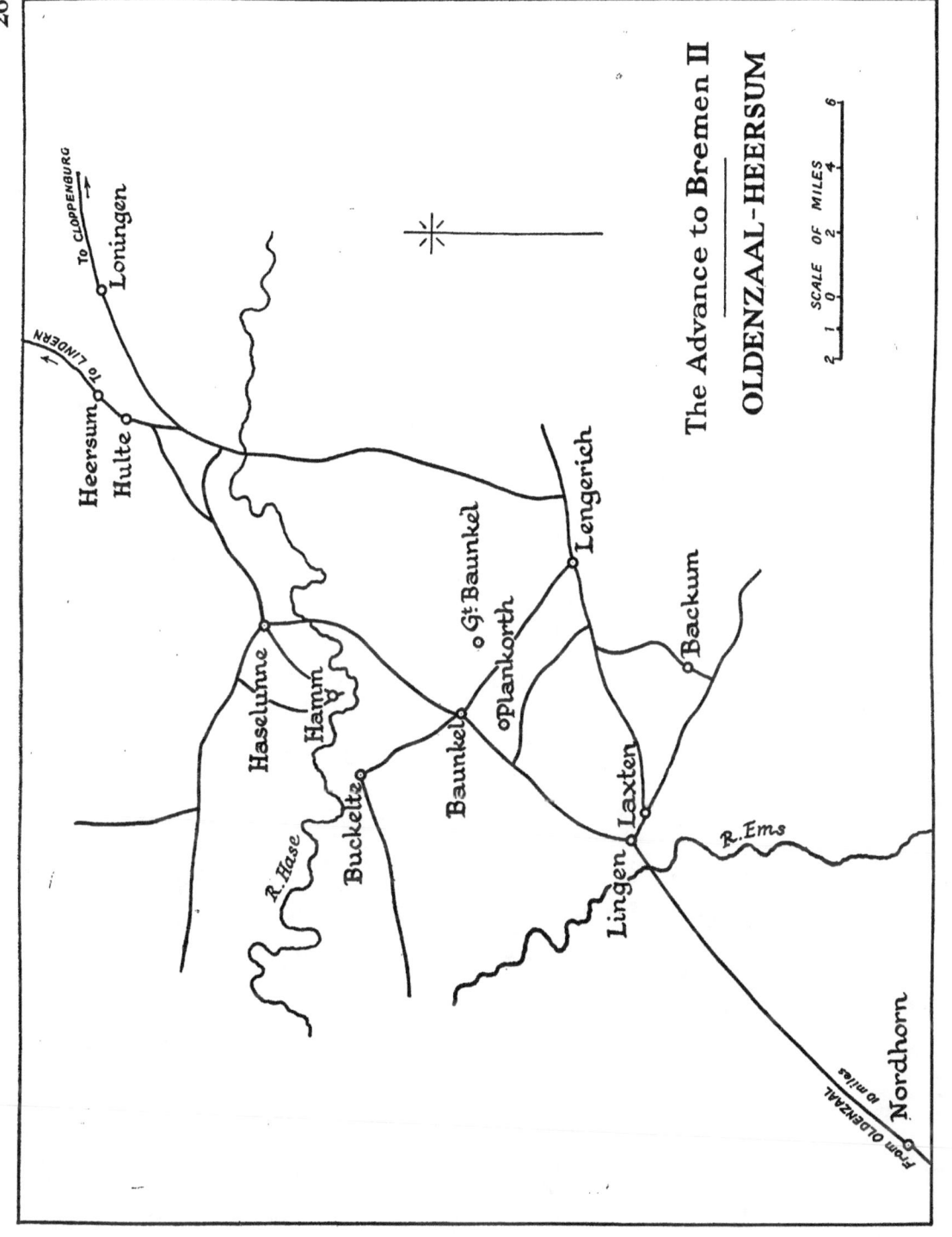

THE RHINE TO THE ELBE

Gdynia and continued the drive through Poland and into the Carpathians. On 30th March they took Danzig. On 9th April Konigsberg fell and by 13th April, Vienna had been liberated.

On the western front, south of 2nd British Army, 9th U.S. Army had been closing up to the line of the R. Weser, while still further south, 3rd U.S. Army took Eisenach and Mulhausen and 1st French Army entered Karlsruhe. On 6th April, 9th U.S. Army crossed the R. Weser at Hammeln, while 1st U.S. Army reached the river below Cassel, extending the Allied front on the R. Weser to 90 miles. While 8 Corps of 2nd British Army was crossing the R. Leine, 1st U.S. Army took Weimar and 9th U.S. Army, driving forward through Essen, reached the R. Elbe, south of Magdeburg. On 12th April, the R. Elbe was crossed and Brunswick entered. To the south, 3rd U.S. Army took Erfurt and 1st French Army occupied Baden Baden and Rastadt.

By 15th April, 1st and 9th U.S. Armies had linked up at Wetter in the Ruhr, the Ruhr "Pocket" being eliminated on 18th April. 3rd U.S. Army was in Bayreuth, while, in the extreme north, 1st Canadian Army reached the sea in North Holland. The German armies were disintegrating rapidly and any attempts on their part to re-group, were made more difficult by intensive Allied bombing.

30 CORPS (*Maps 27 and 28*)

It was now probable that 43rd Division would be entrusted with the task of taking Bremen.

214th Brigade was following 130th Brigade. The latter attacked Cloppenburg on 13th April and the same day, at 0900 hours, 7 Somerset L.I. moved up to Meerdorf. In 129th Brigade, 4 Somerset L.I. moved up, in the evening, from Peheim, to lager at Vahren. On 14th April, at 0700 hours, 5 D.C.L.I. attacked and took Bethen and at 1600 hours, 4 Somerset L.I. moved up to clear some woods near that place.

On 15th April, 129th Brigade was ordered to relieve 152nd Brigade of 51st (H) Division, in the area Morbergen–Cloppenburg–Emster–Visbek. 4 Wilts Regt. moved to Varnhorn and 5 Wilts Regt. to Visbek. At 1900 hours, 129th Brigade was ordered to take over from 153rd Brigade of 51st (H) Division, which was in contact with the enemy in the area Dotlingen–Iserloy.

On 16th April, 4 Somerset L.I. relieved a battalion of 153rd Brigade at Holzhausen and the next day relieved 4 Wilts Regt. at Wildeshausen, where it was in contact with the enemy. During the day, while on patrol, Lieut. Priani was wounded.

In the meantime 214th Brigade, on the 15th April, led the advance eastwards from Cloppenburg. 1 Worcs Regt., the leading battalion, was held up by a blown bridge and opposition at Leyte. 7 Somerset L.I. cleared woods on either side of the axis of advance, on a front of 3,000 yards. On 16th April, 1 Worcs Regt. was counter-attacked near Neulette by a tiger tank and 200 infantry. This attack was beaten off. 7 Somerset L.I. was put in to attack on the left of 1 Worcs Regt., directed on Ahlhorn. The transport had been held up by blown bridges and the attack was unsupported. C company advanced on the right and B company on the left, with A and D companies in support. 1 Worcs Regt. then pressed forward on the right. All objectives were quickly taken, together with 100 P.O.W.

On 17th April, 43rd Division was ordered, after taking over from 51st (H) Division, to move off the route to Cloppenburg, to clear it for 2 Canadian Corps. 43rd Division was, then, to go into an area vacated by Guards Armd. Division and protect the left flank of 30 Corps. 2 Canadian Corps now began to move on the left of 30 Corps. These orders arose from the fact that 2nd British Army was now beginning to converge on the focal point of Bremen and was, also, being crowded by 1st Canadian Army on its left.

129th Brigade spent the 18th April in patrolling. On 19th April, 4 Somerset L.I. attacked, with A and B companies forward, and gained a further 1,000 yards under heavy shell-fire and over mine-fields. In 214th Brigade sector, 5 D.C.L.I. passed through 7 Somerset L.I. and gained Ahlhorn without opposition on 19th April. At 0400 hours, the same day, 7 Somerset L.I. was relieved by the Royal Regiment of Canada and moved to Visbek to rest. 130th Brigade moved up to the area Reide–Intschede–Martfeld and came under command of 52nd Division. 43rd Division was now ordered to take Bremen, if it had not been taken by 52nd Division.

On 20th April, 43rd Division was ordered to take Bretthof and Hengersholz. 129th Brigade led the advance. 4 Somerset L.I. attacked and C company took Bretthof, the Battalion concentrating there. In the meantime 4 Wilts Regt. took Hengersholz. There was slight opposition, but many mines.

The 7th battalion here suffered a great loss when the Quartermaster, Captain J. W. Grant, received serious injuries in a motor accident and had to be evacuated. Very deep patrolling was carried out into Sage by C.S.M. Clarke and Sgt. Hinnels, of the battalion snipers, for which both received the immediate award of the M.M.

On 21st April, 43rd Division was ordered to hold the front between Hengersholz and Dotlingen, but at 1715 hours, received further orders to concentrate in the area Verden–Martfeld–Reide–Intschede. Here it was to be prepared to destroy the enemy south of the R. Weser, between Intschede and Reide and push on to Bremen on the right of 52nd Division. 129th Brigade was now on a front of 14,000 yards and, at 2350 hours, 5 Wilts Regt. was moved up to fill the gap between 4 Somerset L.I. and 4 Wilts Regt.

On 22nd April, 4 Somerset L.I. found Klattenhof clear. Captain J. W. Morris, commanding the Carrier Platoon, was wounded while on patrol. 129th Brigade now came under command of 51st (H) Division. On the left 2 Canadian Corps was moving up and 6th Canadian Brigade passed through to attack and take Neerstedt. 214th Brigade now began to move up.

On 23rd April, 4 Somerset L.I. came under command of 214th Brigade. At 0800 hours, 7 Somerset L.I. advanced and at 1300 hours relieved 2 K.R.R.C. near Langwedee, east of Bremen. 4 Somerset L.I. moved to lager, at 1800

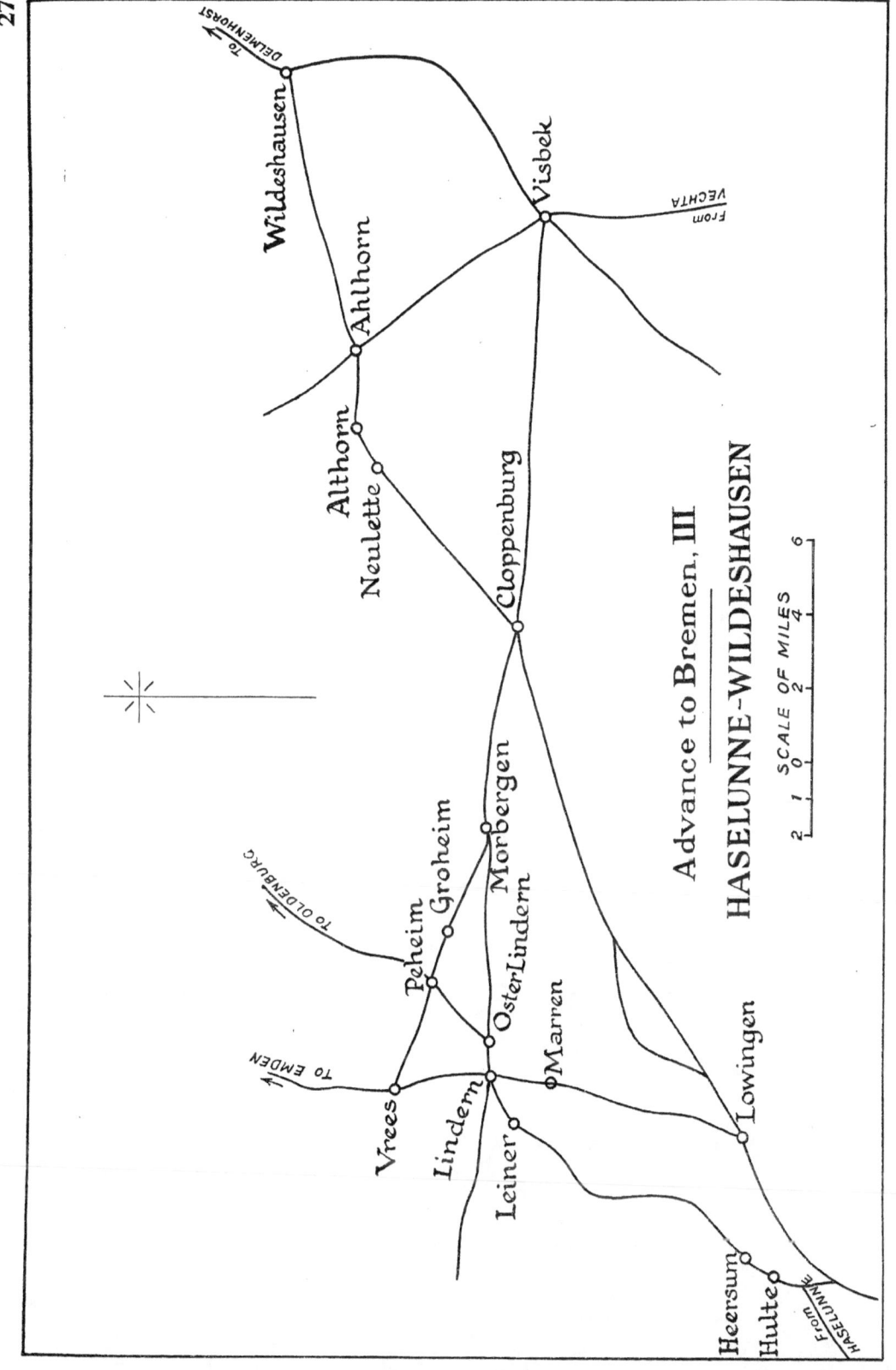

hours, at Eminghausen. This move was preparatory to crossing the R. Weser and assaulting Bremen.

On 24th April, owing to the congestion caused by the convergence of formations on Bremen, 129th Brigade was "pinched out" by troops of 2nd Canadian Division coming in from the north. 52nd (L) Division was, already, eating its way into Bremen from the east. 43rd Division was warned to prepare to take over the area Oyten–Verden.

At 1010 hours, 4 Somerset L.I. crossed the R. Weser and took over an area from 4th Armd. Brigade. In the meantime, in 214th Brigade sector, B company 7 Somerset L.I. advanced at 0001 hours against a strong point between Hintzendorf and Allerdorf, to open the road to Bremen. The plan was to move round the flank and take the position from the rear. The attack went well, Lieuts. Wilson and Jenkins being wounded while dealing with pockets of resistance. At dawn, B company gained the objective and C and A companies passed through, burning out further strong points with "Wasps".

At 1200 hours, 7 Somerset L.I. was ordered to capture Wummingen. At 1430 hours, D company advanced in the face of strong opposition, but gained the objective by 1645 hours. A company then passed through and seized the crossing on the Bremen–Hamburg autobahn, with the aid of "Wasps" under Captain J. M. Taylor for which successful attack he was awarded the M.C.

On 25th April, at 1100 hours, 4 Somerset L.I. reverted to 129th Brigade and was employed in destroying guns, shells and mines. In 214th Brigade, C company, 7 Somerset L.I. was sent, at 0500 hours, to destroy a bridge at Ottersburg. 3rd Division had now moved up and was attacking Bremen from the south.

THE CLEARANCE OF BREMEN

On 26th April, 43rd Division was ordered to clear Bremen, to the north of 52nd Division. 129th Brigade was ordered to attack through 130th Brigade at first light. At 0700 hours, 5 Wilts Regt. followed by 4 Wilts Regt., advanced. 4 Somerset L.I. was in reserve. The attack was held up and 4 Somerset L.I. was directed to attack in the Burger Park area, using Crocodiles. The main opposition was located at a road junction at the south-east corner of the Park, known as "Hyde Park Corner". The plan was for C company to capture this area and A and B companies were, then, to attack northwards. A company was to advance along the eastern edge of the Park and, later, D company was to exploit westwards to the south-west corner of the Park. The fighting was within the city and was, therefore, street fighting.

At 2000 hours C company advanced and after a stiff fight gained the road junction by 2130 hours. The enemy was well dug in and using panzerfaust and small arms fire from houses and cellars. No. 13 Platoon, under Lieut. Lockerby and No. 14 Platoon, under Sergeant Burgess, aided by the "crocodiles" and the light from burning houses, did very well here. For his conduct of this part of the battle, Major A. B. Watts received the M.C.

A and B companies now passed through moving northwards. A company attacked a huge concrete bunker, square and some 30 feet high, with only one entrance. This was expected to house the enemy headquarters in Bremen. When Major V. W. Beckhurst entered it, without opposition, he received the surrender of Major-General Siebel, 2nd-in-Command of the Bremen defences and 25 officers of his Staff. By 2300 hours A and B companies had gained their objectives and D company passed through to the south-west road junction as planned. Casualties were light, but Lance-Corporal Stephens, M.M., of A company, who had been a stretcher-bearer throughout the whole campaign, was killed by a grenade as he went to tend a wounded man. Some 250 prisoners were taken. On 26th April 7 Somerset L.I. rested at Osterholz.

On 27th and 28th April, the clearing of Bremen continued, with considerable street fighting and the reduction of "bunkers". 1 Worcs Regt., of 214th Brigade, passed through 4 Somerset L.I. 4 Wilts Regt. captured Lieut.-General Becker and his Staff, but the local S.A. leader and his wife escaped by committing suicide.

7TH BATTALION (L.I.)

While 30 Corps was advancing on Bremen, 8 Corps, on the right of 2nd British Army, had met little resistance and made rapid strides forward. After the capture of Osnabruch by 6th Airborne Division and Minden, by 11th Armd. Division, 8 Corps advanced across the R. Weser, taking Celle and bridgeheads over the R. Aller. The advance on Uelzen and Luneberg then began, passing south of Bremen to strike the R. Elbe, south of Hamburg.

Between 14th and 15th April, 7th Battalion (L.I.) was resting at Celle. On 16th April, at 1540 hours, it moved by M.T. to Bokel and the next day, starting at 0600 hours, marched to Nettlekamp. On the 18th April, still on foot, it reached Harstadt.

On 20th April, at 1100 hours, it again advanced by march route, reaching Suhlendorf at 1330 hours. At 1830 hours, patrols reported Noventhein clear and some P.O.W. were brought in. Between 21st and 26th April the Battalion rested and at 1830 hours on 27th April, moved by M.T. to Tellmer. Here it searched woods on 28th April, finding them clear. On 30th April, it reached Horndorf and, finally, Holtzen, close to the R. Elbe.

43RD DIVISION

On 29th April, the clearance of Bremen being completed, 43rd Division was ordered:

(*a*) to advance on the axis Ottersburg–Quelkhorn–Tarmstadt;
(*b*) to relieve 51st (H) Division;
(*c*) to sweep areas as far east as the Hamme Canal and as far south as the R. Wumme, securing all crossings between Klenkendorf, on the Canal, and the R. Wumme;
(*d*) thereafter to advance via Glinstedt–Kuhstedt and capture a bridgehead across the Hamme Canal.

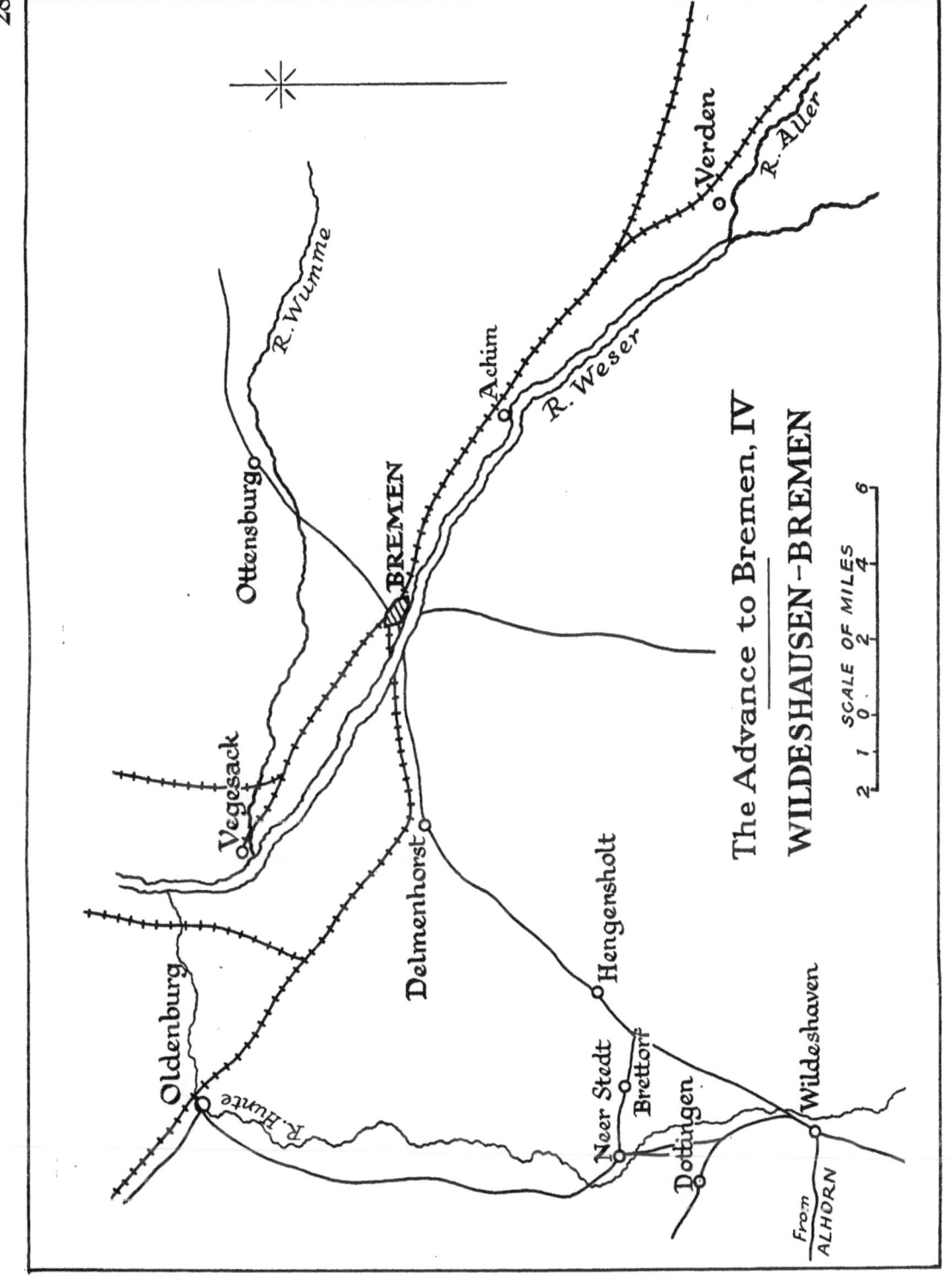

THE RHINE TO THE ELBE

130th Brigade led the advance and was much delayed by deep craters and mines. 129th Brigade was relieved by 155th Brigade of 52nd (L) Division and moved to Oyten, with 4 Somerset L.I. in reserve. 214th Brigade moved at 1425 hours, in T.C.V.s to clear an area near Quelkhorn.

At 1930 hours, 7 Somerset L.I. gained their objectives and moved forward under heavy shell-fire, having their last two fatal casualties of the war in this minor operation.

On 30th April there was heavy rain. 129th Brigade moved on from Oyten by march route; 5 Wilts Regt. to Tarmstadt; 4 Wilts Regt. to Bucholz; 4 Somerset L.I. to Wilstedt. In 214th Brigade area, 7 Somerset L.I. occupied Quelkhorn at 1200 hours.

THE CLOSING SCENE

While 2nd British Army had been closing up to the line of the R. Elbe, southwards from Hamburg, other formations had been completing the disintegration of the German armies.

Nuremberg fell to U.S. forces on 20th April, while U.S.S.R. troops began to advance west of the R. Oder. On 21st April, U.S. forces entered Blankenberg, Dessau and Asch, as well as a number of towns on the Czech frontier. Stuttgart fell to 1st French Army. On 25th April, U.S.S.R. and U.S. troops met at Torgau, on the R. Elbe, while 3rd U.S. Army crossed the R. Danube, west of Regensburg. The same day the 1st White Russian and 1st Ukrainian Armies, linked up east of Berlin. On 26th April, the day on which Bremen surrendered, U.S.S.R. forces took Stettin.

In Italy, our armies had pressed forward. On 28th April, Mussolini, while attempting to escape into Switzerland, was captured and shot by partisans. The next day we took Venice and Mestre. On 1st May, the German armies in Italy surrendered unconditionally.

In the meantime, on 30th April, Hitler, with Eva Braun, committed suicide in Berlin and was succeeded as Fuhrer by Admiral Donitz.

43RD DIVISION

On 1st May, 43rd Division was ordered to clear the north bank of the R. Wumme in the area Quelkhorn–Tarmstadt and to develop a thrust towards bridgeheads over the Hamme Canal near Kuhstedt.

214th Brigade advanced and, at 0915 hours, 7 Somerset L.I. moved off directed on Worpswede. The town was entered without opposition at 1330 hours. On 2nd May, the Battalion was relieved, at 1600 hours, by 7/9th Royal Scots and moved to a concentration area at Oster Timke. Here it rested. There was no move by 129th Brigade.

7TH BATTALION (L.I.) (*Map* 5)

On 1st May, 7th Battalion (L.I.) moved from Holtzen at 0945 hours, and, after crossing the R. Elbe, reached Bukhusen at 1600 hours. On 2nd

May, at 0545 hours, it moved off in M.T., north-eastwards, towards the Baltic Coast and by 2000 hours had occupied Kletzin and Moidentin, near the port of Wismar. Thousands of P.O.W. were coming in. At 1230 hours, on 4th May, the Battalion contacted U.S.S.R. troops, advancing westwards.

THE SURRENDER

On 2nd May, Berlin surrendered to the 1st White Russian Army, while troops of 2nd British Army reached Lubeck and Wismar. 1st Canadian Army occupied Oldenburg, and negotiations were opened for the surrender of Hamburg. Envoys were sent by Admiral Donitz to 21st Army Group Headquarters with overtures for an armistice.

By 4th May, 43rd Division had been ordered to seize the Kuhstedt bridgehead over the Hamme Canal and develop a thrust on Bremerhaven. 130th Brigade advanced to cross the Canal. At 2030 hours reports of the surrender of Germany were received. F.M. Montgomery reported to Supreme Headquarters that all enemy forces in Holland, North-West Germany and Denmark, had surrendered unconditionally.

At 0800 hours on 5th May the "Cease Fire" was sounded. The War in Europe was over.

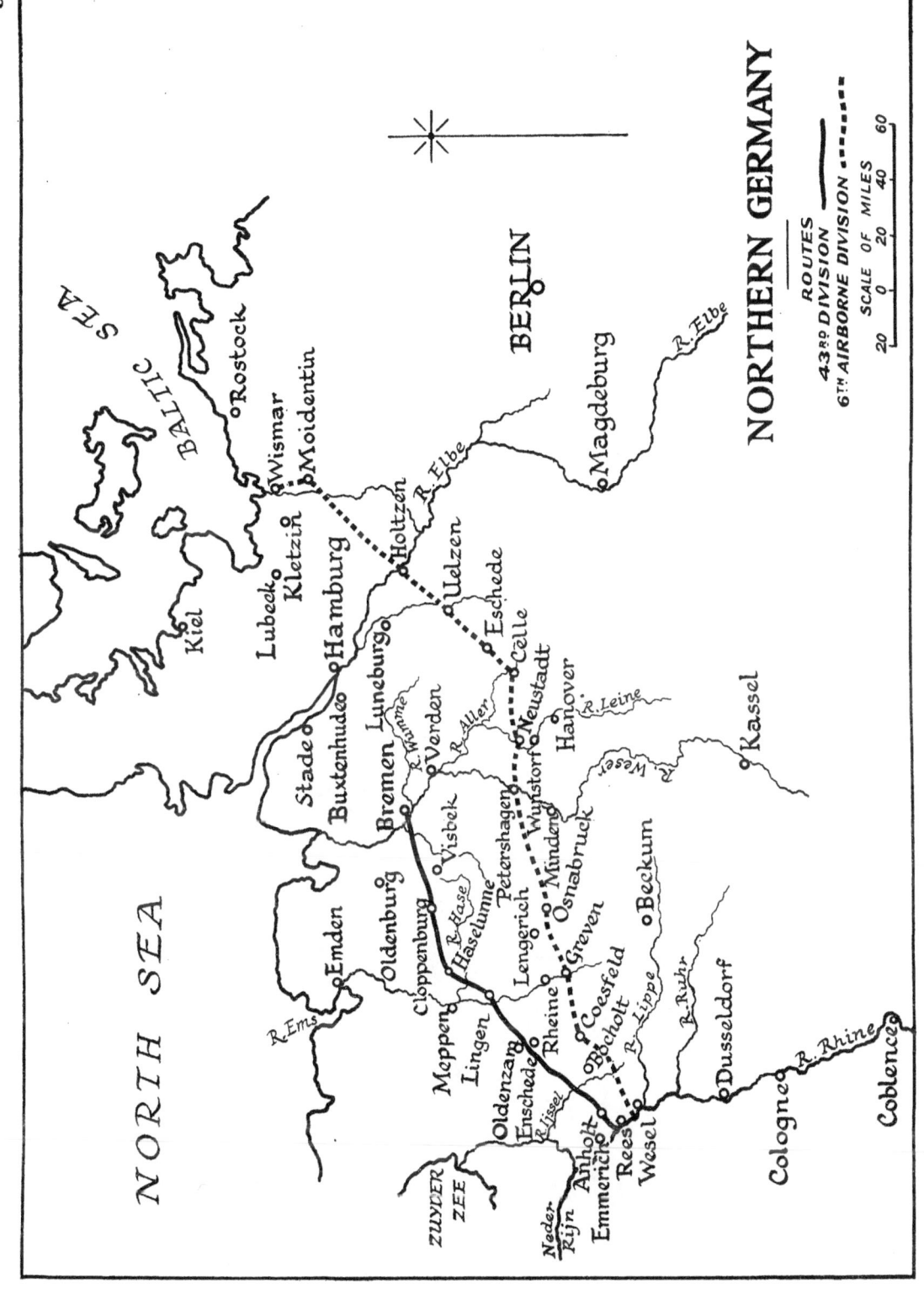

CHAPTER XIX

THE WAR IN GREECE

The beginnings of trouble in Greece—Italian aggression—Invasion of Albania—The Greco-Italian campaign of 1940—The German invasion of Greece in April 1941—Arrival of Imperial troops—Evacuation of Greece—The evacuation of Crete, May 1941—German activities in the eastern Mediterranean—Formation of a new Greek Government, April 1944—The German withdrawal from Greece, September 1944—The Caserta Agreement—Conditions in Greece—4th Division moves to Greece, December 1944—Opening the road to Athens—Street fighting in Athens—The occupation of Greece

THE events of the war in Greece were overshadowed by those in more vital theatres. The history of the aggression which wrecked the Greek economic and political structures had its beginnings before 1939, one of the principal factors being the unpopularity of the monarchical régime. In order to show the part played by British forces in Greece towards the end of the war and during the immediate post-war period, it is necessary to make some mention of the trend of events which led up to what may be described as the "Grecian Tragedy".

It was fairly clear, by the middle of 1940, that few European states could escape the full impact of the war. Italy entered the struggle on 10th June 1940 and she had, in accordance with an aggressive policy, already occupied Albania. Germany began to send troops southwards, through Austria and Hungary, towards the Danubian States. So long as Turkey remained neutral, the German drive to the East was blocked. But Germany had much to gain from the establishment of air and sea bases in Greece and the Ægean Islands, from which to attack our shipping in the eastern Mediterranean and to strike at our bases and installations in Palestine, Egypt, Iraq and the Persian Gulf. Indeed, any enemy bases in the eastern Mediterranean area increased our own considerable difficulties in the protection of communications in that area.

As early as 7th April 1939, Italian troops had landed in Albania. On 13th April, Britain and France, now thoroughly alarmed, gave guarantees to Roumania and Greece. The Italians had not much trouble in the occupation of the Albanian Highlands and their forces concentrated in close proximity to the Greek frontier.

During 1940, in accordance with the usual Axis tactics, Greece was subjected to many minor pin-pricks. On 15th August the Greek cruiser "Helle" was torpedoed by an unidentified submarine, for which Italy denied responsibility. On 16th August, two Greek destroyers were bombed by aircraft. For this Italy apologised.

THE GRECO-ITALIAN CAMPAIGN OF 1940

The "war of nerves" was continued and the situation in Greece became more precarious. At first the Germans left the problem of Greece to the Italians. On 28th October, the latter sent an ultimatum to Greece, which was rejected. Italian troops then crossed the Greek frontier and Patras was bombed. Britain promised immediate help to the Greeks.

By 1st November, Italian forces had reached the R. Kalamas, in Epirus, but their successes were short-lived. The Greek army counter-attacked and, by 19th November, had driven the Italians back. Greek troops entered Koritza, in Albania, on 21st November and gained further successes in December at Premeti, Pogradets and Delvino. Early in January 1941, they took Klisura. This did not suit the German book in any way.

At this time, in spite of discontent with the monarchical régime of King George, the Greeks were united against the Italian foe. But, unfortunately, on 29th January 1941, the Greek Premier, General Metaxas, died and was succeeded by M. Korizis, a leader of somewhat indifferent quality. Bad weather in the mountains restricted any major operations until 9th March, when the Italians opened an offensive in Albania. This did not get very far. It was clear that the Italian troops were of poor quality and badly led.

THE GERMAN INVASION OF GREECE—1941

The Germans were not prepared to have matters delayed by the incompetence of their allies. On 27th March, a revolution had taken place in Yugo-Slavia and King Peter had seized control with a new Cabinet. This, coupled with the debacle in Albania, was too much for Hitler and, on 6th April, he invaded Yugo-Slavia and Greece. King George of the Hellenes issued an appeal to all Greeks to resist to the utmost and the arrival of the promised British and Imperial forces in Greece was announced.

The German troops advanced rapidly and the Yugo-Slav army withdrew, exposing the flank of the Greek forces in northern Greece. By 8th April, German forces had entered Salonika without much difficulty. British forces had been sent northwards into Greece to hold the Florina Gap in northern Greece. Here they were attacked on 9th April. On 10th April, German troops, sweeping south through Macedonia, reached Monastir and Jannitsa.

On 11th April the British were forced to withdraw, in the face of overwhelming numbers, and retreated to the Mount Olympus Line, blocking the German line of advance by the coastal route. On 14th April this position was turned by the loss of the Kleisoura Pass. The British then began a further southwards retreat along the coast. On 17th April the Yugo-Slav army capitulated and King Peter escaped from Kotor in an R.A.F. Sunderland flying-boat. The next day the Greek Premier, M. Korizis, committed suicide and was succeeded by M. Tsouderos. On 20th April, Greek forces in Epirus and Macedonia surrendered and British forces, retreating southwards in Greece, reached Thermopylæ.

THE WAR IN GREECE

The situation was now desperate and the evacuation of the British force began. King George and the Greek Government took refuge in Crete. German air attacks on the airfield at Athens resulted in the virtual destruction of our air forces there. On 26th April, German paratroops dropped on Corinth and the next day German troops entered Athens. By 2nd May, 43,000 British and Imperial troops had been evacuated from Greece. The Germans were in complete control of the country.

THE EVACUATION OF CRETE—MAY 1941

The Germans now began to occupy the Ægean Islands and, on 20th May, began the invasion of Crete, where many of the British forces saved from Greece were now located. The attack started with the landing of 1,500 paratroops. Further troops were landed on 21st May, taking Maleme airfield. A sea convoy was, however, intercepted and destroyed by our naval forces. On 27th May Canea fell. King George and his Government had already escaped to Egypt. By 1st June, all British forces had been evacuated from Crete, but our naval losses in these operations were three cruisers and six destroyers. This was, virtually, the end of the first phase of the war in Greece.

GERMAN ACTIVITIES IN THE EASTERN MEDITERRANEAN

Between 1941 and 1944, the Germans remained in occupation of Greece and the neighbouring islands, while King George and his Government stayed in Egypt. The Germans controlled the sea route to the Dardanelles and Turkey and, from bases in Greece and the Ægean, harassed our shipping in the Mediterranean and carried out air attacks on Egypt and the Middle East. Attempts were made, without success, to bomb the airfields and installations in the Persian Gulf and aid was given, by air, to hostile forces in Syria and Iraq.

FORMATION OF A NEW GREEK GOVERNMENT

The political situation in Greece, adversely affected by the German occupation, deteriorated rapidly. The main factors in the general breakdown were the previous five years' "dictatorship" by the government of King George followed by three years of German ruthlessness and oppression. Two rival resistance groups arose, known, respectively as E.A.M. (of which E.L.A.S. was the military wing) and E.D.E.S. These groups caused little trouble to the Germans, but they engaged in warfare among themselves, with a view to the ultimate gaining of political power. It was not until February 1944 that they were induced to curtail this internecine strife and devote their activities to harassing the Germans.

At the bottom of this civil conflict, was the intense dislike of the rule of King George. In March 1944, this was reflected in mutinies in Greek army and naval units which had escaped to Egypt. King George, who had been in England for some time, returned to Cairo on 11th April 1944. During the next few days he issued a statement on the formation of a new and more popular form of government. M. Tsouderos resigned the Premiership and Colonel Sophocles Venezelos formed a new Cabinet. This only lasted until 28th April, when M. George Papandreou, leader of the Republican Social Democratic Party, who had escaped from Greece, formed a ministry.

M. Papandreou summoned a conference, which included leaders of the resistance groups, to meet in the Lebanon on 14th May. In the meantime, on 22nd April, three Greek battleships at Alexandria, which had, for political reasons, refused to obey orders, were boarded and recovered under the orders of Vice-Admiral Voulgaus, the Greek C.-in-C. On 24th April, the mutineers in 1st Greek Brigade were finally suppressed. The result of the conference in the Lebanon was to agree to disband all "party armies", and to form a National Army. The delegates of E.A.M. were, however, very suspicious and took a long time to obtain the agreement of their Party. It was not until 8th June that a new Cabinet could be formed. Even so, civil war was by no means at an end in Greece. Further clashes between the Parties upset the new National Charter and, on 6th July, M. Papandreou laid the blame for this on E.A.M. On 2nd September, however, M. Papandreou announced the formation of a National All-Party Government and the achievement of complete unity. This result was not, however, borne out by later events.

THE GERMAN WITHDRAWAL FROM GREECE

Early in September 1944, owing to the increasing pressure in other theatres of war, the Germans began to withdraw from Greece and the Ægean Islands. On the night 15th/16th September British troops from 8th Army in Italy made an unopposed landing on Kythera Island, south of the Peloponnesus. The next day the Germans began to evacuate Samos. Shortly afterwards, partisan forces under Marshal Tito, liberated most of the Dalmatian Islands in the Adriatic, aided by a landing of British commandos on Solta.

THE CASERTA AGREEMENT

On 24th September, Major-General Scobie was appointed G.O.C. British forces in Greece. On 26th September, a conference was held at Caserta, at which General Scobie, The G.O.C.-in-C. Mediterranean, M. Papandreou and the two Greek Guerilla leaders were present. All guerilla forces agreed to serve under General Scobie and to accept the orders of the Greek Government.

On 5th October, British forces landed on the mainland of Greece—entering Patras—and also landing on the Greek Islands and in Albania. Corinth and Samos were occupied on 8th October and on 12th October, Allied paratroops seized the airfield at Athens. On 10th October, General Sir B. Paget, G.O.C.-in-C. Middle East, appealed to the Greek Guerillas for unity, but on 15th October there were further clashes between E.A.M. and E.D.E.S. On 18th October, the Greek Government landed at Heraklia, while British troops occupied Lamia on 24th October. On 30th October, the Greek

Government issued a decree disbanding the Militia formed by E.L.A.S. By 5th November, British forces had landed patrols at Salonika.

CONDITIONS IN GREECE

On their withdrawal, the Germans left Greece in an appalling state, with inflated currency, transport and communications wrecked, industries looted, starvation in the cities and dissension everywhere. During November 1944, a financial stabilisation scheme was put into operation and supplies, to feed the people, were imported at the rate of 130,000 tons a month.

Before sending troops to Greece, the British Government had obtained guarantees of co-operation from all members of the Papandreou Government, as well as from the two leaders of the rival resistance forces. Collisions between the two parties were, however, frequent, the leaders of E.A.M. demanding that military forces raised in Egypt, as well as irregulars, should be disbanded. On 1st December, General Scobie announced his intention of supporting the existing government, which was constitutional in nature, until the Greek State could be re-established and free elections held. He also directed that the forces of both E.A.M. (E.L.A.S.) and E.D.E.S. should disband on 10th September.

As a result of this announcement, six of the representatives of E.A.M. in the Government resigned and on 3rd December indiscriminate shooting, followed by civil war, began in Athens. General Scobie called on all troops and police raised by E.A.M., and belonging to E.L.A.S., to leave Athens by 6th December. An attack on British Naval Headquarters in the city followed, with sharp fighting between British and E.L.A.S. troops, the former being hard pressed for some time.

The defection of the representatives of E.A.M. left the Government at the mercy of the Royalist right wing and other reactionaries, while the centre parties were not strong enough to exert any restraining influence. In Athens the people were starving and there was much material damage from E.L.A.S. mortar bombs. British troops were embittered by the presence in the city of un-uniformed and ill-disciplined civilians who supported E.A.M. and E.L.A.S. On 12th December, General Scobie called on E.A.M. to disarm its troops in Athens. This had no effect. This was the situation when 2 Somerset L.I. reached Greece.

4TH DIVISION MOVES FROM ITALY TO GREECE

On 24th November, 1944, 2 Somerset L.I. came out of the line to Forli, as described in Chapter XVII. The same evening orders came for 4th Division to proceed at once to Greece. 2 Somerset L.I. moved first to Lanciano, where it was billeted. On 29th November it moved by bus to Pescara and on the 1st December to Ortona, where it entrained for Taranto, arriving there on 3rd December.

On 9th December orders were received for 28th Brigade to proceed at once to Greece, where the situation had become critical. 2 King's Regt. and

2/4 Hampshire Regt. were flown over. On 11th December, 2 Somerset L.I. embarked at Taranto on s.s. "Banfora" and, sailing at 1600 hours on 12th December, reached Piræus, the port of Athens, on 15th December. In the afternoon it disembarked and moved to billets in the Faliron quarter of Piræus.

OPENING THE ROAD TO ATHENS

By this time troops of E.L.A.S. were athwart the road to Athens and along the hills flanking the R. Ilissus. British forces now available in the area Athens–Piræus, were:

H.Q. 3 Corps.
"Ark Force."
12th Brigade of 4th Division.
2 Somerset L.I. and 2 King's Regt. of 28th Brigade, 4th Division.
23rd Armd. Brigade.
5 and 6 Para Battalions.

Isolated parties and convoys moving between Piræus and Athens were being attacked by E.L.A.S. 4th Division plan was to open the road to Athens, with 28th Brigade leading, and 12th Brigade in support. 2 Somerset L.I. was directed to capture high ground, west of the road, at Lofos Sikelias, but at 1700 hours on 16th December, this plan was postponed for 24 hours.

At 2330 hours on 17th December, the advance began, with 2 Somerset L.I. moving up the road towards Athens. At first there was no opposition and by 0545 hours, on 18th December, the Battalion reached its objective. 2/4 Hampshire Regt., which had just arrived, then passed through, with some minor sniping. Otherwise things were quiet.

The Battalion remained on the hill at Lofos Sikelias until 23rd December, being troubled with snipers from across the R. Ilissus, 2 Other Ranks being killed and 2 wounded on 19th December. There was, also, some spasmodic mortar fire. On 20th December, 2/4 Hampshire Regt. cleared the area across the river and the sniping stopped. By 1400 hours on 21st December, the road was nearly cleared and, at 1500 hours, B company, 2 Somerset L.I. supported by tanks cleared an area near the Rubber Factory, on the outskirts of Athens.

On 23rd December, the Battalion was relieved by companies from 2 Royal Fusiliers and 6 Black Watch and at 1630 hours had cleared the streets leading up to the Rouf Barracks, south-west of Athens, where there was some sniping and mortaring during the evening. Here defences were constructed.

On 25th December, working from the Rouf Barracks, the street of Leoforos Konstandinopoulos, was cleared. This lies parallel and to the east of the railway from Piræus and is the main entry to Athens from the south-west. At 2345 hours hostile bands fired on C company positions, near the Rouf Barracks, from houses to the west and were dispersed by mortar and

P.I.A.T. fire. On 26th December, C company was relieved by 6 Black Watch and moved to a new position east of the Barracks.

The situation was so serious that, on 25th December, Mr. Churchill, Mr. Eden and Field-Marshal Alexander flew to Athens to confer with M. Papandreou. Representatives of Greek public opinion were, also, present. The only result of this conference was that Archbishop Damaskinos was appointed Regent. To this King George, who was now again in London, agreed. He stated that he would not return to Greece unless summoned by a free and firm expression of the national will. M. Papandreou resigned from the Government, but the fighting in Athens, between the rival parties, though less intense, still continued.

On 27th December, Mr. Churchill and Field-Marshal Alexander visited 2 Somerset L.I.

On 28th and 29th December, the Rouf Barracks area was shelled by E.L.A.S. and 1 Other Rank was wounded. Ambushes were laid and a patrol of B company killed four men of E.L.A.S. On 30th December, the Battalion was relieved by 1 R.W.K. and moved north-eastwards to take over an area near the Stadium from 11 K.R.R.C. Here it had two companies of the Greek National Guard under command. At the end of the year the strength of the Battalion was 20 Officers and 694 Other Ranks.

STREET FIGHTING IN ATHENS

The problem now was to turn E.L.A.S. out of Athens by force, since all efforts at persuasion had failed. On 1st January 1945, 28th Brigade received orders to capture the area north of the street Leoforos Alexandras. At 1400 hours on 2nd January, 2 Somerset L.I. moved north to the Goudhi Barracks, where 2/4 Hampshire Regt. was already located. At 2200 hours 2/4 Hampshire Regt. began to attack west of the Barracks.

By 0500 hours on 3rd January, 2/4 Hampshire Regt. were meeting strong opposition in the built-up area. At 0730 hours a further attack supported by tanks was put in and the objectives gained. At 1200 hours 2 King's Regt. passed through 2/4 Hampshire Regt. and gained the final objectives by 1600 hours. At 1500 hours, 2 Somerset L.I. moved forward and started to clear streets and houses in the neighbourhood of Vatheos Street, being supported by tanks. By 1800 hours the Battalion was established on the line of this street, with only slight opposition. 9 P.O.W. as well as large quantities of ammunition and equipment were collected.

At 0545 hours on 4th January B and C companies started to comb out blocks of flats and houses near the Hospital Buildings in the quarter. This task was accomplished by 1400 hours, B company having one casualty. At 1500 hours, A company passed through B and C companies and occupied the Prison.

The night 4th/5th January was quiet. At 1715 hours on 5th January C company, followed by B company, attacked towards Gizi Street, lying west of the Prison, towards Patission Road. By 1000 hours Gizi Street had been reached. All this movement had been designed to force a way into Athens from the east, cutting the city, roughly, into two parts. Troops of E.L.A.S. now began to withdraw northwards from Athens, along the Patission Road. 2 Somerset L.I. followed up, moving forward at 1130 hours and by nightfall was established along the line of the street leading from the Prison to the Patission Road.

On 6th January, 2 Somerset L.I. moved northwards on a broad front, clearing the area east of Pattission Road. The quarter between Fokionos Negri and Leoforos Galatsiou streets was cleared by evening with little opposition. By 1500 hours, 2 King's Regt. was slightly to the north of this area, with 2 Somerset L.I. in the centre and 2/4 Hampshire Regt. to the south.

On 8th January fighting in Athens ceased. Troops of E.L.A.S. withdrew to the surrounding country districts. 10th and 12th Brigades of 4th Division were sent north to guard the approaches to the Attica Peninsula, while 28th Brigade remained in Athens to support the National Guard and provide a mobile reserve. Mopping up in Athens and training began, continuing until 15th January. On that day a truce was signed with E.L.A.S. and hostilities ceased in Greece.

THE OCCUPATION OF GREECE

The 2nd Battalion saw no further fighting in this theatre. On 22nd January, Lieut. A. A. Breton, M.C., while an instructor at 28th Brigade Junior Leaders' School, was killed when his carrier ran over a mine. He was buried at Faliron (Piræus).

At the end of January, 28th Brigade was sent up to relieve 12th Brigade in the Aliartos–Levahdia–Petromagoula area. There were reports of raids by communists and 2 Somerset L.I. was sent to search Akrafinon and Kokkinon.

On 17th March, 2 Somerset L.I. moved to Khalkis for training and on 11th April returned to Athens, being billeted in the Patission area. Here it was employed on guard duties in Athens and Piræus. In April, Major-General A. Dudley Ward, C.B.E., D.S.O., was succeeded in command of 4th Division by Major-General C. B. Callander, C.B., M.C. On 20th April, 2 Somerset L.I. moved to Vouliagmeni, near Piræus, where it took over guard duties in the Port area.

In August 1945 it moved to Prevesa, where it camped among olive groves for training and in October it returned to winter quarters at Patras, with D company at Araxos, guarding a P.O.W. camp. Releases now began, the strength of the Battalion then being 30 Officers and 840 Other Ranks.

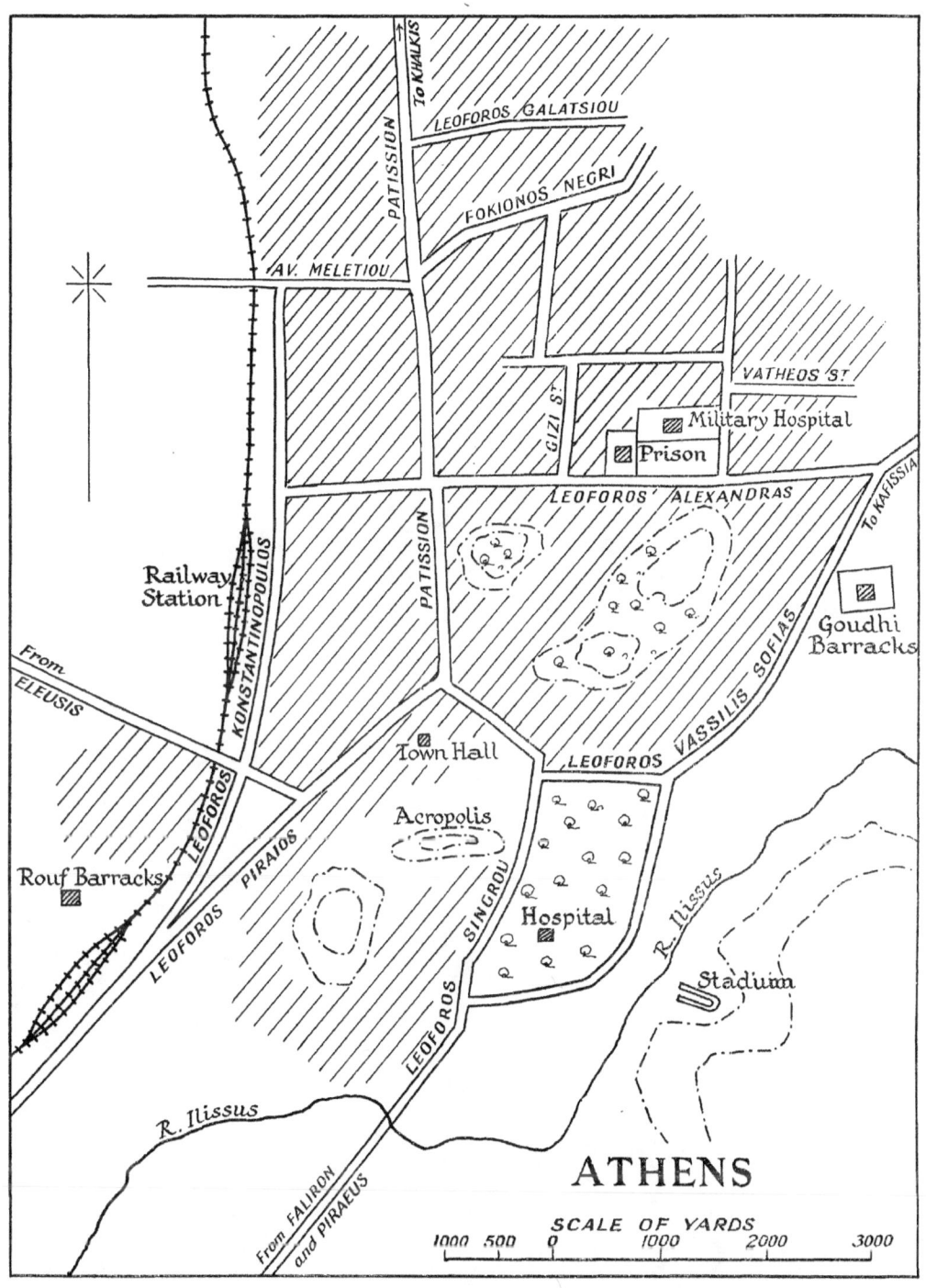

CHAPTER XX

THE CURTAIN FALLS

7th Battalion in Germany—Disbanded at Buxtehude, October 1946—4th Battalion in Germany—Disbanded at Buxtehude, Autumn 1946—7th Battalion (L.I.)—Move to India—End of War with Japan—Move to Singapore and Netherlands East Indies—30th Battalion in Italy—Disbanded at Rome, January 1946—5th Battalion in England—Joins 61st (Light) Division—Disbanded, January 1946—Presentation of Silver Bugle to R.H.L.I.—1st Battalion in India—2nd Battalion—Move to Salonika and Western Macedonia

ALTHOUGH the war in Europe ended on 5th May 1945, two considerations affected the early demobilisation of the armed forces. These were:

(a) the necessity to disarm the enemy forces and occupy enemy territory. The mistakes of 1918 could not be repeated;

(b) the overthrow of Japan.

7TH BATTALION

During May 1945, the 7th Battalion moved to Bevensen a small town near Luneberg. Battalion appointments were:

Commanding Officer: Lieut.-Colonel C. Brooke Smith.
2nd-in-Command: Major K. J. Whitehead, M.C.
Adjutant: Captain J. A. H. Clarke.
I.O.: Lieut. R. A. Wollheim.
Signals: Lieut. H. Procter.
Quartermaster: Captain H. J. R. Catford.
R.S.M.: H. E. Knight.

The Battalion was engaged in guarding large P.O.W. camps, with detachments in villages and at a large underground Oil Refinery and with assistance to the Control Commission on Farming, carriers being used to assist in ploughing. In August a Band was formed, under Corporal Osborne, which, together with a Bugle Band, 20 strong, played Retreat, weekly, at Velzeu, Luchow and Luneberg.

Recreation was a serious problem and successful Cricket, Football and Hockey Teams were started. A "Willing Horse" restaurant was opened. A "XIII Club" was, also, opened on the R. Elbe, but closed down when the Battalion moved to Luchow. A *XIII Magazine* was also popular, and ran to 13 monthly editions. The problem of fraternisation was difficult at first. As time went on restrictions were relaxed and there was gradual improvement in relations with local inhabitants.

During September, Major J. K. Whitehead assumed command and Lieut. R. E. Knowlson became Adjutant. At a ceremonial parade at Celle, Major D. B. M. Durie and Corporal Comm received, respectively, the M.C. and D.C.M. from Field-Marshal Montgomery. At a subsequent parade a French General presented Major Durie and Corporal Yorke with the Croix de Guerre. Other awards received were the M.C. to Major E. R. H. Harvey and Captain H. H. Marshall (who had been Medical Officer with the battalion throughout the campaign); the M.M. to Sergeant Jones and C.-in-C.s certificates for Good Service to C.S.M. Sully, Corporals Willis and Blackwell and Private Parsons.

During January 1946, Major L. Roberts and Lieut.-Colonel C. L. C. Ward, Ox. and Bucks L.I. were in command. In April, Captain T. R. Fox became Adjutant. In March, 43rd Division and its brigades were broken up and the Battalion came under 6th Guards Brigade (Brigadier Greenacre) at Hamburg. In May it relieved 7 Midx. Regt. at Luchow and, in July, moved to Buxtehude. In June, Lieut.-Colonel Woolsy, D.S.O. (Manchester Regt.) assumed command.

In July the 4th and 7th battalions, now accommodated in the same ex-German Naval Barracks at Buxtehude in the Wilhelmshaven peninsula, were inspected on parade by Major-General V. H. B. Majendie, C.B., D.S.O., Colonel of the Somerset Light Infantry. He later attended an inter-battalion football match and a sergeants' dance In the evening combined buglers of both battalions beat Retreat. This was the final big event for both battalions who, slowly running down in numbers owing to demobilisation, were eventually disbanded simultaneously, at Buxtehude, in October 1946.

4TH BATTALION

The 4th Battalion fate was much the same as that of the 7th Battalion. During May 1945, it was employed in collecting war material and destroying dumps and mines. It worked over a wide area in Wichmansberg, Bruchdorf, Winsen and Grossbugwedel. Finally it took over from the U.S. troops at Faliersleben. For services in the campaign Major P. D. Maud and R.S.M. Smith received the M.B.E., Lieut. Priani the M.C., and Sergt. McQuillan the M.M.

In July the Battalion moved south to the area of Celle, with B company at Eldingen and D company at Weinhausen. Here it was employed on guard duties, training and education. In December it moved into the Heidekaserne Barracks at Celle, which were re-named "Taunton Barracks". The release of key men now began.

During January 1946 the release of Groups began, with Group No. 26. On 7th April Jellalabad Day was celebrated. The Battalion was then re-organised into H.Q., B, C and S Companies. In June it moved to Spey Barracks, at Buxtehude, near Bremen, where, on the break up of 43rd Division, it came under 6th Guards Brigade. Here, during the autumn of 1946, it was disbanded at about the same time as the 7th Battalion.

THE CURTAIN FALLS

When concluding the history of World War II, so far as the 4th and 7th Battalions are concerned, mention should be made of the regiments of the 8th Armoured Brigade, who formed part of the Order of Battle of the 43rd Division and were only absent on some two occasions when the Division was engaged after leaving Normandy. The constant and sterling support which these Armoured units gave to these two battalions of the Regiment contributed very greatly to the lustre of their achievements and to the laurels which they won.

7TH BATTALION (L.I.)

During May 1945, the 7th Battalion (L.I.) was relieved near Wismar, on the Baltic Coast, by 17th Brigade of 5th Division. On 19th May it moved to Luneberg airfield and was taken, in Dakotas, to England, concentrating at Bulford, by 21st May.

In July 1945, it moved by ship to India, in preparation for operations against the Japanese in Malaya. 25 Officers and 537 Other Ranks landed at Bombay on 7th August and moved to Kalyan. On 16th August, the War with Japan ended.

On 8th September, 32 Officers and 617 Other Ranks embarked at Bombay and reached Singapore on 21st September. In December the Battalion sailed for Java, landing at Batavia on 14th December. Here it was engaged in clearing the town.

In January 1946 the Battalion moved to Semarang, Java, where it fought many actions against the Indonesians. Included in the Brigade was a Japanese Battalion which had been co-opted owing to shortage of troops. It fought hard and well. The 7th Battalion finally returned to Singapore on 19th March 1946, and was moved up-country to deal with bandits. In the course of these actions it entered Siam and operated there, successfully, for some months. In August 1946 it moved to Palestine.

30TH BATTALION

During May, 1945, the 30th Battalion was relieved in the area south of Naples, by 525th Italian Guard Battalion and, in the area Naples–Caserta, by 605th Regt., R.A. It then moved to Rome, with A company at Falconara and C company at Fabriano–Mondolfo. Appointments at this time included:

H.Q. Company: Captain H. Ferdinand.
A company: Major H. G. Robbins.
B company: Captain G. F. Stevens.
C company: Captain L. W. C. Whitehead.
D company: Captain R. G. R. Arch.
R.S.M.: E. Saunders.

The release scheme started in May, when the strength was 25 Officers and 705 Other Ranks. In June, Captain H. Ferdinand was appointed Adjutant.

During August, A and C companies were relieved by 507th Italian Guard Battalion and moved to Rome, B company remaining at Terni. During September, the release of Group 17 was completed. On 31st December, orders were received for disbandment, to be completed by 11th January 1946. The strength was then 21 Officers and 587 Other Ranks.

In January 1946, disbandment began. On 8th January all remaining railway commitments were handed over to 13th L.A.A. Regt., R.A. On 14th January A, B, C, and D companies closed down. On 19th January 1946 the 30th Battalion was finally disbanded at Rome. The bulk of the men were sent to England for release. Eligible men were posted to other units and a small draft sent to join the 2nd Battalion in Greece.

THE 5TH BATTALION

Mention was last made of the 5th Battalion in Chapter X, when it moved to Seaford in June 1944. It had then become a draft-finding unit. At that time appointments included:

Commanding:	Lieut.-Colonel W. Q. Roberts.
2nd-in-Command:	Major E. H. T. Ubsdell.
Adjutant:	Captain J. C. Griffin.
Quartermaster:	Captain E. Thrift.
R.S.M.:	R. Baldwin.
R.Q.M.S.:	R. W. Viveash.

During July and August the Battalion came under 164th Infantry Brigade of 55th Division, in Home Forces Command, under Lieut.-General Sir H. E. Franklyn, K.C.B., D.S.O., M.C. It was reorganised into four companies to train fourteen platoons of Royal Artillery (L.A.A.). Lieut.-Colonel C. L. Firbank commanded for a time and was succeeded by Lieut.-Colonel C. C. Strong, O.B.E., on 5th August. R.S.M. G. Cooke, succeeded R.S.M. Baldwin. Later, Captain E. A. Batten became Adjutant.

In January 1945, the strength was 41 Officers and 371 Other Ranks. On 18th April, the Battalion moved to Whetstone Camp, Pembroke, South Wales, remaining under 55th Division (Major-General Berney-Ficklin, D.S.O., M.C.). In June it moved to Crowborough, Sussex. Here it was reorganised as an infantry battalion, to form part of 61st (Light) Division (Major-General Wainwright, C.B.). Drafts were received and the strength rose to 31 Officers and 662 Other Ranks. In July, Lieut.-Colonel J. R. I. Platt, D.S.O., took command with Major T. L. Ingram as 2nd-in-Command.

The Battalion had been undergoing intensive training as part of a Light Division, which was to be air transportable and was to be used against the Japanese. In August, however, the war with Japan came to an end, and the 5th Battalion lost its last chance of seeing active service.

A period ensued during which the Battalion was uncertain of its destiny, which was continually being changed.

THE CURTAIN FALLS

General Sir Walter Braithwaite, who had been Colonel of the Regiment from 1929–38, died on 8th September 1945. The 5th Battalion provided the Buglers for his funeral at Chelsea Hospital.

On 11th November a party from the Royal Hamilton Light Infantry, consisting of Officers, Warrant Officers and Sergeants, under the Commanding Officer, Lieut.-Colonel Hugh Arrell, visited the 5th Battalion and spent the day, prior to their departure for Canada in the "Queen Elizabeth" the following day. During their visit a formal parade was held, at which Lieut.-Colonel Platt, on behalf of the Colonel of the Regiment, presented to Lieut.-Colonel Arrell a Silver Bugle, to commemorate the close association of the two regiments during the War.

On 23rd November, orders for disbandment were received and drafts began to leave the Battalion. On 1st January 1946, the remaining 64 Other Ranks were posted to 16th Infantry Holding Battalion at Plymouth and the 5th Battalion was disbanded.

THE 1st BATTALION

In June 1944 Lieut.-Colonel C. S. Howard relieved Lieut.-Colonel P. Lewis in command of the Battalion in Peshawar. It continued to train for frontier warfare, but much time was given to preparation for a return to Burma. During the hot weather of 1944 and 1945 the majority of the Battalion was moved up to Cherat where it had been forty years before.

In August 1945 orders were received that the Battalion was to proceed to Ranchi for intensive jungle training prior to a return to Burma, but no sooner had this news arrived than V-J Day was announced.

In October of the same year the Battalion moved to Shargarh in the Central Provinces to form the British element of 17th Indian Infantry Brigade in 8th Indian Division. The 1/12 Frontier Force and 1/5 Gurkhas made up the Brigade under Brigadier P. McNamara, D.S.O. A high standard of training had been reached in the new Brigade when on the 28th February 1946 a telephone message from Divisional Headquarters said that the Battalion was to move to Jubbulpore that night by road. It transpired that there had been a Mutiny among the Indian Signals and a serious situation was threatened. The move at short notice was highly successful and within a week the situation in Jubbulpore was restored. The Battalion was kept in the station until mid-April, when it moved to Deolali to form the new 29th British Independent Brigade Group. The 1st Gloucesters and 2nd K.O.Y.L.I. made up the Infantry component of the group.

In February 1947 Lieut.-Colonel C. S. Howard was posted to the Staff College at Quetta and Major F. M. De Butts assumed command until the arrival of Lieut.-Colonel J. R. I. Platt. During this period the Battalion moved to Bombay where it was to remain until the final evacuation in April 1948.

THE 2ND BATTALION

In January 1946 the advance party of the 2nd Battalion embarked at Piræus, Greece, and reached Salonika on 8th January. The remainder of the Battalion moved from Patras to Athens and embarked on s.s. "Ocean Vigour" on 17th January, landing at Salonika the next day. This move was part of the relief of 4th Indian Division by 4th British Division.

The Battalion then moved, through Drama, to Komotini, D company remaining at Salonika for guard duties.

In January Lieut.-Colonel A. Hunt assumed Command. The Battalion remained in the Komotini area until October 1946, when it moved to Serres in Western Macedonia.

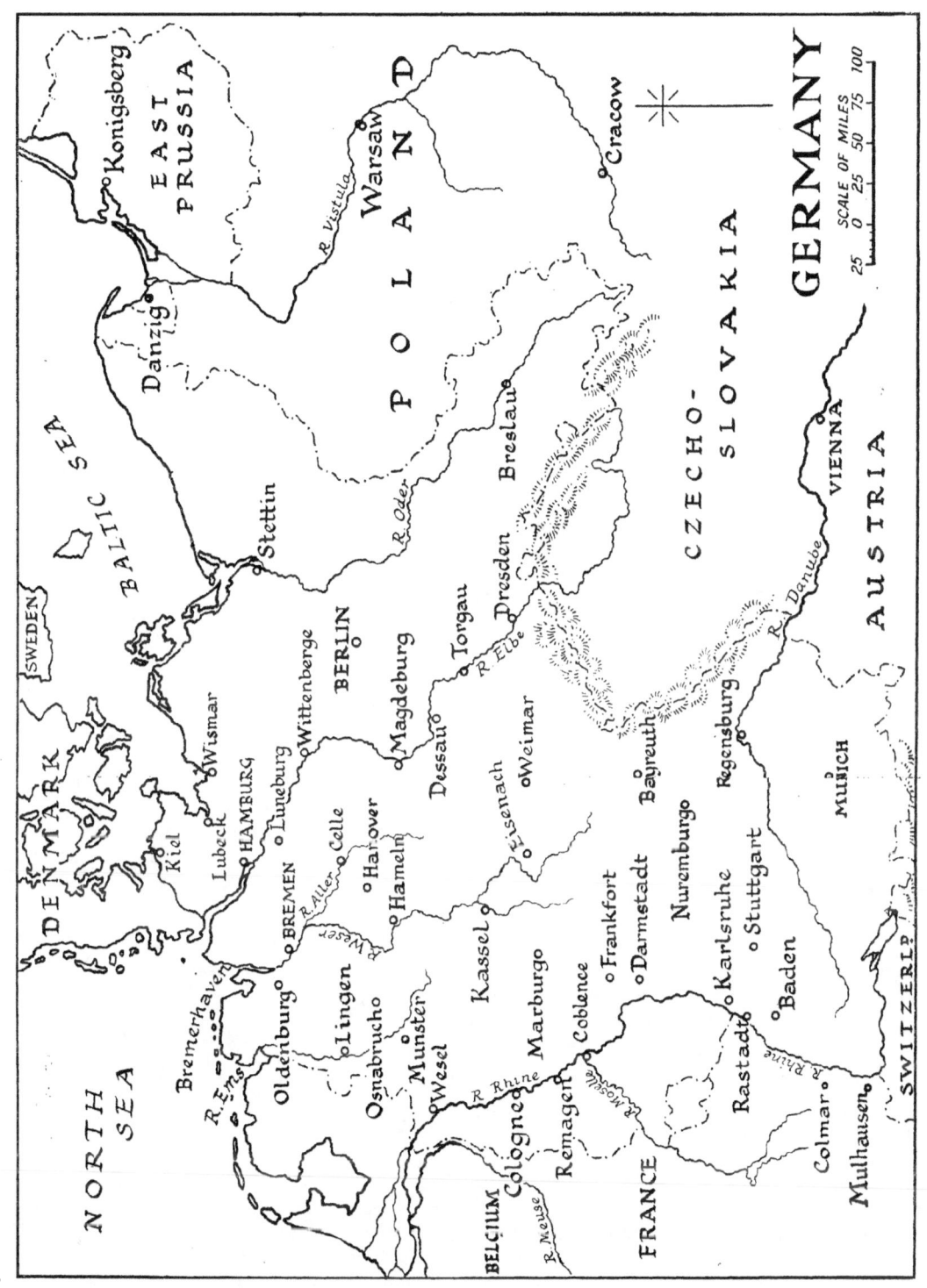

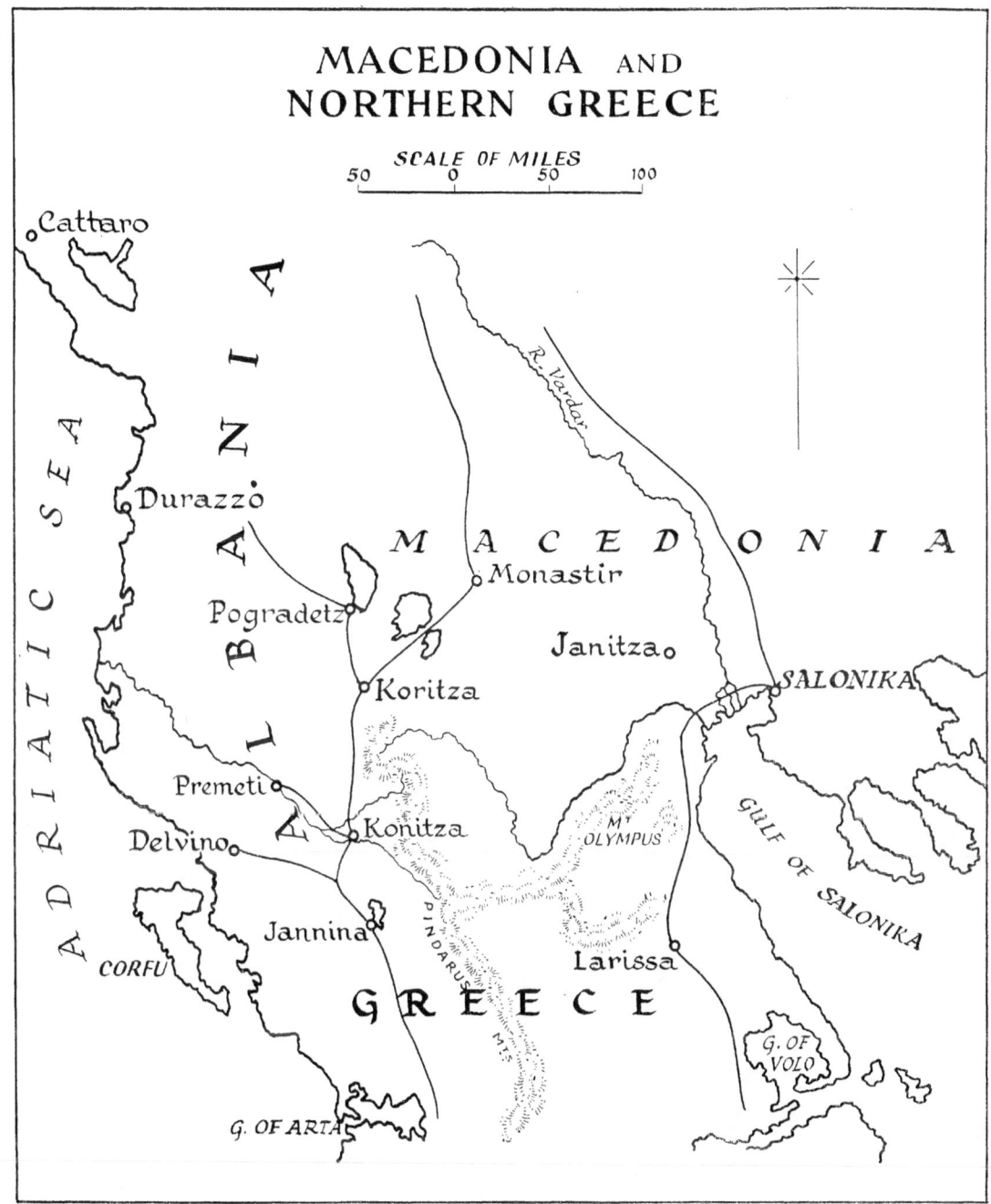

EPILOGUE

THUS the curtain falls on yet another period in the history of a great Regiment. The actors have played their parts and pass from the stage; the scene fades and the lights of war are dimmed. It remains only for the audience to record their applause of a record of self-sacrifice, fortitude under suffering, loyalty and devotion to duty which is second to none.

Throughout the history of The Somerset Light Infantry, as indeed throughout the histories of British Regiments of the Line, runs an ever changing pattern of progress and development. Starting with the old "Private Army", with its units raised and sponsored by noblemen, its curious system of supplying Officers, its "private soldiers" and adventurers, its picturesque uniforms and its aloofness from the general life of the people, the scene passes to the Professional Army of the State, to the National Army and, finally, to the Nation in Arms. The old systems of Commissariat and Supply become more and more controlled and complex as the years go on. The "specialised" wars of previous centuries have become the Nationalised wars of today. The horse has gone and is replaced by mechanical horse-power. Oats have given way to petrol.

With the closer linking of military science and practice to national development and production, the soldier himself tends to become more and more of a technician. During the present century he has had to learn the use of many varied and complex weapons and machines and protect himself not only from enemies on the ground, but from devastating attack from the air. He has, also, had to learn how to go into the air himself and thus to strike and maintain himself at long distances from his bases. He has had to learn how to fight and live in strange countries and climates and how to adapt himself and his tactics to co-operation with allies. He has had to be prepared to fight, under many varying conditions, on sea, land and from the air.

Throughout all these changes, two basic facts emerge. Firstly, whatever may be the increase in military weapons, or armour, the need for the infantry soldier, to fight on the ground with whatever weapon may come to his hand, still remains. The man and not the machine is the ultimate arbiter of war. Secondly, the character of the British soldier, his courage, cheerfulness and fortitude has not changed. Better education and conditions have not in any way impaired his basic qualities. Possibly, this is the major lesson to be learned from this narrative of the War 1939–45.

In the three volumes of the Regimental History, the spirit of the individual and of the Regiment has survived the shock of the big battalions and horsed cavalry; the open warfare conditions where the rifle and the bayonet predominated; the intense artillery fire and chemical warfare of World War I;

and the air and armoured assaults of World War II. There is no reason whatsoever why they should not survive, with glory, the coming of warfare in the Atomic Age, with guided missiles, electronic developments, bacterial warfare and, undoubtedly, many other unpleasantnesses which have not yet seen the light of publicity. The next war will not be like the last. But, whatever may be in store, the Light Bob will bear himself as he has always done.

Personal courage is a matter of National characteristics. Collective courage and fortitude need training, tradition and confidence in leadership. Nowhere can these be better inculcated than by a study of Regimental history. A man may, in his own soul, be a poltroon. To few is it given to be impervious to fear of death and wounds. But a study of Regimental History shows the individual what has been achieved by a team spirit in the past and that he is part of a great tradition whose untarnished record must, at all costs, be maintained and enhanced.

There is no greater record of a Regiment than is contained in this volume and in those which preceded it. It is worth while studying and storing in mind. Our American friends, with whom we may have to work very closely in the future, expressed this well in their songs of the Civil War;

> John Brown's body lies mouldering in the grave,
> But his *soul* goes marching on.

GENERAL SIR WALTER P. BRAITHWAITE, G.C.B.
COLONEL OF THE REGIMENT AUGUST 1929—OCTOBER 1938

APPENDIX A

SUCCESSION OF COLONELS OF THE SOMERSET LIGHT INFANTRY

(Continued from Volume I)

LIEUT.-GENERAL SIR THOMAS D'OYLY SNOW, K.C.B., K.C.M.G.

He was born on 5th May 1858 and educated at Eton College, and Cambridge, entering the Somerset Light Infantry in 1879. He served with the 1st Battalion in the Zulu War of 1879 and with the Mounted Infantry Regiment of the Camel Corps in the Soudan Expedition of 1884–5, being present at the actions of Abu Klea and El Gubat (where he was severely wounded). He also served in the Soudan Campaign of 1898, as Brigade Major, British Brigade and, later, in 1st Brigade, British Division, being mentioned in despatches twice and promoted Brevet Lieut.-Colonel. He received his majority by promotion into The Royal Inniskilling Fusiliers and, later, commanded the 2nd Battalion The Northamptonshire Regiment. Between 1911–14 he commanded the 4th Division. During the 1914–18 War he commanded the 27th Division in 1915 and VII Corps from 1915 to 1918 on the Western Front. He was mentioned in despatches six times, receiving the honours of Commander of the Legion of Honour and Grand Officier of the Order of Leopold. He was created K.C.B. and K.C.M.G. for his services. In 1918 he was promoted Lieut.-General. On retirement he became a Justice of the Peace for the County of Dorset. In 1897 he married Geraldine, daughter of the late Major-General Talbot Coke of Trusley and had two sons and two daughters. He died in 1940. He was Colonel of the Regiment from 1920 to 1929.

GENERAL SIR WALTER PIPON BRAITHWAITE, G.C.B., A.D.C.

He was born on 11th November 1865 and educated at Bedford School and the Royal Military College, Sandhurst. He joined the Somerset Light Infantry in 1886, being promoted Captain in 1894, Major in 1906 and Lieut.-Colonel in 1906. Between 1886–7 he served with the Regiment in Burma, receiving the medal with clasp and being mentioned in despatches. In 1899–1902 he served with the Regiment in South Africa, receiving the Queen's Medal and six clasps, the King's Medal and two clasps, three mentions in despatches and the Brevet of Major. Between 1900–2 he served in the South African War as D.A.A.G. From 1902 to 1904 he was D.A.Q.M.G., 2nd Army Corps and Southern Command and a G.S.O. II, Southern Command, in 1905. Thence he went as General Staff Officer, to the Staff College, Camberley, 1906–9, and after a spell of duty at the War Office, was appointed Commandant of The Staff College, Quetta, 1911–14. He had been promoted Colonel in 1909 and Brigadier-General in 1911. In 1914 he returned to the War Office as Director of Staff Duties and from March–October 1915, was Chief of the General Staff, M.E.F. In that year he was promoted Major-General and in December took command of the 62nd Division. In August 1918 he was appointed to command IX Corps.

For his services in the 1914–18 War he received nine mentions in despatches, Commander of the Legion of Honour, Grand Officier Ordre de la Couronne, the French Croix de Guerre with two palms, the Belgian Croix de Guerre. He was promoted Major-General in 1915 and Lieut.-General in 1919. Between 1920–3 he was G.O.C.-in-C., Western Command, India; G.O.C.-in-C., Scottish Command, 1923–6; and G.O.C.-in-C., Eastern Command, 1926–7. In the latter year he became Adjutant-General to the Forces. He retired in 1931, serving as Governor, The Royal Hospital, Chelsea, 1931–8. In 1933 he became Bath King of Arms. In 1895 he married Jessie Adine, daughter of the late Caldwell Ashworth, Esq. He died on 8 September 1945. He was Colonel of the Regiment from 1929 to 1938.

MAJOR-GENERAL VIVIAN HENRY BRUCE MAJENDIE, C.B., D.S.O.

He was born in 1886, educated at Winchester College, R.M.C., Sandhurst, and entered The Somerset Light Infantry in 1905, being promoted Captain in 1915. Between 1908–13 he was employed with the West African Field Force. Between 1915–18 he saw much distinguished service with the 1st Battalion in France and Belgium, all of which is recounted in detail in Volume II of the Regimental History. For his services he was mentioned in despatches four times and received the 1914–15 Star, British War Medal, D.S.O., and the Brevet of Major. In 1919 he was Commander (Class X) of Amiens Sub Area, France, and during 1922 was Brigade Major, Irish Command. Between 1922–4 he commanded a company of Gentlemen Cadets (G.S.O. II) Sandhurst, and from 1924 to 1928 was Staff Officer to the Inspector General Royal West African Field Force. In 1933 he was appointed G.S.O. I, The Staff College, Camberley. He received the Brevets of both Lieut.-Colonel and Colonel, being promoted substantive Colonel in 1933. He was a graduate of the Staff and Imperial Defence Colleges. He was appointed Director of Military Training India, 1936–8. Between 1929–33 he commanded the 2nd Battalion, The Somerset Light Infantry. His services during the 1939–45 War are given in Appendix F to this Volume. He was Colonel of the Regiment from 1938 to 1947.

MAJOR-GENERAL V. H. B. MAJENDIE, C.B., D.S.O.
COLONEL OF THE REGIMENT OCTOBER 1938–OCTOBER 1947

APPENDIX B

Succession of Lieutenant-Colonels commanding regular battalions between 1919 and the outbreak of war in 1939.

1st Battalion

Penrose Mark Wardlaw	1919–1920
Arthur Hamilton Yatman	1920–1924
John Sandbach Noel Harrison	1924–1928
Cecil Hunter Little	1928–1932
Gerald Eden Mynors Whittuck	1932–1936
Victor Wellesley Roche	1936–1939
Allan Francis Harding	1939–1940

2nd Battalion

William James Bowker	1919–1921
Arthur William Sibbald Paterson	1921–1925
Henry Irving Rodney Allfrey	1925–1929
Vivian Henry Bruce Majendie	1929–1933
Richard Henry Waddy	1933–1937
Owen George Bridger Philby	1937–1940

APPENDIX C

Succession of Adjutants of regular battalions between 1919 and the outbreak of war in 1939.

1st Battalion

Lieut. Eric Herbert Cokayne Frith	1919–1922
Lieut. Felix Clement Vincent Digby Caillard	1922–1923
Capt. John George des Reaux Swayne	1923–1925
Capt. Owen George Bridger Philby	1925–1928
Capt. Stanley Charles Gordon Young	1928
Lieut. Ralph Nevill Thicknesse	1928–1931
Lieut. John Rowley Innes Platt	1931–1934
Lieut. Charles Storrs Howard	1934–1937
Major Ashton Hunt	1937–1940

2nd Battalion

Lieut. Gerald Harrison Cole	1919–1922
Capt. Allan Francis Harding	1922–1925
Lieut. Theodore Mackillop Thring	1925–1928
Capt. Hugh William Spurrell	1928–1931
Lieut. John Charles Douglas Bruce	1931–1934
Lieut. Hilaro Nelson Barlow	1934–1937
Lieut. Philip David Maud	1937–1940

REGULAR QUARTERMASTERS 1919 TO 1939

1st Battalion

Captain A. Neate	1919–1926
Lieut. J. A. Trevelyan	1926–1934
Major J. S. Webber, M.B.E.	1934–1939
Lieut. T. J. Johnson, M.C.	1939

2nd Battalion

Major D. J. Owens	1919–1924
Lieut. F. Goldby	1924–1926
Lieut. J. S. Webber, M.B.E.	1926–1934
Captain J. A. Trevelyan	1934–1939

Depot

Major H. French, D.C.M.	1919–1922
Lieut.-Col. C. Smyth	1922–1924
Lieut.-Col. D. J. Owens	1924–1926
Major F. Goldby	1926–1939
Major J. S. Webber, M.B.E.	1939

APPENDIX D

List of Regimental Sergeant-Majors of regular battalions and the depot between 1919 and the outbreak of war in 1939

1st Battalion
W. Male	1918–1923	E. J. O'Hare	1926–1936
J. A. Trevelyan	1923–1926	G. Farmer	1936–1940

2nd Battalion
F. Goldby	1918–1923	A. H. Cook	1926–1930
G. Pearce	1923–1925	T. J. Johnson	1930–1939
J. S. Webber	1925–1926	J. Lumbers	1939–1940

Depot
E. Gange	1918–1923	A. H. Cook	1930–1932
F. Goldby	1923–1924	T. J. Wilkins	1932–1936
T. J. Johnson	1924–1930	W. J. Atkins	1936–1939

APPENDIX E

Records of Service of some Old Comrades, who died in the period between the two wars

POLLOCK, A. W. Alsager, Lieut.-Colonel.
    Died 2nd July 1923. Aged 69. Joined Regiment in 1875. Served in Kaffir and Zulu Wars and Suakin Operations of 1885. Later, became editor of *United Service Magazine* and was correspondent of *The Times* in the South African War. Assisted Mr. L. S. Amery in preparation of *Times History of South African War*. While commanding the Depot at Taunton, his original methods of training recruits attracted much attention. Later, under the auspices of the *Spectator* he trained a company of 100 men, as a test, at Hounslow. His aim was to produce a Reserve Army fit to relieve regulars from garrison duties in time of war. Commanded 10th Service Battalion, K.O.Y.L.I at Loos and during war 1914–18, but was gassed and, later, invalided and served on L. of C. in France.

GUEST, Richard William, Colour-Sergeant.
    Died 2nd January 1927. Aged 73. Joined the Regiment in 1870 after serving as a boy in the Navy. Went to South Africa in 1876, to Pretoria and Utrecht. Present at crossing of the Blood River in 1879 and at Kambula. Held Zulu War and Long Service and Good Conduct Medals. Saved life on three occasions and held Humane Society's Bronze Medal and Certificate.

TOBIN, Thomas.
    Died 1st October 1923 on his Diamond Wedding Day. Was an Indian Mutiny Veteran. Joined the Regiment on 6th August 1854 and was invalided out as a Private in 1861. He drew his army pension for 61 years.

BORTON, A. C., Colonel, D.L., J.P.
    Died 9th October 1927. Aged 76. Joined the 2nd Battalion in 1869. Adjutant, 1874–8. Commanded 1st Battalion from November 1874. Served on North-West Frontier India and with Mohmand Field Force, 1897.

EMBERSON, Henry, Bugle-Major.
    Died 20th July 1924. Aged 72. Joined the Regiment in 1867, when 15 years of age. Served at Gibraltar, 1868, Malta, 1872. Zulu Wars and expedition against Sekukini in 1880. Battle of Ulundi, 1879 Medal and clasp for Zulu Wars. Became Bugle-major in 1880 and from 1890 to 1898 was Bandmaster at the Depot. Long Service and Good Conduct Medal. Meritorious Service Medal.

WALL, Charles.
   Died in 1925. Served with Regiment during Zulu War 1879. He was one of the party which assisted in the recovery of the body of the Prince Imperial, only son of Napoleon III, who was ambushed and killed by Zulus.

BAKER, John, Sergeant-Major.
   Died 16th July 1925. Aged 76. His father was a Sergeant-Major in 1st Royal Regiment and, later, in the 13th Light Infantry. Joined the Regiment in 1864. Served at Kambula and Ulundi in 1879. Discharged in 1891, but continued as a drill instructor and recruiter with the R.A.S.C. until 1915. Zulu War, Long Service and Good Conduct and Meritorious Service Medals. Humane Society's Certificate for saving life.

MALONEY, James, Lance-Corporal, No. 521.
   Died 20th December 1924. Aged 59. Chelsea Pensioner. Indian General Service Medal with clasp, Burma, 1885–7; Clasp, Punjab, 1879–8; Long Service and Good Conduct Medal.

BUCKLEY, Patrick, Joseph, Sergeant.
   Died 1926. Aged 78. Joined 13th Foot in 1867 and served for 30 years. Present at battles of Kambula and Ulundi 1879. His five sons all served in the Regiment during the 1914–18 War, one being killed. This family possesses some 40 medals, including two Meritorious Service Medals.

WADDY, J. M. E., Lieut.-Colonel.
   Died 27th May 1928. Aged 81. Joined the Regiment in 1867. Adjutant 1st Battalion. Served in Kaffir and Zulu wars 1878–9, being present at Kambula and Ulundi. Commanded 2nd Battalion, 1894–8. After retirement served for 5 years as Adjutant of 3rd Battalion. In 1914, at age of 67, took a commission as Major in the Territorial Army and commanded the 2/4th Battalion in India, becoming a Lieut.-Colonel in 1915.

SWAYNE, E. H., Lieut.-Colonel, O.B.E.
   Died 23rd October 1932. Joined 1st Battalion in 1885. Adjutant, 2nd Battalion, 1896–1900. Commanded 1st Battalion, 1913, and took it to France in 1914. Invalided after retreat from Mons. Commanded 9th (Reserve) and 12th (Home Service) Battalions. Retired in 1919. Burmese Expedition (1885–7), Chin-Lushai Expedition (1889–90), South Africa (1899–1901), Great War (1914–18).

LOVETT, H. W., Lieut.-Colonel.
   Died 7th November 1932. Joined the Regiment in 1878. Zulu War (Medal and clasp, 1879). Employed with Egyptian Army and received Medal and clasp (1884–5). Burma Medal and clasp (1885–7). Khedives Bronze Star and Order of Medjidieh 4th Class. Humane Society's Bronze Medal 1891. Retired in 1899.

APPENDIX E

COMPTON, C. W., Brigadier-General, C.B., C.M.G.
Died 23rd November 1933. Aged 64. Joined the Regiment in 1889. North-West Frontier, India, 1897–8 (Medal and clasp) with 1st Battalion. 2nd-in-Command 1st Battalion, 1914. Wounded at Fontaine, August 1914. Commanded 1st Battalion, June 1915–November 1916. Commanded 11th Infantry Brigade November 1916–November 1917.

RANDALL, J. R., Private.
Died 5th December 1933. Aged 97. Joined 13th Foot at Bath in 1857. Served in Indian Mutiny under Lord Mark Kerr; Medal and clasp. Discharged 1868.

COUCHMAN, G. H. H., Colonel, D.S.O.
Died 25th February 1936. Joined the Regiment in May 1878. Burma Expedition, 1885–6–7; two mentions in despatches and D.S.O. North-East Column, Burma, 1891. Commanded 1st Battalion. Brigade Commander in France during 1914–18 War. Mentioned in despatches. 1914–15 Star, Great War and Victory Medals.

DUNHAM, J., Private.
Died 3rd January 1936. Zulu War 1878–9. Present at Kambula and Ulundi. Medal and clasps. Re-enlisted in Regiment for South African war. Medals and clasps.

TOBIAS, T., Regimental Sergeant-Major, D.C.M.
Died 23rd March 1936. Aged 76. Joined the Regiment in 1878. Discharged 1908. Rejoined in 1914 but was invalided. 30 years' service. Zulu War, South African War (King's and Queen's medals and clasps), Distinguished Conduct and Long Service and Good Conduct medals.

MORAN, Patrick, Major.
Died 3rd August 1933. Aged 70. Joined the Regiment in 1873, serving with 2nd Battalion. Lieut. and Quartermaster at the Depot, 1897. Quartermaster, 2nd Battalion, 1907. Retired as Major and Quartermaster, 1910. Rejoined for War, 1914–15, as S.D.O., R.A.S.C., Gosport. Total service, 42 years. Burma, 1885–7, and South African War medals. Two mentions in despatches.

OATES, T., Regimental Sergeant-Major, D.S.M.
Died 29th April 1937. Served in 2nd Battalion. Relief of Chitral 1895, Tirah, 1897, Punjab Frontier, 1898, Transvaal, 1899, Relief of Ladysmith, Orange River, Tugela Heights, Cape Colony. He won the D.S.M. at Colenso.

POTTER, E., Private, No. 4474.
Died 30th July 1937. Aged 88. Joined the Regiment in 1869. Joined reserve 1903. Served in Essex Regiment in 1914–18 War. Indian G.S. Medal, 1895, and clasp; Punjab Frontier, 1897–8; South African medal with clasps, Transvaal and S.A., 1902; 1914 Star, British War and Victory medals.

HAWKINS, E., Private.
Died 27th March 1937. Aged 80. Joined the Regiment in 1874. Transvaal, 1879. Present at Kambula and Ulundi. Zulu War medal and clasp, 1878–9.

STEVENS, W., Private.
Died 16th December 1937. Aged 86. Joined the Regiment in 1875. Sekukini Campaign. Present at Kambula and Ulundi. Medal and clasp, 1878–9.

APPENDIX F

Records of Service of General Officers, 1939–45

MAJENDIE, V. H. B., Major General, C.B., D.S.O., p.s.c., i.d.c.

Promoted Major-General in 1938 and appointed to command 55th (West Lancashire) Division T.A. Succeeded General Sir Walter Braithwaite as Colonel of the Regiment in 1938. In 1941 was created C.B., and took command of Northern Ireland District. In addition to these duties he was most active, as Colonel of the Regiment, in visiting and inspecting Battalions of the Regiment during the years 1939–45. In 1943 was appointed President of the War Office Regular Commission Board and held this appointment until he retired from the Service in 1946. While President of the Board he visited Egypt, India, Kenya, Italy and Germany. During the early years of the war his 55th Division first held part of the East Anglian Coast and, later, the Sussex Coast.

SWAYNE, Sir John, Lieut.-General, K.C.B., C.B.E., p.s.c., i.d.c.

From September 1939 to June 1940 was Brigadier and Head of British Mission to G.Q.G., France. Between June 1940 and October 1940, served as Deputy Chief of the General Staff (Brigadier), Home Forces. From October 1940 to March 1942, as Major-General, commanded 4th Division. In March 1942, as Lieut.-General, became Chief of the General Staff, Home Forces, and served in this capacity until October 1942, when he was appointed G.O.C.-in-C., South-Eastern Command, England. In March 1944 he went to G.H.Q., India, as Chief of the General Staff, India, serving there until January 1946. Created C.B.E. in 1940, C.B. in 1942, and K.C.B. in 1944.

HARDING, Sir John, Lieut.-General, K.C.B., C.B.E., D.S.O., M.C., p.s.c., i.d.c.

Alan Francis Harding was born in South Petherton, Somerset, on 10th February 1896, the son of a solicitor, and was educated at Ilminster Grammar School.

On leaving school he was employed in the G.P.O., London, and in May 1914 was commissioned in 1/11 Battalion the London Regiment. He subsequently transferred to the Machine Gun Corps, a battalion of which he commanded during the 1914–18 war. He saw action in Gallipoli, was awarded the M.C. (*London Gazette*, 1/1/18) and mentioned in despatches, and at little more than twenty years of age commanded a brigade in action until he was wounded. Later he saw further action in the Palestine campaign.

He was given a regular commission in the Regiment as a lieutenant to date March 1917. He was appointed adjutant of the 2nd Battalion in India in 1922.

LIEUTENANT-GENERAL SIR JOHN HARDING, K.C.B., C.B.E., D.S.O., M.C.

APPENDIX F

After qualifying at the Staff College in 1930, he held staff appointments at Southern Command and Catterick, with the International Force in the Saar, and at the War Office. In 1939 he assumed command of the 1st Battalion in India and led it in action in the Ahmedzai Salient, being mentioned in despatches.

In September 1940 he was ordered to the Middle East as G.S.O. I of 6 Division and served there for over two years, holding the following appointments: B.G.S., Western Desert Force, December 1940–September 1941; B.G.S., 13 Corps, September 1941–January 1942; D.M.T., Middle East, January–August 1942; D.C.G.S., Middle East, August–September 1942; appointed in September 1942 Commander 7 Armd. Division which he led from El Alamein until he was severely wounded in January 1943 by a direct hit on his tank outside Tripoli.

Having recovered from his wounds, he was given command in November 1943 of 8 Corps in the U.K., destined for the invasion of Europe, but in January 1944 he was transferred to Italy as C.G.S., 15 Army Group. In December 1944 he became Lieut.-General, G.S., C. of S. Section, C.M.F., and in March 1945 Commander 13 Corps. After the end of hostilities he was responsible for handling the delicate situation in the Trieste area. Having been promoted substantive Lieut.-General, he held the appointment of G.O.C.-in-C., C.M.F., from October 1946 to July 1947.

For his services he was awarded the D.S.O. with two bars (30/12/41, 24/2/42, 28/1/43), and appointed C.B.E. (8/7/41) and K.C.B. (16/6/44). He obtained His Majesty's permission to be knighted as Sir John, since he had been known throughout the army by that name. The change of Christian name was notified in the *London Gazette* of September 1944. He was also awarded the American Legion of Merit, and the French Legion of Honour and Croix de Guerre.

APPENDIX G

Records of Service of Brigadiers and Colonels who served away from the Regiment 1939–45

ALMS, J H., Brigadier, O.B.E.
Served on the staff in various appointments until promoted Acting Colonel on 23rd May 1945 for duty with S.H.A.E.F. After VE-day was appointed A.A.G., Alfsea, and, later, Brigadier (Intelligence), in which appointment he was killed in an air crash on 26th February 1947.

ANSTEY, J., Brigadier, C.B.E.
Served on the staff in various appointments until appointed Colonel General Staff, attached H.Q. 8th (U.S. Army on 21st June 1944, serving with that formation in North Africa and Southern France. On 10th November 1944, appointed B.G.S. H.Q., Sacsea, South-East Asia Command, where he remained until 1st February 1946.

BARLOW, H. N., Colonel.
Raised and commanded 7th. Battalion (L.I.) Appointed Acting Colonel on 21st February 1944 and Deputy Commander, 1st Air-Landing Brigade, 1st Airborne Division. Landed with this formation at Arnhem on 19th September 1944 and was reported "missing believed killed" on 25th September 1944.

BARRY, R. H., Colonel, O.B.E.
On 1st July 1943 promoted Acting Colonel and appointed Colonel General Staff, H.Q. Special Forces in the United Kingdom. On 1st January 1945 was appointed Colonel General Staff and Deputy Director of Plans, War Office, where he remained till the end of the war.

CAILLARD, F. C. V. D., Colonel, M.C.
Promoted Colonel in October 1940 and appointed President of a War Office Selection Board until May 1942.

COSSENS, J. B., Colonel, M.B.E.
Promoted Acting Colonel in May 1945 and held the following appointments in France, Germany and Austria; Head of G 1., S.H.A.E.F., until August 1945; Head of Combined Administrative Liquidating Agency until December 1945; Second-in-command (Technical) Field Information Agency until June 1946; Head of Field Information Agency, Technical and Commander British Troops, Frankfurt Area, U.S. Zone, until March 1947.

CURTIS, W. S. C., Colonel, M.C.
Promoted Colonel on 26th October 1944 and appointed Commandant Reinforcement Group, B.L.A., until 8th October 1945.

APPENDIX G

ELLIS, R. W., Colonel.
: Commanded an I.T.C. and served at the Record Office, Exeter. Promoted Colonel on 3rd March 1943 and was subsequently Officer in Charge of Records, Edinburgh, Army Air Corps and A.C.C., Perth and A.A.C., A.C.C. and General Service Corps, Edinburgh. He retired on 18th January 1946.

FIRBANK, C. L. Brigadier, D.S.O.
: Commanded a battalion of the Lincolnshire Regiment. Promoted Acting Brigadier on 24th April 1945 and appointed to command 71st Infantry Brigade, B.L.A.

FRITH, E. H. C., Brigadier, C.B.E.
: Promoted Acting Brigadier on 23rd March 1942 and appointed to command 131st Infantry Brigade, which he took out for service with M.E.F. in the Western Desert. In January 1943 was appointed Colonel, General Staff, British Military Mission to Egyptian Army, until 27th December 1943. On 28th December 1943 was appointed to command (Temporary Brigadier) 26th British Liaison Unit attached H.Q., 2nd Polish Corps. Went with this Corps to Italy in January 1944 and served with them throughout the Italian Campaign.

McCRIRICK, D. G. H., Colonel.
: Promoted Acting Colonel on 5th July 1942 and appointed to command an area in Northern Ireland. From 23rd October 1943 to 4th May 1945 commanded Border Sub-District, Galashiels.

ROCHE, V. W., Colonel.
: Appointed Commandant (Colonel), School of Military Administration, from February 1940 to April 1944. From May 1944 to July 1945 was Deputy Chief, Psychological Warfare Division, S.H.A.E.F. From July to October 1945 was Chief, Psychological Division, Cala. He was then seconded to U.N.R.R.A and was on duty with the Personnel Division, European Regional Office until April 1947.

SNOW, A. E., Brigadier, O.B.E.
: Promoted Acting Brigadier on 14th May 1945 and appointed to command 115th Infantry Brigade until July 1944. Then transferred to command Force 135 designated for the relief of the Channel Islands. In May 1945 he received the surrender of the German Forces in the Channel Islands and remained there as commander of the Armed Forces until August 1945.

WHITTUCK, G. E. M., Brigadier, M.C.
: At outbreak of war he was commanding 129th Infantry Brigade. In September 1940 was appointed to command Cornwall Sub-area and 203rd Infantry Brigade. Between August 1941 and November 1944, as a retired officer, he commanded, successively, North Hampshire Sub-area and Leeds Sub-District. Later he underwent training and was posted to work with U.N.R.R.A in Germany.

APPENDIX H

Note on No. 7 (Somerset Light Infantry) Troop, No. 8 (London District) Commando

No. 8 (London District) Commando, was formed in London about July 1940. Soon afterwards it moved to Burnham-on-Crouch, Essex, where the various troops were completed and training began.

No. 8 Commando consisted of ten troops, each troop being designated by the name of the corps or unit which sponsored it and supplied recruits. The organisation was as follows:

Commander: Lieut.-Colonel R. Laycock, Royal Horse Guards.
2nd-in-Command: Major W. S. C. Curtis, Somerset Light Infantry.
Adjutant: Captain J. D. Majendie, Somerset Light Infantry.

TROOPS

1. Household Cavalry.
2. Grenadier Guards.
3. Coldstream Guards.
4. Scots Guards.
5. Irish and Welsh Guards
6. Cavalry of the Line.
7. Somerset Light Infantry.
8. 12 Corps.
9. 12 Corps.
10. Royal Marines, Royal Artillery, Royal Engineers.

Troops were armed and equipped as for a normal infantry platoon, *plus* scaling ladders, toggle-ropes, explosives, etc. Much experimental work was carried out during Home training as well as for Combined Operations. Bases were used at Burnham, Inveraray, Largs, Isle of Arran and on H.M.S. "Glenroy" and "Karanja". Since two of the senior officers of the commando belonged to the Somerset Light Infantry, they saw to it that the Regiment was adequately represented. The personnel for No. 7 Troop were all volunteers and came, mainly, from the 5th, 6th and 7th Battalions.

The commander of the troop was Major Geoffrey Lance, who was killed later when serving with the 7th Battalion in northern Europe. Captains Barkworth and Laurence were officers with the troop, the former becoming Intelligence Officer of No. 8 Troop, at a later date. Captain Laurence was captured by the Germans in Greece. He escaped, joined the Yugoslav partisans and has, since, written and published an account of his adventures. The strength of the troop was 47 Other Ranks.

No. 8 Commando sailed for North Africa early in 1941. It served in North Africa, Greece and Crete. It also sailed on an expedition to capture Pantellaria, but was recalled before a landing could be made. It was disbanded late in 1942, or early 1943.

APPENDIX I

Note on the services of 13th and 2/13th Australian Infantry Battalions in the War 1939–45 (see also Chapter III)

Under the universal training scheme introduced under the advice of Lord Kitchener in 1911, Australia raised 93 Battalions. These were numbered from 1 in North Queensland, round to Western Australia, the highest number —93—being in Tasmania. In the same way the military districts were numbered from 1 to 6, from Queensland in the north to Western Australia and Tasmania. In 1918 the nomenclature of the battalions was changed, so as to provide for the perpetuation of the titles and traditions of the 60 infantry battalions and 5 pioneer battalions which constituted the First A.I.F. In this reorganisation the names of the A.I.F. battalions were given, so far as possible, to the areas in which the personnel who comprised those battalions were recruited. It was about this time, therefore, that the 13th Australian Infantry received the title of "The Maitland Regiment".

In February 1942, 1/13th Australian Infantry was engaged on coast defence duties in the Nelson's Bay area of New South Wales, under the command of Lieut.-Colonel G. A. Patterson. In March 1942 it moved to Greta Camp, (N.S.W.) for a period of training, thereafter returning to Nelson's Bay.

On 30th April 1940, Headquarters 2/13th Australian Infantry came into being at Sydney. In June 1940, Lieut.-Colonel F. A. Burrows, M.M., E.D., assumed command. Preliminary training and organisation was carried out at Ingleburn Camp and, in August 1940, the battalion marched to Bathurst (N.S.W.), where training continued until October 1940.

The Regiment now had two battalions and it will be convenient to deal with these separately, since the 1st Battalion served in Australia, while the 2nd Battalion proceeded overseas.

1/13TH AUSTRALIAN INFANTRY

In June 1942, Major J. W. Whitmore succeeded Lieut.-Colonel Patterson in command and was succeeded, in August 1942, by Lieut.-Colonel H. H. M. Chilton. In September the Battalion—now termed the 13/33rd Battalion—moved to St. Ives, near Sydney. The 13th and 33rd Australian Infantry Battalions had been amalgamated at Rutherford (N.S.W.). The new Battalion formed part of 1st Australian Infantry Brigade.

On 30th October 1943, Lieut.-Colonel Chilton was given a new command and was succeeded by Major G. V. Johnson. The latter handed over to Major M. B. Moran, who commanded until February 1944, when Lieut.-Colonel R. Joshua assumed command.

During the period 1942–4 there had been a long spell of training and patrol duties at St. Ives, but on 27th April 1944, the Battalion moved to

French's Forest and began a period of duty on the Sydney wharves. During this time A company was detached for duty in Queensland and 343 all ranks performed guard duties, for a time, at a P.O.W. camp at Cowra (N.S.W.).

On 18th September 1944, the Battalion marched to Singleton (N.S.W.), completing the 147 miles' march by 26th September. The rôle of the Battalion was now a holding unit for "young soldiers" up to the age of 19 years, pending drafting as general reinforcements to the Jungle Warfare Training Centre at Canungra (Queensland). It also was responsible for the "conversion" to infantry of troops from other arms and services of the army. The Battalion continued in this rôle until September 1946, after which month War Diaries were no longer submitted.

2/13TH AUSTRALIAN INFANTRY BATTALION

This Battalion formed part of 20th Australian Infantry Brigade. On 19th October it embarked on H.M.T. "Q.X." at Sydney and disembarked at Bombay on 7th November. From there it moved to Deolali Camp, 125 miles north-east of Bombay. On 11th November it re-embarked at Bombay on s.s. "K. 306" and arrived at Kantara, Egypt, on 26th November, moving by train to Kilo 89, where intensive training began. It arrived at Mersa Matruh, Egypt, on 27th February 1941.

During February 1941, the British counter-offensives in Abyssinia and Somaliland were in progress. In April, the First German-Italian counter-offensive in Libya started. By 28th April, Benghazi and Bardia had been lost, Tobruk encircled and the enemy had reached Sollum.

In May 1941, the Battalion was sent to reinforce the garrison at Tobruk. British operations in Libya remained somewhat stagnant. Both sides were awaiting reinforcements and building up resources. On 18th November the 8th Army opened the Second Western Desert Offensive and tank battles raged in the area Tobruk–Sollum–Sidi Omar–El Gobi. On 17th December the enemy front crumbled and by 24th December the 8th Army had retaken Benghazi. Tobruk was relieved on 16th December. 2/13th Australian Infantry then moved by stages to Hill 69 (Palestine). During the operations in Tobruk, Lieut.-Colonel Burrows was wounded and was evacuated on 1st December. A few days earlier he had been decorated, by Major-General Kopanski, with the Polish Military Cross. He was succeeded by Major G. E. Colvin. On 27th December, Lieut.-Colonel R. W. N. Turner was appointed to command.

The Battalion remained in Syria until 30th June 1942 and then returned to Egypt for further operations in the Western Desert. Late in July it arrived in the "Ruin Ridge" area and later moved to Tel El Eisa and El Alamein.

The Third German Offensive in North Africa had opened on 26th May 1942. After fluctuating battles south of Tobruk, the 8th Army began to withdraw on 14th June. On 21st June Tobruk fell and the enemy reached Bardia. On 27th June the Battle for Egypt began at Mersa Matruh and by 14th July British and German forces faced each other on the Ruwaisat Ridge, south of El Alamein.

APPENDIX I

The Battle of El Alamein was fought between 24th October and 3rd November, 2/13th Australian Infantry taking part. On 24th October, Lieut.-Colonel Turner was wounded and the command passed to Lieut.-Colonel G. E. Colvin. On 29th October the latter was wounded and Major J. L. A. Kelly temporarily assumed command until the return of Lieut.-Colonel Colvin on 8th November. On 5th November, 8th Army began to advance and by 12th November had retaken Sollum, Bardia and Tobruk. Early in December, 2/13th Australian Infantry moved to Julis (Palestine) for reorganisation and re-equipping.

On 26th January 1943, the Battalion embarked on H.M.T. "Aquitania" at Suez, and arrived at Sydney on 27th February. After a short leave period it moved to Atherton Table-lands, North Queensland, early in April 1943, for training in Jungle Warfare.

During 1942, the Japanese had been penetrating southwards in the Pacific. Their advance towards Australia was checked, in May 1942, by the successful naval battle of the Coral Sea. Thereafter amphibious operations began in the whole area of the Pacific Islands, stretching from the Solomons on the east, through New Guinea, to the Netherlands East Indies, Borneo and northwards towards the Philippines. In these operations, particularly in the Solomons Group, Guadalcanal and New Guinea, Australian forces played a major part, in conjunction with United States forces. By February 1943, the Japanese had been cleared from Guadalcanal and on 2nd March the naval Battle of the Bismarck Sea went in the Allies' favour.

On 26th July 1943, 2/13th Australian Infantry embarked at Cairns on U.S.S. "X 12" (Maetsuyoker) and landed at Milne Bay, New Guinea, on 30th July 1943. During 1943 and 1944 it took part in the Lae–Finschhafen–Satelburg operations.

On 1st March 1944, the Battalion embarked at Milne Bay and arrived at Cairns on 7th March. After a period of leave, it concentrated at Atherton Table-lands for further training. On 28th April 1945, it embarked at Cairns and arrived at Morotai on 9th May. By this time, the Japanese had been driven northwards in the Pacific. In June 1944, U.S. forces had landed on Leyte, in the Philippines. Guam was taken in August 1944. During October, the Japanese fleet was heavily defeated in the Second Naval Battle of the Philippines. Early in 1945, the stage was set for operations in Borneo.

On 10th June, 2/13th Australian Infantry landed at Brunei, Borneo, and was engaged in operations there when hostilities ceased on 15th August 1945. On 21st September Lieut.-Colonel Colvin took command of 20th Australian Infantry Brigade and was succeeded in command of the Battalion by Captain D. F. Faulkner. Colonel Colvin was later appointed to command 66th Australian Infantry Battalion, then being raised as part of the Australian component of B.C.O.F.

In September 1945, Long Service discharge (5 years) began and general demobilisation preparations started. On 7th November, the Battalion arrived at Labuan and, on 9th December, the remaining personnel embarked for Australia.

APPENDIX J

ROLL OF HONOUR

(The following lost their lives while serving with The Somerset Light Infantry (Prince Albert's) during the war 1939–1945)

65 Officers
883 Other Ranks.

Their names are recorded in the Regimental Book of Remembrance which is deposited in the Church of St. Mary Magdalen, Taunton.

The above figures include those only who either belonged to the Regiment before the war or were posted to it during the war. As lists of casualties kept by the War Office are arranged according to the regiments to which officers or men were first commissioned or posted, it has not been found possible to include many who were commissioned in or posted to other regiments but actually carried out most of their war service, if not all, with battalions of The Somerset Light Infantry (Prince Albert's): nor do the figures include all those who lost their lives whilst serving in the 7th Parachute Battalion (L.I.) which became part of the Army Air Corps.

LIEUTENANT GEORGE ALBERT CAIRNS, V.C.
THE SOMERSET LIGHT INFANTRY

The *London Gazette* of 20th May 1949:

"The King has been graciously pleased to approve the posthumous award of the Victoria Cross to Lieut. George A. Cairns, The Somerset Light Infantry, attached South Staffordshire Regiment.

"On March 12, 1944, columns from the South Staffordshire Regiment and 3/6 Gurkha Rifles established a road and railblock across the Japanese lines of communication at Henu Block. The Japanese counter-attacked this position heavily in the early morning of the 13th, and the South Staffordshire Regiment was ordered to attack a hill-top which formed the basis of the Japanese attack. During this action, in which Lieut. Cairns took a foremost part, he was attacked by a Japanese Officer, who, with his sword, hacked off Lieut. Cairn's left arm.

"Lieut. Cairns killed this Officer, picked up his sword and continued to lead his men in the attack and, slashing left and right with the captured sword, killed and wounded several Japanese before he himself fell to the ground. Lieut. Cairns subsequently died from his wounds.

"His action so inspired all his comrades that, later, the Japanese were completely routed, a very rare occurrence at that time."

On joining The Somerset Light Infantry in 1941, Lieut. Cairns was posted to the 6th Battalion. Subsequently he went to India, where he was attached to the South Staffordshire Regiment.

LIEUTENANT G. A. CAIRNS, V.C.

APPENDIX K

HONOURS AND AWARDS

The following is a list of Honours, Awards, Mentions in Despatches and Foreign Decorations gained by Officers, N.C.O.s and Men of the Regiment. It does not include personnel of other Regiments who may have gained awards whilst attached to the Regiment. Ranks shown are the ranks held at the time of the award, according to War Office Records.

VICTORIA CROSS
Cairns, Lieut. G. A.

GEORGE CROSS
Silk, Pte. J. H.

K.C.B.
Harding, Lieut.-General A. F.
Swayne, Lieut.-General J. G. des R.

C.B.
Majendie, Major-General V. H. B.
Swayne, Major-General J. G. des R.

C.B.E.
Anstey, Brigadier J.
Frith, Brigadier E. H. C.
Harding, Brigadier A. F.
Swayne, Brigadier J. G. des R.

D.S.O.
Bartholomew, Major P. I.
Brind, Lieut.-Col. J. L.
Firbank, Lieut.-Col. C. L.
Harding, Brigadier A. F.
Hood, Major E. H. M.
Lance, Lieut.-Col. G. C. P.
Lipscomb, Lieut.-Col. C. G.
Platt, Lieut.-Col. J. R. I.
Roberts, Lieut.-Col. W. Q.
Worrall, Major E. W. H.

BAR TO D.S.O.
Firbank, Lieut.-Col. C. L.
Harding, Brigadier A. F.
Lipscomb, Lieut.-Col. C. G.
Roberts, Lieut.-Col. W. Q.

SECOND BAR TO D.S.O.
Harding, Major-General A. F.

O.B.E.
Akerman, Lieut.-Col. E. J. B.
Alms, Lieut.-Col. J. H.
Barry, Lieut.-Col. R. H.
Dennys, Lieut.-Col. K. G. G.
Ellis, Lieut.-Col. W. R. F.
Howard, Lieut.-Col. C. S.
King, Lieut.-Col. L. T.
Snow, Major A. E.

M.B.E.
Aubrey-Smith, Major D. H.
Besley, Major R. G. P.
de L. Byrde, Capt. C. M.
Cossens, Major J. B.
De Butts, Major F. M.
Denison, Major J. L.
Edmunds, Lieut. J. H.
Farmer, Capt. (Q.M.) G. H.
Fear, Major F.
Fortnum, Capt. (Q.M.) R. P.
Green, Major A. J.
Hale, Capt. (Q.M.) F. G.
Hartnell, Major C. R.
Maud, Capt. P. D.
Milton, Major T. A. H.
Mounter, W.O.I J. S. W.
Preston, Capt. D. H.

Smart, Capt. (Q.M.) C. W.
Smith, W.O.I H. J.
Taylor, Major J. B.

M.C.

Bean, Lieut. D. F.
Beckhurst, Major V. W.
Blackler, Major G. G. J.
Bonny, Capt. E. A. W.
Braithwaite, Major T. M.
Breton, Lieut. A. A.
Carfrae, Major C. C. A.
Cooke, Lieut. J.
Davies, Lieut. R. G.
Delafield, Major A.
Durie, Capt. D. B. M.
Goudie, Capt. W. H.
Harvey, Major E. R. H.
Hutchinson, Capt. J. F. M.
Luckock, Major T. P.
Millard, Lieut. R. J.
Molloy, Major P. G.
Ovenden, Capt. R. E.
Parsons, Lieut. G. A.
Perks, Capt. J. C.
Pitt, Lieut. P. M.
Wallis, Lieut. G. C. W.
Watts, Capt. B. A.
Whittaker, Lieut. K. H.
Whitehead, Capt. K. J.
Worrall, Major E. W. H.
Young, Capt. S. C. W.

BAR TO M.C.

Hutchinson, Capt. J. F. M.
Whittaker, Capt. K. H.

D.C.M.

Comm, Pte. P. A.
Grant, Cpl. N. G. A.
Leeks, Cpl. R.
Moody, Sgt. J. J.
Pegler, L/Cpl. L. A.

M.M.

Barrell, Pte. G. F. E.
Bartram, Pte. G. C.
Bond, Pte. W.
Burgess, Sgt. A.
Carpenter, Pte. L. H.
Chinnock, Sgt. J.
Clarke, W.O.II D. E.
Cockayne, L/Cpl. A. L.
Coles, Cpl. J. H. B.
Comer, L/Sgt. L.
Cross, Pte. E. S.
Evans, C/Sgt. L.
Gant, Pte. J. E.
Garrod, Pte. D.
Graham, Pte. N.
Green, Sgt. J.
Hayman, Sgt. R.
Higgins, L/Sgt. W. M.
Hinnells, L/Sgt. B. G.
Homer, Pte. R. N.
James, Pte. J. W.
Jones, Sgt. A.
Jones, L/Cpl. B.
Lambert, Pte. B. J.
Love, L/Sgt. R. W. T.
Martin, L/Cpl. R. H. P.
Maskell, Sgt. P. A.
McClernon, Cpl. J. H. L.
McQuillan, Sgt. W. A.
Myram, Sgt. A. E.
Partridge, Sgt. W. J.
Shepperd, L/Cpl. S. F.
Sims, L/Cpl. R. W.
Stevens, L/Cpl. J.
Stevens, Sgt. W. H.
Stigger, L/Cpl. L. J.
Tipple, Pte. H. A.
Vallard, Pte. A. G. J.
Wheadon, Sgt. D. W.
Wheeler, Sgt. F. K. C. M.
White, L/Cpl. G. R.

Bar to M.M.

Hayman, Sgt. R.

B.E.M.

Ashman, Sgt. S.
Booth, C.Q.M.S. E. L.

APPENDIX K

Bryant, Sgt. A. L.
Chapman, C/Sgt. W. E.
Cotton, Sgt. E. V.
Langdon, Sgt. W. F.

Mentions in Despatches

(A second or further Mention is shown by figures in parentheses giving total number of Mentions

Allen, Capt. B. O.
Anstey, Brigadier J.
Arch, Pte. F. W.
Aubrey-Smith, Major D. H.
Barford, Lieut. A. J.
Barnes, Lieut.-Col. R. J.
Bath, Pte. E.
Beach, Capt. R. G.
Bennetts, Lieut. G. V.
Biggs, Capt. R. A.
Biles, Pte. J.
Bond, Major G. D.
Bond, Lieut. H. W.
Bonny, Capt. E. A. W.
Bret, Capt. C. G.
Broughton, Major B. J.
Brown, Pte. V.
Bruford, Major E. J.
Bryant, Sgt. A. L.
Butcher, Cpl. H. L.
de L. Byrde, Capt. C. M.
Cairns, Lieut. G. A.
Castle, Capt. H.
Cheeseman, Cpl. O. W.
Chetwynd-Stapylton, Lieut.-Col. G. R.
Chiffers, Sgt. D. N.
Clarke, Capt. J. E. C.
Coleman, Sgt. L. W.
Connett, W.O.II W. C.
Cossens, Major J. B.
Curtis, Col. W. S. C.
Dagger, Sgt. S. G.
Darbyshire, Capt. G. M.
Davidson, Pte. W. J.
De Butts, Major F. M. (2)
Costabadie, Major H.
Denison, Capt. J. L.
Dicken, Major E. W. T.
Dodd, Lieut. A. J.
Drewitt, Capt. R. W.
Eatwell, Sgt. L. G.
Elliott, Capt. D. T.
Elliott, L/Sgt. G.
Ellis, Major, A. R. (2)
Ellis, Lieut.-Col. W. R. F.
Evers, Pte. T.
Follett, W.O.II H. A.
Ford, C/Sgt. H.
Ford, C.Q.M.S. J. B.
Fry, Lieut. N. H.
Garbutt, Capt. F. A. W.
Gatehouse, Pte. K. W.
Gingell, Cpl. F. R. G.
Glennie, Capt. F. R.
Gough, Capt. V. A.
Gouldsworthy, Lieut. R. J.
Grant, Capt.(Q.M.) J. A.
Grover, Pte. R. A.
Hale, Major S. A. G.
Harding, Brigadier A. F. (3) (3rd as Major-General)
Hartnell, Major C. R.
Harvey, Major E. R. H.
Hemmings, L/Cpl. W. R.
Herbert, Capt. E. S. A.
Heritage, Sgt. R. S.
Hiles, Pte. T. R.
Holder, Capt. R. B.
Hood, Major E. H. M.
Howarth, Pte. P.
Hudson, W.O.II W. A.
Hunt, Capt. N. G.
Hunter, Major A. D. W.
Hyatt, Capt. A. J. R.
Jessel, Major R. G. (2)
Johnson, Pte. J. D.
Jones, Sgt. A.
Jordan, Pte. J. T.
Kessler, Capt. C. W. E.
King, L/Cpl. C.

Kingston, Sgt. J. A.
Knight, Sgt. P. H.
Law, C.Q.M.S. A.
Lawrence, Capt. C. N.
Locke, Capt. W. J.
Long, Capt. H. A.
Lowe, Sgt. F.
Lyons, Lieut. R. B.
Mallalieu, Major G. N. A. W.
Mann, Pte. S. R. C.
Mansell, L/Cpl. J.
Marshall, L/Cpl. W. W.
Martin, Lieut. L. T.
Mayne, Capt. J. R. D.
McQuillan, L/Sgt. W. A.
Mee, Capt. A. J.
Miller, Pte. R.
Milton, Major, T. A. H.
Molloy, Capt. P. G.
Morgan, Capt. A. G.
Munnings, Sgt. S. W.
Nunneley, Lieut. J. H.
Ogilvie, Major J. J.
Paton, Capt. P. C.
Pitt, Lieut. P. M.
Platt, Lieut.-Col. J. R. I.
Plenty, W.O.II H. J.
Pollard, Major G. J.
Poole, Cpl. H. J.
Preston, Capt. D. H.
Reader, Capt. V. A.
Richardson, Sgt. T.
Robinson, L/Cpl. C. C.
Robinson, Pte. G.
Rose, Cpl. R. W.
Saffin, Pte. E. E.
Salter, Pte. J. A.
Salter, Lieut. K. W.
Sanders, Sgt. A. A.
Sealy, Major J.
Sedgwick, Cpl. J. T.
Sharp, Sgt. C. J.
Sharp, Pte. R. C.

Smart, W.O.I C. W. (2) (2nd as Lieut.(Q.M.))
Smith, Sgt. G. R.
Smith, W.O.I H. J.
Snow, Capt. J. F. (2) (2nd as Lieut.-Col.)
Speed-Andrews, Major, H. J.
Spencer, Cpl. J. W.
Spicer, W.O.I W. W. S.
Spurrell, Lieut.-Col. H. W. (3)
Stevens, L/Cpl. J. J.
Stone, Pte. J.
Strachey, Major-Hon. A. E. T.
Strickland, Lieut. R. D. W.
Stride, Capt. R. T.
Surridge, Sgt. G. O. R.
Suter, Major M. E. H. (2)
Sutton-Pryce, Major, E. A.
Swayne, Brigadier J. G. des R.
Swinney, Capt. T. A.
Tappenden, Sgt. K. G.
Taylor, W.O.II E. G.
Thompson, L/Cpl. A. T.
Thring, Major T. M.
Tompkins, Cpl. K. W.
Toms, Lieut. H. (2)
Unsworth, L/Sgt. R.
Walker, Pte. W. N.
Walking, Pte. B. E.
Walliss, Lieut. G. C. W.
Warren, Pte. H.
Watson, Capt. T. M.
Weeks, Major A. J. (2)
Weston, Sgt. J.
Weston, Cpl. W. R.
Wiggins, Lieut. R. R.
Williams, Pte. E. W.
Williams, C/Sgt. F. H.
Williams, L/Cpl. J. B.
Williams, C.Q.M.S. R. R.
Wise, Cpl. L. G.
Woodcock, L/Sgt. G. W.
Wooton, Sgt. A. J

APPENDIX K

SUMMARY

V.C.	1	M.B.E.	20
G.C.	1	M.C.	27
K.C.B.	2	Bar to M.C.	2
C.B.	2	D.C.M.	5
C.B.E.	4	M.M.	41
D.S.O.	10	Bar to M.M.	1
Bars to D.S.O.	5	B.E.M.	6
O.B.E.	8	Mentions	176

Decorations awarded to Members of the Regiment by Allied Foreign Governments for services during the 1939–45 War

BELGIUM

Chevalier of the Order of Leopold II with Palme

Bret, Capt. C. G.
Phillips, Capt. N. C.
Rice, Capt. N. D.

Croix de Guerre with Palme

Bret, Capt. C. G.
Phillips, Capt. N. C.

Decoration Militaire 2nd Classe

Mott, C.S.M. D. V.

FRANCE

Officer of the Legion of Honour

Harding, Lieut.-General Sir John
Swayne, Brigadier J. G. des R.

Chevalier of the Legion of Honour

Alms, Col. J. H.
Anstey, Brigadier J.
Corballis, Lieut.-Col. B. J.
Roche, Col. V. W.

Croix de Guerre with Palme

Alms, Col. J. H.
Anstey, Brigadier J.
Cossens, Col. J. B.
Harding, Lieut.-General Sir John
Roche, Col. V. W.

APPENDIX K

Croix de Guerre Vermeil

Durie, Major D. B. M.

Croix de Guerre with Silver Star

Gough, Capt. V. A.

Croix de Guerre with Bronze Star

Hole, Sgt. J. W.
Hood, Major E. H. M.
Yorke, Cpl. D. A.

HOLLAND

Bronze Star

Hogg, Sgt. S. F.

POLAND

Order of Polonia Restituta 3rd Class

Frith, Brigadier E. H. C.

Gold Cross of Merit

Alms, Col. J. H.

UNITED STATES OF AMERICA

Commander of the Legion of Merit

Harding, Lieut.-General Sir John

Officer of the Legion of Merit

Alms, Capt. J. H.
Anstey, Brigadier J.
Cossens, Col. J. B.
Roche, Col. V. W.

Medal of Freedom with Silver Palme

Frith, Brigadier E. H. C.

APPENDIX L

HISTORY OF REGIMENTAL DINNER CLUB

This was first inaugurated by Major-General Lord Mark Kerr, C.B., in June 1870. The first dinner was held at Willis' Rooms, London, at 8.0 p.m. on 4th July 1870; 23 members were present. A committee was elected and rules proposed. The annual subscription was fixed at ten shillings, those serving abroad paying five shillings only. The tickets for the first dinner were thirty-five shillings.

In 1879 only six members attended the dinner, to support the Colonel of the Regiment, General Phillip Spencer Stanhope. This produced a letter to all members which contained the following remarks:

"The want of *esprit de corps* which this poor attendance exhibits, is the more remarkable when it is considered how distinguished a Corps is the 13th Light Infantry, with a history which many Regiments (whose officers year after year find it a pleasure as well as a duty to attend their annual dinner in numbers varying from 20 to 150) would be proud to possess. It is truly disheartening ..."

In 1891 a farewell dinner to the 1st Battalion on embarkation for foreign service was held at the Grand Hotel, London; 57 members were present. In 1899 Lord Mark Kerr dined with the members for the last time. In 1903 all officers who served with the 2nd Battalion in South Africa were guests of past officers of the Regiment. There were 22 guests and 32 hosts.

In 1908, on 26th October, a farewell dinner was given to the 2nd Battalion, leaving for foreign service. There were 14 hosts and 18 guests.

In 1922 H.R.H. The Duke of York, Colonel-in-Chief, first dined with the members. Certainly General Stanhope's reproof in 1879 appears to have served its purpose. For many years Regimental dinners have been attended by large numbers of serving and retired officers; and Territorial Army Officers can also be members of the Club and are welcomed at the Dinner. No dinners were held in:

  1900:   The South African War.
  1910:   The death of King Edward VII.
  1915–19: The War of 1914–18.
  1940–45: The Second World War.

In August 1933 the Somerset Light Infantry Regimental Club was formed.

www.ingramcontent.com/pod-product-compliance
Lightning Source LLC
Chambersburg PA
CBHW082034230426
43670CB00016B/2650